Cooking with the Bible

Cooking with
THE BIBLE

Biblical Food, Feasts, and Lore

Anthony F. Chiffolo and Rayner W. Hesse, Jr.

GREENWOOD PRESS
Westport, Connecticut • London

Library of Congress Cataloging-in-Publication Data

Chiffolo, Anthony F., 1959–
    Cooking with the Bible : biblical food, feasts, and lore / Anthony F. Chiffolo
and Rayner W. Hesse, Jr.
        p.   cm.
    Includes bibliographical references and index.
    ISBN 0–313–33410–2 (alk. paper)
    1. Food in the Bible.   2. Food—Religious aspects—Christianity.
3. Recipes.   I. Hesse, Rayner W.   II. Title.
    BS680.F6C45   2006
    220.8'641—dc22   2006014785

British Library Cataloguing in Publication Data is available.

Library of Congress Catalog Card Number: 2006014785
ISBN: 0–313–33410–2

First published in 2006

Greenwood Press, 88 Post Road West, Westport, CT 06881
An imprint of Greenwood Publishing Group, Inc.
www.greenwood.com

Printed in the United States of America

The paper used in this book complies with the
Permanent Paper Standard issued by the National
Information Standards Organization (Z39.48–1984).

10 9 8 7 6 5 4 3 2 1

The publisher has done its best to make sure the instructions and/or
recipes in this book are correct. However, users should apply judgment and experience when preparing recipes, especially parents and
teachers working with young people. The publisher accepts no responsibility for the outcome of any recipe included in this volume.

Contents

Contents

Preface

When we first conceived of the idea of a biblical cookbook, the question fast arose concerning its potential audience. Who would find a book of recipes based on biblical meals of interest? Women's groups at churches or synagogues? Bible enthusiasts? Cooking classes or clubs? Adult study programs? We soon found a more than willing audience in the bible class participants of the parish we both attend.

For the first meal we presented, we invited nearly thirty people to our home for a dinner that took all day to prepare. We photographed every ingredient that was part of the menu, and just prior to serving, with placards set in front of each dish to be sampled, we took photos of the entire spread. The dining table, covered by a 19th-century paisley remnant, boasted exotic-sounding dishes surrounded by burning Israeli oil amphorae and 1st-century coins. The initial impression was as we had hoped, and our invited audience oohed and aahed. Little did they know what a chore we had undertaken for hours prior to their arrival!

The baking of the bread was our greatest challenge in that the recipe, though tasty, did not result in what we thought should be the desired outcome. We kept asking each other, "Is this what it is supposed to look like?" After all, we had created the recipe in our heads, based on others' and our own research. Finally, on the third try, we felt we had gotten it right. And boy did we get it right! It was so delicious when hot and served with sheep's milk cheese that our invitees were content (spurred on with a little red wine) to make the bread and cheese the entire meal. By the time we served the shish kebab, most everyone was so stuffed that few were interested in eating another bite. But they did anyway. Clearly, the hit of the evening had been the wheatberry soup; requests came in for days by e-mail and phone for that recipe. We were very pleased at the group's response, so we planned our next chapter and set the date to cook another meal. And another. And another.

It didn't take long before we realized that it was not good for the two of us to be doing all the cooking, if our intended market were church groups, women's groups, cooking clubs, and so forth. So after we had finished our fourth chapter, we distributed the recipes to the members of the bible class at our church with the suggestion that they try their hand at preparing the meals we had conceived and bring them to class. We named the event a "Potluck Biblical Supper" and allowed folks to choose what they wanted to make. (We made one of everything ourselves, just in case there were no-shows come dinnertime.) The resulting meal was nothing short of spectacular. We quickly learned that each cook made his or her own adaptations, all of which were quite acceptable to taste and appearance, with the exception of one baker who used a bread machine where the recipe specifically advised otherwise. Her bread was reduced to a bunch of dry crumbs. But since she had brought them along as evidence, they were sprinkled over one of the rice dishes, and participants found the new creation quite to their liking.

For the next few chapters, the bible class became our testing medium. Each meal became more elaborate as more and more cooks joined the fray. Word spread about our dinners, which led to our first speaking invitation from a neighboring church's women's group. It was proposed that we come to talk about our book, but that the lecture be centered around a meal. Once again, recipes from one of our chapters were distributed to all the members of the group; because it had a large membership, two or three people signed up to cook each recipe. On the day that the meal was to be "tasted," we arrived at the church hall to an aura of anticipation. One by one the dishes were put in place, and the arrangement of such a variety of foods on the table was an incredible vista. All in all, more than thirty people showed up for lunch that day, including quite a few men who didn't want to be left out. In fact, several husbands had done the cooking themselves, relegating their wives to merely choosing the right serving dish or container. The meal was delicious, and the variety of interpretations of the same recipe was fascinating. The group leader proclaimed that it was one of their most successful programs ever, and we are already signed up for a visit again next year.

Following the warm reception from the churchwomen's group, we decided to branch out. To date, we have offered biblical cooking classes at the local evening adult school, traded recipes with attendees at the American Academy of Religion Conference in San Antonio, set up a fund-raising dinner using portions of our work for a book club in Maryland, gone on the lecture circuit at various church functions, and entertained proposals about opening our own restaurant. The writing of this cookbook has also encouraged a new boldness in how we prepare everyday meals: spices like *zaatar*, sumac, and turmeric, which we had never used, now show up regularly in the dishes we eat. Plus, we've learned not to be shy about trying any recipe, no matter how strange it seems, and we've been accepting cooking challenges we'd have never dreamed of taking on previously. In fact, we recently catered a luau for over 160 people, using many of the techniques and variations on some of the recipes we had written while composing this book.

Pondering what other possibilities and opportunities lie ahead has become a most intriguing pastime.

Someone we know quite well once commented, "If you can read, you can cook"—a motto we have taken to heart. We invite you, therefore, to read *Cooking with the Bible*—and then *cook;* and we trust that we have provided ample interesting culinary challenges in the pages ahead, and along with them, plenty of food for thought.

ACKNOWLEDGMENTS

We wish to thank the parishioners of St. John's Episcopal Church in New Rochelle, New York, for their assistance in testing the recipes included in this book. Special thanks to Peter Smith for helping to prepare the meals—without his aid in the kitchen, we would not have been able to satisfy the hunger of so many eager diners—and to Lisa Chiffolo, who pitched in to chop vegetables, mix ingredients, set the table, and clean up afterward. Many thanks also to Raymund Peckauskas and Irene Schindler for help in proofreading the manuscript; and to Armen Benlian at Yaranush Mediterranean Foods in White Plains, New York, for her recipe and cooking advice.

Thanks also to Michael Hermann, senior editor at Greenwood, for his support and encouragement along the way, and to the many production hands at Greenwood: Erin Ryan, Bridget Austiguy-Preschel, Rebecca Homiski, and Jo-Ann Parks.

ABBREVIATIONS

JB	The Jerusalem Bible
KJV	King James Version
NIV	New International Version
NIV–UK	New International Version–United Kingdom
NRSV	New Revised Standard Version
RSV	Revised Standard Version

Introduction

And I will say to my soul,
"Soul, you have many goods laid up for many years;
take your ease; eat, drink, and be merry."

Luke 12:19, King James Version

When we first set out to write a cookbook with a biblical theme, we never dreamed what a challenge it would be to make sense of thousands of years of food preparation. Our primary research confirmed what we already knew: the Judeo-Christian lifestyle, influenced by both Eastern and Western cultures, was centered around meals, primarily the noonday meal (what in some places is known today as "supper") and the meal closest to sundown ("dinner"). That these terms in modern times are used interchangeably is just one indication of how blurred the lines have become between what were once two distinct events with their own unique, traditionally prescribed menus. And despite nutritionists' insistence that breakfast should be and is the most important meal of the day, the current gastronomical focus is centered on what is served at dinnertime; and in Western culture, if not elsewhere as well, it is at this meal, as in the biblical era, that we tend to gather our families and do most of our entertaining.

In biblical times, an invitation to dine, whether with family and friends or with complete strangers, was taken most seriously. The Middle Eastern code of ethics held strongly to a belief that good hospitality was the command of The Divine, and the offer to partake of a meal was sacred. In deference to and respect for God, the Jews of the biblical era began all meals with a ritual washing of hands (demonstrating an understanding of the connection to the sacrifices offered to God at the Temple) and with the asking of God's blessing over the food and drink that was about to be consumed. Strangers at a meal were a *mitzvah* (Hebrew for "blessing"), as acknowledged by the author of the Letter to the Hebrews, who imparts (13:2), "Be not forgetful to entertain strangers, for thereby some have entertained angels unawares." Often, as at the Passover meal, an extra place was set at table and a portion set aside in anticipation of the arrival of one more for dinner.

The biblical landscape is peppered with meal stories that often describe a menu and, in a few instances, instructions on how the food is to be eaten. Oddly, despite a frequent penchant for detail, scriptural redactors provided no recipes for their repasts.[1] This lack of information encouraged some food for thought on our part: namely, if one were to prepare the meals mentioned in the Bible, using materials and techniques available today, how might this be accomplished? Hence the premise for this book.

In *Cooking with the Bible,* we present eighteen meals found in the scriptures, along with complete menus. Our attempt is to provide the reader with all the ingredients necessary to better understand what is at stake in the text, while at the same moment allowing the hermeneutic to come into play (a discovery aid that tries to answer how the words of the Bible can be relevant to those encountering them today). Through this process we intend that the ancient text become more alive and vibrant through the preparation and cooking of a meal that relates to it. *Cooking with the Bible* has sixteen menus for dinner, one for the noontime meal (from the story of Ruth), and one breakfast (Jesus cooking for the disciples on the shore of Lake Genessaret).

The ingredients of these varied menus could best be described as what one might expect, given the era and the location of the meal they comprise (which is to say that they are hardly exotic); yet they are, at close examination, certainly not foreign to any contemporary dining experience nor to our present-day mania for healthy eating. Most families described in the stories of the biblical era were undoubtedly vegetarian (as the Israelites, whether in nomadic mode or more settled, were the keepers of an agrarian lifestyle); so we have taken care to include a large variety of vegetables in our menus, whether they be specifically mentioned in the biblical passage or not, in full knowledge that a typical Middle Eastern meal included all types of vegetarian fare, especially beans, cucumbers, garlic, herbs, leeks, lentils, olives, onions, and grains with their byproducts (such as flour). We have also included menus with rice, eggplant, and tomatoes, all three of which, while not biblical, are common in the pantries of modern Middle Eastern kitchens.

Of equal importance in the diet of biblical diners were fruits (dried, fresh, or in liquid form) and nuts, especially grapes, apricots, pomegranates, melons, dates, figs, almonds, and pistachios. Many of the recipes of the following chapters include this shopping list, but in keeping with what can now be found in most markets of the Middle East, we have included a few other specimens that will spice up a meal.

Because Israel was known as "the land flowing with milk and honey," we were generous in using milk and milk products (cheese, yogurt, curds, butter) and in substituting honey for granulated sugar (sugar cane was known, yet not pro-cessed in the ancient world) wherever we thought it made sense and would add to the flavor of the dish.

Many of our menus include fish. Though rarely mentioned in the Hebrew scriptures, our research determined that fish was a goodly part of the Middle Eastern diet and that it was actively traded, as evidenced by the mention of the selling of fish outside of Jerusalem in the books of Nehemiah (13:16) and Zephaniah (1:10). In the Christian New Testament, a few of the disciples of Jesus were fishermen, and Jesus himself prepares them a fish meal in the Gospel of John (21:9ff.). Because some of the biblical meals take place in Egypt, and given evi-dence that the Israelites were actively bartering with seafaring peoples from other lands, we have written recipes for fish that were known to be available at market, either from the Nile, the River Jordan, the Sea of Galilee, or the Mediterranean itself.

It is a well-known fact that all kinds of "meat" were prepared and eaten in biblical times, everything from venison to goat, from lamb to oxen and kine (cows), and from quail and duck to pigeons, sparrows, doves, and geese. Most of these meats were reserved for religious or festive occasions (such as the arrival of a guest or a wedding celebration); yet, as always, the rich and royal feasted much better and more often on these domesticated or hunted animals. Chicken was not unknown (having made its way, some say, from or through Persia), so we have included it as well, in full knowledge that the peoples of the Bible must have learned some new recipes from their captors and those who ruled over them in Egypt, after the fall of what remained of the divided kingdoms of Judah and Israel in the 6th century B.C.E., and under Roman occupation.

As Jewish law forbids adherents to eat animals that were considered "un-clean," we have refrained from recipes that use "forbidden foods," such as pork, rabbit, birds of prey, and fish without scales (such as shellfish, catfish, and eels). We have included yogurt made from camel's milk (*kefir*), yet no recipes using the flesh of the camel (also forbidden), although Bedouins and other nomads now (and then) have used it as a form of sustenance.

It was customary to serve bread and red wine (or some liquid product of the fruit of the vine) with every meal.[2] The menus in this book include both at times, specifically (but not always) if one or the other is mentioned in the biblical passage that is the focus of the chapter. The cook, or whoever is planning the menu, should feel free to include bread and wine in the meal as being representative of the era and authentic to the experience of Middle Eastern gastronomy.

A major difference between scripturally based meals and the more Western dining experience is in the order of the meal and in what constitutes "dessert." Most likely, bread and wine were first on the menu of most biblical meals, as they were blessed when the meal began. A typical meal continued with something pickled in brine or vinegar, because it was thought that such stimulated the appetite. What one might consider "appetizers," such as cheese, raw vegetables,

soups, and salads, were usually served next along with the main meat or vegetable course. Dessert, which often consisted of dried or fresh fruits, puddings, or
"dainties" (delicacies that were sweet), came last (if indeed it were part of the
meal at all). The concept of sweet baked goods as a dessert, e.g., cakes or cookies,
is a fairly new occurrence at Middle Eastern meals.

In an attempt to bridge the old with the new, we have provided recipes for
more modern delectables at the end of each menu, often with ingredients that
play to the theme of the chapter—e.g., *Angel Food Cake* for the story of the angels'
visit to Abraham and Sarah; *Abigail Fritters* for the story of Abigail's encounter
with King David; and *Governor's Cake* in the chapter on Nehemiah's gubernatorial reign. We do so "tongue-in-cheek"; we know, and we are confident that
the reader is also aware, that these recipes are not biblical; still we thought, and
we hope the audience you are cooking for will appreciate too, that a few such
recipes might add a bit of levity to the presentation of the meal ("presentation is
everything"), while serving to highlight a central theme of the story.

A major portion of *Cooking with the Bible* has been given over to a historical
overview of the list of ingredients used in the meals we have created. We've attempted to describe every foodstuff that is mentioned in the recipes, providing
the reader with etymological, botanical, culinary, practical, and folkloric information for each biblical entry; we have provided similar descriptions for all
nonscriptural items as well. In many ways, this has been the most fascinating
aspect of our work: the research into the properties of the foods about which
we were writing encouraged us time and again to experiment with interesting
combinations of ingredients that complemented one another in nontraditional
but savory ways.

So as to further understand the *sitz im leben* (historical setting) of the biblical
passage, we have provided maps of the places cited in each story that will provide
the reader with insight into the distances traveled between places, as well as their
proximity to water sources, neighboring kingdoms, and Jerusalem itself, the capital focus of many of the Bible stories presented.

A table listing biblical weights and measures and their equivalents is also
included for the more mathematical cooks amongst us. By nature, we see ourselves as intuitive in our approach to cooking; but we have learned the hard way,
especially in the making of certain breads, that when an *exact* amount is required,
nothing more or less will do!

With regard to cooking methods, an attempt has been made to cover all bases.
Though most biblical fare was parboiled in cauldrons or cooked in clay pots
hanging over an open fire, fried on hot stones or hard earth with coals set on top
of the food, or sometimes baked in makeshift ovens, the truth is that there is not a
whole lot of archaeological or written evidence about how food was cooked in
biblical times. Fish and meats were often hung out raw, then smoked or buried
until used, or else they were preserved by sun drying, often in salt. No further

cooking was required in these instances. Utensils were used to aid in cooking, but not for eating. Biblical diners ate with their fingers, often using bread to scoop or sop up what was not easily handled. The meals we have put together presume the use of knife, fork, spoon, and other utensils, yet this does not preclude using one's hands, especially if good bread is available and tasty juices are left on the plate! To make cooking easier, and assuming that most cooks do not have industrial kitchens at their beck and call, we have varied the food-preparation methods in our recipes to include use of an oven, a charcoal or gas grill (or outdoor fire), electric frying pan, pots on the stove, microwave, refrigerator, toaster oven, blender, hand mixer, bread machine, food processor, and even a fondue pot! We have also taken into account that some foods might be easier to locate in frozen form, and many of our recipes call for dried herbs and spices at times when fresh varieties might not be readily available.

The chapters that follow are arranged in a standard format. At the start of each chapter is the biblical text. We have not employed one sole translation of the Bible for our work here. A variety of English translations have been used, from one of the oldest (King James Version, or KJV) to one of the newest (The Message), choosing the one that best elucidated the ingredients of the meal described therein. We cannot sufficiently underscore the value of the text to speak for itself (in whatever translation), and so we have given each excerpt its own special place, using as much of the passage as clearly conveys the story. We recommend that you provide a copy of the text (or read it) to those you've invited to the meal, as it wonderfully sets the stage for all that has been prepared and is about to be enjoyed.

As some of the texts are a bit obscure or lesser-known to even the most ardent readers of the scriptures, a commentary accompanies each biblical passage. Portions of their content are exegetical in nature, so they include word studies, as well as literary, critical, sociological, and historical background material—all of which are intended to further illuminate what has sadly been lost in translation from the original languages of our forebears who passed these stories down to us. This framework also seeks to establish a place on the map and on the timeline for the story at hand, regardless of the mythic elements that often surround it. (In other words, one does not have to believe that every aspect of what the story relates actually happened in order to learn something from it.)

The menu and the recipes are last, but not least. After all, this is a cookbook! You should know that no fancy test kitchens were used to test these recipes. All the meals can be created in a home kitchen without any special equipment. Hopefully, you will come to an understanding of the Middle Eastern way of cooking, a gastronomical exercise that has its own unique preparation and taste and presentation, rich in tradition but adaptable to its surroundings and joyous in its expression of the earthly bounty and its culinary inheritance. In the Middle East, eating is not only for daily sustenance—it is a way of life!

NOTES

1. That is to say, unless one counts the instructions from God regarding the Passover meal, in which the Israelites are told to *roast* the lamb shank (versus the usual boiling method); or the mixed grain and pulse bread of Ezekiel 4:9, which gives a list of ingredients but no specifics of quantity.

2. Regarding other beverages, although we do include coffee or tea in some of our recipes, coffee may have been unknown in the Middle East during biblical times. Cooks of that era might have understood the nature of creating infusions (such as mint or some other herb) or adding citrus to heated water to create a kind of "tea"; but we have no evidence that it was a common beverage choice.

Chronology

1900 B.C.E.	Setting of Genesis 18:1–8; 25:24–34; 27:1–29 (Abraham, Isaac, Jacob and Esau)
1800 B.C.E.	Joseph in Egypt (Genesis 43:11ff.)
1700–1280 B.C.E.	Jacob's descendants are enslaved in Egypt
1290–1250 B.C.E.	Exodus from Egypt (Exodus 12:1–11); Wanderings in the Wilderness (Numbers 11:5ff.)
1150 B.C.E.	Period of the Judges and Story of Ruth (2:14–16)
1010 B.C.E.	David and Abigail; David's nuptials (I Samuel 25:14–25a; 39b–42)
970 B.C.E.	Solomon (Song of Songs 5:1ff.)
931–722 B.C.E.	The Divided Kingdom: Elisha (II Kings 4:38–42)
722 B.C.E.	Fall of Samaria
586 B.C.E.	Fall of Jerusalem; beginning of Babylonian Captivity
538 B.C.E.	Beginning of return of Jews to Jerusalem
480 B.C.E.	King Xerxes and Esther (Esther 5:4ff.)
445 B.C.E.	Nehemiah is Governor of Syria (Nehemiah 5:14–19)
400 B.C.E.	Beginning of the Second Temple Period
323 B.C.E.	Death of Alexander the Great
167 B.C.E.	Jewish Wars

44 B.C.E.	Julius Caesar comes to power in Rome and is killed in the same year
30 B.C.E.	Octavian (Augustus Caesar) comes to the throne and becomes first Roman Emperor
4 B.C.E.	Jesus born in Nazareth
14 C.E.	Augustus dies; Tiberias assumes role as emperor
26 C.E.?	Appearance of John the Baptist at the Jordan (Matthew 3:4–6)
26 C.E.–?	Ministry of Jesus (Luke 11:37–42; 15:11–32; John 2:1–11; 21:1–14)
35–44 C.E.	Paul is converted; founds various churches throughout Asia Minor
60 C.E.–120 C.E.	Probable dating of the writing of the gospels
62 C.E.	Death of Peter and James
70 C.E.	Fall of the Second Temple

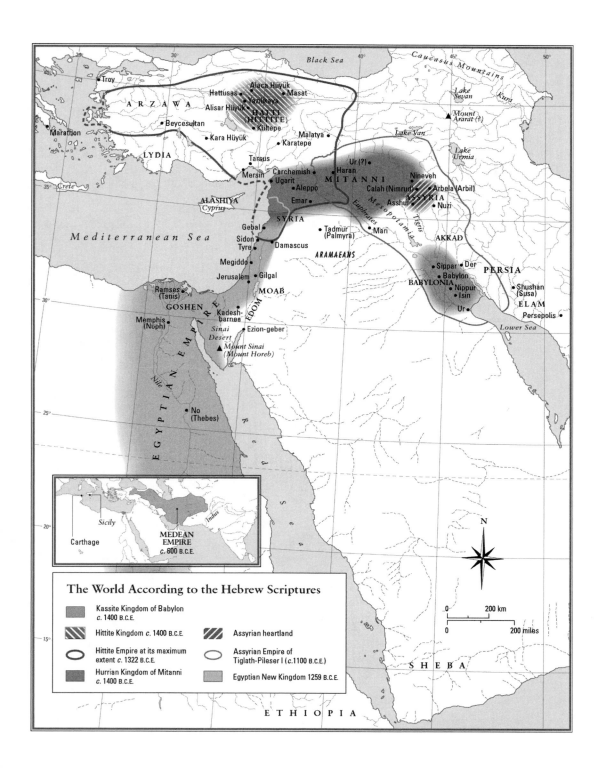

The World According to the Hebrew Scriptures

Kassite Kingdom of Babylon
c. 1400 B.C.E.

Hittite Kingdom c. 1400 B.C.E.

Hittite Empire at its maximum
extent c. 1322 B.C.E.

Hurrian Kingdom of Mitanni
c. 1400 B.C.E.

Assyrian heartland

Assyrian Empire of
Tiglath-Pileser I (c. 1100 B.C.E.)

Egyptian New Kingdom 1259 B.C.E.

The World According to
the Hebrew Scriptures

Kingdoms of Israel
and Judah

ISRAEL

JUDAH

33°

GALILEE

BASHAN

Sea of
Galilee

Mt. Carmel

Nazareth •

• Sepphoris

Shunem

Plain of
Esdraelon

• Megiddo

Mt. Tabor

Yarmuk

Mt. Gilboa

Salim
Aenon

Samaria •

Mt. Ebal

Shechem

Jordan

Jabbok

Mt. Gerizim

Apollonia •

Baal Shalishbah

GILEAD

Jebelyusha

32°

Joppa •

Ephraim •

Arimathea •

Bethel •

• Ai

Gilgal

Ephraim •

Mt. of Olives

Gibeah • Jericho

AMMON

Jerusalem •

Mt. Moriah

Plains
of Moab

Mt. Nebo

Bethlehem •

Mediterranean

Sea

Soreq

Ascalon •

Hebron •

Dead
Sea

CANAAN

PHILISTINES

Gaza •

Shiqma

Engaddi •

Arnon

Masada •

MOAB

Besor

• Beersheba

N e g e v

N

AMORITES

W i l d e r n e s s

o f   S i n

0   25 km

AMELEKITES

0   25 miles

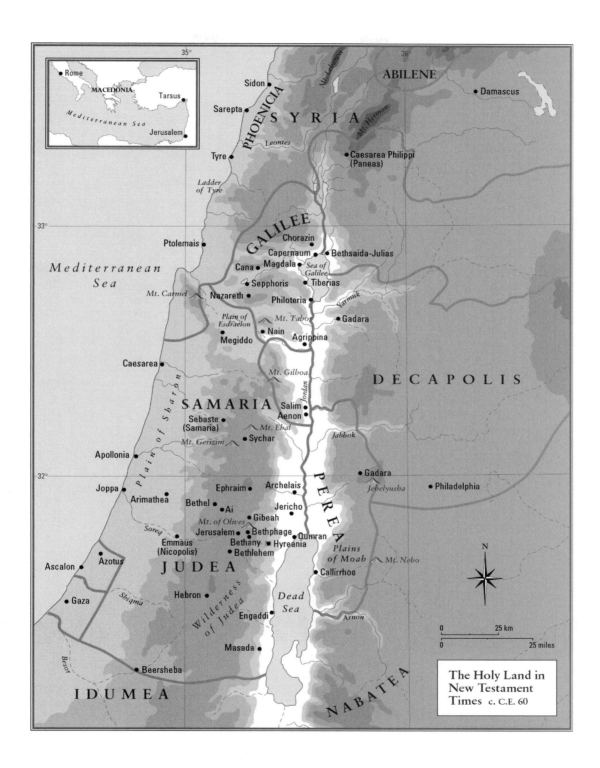

The Holy Land in
New Testament
Times c. C.E. 60

PART I
THE MEALS

1

Entertaining Angels Unawares

THE TEXT

The LORD appeared to Abraham by the oaks of Mamre as he sat at the entrance of his tent in the heat of the day. He looked up and saw three men standing near him. When he saw them, he ran from the tent entrance to meet them, and bowed down to the ground. He said, "My lord, if I find favor with you, do not pass by your servant.

Abraham cooked the meat by cutting it into small pieces and broiling them on skewers over an open fire.

Let a little water be brought, and wash your feet, and rest yourselves under the tree. Let me bring a little bread, that you may refresh yourselves, and after that you may pass on—since you have come to your servant." So they said, "Do as you have said." And Abraham hastened into the tent to Sarah, and said, "Make ready quickly three measures of choice flour, knead it, and make cakes." Abraham ran to the herd, and took a calf, tender and good, and gave it to the servant, who hastened to prepare it. Then he took curds and milk and the calf that he had prepared, and set it before them; and he stood by them under the tree while they ate.

Genesis 18:1–8, New Revised Standard Version

THE HISTORY

The story begins approximately 3,900 years ago (about 1900 B.C.E.), in the city of Ur in Babylonia. There, according to Jewish tradition, a boy named Abram

(Abu-ramu in Assyrian, or Avram in transliterated Hebrew) was born to Terah (or Terach), a seller of religious idols, and his wife.

At that time, the city of Ur, otherwise known as Ur Kasdim or Ur of the Chaldees (an indication that the city was located in southern Babylonia), was a busy cosmopolitan area, situated at the crossroads of ancient migration pathways. Centered on the nearby Tigris and Euphrates Rivers, Mesopotamia, as this part of what is now Iraq was known, was and still is a giant floodplain. With no natural defenses, it was often invaded by peoples from the east and the north, who desired to farm its vast expanse of fertile land. The Tigris and Euphrates themselves carried a heavy traffic of both trading goods and migrants, downstream to what is now known as the Persian Gulf and upstream as far north as modern-day Syria and Turkey. Until about 1900 B.C.E., Mesopotamia was ruled by the Sumerians, who were the first to develop writing in order to keep track of their administrative records. But then a tribe known as the Amorites moved south from the Syrian desert and conquered Sumer, laying the foundation for the Babylonian Empire.

Ur was dedicated to Nannar, the moon god. According to recent archaeological studies, nearly one-quarter of Ur was set aside as temple grounds for Nannar. The other Babylonian deities had temples scattered throughout the rest of the city. The polytheism of Ur—indeed, of all of Mesopotamian civilization in this age—reveals just how radical Abram/Abraham's monotheism was; so revolutionary, in fact, that it can be said to have changed the course of history.

The exact date of Abram's birth is uncertain. In fact, as there are no extra-biblical sources for his biography, scholars disagree about whether he was a historical personage or a religious allegory—that is, a personification of one particular nomadic tribe. As the book of Genesis relates the story, Abram's life in Ur was unremarkable. He married a woman named Sarai, but they were unable to have children. At some point, Terah took Abram, Sarai, and their nephew Lot to Haran, a flourishing city some 600 miles northwest of Ur, on the trade routes to Damascus. Like Ur, Haran was the seat of worship of the moon god. There they settled, until the death of Terah.

Soon thereafter, as the story goes, when Abram was seventy-five years old, he received a call from God to leave Haran and travel to Canaan, the land between the Mediterranean Sea and the Dead Sea/Jordan River (roughly the area occupied by present-day Israel). To follow this call, Abram had to leave his own people, travel across the desert, and settle among strangers. What's more, Abram had to pledge his allegiance to one god. In Sumeria/Babylonia and in Canaan, the people worshipped a whole pantheon of gods, offering sacrifices to this one for good harvests, to that one for good commerce, and so forth. By agreeing to follow God's call, Abram was turning his back on the gods of his youth and committing himself to the idea that Yahweh was the one and only God, and that all other so-called gods were imposters or shams. Thus, Abram is considered the father of monotheism. In return, God promised to create a great nation through Abram. When Abram arrived in Canaan with his wife and nephew, God amplified the promise by pledging that Abram's offspring would possess that land—even though Abram was already advanced in years and he and his wife were unable to conceive.

In this age (the Middle Bronze Age, c. 2200–1550 B.C.E.), the area now known as Israel/Palestine was thinly populated, with few sedentary populations, as there was little arable land. Cisterns, or wells, had not come into general use, and springs were rare. Virtually all the towns were located in the Coastal Plain, the Plain of Esdraelon, and the Valley of the Jordan and of the Dead Sea. Most of the inhabitants were seminomadic, wandering freely over the heavily forested hills of the central region and the dry areas to the south. So it is not unusual that in the following years, Abram and his household moved south into the Negev desert, sojourned in Egypt, then returned to the Negev, accumulating large herds of sheep, oxen, donkeys, and camels and becoming rich in silver and gold. After a falling out with Lot, Abram sent his nephew east toward the plain of the Jordan and took the rest of his household north to Canaan, settling "by the oaks of Mamre," near present-day Hebron. Though Abram and Sarai continued childless, God still promised to make Abram's descendants as numerous as the stars.

Because a man's wealth was measured not only in gold and livestock but also in wives and children, Abram was a laughingstock among his neighbors, for he had wealth but no direct heirs and only one wife. Feeling this disgrace herself, Sarai, also advanced in years, urged her husband to have children with her Egyptian slave-girl Hagar, who was (according to some legends) a daughter of Pharaoh. Hagar bore a son and called him Ishmael. But Sarai felt even more disgraced by her childlessness, and she jealously drove Hagar and her son out of the household and into the desert. By this time, Abram was eighty-six years old and despaired of having any so-called legitimate heirs.

But as Genesis relates, God intervened. When Abram was ninety-nine years old, God appeared to Abram and established a covenant (contract) with him: God gave Abram the name *Abraham* (or *Avraham,* in transliterated Hebrew), gave Sarai the name *Sarah,* and promised that they would bear a son in a year. In return, Abraham and all the male members of his household would be circumcised, as a reminder that they and all their offspring were God's people. Genesis offers two accounts of this promise to Sarah, and one of them is the story of how Abraham provides a special meal to "three men," or perhaps God and two angels, who appeared to him while he was sitting at the entrance to his tent—as related in the scripture text above. A year after this meal, Abraham's son Isaac was born of Sarah.

Thus, according to Jewish tradition, through Isaac and his children, Abraham became the father of the Jewish people. According to Arab traditions, through Ishmael, Abraham was the father of all the Arab peoples. Jews and Muslims as well as Christians revere Abraham for his faith in God's covenant and his belief in the face of seeming impossibilities, and all three monotheistic religions cite his hospitality to strangers as an ideal to be followed.

BIBLICAL PASSAGE NOTES

"The Oaks of Mamre": In Hebrew, *Elonei Mamre* or *Alonei Mamre,* the place where Abram settled and built an altar to God after dividing his household between himself and Lot. Some scholars have connected the place with ancient tree-worshipping cults, and such a connection would seem to emphasize the difficulty of Abram/Abraham's break from polytheistic traditions. Others indicate that *Mamre* was the name of an Amorite inhabitant of the area (that is, someone from the hill country or the vicinity of Jerusalem). Over the ensuing millennia, pilgrims have venerated the site because of Abram/Abraham's commitment to monotheism, though there is some question about the precise location of the oaks. Constantine, the 4th-century C.E. Roman emperor, consecrated one spot with the Basilica of the Terebinth of Mamre, but during the time of Saint Jerome, pilgrims held fairs under a growing oak tree. The Crusades brought renewed interest, and pilgrims celebrated the Feast of the Trinity at a supposedly original site, remembering the three strangers (God and two angels) who visited Abram/Abraham there.

The name *Abu-ramu* is sometimes taken to mean "lofty father," but this is a doubtful translation of the Assyrian. The name *Abraham* is also thought to mean "ancestor of a multitude," though that meaning is probably folklore, and there seems to be no linguistic evidence to support it. It is probable that *Abraham* is merely a dialectical variation of *Abram.*

THE MENU

Sarah's Flat Barley Bread
Wheatberry Soup *or* Middle Eastern Vegetable Casserole
Camel's Milk
Dates with Honey and Ricotta Curds Spread
Grilled Kebab with Sumac Garnish
Angel Food Cake

THE PREPARATION

This was a simple meal that Abraham prepared for his visitors, and probably the first instance of fast food in the Bible. It takes place near Hebron, about twenty-three miles south of present-day Jerusalem. The city itself is situated on a plain about 3,000 feet above sea level. To this place the three visitors arrived, we are told, and Abraham "hastened" to prepare a meal, as he was not expecting strangers, especially at hot midday, when one usually rests. Sarah was given the task of making the bread, the daily custom of grinding and baking reserved for the women of the household, most often the wife. Generally, flour was mixed with water, made into dough, and rolled out into cakes. The cakes were then placed on ground previously heated by fire, then covered with hot embers till baked. It was a quick process.[1]

Luckily the visitors were not in too much of a hurry, as preparing a calf from pasture to palate would take a bit longer. In the interest of time and hospitality, the calf would probably have been cooked either by roasting it whole (no fancy preparation or cuts) or by cutting it up into small, hacked pieces and broiling them on skewers over the fire. Many scholars point out that the meat would have been served with some sort of grain and vegetable dish (the KJV speaks of "corn," but as it was originally a North American plant, probably barley or some other large grain was used). A bowl of camel's milk and some cheese or curds served as dessert; the 21st-century cook with a sense of humor might add or substitute Angel Food Cake.

Abraham served this meal, or something like it, at the terebinth of Mamre, a tall spreading tree or grove of trees, an ideal setting for today's cookout or picnic meal. The recipes that follow comprise an entire meal for six to eight people, yet they require some planning and advance preparation.

Many of the ingredients for these recipes are found in the Bible: yeast (Leviticus 10:12), flour (Numbers 15:4), salt (Ezra 6:9), saffron (Song of Songs 4:14), honey (I Kings 14:3), walnuts (Song of Songs 6:11), cinnamon (Exodus 30:23), mint (Luke 11:42), endive (one of the "bitter herbs" of Exodus 12:8), leeks and garlic (Numbers 11:5), olive oil (Luke 16:6), egg whites (Job 6:6), veal (I Samuel 28), cumin (Isaiah 28:25, 27), cucumbers (Isaiah 1:8), and goat cheese (II Samuel 17:29), but feel free to substitute or adapt as needed. It will still be a heavenly meal!

THE RECIPES

✌ Sarah's Flat Barley Bread

1 tsp. active dry yeast	½ cup chickpea flour
¼ cup warm water	½ cup whole wheat flour
1 cup sour milk	½ tsp. salt
½ tsp. baking soda	½ cup caraway seeds
½ cup barley flour	a few Tbsp. olive oil
½ cup rye flour	

Dissolve the yeast in warm water.

Stir the sour milk into the baking soda. Combine the flours in a mixing bowl with the salt. Add the yeast mixture and the milk. Toss in the caraway seeds, then knead by hand for about 10 minutes.

Cover the bowl with plastic wrap and let the dough rise in a warm place for about 2 hours, or until doubled in size. Turn the dough out onto a heavily floured board and knead for a few minutes, then divide it into 8 equal portions, rolling it into balls.

Flatten each ball into a small circle about 6″ in diameter. Cover with a damp cloth and let sit for about 20 minutes.

Heat a griddle or electric frying pan to medium-high heat. Add a few tablespoons of olive oil and put one dough circle into the pan; press with the back of a spoon so that small bubbles form, as when cooking pancakes. Cook for 2 minutes on each side. Repeat until all circles are cooked.

Wrap each flat bread to keep it warm, and serve as soon as possible.

Yield: 8 servings

❧ Wheatberry Soup

1 cup wheatberries

cold water for soaking (or 4 cups boiling water as an alternative)

5 cups plain tomato sauce

1½ cups navy beans

6 new potatoes, diced

1 large onion, sliced

4 cloves garlic, minced

5 tsp. ground cumin

1 Tbsp. turmeric

½ tsp. ground black pepper

2 green peppers, chopped

A soup made with wheatberries is a hearty, healthy beginning to a tasty biblical meal.

Soak the wheatberries overnight in cold water. If this is not possible, put 1 cup of wheatberries in a small pot with boiling water and simmer till all water evaporates. Berries will then be open and full.

Add berries to remaining ingredients in a large pot and cook for 1 hour on a low flame. Serve piping hot.

Yield: 8 servings

❧ Middle Eastern Vegetable Casserole

2 large eggplants

salt, as needed

2 large cucumbers

2 small green peppers

1 small red pepper

1 small yellow pepper

¼ lb. green beans, sliced

½ cup olive oil

2 large sweet onions

3 cloves garlic, crushed

2 yellow squash, cubed

20 cherry tomatoes, halved

½ tsp. salt

¼ tsp. fresh ground pepper

¼ lb. lima beans (optional)

handful of fresh chopped basil (optional)

¼ cup water

1 cup fresh seasoned breadcrumbs

goat cheese (optional)

Preheat oven to 350°F.

Peel the eggplant, cut into slices, and sprinkle with a little salt. Place in a bowl or on a plate and set aside. Keeping all ingredients separate, cut the cucumbers into small pieces; dice the peppers; cut the green beans in half.

Fry the eggplant using half the olive oil, flipping frequently, until lightly brown on both sides. Set eggplant aside; do not discard oil. Add second ¼ cup of oil and fry the onions until very soft and gleaming. Stir in garlic, cover pan, and cook for 1 minute. Do not overcook.

Starting at the bottom of a large casserole dish, layer, in order, the eggplant, then the

This casserole contains a wide variety of Middle Eastern vegetables and legumes, from eggplant and cucumbers to beans and squash.

cucumbers, the yellow squash, the peppers, and the green beans. Add a portion of the onion and garlic mixture, then place a handful of halved cherry tomatoes on top. Sprinkle with salt and pepper. Repeat this, if necessary, until all ingredients are used.

When lima beans are included, place them at the top of the casserole with the last of the onion and garlic spread and a few odd pieces of eggplant. Sprinkle with basil, salt, and pepper; add water over the vegetable mixture, and top with seasoned breadcrumbs. Bake for 1–1½ hours until vegetables are very tender. May be served with goat cheese, if desired.

Yield: 8 servings

Camel's Milk

Camel's milk has a very strong taste, much more so than cow's or goat's milk. It also must be consumed very slowly for it to be digestible. Once prepared, it should be served cold after hours of refrigeration, or warmed, as in the following recipe.

6 cups fresh camel's milk

2–3 tsp. sugar

1 tsp. saffron

½ tsp. cardamom or nutmeg

Pour milk and sugar into a pot and bring to a boil at low heat. Add the saffron and cardamom or nutmeg and boil for 2–3 minutes. Add more sugar if desired to sweeten further. Serve in warmed mugs.

Yield: 8–12 servings

❧ Dates with Honey and Ricotta Curds Spread

2 cups rich fresh ricotta curds   ¼ tsp. ground cinnamon

2 Tbsp. honey   ⅛ tsp. nutmeg

1 Tbsp. ground walnuts   sprig of fresh mint

Mix the curds, honey, walnuts, cinnamon, and nutmeg in a small, deep, chilled bowl. Stir until well combined. Chop the mint leaves and sprinkle over the mixture.

Use as a filling for pitted dates or as a topping on celery or endive; it is also fine on toasted cinnamon bread.

Yield: 6–8 servings

❧ Grilled Kebab

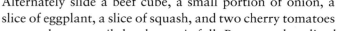

2 lb. beef (or veal), cut in cubes

6 small onions or leeks

1 large eggplant, sliced

2 yellow squash, sliced

handful of cherry tomatoes

several (as needed) cloves garlic, mashed

salt and pepper

allspice

yogurt and apricot sauce or peach jam sauce

thick-crusted bread

A kebab is the most efficient way to cook a large amount of meat in a short amount of time.

Alternately slide a beef cube, a small portion of onion, a slice of eggplant, a slice of squash, and two cherry tomatoes onto a skewer until the skewer is full. Put several garlic cloves through a fine press and into a small bowl; use a small brush or rub the garlic by hand over portions of the meat and vegetables. Mix together the salt, pepper, and allspice in a cup; sprinkle over each skewer. Grill over charcoal, turning several times to prevent overcooking.

If desired for added flavor, baste with a yogurt and apricot or peach jam sauce while cooking. Remove the skewers and serve in a piece of hollowed-out, thick-crusted bread. Sprinkle with 1 or 2 Tbsp. sumac garnish.

Sumac Garnish

1 onion, chopped very fine

½ cup minced parsley

1 tsp. sumac

Yield: 8–12 servings

❧ Angel Food Cake

1 cup cake flour

1½ cups confectioners' sugar

12 egg whites

2 Tbsp. cold water

1½ tsp. cream of tartar

1 cup granulated sugar

½ tsp. salt

1½ tsp. vanilla extract

½ tsp. almond extract

whipped cream

1 cup mulberries, drained (other berries can be substituted)

Preheat oven to 350°F.

Sift cake flour into large metal bowl. Add confectioners' sugar and sift entire mixture two or three times. Beat egg whites, water, and cream of tartar in large mixing bowl until foamy. Sift the granulated sugar and fold in, 2 Tbsp. at a time; continue beating until glossy. Add salt and extracts, and continue to beat until very stiff.

Sprinkle flour and confectioners' sugar mixture over egg mixture a bit at a time until it barely disappears. Scoop batter into an ungreased tube pan.

If you've never had homemade angel food cake, you're in for a real treat!

Bake approximately 35–40 minutes, until top springs back when touched lightly, or until a broom straw comes out clean. Invert pan and let sit until cool, then remove to a plate. Serve with whipped cream or mulberries (or other berries), if desired.

Yield: 8 servings

NOTES

1. See Gerhard von Rad, *Genesis: A Commentary* (Philadelphia: Westminster Press, 1972), 206.

2

A Birthright Worth Beans

The Text

24 When Rebekah's time to give birth came, sure enough, there were twins in her womb.

25 The first came out reddish, as if snugly wrapped in a hairy blanket; they named him Esau.

26 His brother followed, his fist clutched tight to Esau's heel; they named him Jacob. Isaac was sixty years old when they were born.

27 The boys grew up. Esau became an expert hunter, an outdoorsman. Jacob was a quiet man preferring life indoors among the tents.

Jacob gave Esau bread and a stew of lentils in exchange for the older brother's birthright.

28 Isaac loved Esau because he loved Esau's game, but Rebekah loved Jacob.

29 One day Jacob was cooking a stew. Esau came in from the field, starved.

30 Esau said to Jacob, "Give me some of that red stew—I'm starved!" That's how he came to be called Edom.

31 Jacob said, "Make me a trade: my stew for your rights as the firstborn."

32 Esau said, "I'm starving! What good is a birthright if I'm dead?"

33 Jacob said, "First, swear to me." And he did it. On oath Esau traded away his rights as the firstborn.

34 Jacob gave him bread and the stew of lentils. He ate and drank, got up and left. That's how Esau shrugged off his rights as the firstborn.

Genesis 25:24–34, adapted from The Message

THE HISTORY

As recounted in Chapter 1, God made a covenant with Abraham, promising him descendants that would be as numerous as the stars in return for Abraham's fealty to the One God. Although past child-bearing age (tradition indicates that she was ninety years old), Sarah, Abraham's wife, gave birth to a son. They called him Isaac (Yitzchak), which is believed to mean "laughter" in ancient Hebrew, because Sarah laughed when the angels who feasted with Abraham told her that she would have a son within the year, and because the son's conception brought the parents joy.

Isaac was not Abraham's firstborn or heir, however. At Sarah's urging, he had had a child with her servant, Hagar, and the boy had been named Ishmael. After Isaac's birth, Sarah urged Abraham to disinherit his firstborn son, so he banished Hagar and her child to the desert. According to tradition, God's angels saved Hagar and Ishmael, who himself became the ancestor of many people (some say he was the father of the Arab peoples).

At some point during Isaac's youth, Abraham received an extremely disturbing message from God: he was to take Isaac to the top of Mount Moriah and sacrifice him there. Abraham was thunderstruck: the gods he had abandoned in Ur might have required sacrifices, but was the One God no different? Libraries of books have been written about this event. As related in the book of Genesis, Abraham did as he was commanded, and Isaac, though strong and swift, obeyed his centenarian father and allowed himself to be bound on the sacrificial altar. Just as Abraham was about to slit his son's throat, God commanded him to stop, pleased that the man would withhold nothing, not even his son, from God. Moved by this display of fealty, God provided a ram for the sacrifice in place of Isaac. This event, or test of Abraham's faith, is known as the *Akeidah*, which means "binding." One can imagine the emotional trauma that Isaac might have had to live with for many years, if not his whole life.

After the death of Sarah, Abraham sent a servant to find a wife for Isaac among their relatives in Ur. The servant, Eliezer, returned with a young maiden named Rebekah (sometimes called Rivka), who became Isaac's wife. He was about forty years old at this time. They settled in the land of the Philistines, and the people of that region prospered. However, the Philistine king, Abimelech, tried to take Rebekah away; but when he discovered that she was Isaac's wife he forced all of Isaac's people out of the country. The fortunes of the Philistines plummeted, and eventually Abimelech invited Isaac's tribe back to Philistia.

Meanwhile, Abraham had married again, to Keturah, who bore six children, and he had additional children with his concubines. But he left everything he owned to Isaac and sent his other sons away. When Abraham died at the age of 175, his sons Isaac and Ishmael (they must have reconciled at some point) buried him next to Sarah, in the tomb Abraham had purchased from the Hittites, probably a branch of the Canaanite peoples who lived in the area of Hebron.

According to the biblical account, Isaac and Rebekah suffered from the same infertility that had afflicted Abraham and Sarah, but after twenty years Rebekah became pregnant. She gave birth to twins who were completely dissimilar. The older boy was called Esau because he was red and covered with hair (*Esau* means "hairy" in ancient Hebrew; he was also known as Edom, which means "red"). The younger child was named Jacob (Ya'akov) because he was holding onto Esau's heel (*Ya'akov* means "he grasps the heel," but that expression signifies "one who deceives" or "one who supplants"—and indeed, Jacob would prove to be the deceiver who supplanted his brother). Esau grew up to be a strong man, a skilled hunter and outdoorsman and Isaac's favorite; Jacob grew up to be a quiet man who preferred to remain in the camp, tending the flocks, and he was Rebekah's favorite. The parents' favoritism became a source of conflict, jealousy, and enmity between the two young men.

It is not surprising, then, that Jacob would attempt to trick Esau and "steal" his birthright. The opportunity came when Esau returned to the camp from what had probably been a long, unsuccessful hunt. Exhausted and famished, he happened to find Jacob in the middle of making a fine pot of red lentil stew. Esau asked for a bowl of the stew, to which, as the older brother, he was legally entitled. Taking advantage of Esau's fatigue, Jacob slyly began to negotiate: was Esau hungry enough to trade his birthright for a plate of food? Esau may have thought it was a joke—or he may have been too hungry to pay it much heed—or he may not have cared about his spiritual leadership of the tribe—but he swore an oath, giving his birthright to his younger brother.

The birthright was and continued to be extremely important among the descendants of Abraham. The first son born to the father took priority over all of his brothers and sisters. He usually inherited most of the father's wealth, and the law of Deuteronomy eventually fixed his inheritance as a double portion of all of the father's possessions; in fact, the Deuteronomic law forbade a father from favoring a younger son over the firstborn. When the father died, the firstborn became the head of the family, with all the rights (respect and property) and responsibilities (caring for his father's widows, all unmarried sisters, and any boys who had not reached adulthood) of that position. At some point in the history of the ancient Hebrews it became the custom to consecrate the firstborn to God; another custom permitted an animal sacrifice to redeem the firstborn. This may be a secondary explanation for the story of Isaac's near-sacrifice at the hand of Abraham. At any rate, the birthright was a valuable possession, and Esau should have been warier of his brother's intentions.

Biblical Passage Notes

This simple but very famous biblical story has as its center the elements of hunger, greed, ignorance, and a bit of sibling rivalry thrown in for good measure—a perfect tale around which to build a great meal! Here also we have an insight into the two typical ways of life in ancient Palestine, where Jacob and his twin brother, Esau, grew up: the shepherd (Jacob) and the hunter (Esau) personify two differing but contemporaneous groups that lived off the same landscape and often encountered each other amid their daily routines. The perspective of the text seems to favor Jacob, not only because he wins the big prize of birthright at the end, but also because there is an implied preference for his way of life, which is presented as more cultured, more orderly, less impetuous. True, their father, Isaac, we are told, favors Esau, especially because he is strong and could hunt the big, tasty game whose meat was a delicacy for these early tribesfolk; but shepherd and farmer Jacob has the upper hand, a clue we get at the beginning of the story when he comes out of the womb clutching Esau's heel. From that day forward, Esau would always be looking over his shoulder, fearful of Jacob's mischief and deceit.

Esau arrives at Jacob's tent, bursting with an insatiable need to eat. He doesn't even seem to care what his brother is preparing and most likely did not even recognize the dish; perhaps the chance to dine on the unknown and the wonderful odor of sweet Egyptian beans made the meal irresistibly tempting.[1] But it must have been a satisfying meal, because he appears to gulp it down and then get up and go on his way very quickly.

THE MENU

Bread (*El Khobz*)

Mejeddarah (Lentils with Rice)

Cucumber and Yogurt Salad

Basai Badawi (Onions with Lentils, Nuts, and Fruit)

Esau's Pottage

Baked Goat Cheese with Herbs

Dried Apricots and Whole Shelled Pistachios

Red Velvet Cake

THE PREPARATION

The stew that Jacob feeds his brother is made of lentils, a vegetable that is mentioned only four times in the Bible (II Samuel 17:28 and 23:12; Ezekiel 4:9; and in this chapter of Genesis), but it seems very likely that lentils were widely planted and utilized during the biblical era. Even today they are grown throughout the Middle East and are known as a good source of vitamins A and C, and they are rich in protein and amino acids, making it natural that they became a staple among the poorer inhabitants of the land. Planted during the winter season in very small patches of plowed soil and harvested during late spring or early summer, the plants grow to about one foot tall and sport small bluish-white flowers.[2]

There are two main types of lentils grown in the Middle East. The first is a large, gray bean with a reddish center. This is usually prepared by grinding off the outer layer, the seed coat, leaving the red cotyledons. The seed coat residue is fed to animals.[3] Lentils of this type cook more rapidly than the second type, which is smaller and does not have red cotyledons, although some of the seed coats themselves can have a brownish-red hue. This type of lentil is eaten with the outer coating intact. (Cotyledons are the first part of the plant that pokes out of the ground when a seed sprouts; they keep the new seedling fed until it can make its own food through photosynthesis.)

The recipes below feature the smaller lentils, which require less work in preparation. Two of the lentil dishes are vegetarian; the third dish adds some meat for those who want a heartier stew. All are great dishes for a large group of hungry folk, who'll have to give over very little for a tasty meal!

THE RECIPES

Bread (El Khobz)

1 package active dry yeast

1 tsp. granulated sugar

¼ cup warm water

1 cup semolina flour

2 cups unbleached flour or whole-wheat flour

2 tsp. salt

1 tsp. sesame seeds

2⅓ cups water

2 Tbsp. semolina flour for the countertop

Of all the Middle Eastern flatbreads, *El Khobz* is one of the easiest and tastiest to make.

Preheat oven to 400°F.

In a cup or glass, mix the yeast, sugar, and water; stir, and set in a warm place until the yeast is bubbly and doubled in volume.

Meanwhile, mix the flours, salt, and sesame seeds in a large bowl; slowly add the water, ⅓ cup at a time, then the yeast mixture. Knead the dough by hand for 5–6 minutes until it forms a complete ball; remove from the mixing bowl. Knead the dough by hand again for 2 minutes or so. The dough should have a smooth, elastic consistency. Cut the dough into two pieces. Cover each piece with moist, hot towels and let rest for 2 minutes or so.

Spread some semolina flour on a clean work area and start making a ball with one piece of the dough. Do the same with the other piece. Cover with moist, hot towels and let stand for 3 minutes on a baking sheet. Sprinkle some semolina flour and start flattening the dough to form a disc about 5″ in diameter. Do the same with the other ball. Cover with moist, hot towels and let rise 1 hour in a warm place.

With a sharp knife make incisions on the top and bake 15 minutes. Lower the heat to 325°F and bake 25–35 minutes.

Remove from the oven. The bread is done when it is nicely brown over the top and sounds hollow when you tap the bottom. Cover with a towel and let cool. Cut the bread just before serving.

Yield: 12 hearty diagonal slices

Mejeddarah (Lentils with Rice)

2 cups lentils (about 1 lb.)

8 cups water

2 large Spanish onions, chopped

½ cup olive oil, plus a splash

2 Tbsp. sumac

1 cup brown (or white) rice, uncooked

salt and pepper to taste

With its lentil and onion base, *Mejeddarah* is a staple of many Middle Eastern menus.

Sort through the lentils to remove any small stones that might have gotten mixed in during the drying process. Wash thoroughly, and drain in a colander. Place lentils in a large pot with the water and bring to a boil; lower the heat and continue to cook for about 15 minutes.

Meanwhile, sauté the onions in the olive oil and sumac until they begin to caramelize. Add uncooked rice, onions, and pan residue to the lentils. Continue cooking about 45 minutes until lentils are barely mushy, stirring occasionally. Season to taste.

Serve hot or cold.

Yield: 8 servings

Cucumber and Yogurt Salad

3 large cucumbers

juice of one lemon

1 clove garlic, minced

4–5 sprigs fresh mint, finely chopped

1 pint nonfat yogurt

½ tsp. salt

Peel and slice cucumbers into thin strips. Lay them out around the circumference of a large, chilled glass bowl so they form a kind of "cold crust." Squeeze the juice of one lemon over the cucumbers. Next, place the minced garlic and finely chopped mint leaves into a garlic press and mash thoroughly over the salad. Take what mint and garlic did not mash well and toss it into the yogurt, then add the salt. Pour over cucumber and lemon mixture and refrigerate 1 hour before serving.

Yield: 6 servings

Cool and refreshing, this cucumber and yogurt salad combines sweet and sour tastes to delight the palate.

Basai Badawi *(Onions with Lentils, Nuts, and Fruit)*

This is a vegetarian version of a Bedouin dish. If you serve it with rice, try adding saffron or turmeric to the rice before cooking. It adds a distinctive flavor as well as color, creating "red" rice.

4 large onions (Spanish onions are ideal)

½ cup red lentils, cooked

salt and pepper to taste

¾ cup plain yogurt

2 Tbsp. dates, finely chopped

2 Tbsp. walnuts, chopped

1 Tbsp. raisins or sultanas

2 Tbsp. bread crumbs

1 bunch fresh parsley, chopped

Using lentils, nuts, and fruits, *Basai Badawi* is a vegetarian version of a typical Bedouin dish.

Preheat oven to 350°F.

Peel the onions (do not cut off the ends) and place them in a large pan of boiling water. Reduce the heat and let them simmer for 15–20 minutes, covered, until they are fairly tender. When they are ready, take them out and set aside to cool. Using a knife and fork, carefully remove the top of each onion and trim the base. Remove the center section of the onion, leaving a shell about ¾″ thick. In a bowl, mix together the lentils, salt, pepper, yogurt, dates, walnuts, raisins or sultanas, and bread crumbs. Fill the onions with this mixture. Keep any filling that remains and mix it with the chopped discarded onion centers. Place the filled onions in an oven-proof dish, spoon any remaining mixture around them, and cook for about 20 minutes. Garnish with parsley and serve with bulgur or "red" rice.

Yield: 8 servings

Source: Basai Badawi recipe reprinted by kind permission of the New Internationalist. Copyright New Internationalist (www.newint.org), as found in *The New Internationalist Food Book* by Troth Wells (New Internationalist, 2000).

Esau's Pottage

½ cup olive oil

6 onions, diced

1 lb. lamb, cubed

2 carrots

2 stalks celery

1 green pepper

2 cups tomatoes

1 lb. lentils

2–3 cups water

1 tsp. salt

¼ tsp. black pepper

This hearty stew known as Esau's Pottage is so delicious that a brother might even give up his birthright for a mere taste.

Heat the oil; add the onions and sauté until tender but not brown. Add the cubed meat (it should be as lean as possible) and let simmer while washing and dicing the vegetables. Add the vegetables and lentils to the meat with 2 cups of water, and simmer gently until lentils are tender. It will take about 1½ hours. Add salt and pepper when the lentils are cooked. Shake the pot occasionally or add another cup of water to prevent sticking.* Serve hot in a bowl or on a plate next to a cucumber salad.

Yield: 6–8 servings

*If you double the recipe, you'll keep adding water as needed. Those lentils soak up a lot of liquid!
Source: Adapted from *The Bible Cookbook* by Marian Maeve O'Brien, 203.

Baked Goat Cheese with Herbs

Because Jacob was a shepherd, there was probably a lot of goat's milk and cheese on hand. Therefore, we've added this short but impressive side dish, which will complement any lentil meal.

5 oz. fresh creamy soft goat cheese (not feta, which is too dry)

5 smallish fresh ripe tomatoes, diced

2 tsp. extra virgin olive oil

sprigs of sage and parsley

Preheat oven to 350°F.

Adding a little hot water to the hands, form the goat cheese into an elongated ball. Place in the center of a greased baking pan. Arrange the diced tomatoes all around the cheese. Pour the olive oil over the cheese to help prevent burning and to aid in browning. Sprinkle the chopped herbs on top, and bake approximately 55–60 minutes. Remove from pan and let cool just a bit on a large wooden cutting/serving board. Serve surrounded by the cooked tomatoes. Place bowls of dried apricots and whole shelled pistachios for some color and extra flavor; or spread over El Khobz bread (see recipe).

Yield: 6–8 servings

Dried Apricots and Whole Shelled Pistachios

To liven up the meal a bit, place some dried apricots[4] in one bowl and whole shelled pistachios[5] in another, and let your guests help themselves to some prime biblical fare!

Red Velvet Cake

Red Velvet Cake is a beautifully textured cake with a mild chocolate flavor that just happens to be startlingly red. In order to mask its color before the cake is cut and enhance its redness once it is, Red Velvet Cake is traditionally complemented with a thick, very white frosting.

2¼ cups all-purpose flour, sifted

1 tsp. salt

2 Tbsp. cocoa

2 1-oz. bottles of red food coloring
(equivalent measure is ¼ cup or 4 Tbsp.)

½ cup Crisco or other vegetable shortening

1½ cups sugar

2 large eggs

1 cup buttermilk

1 tsp. vanilla extract

1 tsp. white vinegar

1 tsp. baking soda

Reflecting the meaning of Esau's name ("red"), this Red Velvet Cake crowns the meal with a bright finish.

Preheat oven to 350°F. Grease and flour two 9″ cake pans.

Combine the flour and salt and set aside.

Put the cocoa in a small glass bowl, and add the food coloring gradually, stirring until mixture is smooth. Set aside.

Cream together the shortening and sugar, beating for 4 or 5 minutes at medium speed with an electric mixer until fluffy. Add the eggs, one at a time, beating for at least 30 seconds after each addition.

At low speed, add the flour mixture to the sugar mixture alternately with the buttermilk and vanilla, scraping down the sides of the bowl as necessary. Add the cocoa/food coloring mixture until the color of the batter is uniform. Do not overbeat; overbeaten cake batter will result in a tough cake.

In a small bowl, mix the vinegar with the baking soda. It will foam up. Stir it briefly to mix, and then add it to the cake batter, folding it in to incorporate well, but do not beat.

Pour the batter into the prepared cake pans and bake for 25–30 minutes, or until a cake tester comes out clean. Allow layers to cool on a rack for 10 minutes before turning out. Let the cake cool completely before frosting.

Beautifully Thick White Frosting

1½ cups sugar

½ tsp. cream of tartar

⅛ tsp. salt

½ cup water

4 egg whites (at room temperature)

Combine sugar, cream of tartar, salt, and water in a heavy saucepan. Cook over medium heat, stirring constantly, until the mixture is clear and reaches 240°F on a candy thermometer (soft ball stage).

Beat the egg whites until soft peaks form. Continue to beat while slowly pouring the sugar mixture in a thin stream down the side of the mixer bowl (don't let the sugar mixture come into contact with the beaters). Continue beating until stiff peaks form and the frosting thickens to the desired consistency.

Yield: 10–12 servings

Source: Adapted from a recipe by Patricia Mitchell at www.texascooking.com/features/may99redvelvet .htm

NOTES

1. "It is probable that it was made of Egyptian beans, which Jacob had procured as a dainty; for Esau was a stranger to it. It is very palatable; and to the weary hunter, faint with hunger, its odor must have been irresistibly tempting." Robert Jamieson, A. R. Fausset, and David Brown, *A Commentary, Critical and Explanatory on the Whole Bible* (New York: George H. Doran, 1921), as found at www.searchgodsword.org/com/jfb/view.cgi? book+ge&chapter=025

2. See "All the Plants of the Bible" by Lytton John Musselman, http://web.odu.edu .webroot/instr/sci/plant.nsf/pages/allbibleplantslist

3. Ibid.

4. According to Kitty Morse (*A Biblical Feast: Foods from the Holy Land* [Berkeley, Calif.: Ten Speed Press, 1998], 11), "Some noted biblical botanists now believe that the apple of scripture was an apricot, or perhaps, a quince. The apricot better fits the biblical criteria: a pleasant-tasting, fragrant, golden fruit, from a shady, silver-leafed tree."

5. Ibid., 19. "The nuts mentioned in the Bible were probably pistachios ... which have been widely cultivated since the time of Solomon."

3

All for a Father's Blessing

THE TEXT

1 When Isaac was old and his eyes were so weak that he could no longer see, he called for Esau his older son and said to him, "My son." "Here I am," he answered.

2 Isaac said, "I am now an old man and don't know the day of my death.

3 "Now then, get your weapons—your quiver and bow—and go out to the open country to hunt some wild game for me.

4 "Prepare me the kind of tasty food I like and bring it to me to eat, so that I may give you my blessing before I die."

5 Now Rebekah was listening as Isaac spoke to his son Esau. When Esau left for the open country to hunt game and bring it back,

6 Rebekah said to her son Jacob, "Look, I overheard your father say to your brother Esau,

7 "'Bring me some game and prepare me some tasty food to eat, so that I may give you my blessing in the presence of the LORD before I die.'

8 "Now, my son, listen carefully and do what I tell you:

9 "Go out to the flock and bring me two choice young goats, so I can prepare some tasty food for your father, just the way he likes it.

Rebekah told her younger son Jacob, "Go out to the flock and bring me two choice young goats, so I can prepare some tasty food for your father, just the way he likes it." Deceived by the meal, Isaac gave his blessing to the younger son and had no blessing to give to Esau, the older. Angry and embittered, Esau left his family and settled in Edom ("red"), linking the famous cheese to the tale.

10 "Then take it to your father to eat, so that he may give you his blessing before he dies."

11 Jacob said to Rebekah his mother, "But my brother Esau is a hairy man, and I'm a man with smooth skin.

12 "What if my father touches me? I would appear to be tricking him and would bring down a curse on myself rather than a blessing."

13 His mother said to him, "My son, let the curse fall on me. Just do what I say; go and get them for me."

14 So he went and got them and brought them to his mother, and she prepared some tasty food, just the way his father liked it.

15 Then Rebekah took the best clothes of Esau her older son, which she had in the house, and put them on her younger son Jacob.

16 She also covered his hands and the smooth part of his neck with the goatskins.

17 Then she handed to her son Jacob the tasty food and the bread she had made.

18 He went to his father and said, "My father." "Yes, my son," he answered. "Who is it?"

19 Jacob said to his father, "I am Esau your firstborn. I have done as you told me. Please sit up and eat some of my game so that you may give me your blessing."

20 Isaac asked his son, "How did you find it so quickly, my son?" "The LORD your God gave me success," he replied.

21 Then Isaac said to Jacob, "Come near so I can touch you, my son, to know whether you really are my son Esau or not."

22 Jacob went close to his father Isaac, who touched him and said, "The voice is the voice of Jacob, but the hands are the hands of Esau."

23 He did not recognize him, for his hands were hairy like those of his brother Esau; so he blessed him.

24 "Are you really my son Esau?" he asked. "I am," he replied.

25 Then he said, "My son, bring me some of your game to eat, so that I may give you my blessing." Jacob brought it to him and he ate; and he brought some wine and he drank.

26 Then his father Isaac said to him, "Come here, my son, and kiss me."

27 So he went to him and kissed him. When Isaac caught the smell of his clothes, he blessed him and said,

> "Ah, the smell of my son
> is like the smell of a field
> that the LORD has blessed.

28   May God give you of heaven's dew
> and of earth's richness—
> an abundance of grain and new wine.

29   May nations serve you
and peoples bow down to you.
Be lord over your brothers,
and may the sons of your mother bow down to you.
May those who curse you be cursed
and those who bless you be blessed."

Genesis 27:1–29, New International Version

THE HISTORY

As described in Chapter 2, Jacob tricked his brother, Esau, into trading his birthright for a plate of stew. But their mother, Rebekah, so favored Jacob that she urged him also to steal the blessing of Isaac that rightly belonged to Esau.

Among the ancient Hebrews, the words spoken by parents had power—the power to determine the future, to bring forth good or ill (blessing or curse) upon their children. For example, Noah blessed two of his sons, Shem and Japheth, who had refrained from looking at him when he was naked, and cursed his other son, Ham, who had not turned away; the blessing determined that the offspring of the first two sons would prosper, and the curse, that the descendants of the third son would live in servitude (Genesis 9). Furthermore, the father's blessing (or curse) was believed to be a pronouncement from the One God, and once uttered, the words could not be taken back or redirected or shared with another. The parents' blessing and goodwill were the greatest happiness that a child could desire.

Thus when Isaac felt the approach of death, he wished to bestow his blessing upon his favored son, Esau, to pass on to him all the wealth and power that the family had accumulated, not to mention the covenant that they had made with God. Rebekah, perhaps seeing God's intentions better than her blind husband could, and perhaps knowing that Jacob, not Esau, was the only son strong enough to shoulder the responsibility of the Covenant, directed Jacob to pretend to be Esau in order to steal Isaac's blessing. Other factors may also have been in play: Esau had married outside of the tribe, taking two Hittite women, Judith and Bashemath, as his wives. Later on, he married a half-cousin, one of Ishmael's daughters, but this was no better, as Abraham had disinherited Ishmael.

When Isaac discovered the deception, he was distraught, but God had spoken, and one could neither countermand nor protest God's declaration. However, when Esau discovered the deception, he vowed to kill Jacob upon Isaac's death. Rebekah stepped in again and sent Jacob to Haran to live with her brother Laban until her sons could be reconciled.

BIBLICAL PASSAGE NOTES

Verse 3: The King James Version of this text uses "venison" in place of "wild game." The Hebrew word itself, *tsedah,* and its variant, *tsayid,* most often mean simply "meat" or "provisions that have been hunted." The Hebrew word for gazelle, *tsebi*, which has a similar etymological origin, was probably what the translators had in mind when they looked at this text. Where it appears elsewhere in the Bible, it was translated by the scholars in King James' day as "roedeer," which was better known to Europeans. The question of exactly what type of animal Esau would have hunted for food is rather complicated, given that many animal species common in Palestine when the text was written have since become extinct in that location—for instance, the lion, the ostrich, the fallow deer, the onager, and some antelope species. As a consequence, there are still several animal terms that cannot be translated with certainty,[1] including the animals in this particular biblical passage.

Verse 17: Rebekah gives Jacob bread to serve Isaac with his meal. It is not a loaf, and it is not unleavened (Hebrew *matstsah*). It is the very staple of Middle Eastern life, that which provides sustenance, most likely a semiflat bread that contained some yeast. It is fascinating that the Hebrew word used for bread in this text, *lechem,* can also mean provisions, meat, or food for the feast, just as *tsedah* carries the same meaning in verse 3 (see previous paragraph). Perhaps such closeness in meanings and usage indicates the serving of a type of ritualistic or very traditional meal, one at which the diner would expect certain foods to be present to make the meal complete, all interconnected, one imperfect without the other.[2]

Verse 25: What exactly did Jacob give his father to drink? Was it good red wine, or white wine, or merely juice? The Hebrew word used here is *yayin*, "that which is pressed out, grape juice." It is the most frequently used word for wine in the Hebrew scriptures (other words, *chemer, chamar, tirosh,* are used to describe a thick, syrupy or mixed drink, or mead). Yet *yayin* is the meal wine, sometimes called the banqueting wine, and it is more than grape juice; it is the end process of fermenting the grapes, and it is intoxicating.[3] So suffice it to say, Isaac enjoyed his meal with a nice, full, heavy (and heady) red wine.

Verse 28: Though not part of the recipes in this chapter, it bears mentioning that "the grain" of this verse, rendered "corn" in the KJV, has caused quite a bit of confusion among biblical readers. The New World version of corn, or *maize* as Native Americans called it, was unknown in the Middle East and to the early English translators of the Bible. This verse in Genesis uses the term *dagan,* one of five types of grain mentioned in the Hebrew scriptures. The *Catholic Encyclopedia* says that these grains were barley, spelt (fitches), vetch, millet, or pulse, all of which can be used in the making of bread.[4]

The "new wine" (Hebrew *tirosh*) of this verse is in contrast to the wine discussed in verse 25. *Tirosh* is a sweet wine, new in that it is young, and usually unfermented, a kind of grape juice. Isaac's blessing was meant to confer a vast genesis of good fortune, the land of milk and honey promised to his father, Abraham, a place of ever new beginnings and fine living.

THE MENU

Savory Chevon Ragout

Rice of Beersheba

Rebekah's "Tasty Dish"

Venison Stew

Mouthwatering Date and Walnut Bread

Jacob's Green Bean Salad

Edam Cheese and Seedless Grapes

The Ultimate Deception

THE PREPARATION

This is an intriguing tale, not the least because it involves a small family and a simple meal that affects the fate of entire generations to come. The author of the tale knew a lot about the subjects—especially regarding their needs and greeds—and (s)he capitalizes on all their hungers—the hunger for land, the hunger for power, the hunger to control destiny, the hunger for food—to demonstrate to the reader just how primal our urges are or can become.

The adjectives used by the characters themselves in this passage are both cunning and culinary. One almost gets the feeling that the teller of the tale is as interested in the gastronomical as (s)he is in the recipe for deception. The "tasty" food of verse 4 is more than a compliment to Esau's talents as a chef. This is the language of fairy tales, of the Big Bad Wolf with huge teeth ready to consume an unsuspecting Little Red Riding Hood, or the evil witch in the forest coaxing Hansel and Gretel into the oven. We know that the undoing of someone in the story will be linked to tasting. Isaac is a perfect foil. We learn in verse 1 that he is old, blind, quite feeble, yet astute about his physical limitations. With age might have come the dimming of the taste buds also, so he asks for something "tasty," the implication being that something "spicy" was necessary to pique his appetite. (Some translations of this text substitute the word "savory," a pun, no doubt, as the herb *savory* [*Saturejua hortensis L.*, Hebrew *zaatar*] has been widely used in Middle Eastern cooking for hundreds of generations.)

The same can be said of Rebekah's instructions to Jacob regarding two "choice" goats. The goats were to be *tob* (Hebrew for "good"), which can mean sweet, fine, or pleasing. The translators of the New International Version (used above), in their use of "choice," seem to foreshadow the choice that Isaac makes between his two sons, and underscore the choice that Rebekah has already made as to who is her favorite. That they were also to be "young" goats or kids (in Hebrew, *gedi*) reemphasizes just whom the battle in this story is between: two young twin brothers fighting for their place in the world, asking the blessing of an old goat who is near death. (The biblical text tells us earlier that Isaac is 137 years old!) That the young kids chosen for the meal are sweet to the taste and not as sinewy or tough as the older goats of the flock betrays the writer's experience in the kitchen. In the guise of Rebekah, this cook knows just what will be tasty and pleasing.

To serve Rebekah's meal as a dinner or for a weekend luncheon will require some advance preparation. Though the biblical text gives the idea of a hastily prepared meal, one should plan to give over an entire day to cooking. To make this more facile, we have framed the meal around a ragout. According to some scholars, this was probably the way in which Rebekah would have prepared the meal herself, the young goat meat marinated with salt, onions, garlic, and lemon juice.[5] With enough of all these ingredients, and with the right preparation, goat can taste as good as the finest game of the field.

We know from the biblical text and from the strong storytelling traditions of the Israelites that Isaac and his family, though somewhat settled in Beersheeba, a town in the southernmost part of present-day Israel, were sheep-herding seminomads. This means that though Isaac had grown richer and God blessed him with flocks, herds, and a large household, he also spent some time tilling and keeping the land. The book of Genesis tells us that he was very successful in agriculture, reaping "a hundred-fold the same year" he sowed. Therefore, in contrast to the tents used by full-fledged nomads, Isaac and Rebekah's home was not a temporary shelter (no hastily erected tent) but more of a permanent structure with built-in cooking facilities. Biblical cooks prepared their meals in open courtyards outside their homes,[6] using a pit that had been filled with dry grasses and sticks or cattle dung as fuel. Bread was often baked by placing the coals on top of the dough (as in Chapter 1), or sometimes on a griddle or earthen oven. Archaeological evidence has turned up clay cooking pots, cauldrons, and even frying pans, along with some utensils for carving or stirring, but undoubtedly most meals were eaten with the hands, using the folded bread as both a scoop and a sponge, while the fingers picked up the larger or more slippery morsels.

To prepare the following recipes, a modern stove and oven are key; yet some of the same time-tested, ancient methods of food production will be used to create the meal. When serving, to lend an air of authenticity, use large clay bowls or casserole dishes, and maybe some pottery pitchers and drinking vessels. And be bold! Leave the knives and forks in the drawer, and let everyone fend for themselves!

THE RECIPES

❧ *Savory Chevon Ragout*

1 large bag of frozen cubed goat meat	1 cup onions, minced
4–5 large garlic cloves, minced	¾ cup olive oil

1 red bell pepper, chopped

1 green bell pepper, chopped

5 large, very ripe tomatoes, finely cut

3 Tbsp. cumin

1 Tbsp. ground coriander

2 tsp. salt

1 tsp. ground black pepper

½–1 cup water

¼ cup flour

juice of one lemon

bed of rice

fresh mint

crumbled goat cheese

Place frozen goat cubes in boiling water and simmer slowly, stirring about every 5 minutes. Cover slightly and continue simmering (about 15 minutes) until meat is very tender and a bit stringy. Discard water and cover. In a large frying pan, combine the garlic and onions and cook at medium heat in olive oil; toss in chopped peppers, cooking slowly until all are tender and lightly browned. Add goat cubes and allow them to cook about 5–10 minutes on low to medium heat, taking care to allow them to brown and pick up the flavor of the garlic-

Although requiring a lot of preparation, this delicious goat stew is well worth the effort.

onion-pepper mixture. Next add tomatoes, spices, and water and let cook on low heat for 25–30 minutes, stirring occasionally so that there is no burning. (If there does not seem to be enough liquid in the pan, add another ½ cup water.) As dish thickens, add flour and lemon juice. Serve piping hot over rice, with sprigs of mint and a sprinkling of goat cheese on top.

For a nice presentation, have several bottles of full-bodied red wine on hand, and be generous as you pour, just as Jacob was when he served the meal to his father.

Yield: 8–12 servings

Rice of Beersheba

1½ cups water

1½ cups chicken broth

1 tsp. salt

1 Tbsp. butter or olive oil

1½ cups basmati rice

½ cup fresh dill, finely cut

⅛ cup capers

Fill a large saucepan with the water and broth; add salt and butter or olive oil, and bring to a boil. Stir in rice. Quickly cover and simmer on lowest heat possible, stirring once or twice to help prevent clumping. Pour into a large wooden bowl and mix in dill and capers. Toss like a salad just prior to serving.

Yield: 6 large servings

For those who have never sampled savory and fragrant basmati rice, Rice of Beersheba will convince you to use it at every turn.

Rebekah's "Tasty Dish"

For folks whose nose wrinkles or stomach turns at the thought of eating goat, here's a recipe along the same lines that uses lamb instead.

3 lb. lamb, boned

2–3 medium onions, chopped fine

1 clove garlic, crushed

1 cup wine vinegar

1 cup water

10–12 whole peppercorns

1 Tbsp. salt

2–3 bay leaves

1 tsp. caraway seeds

1 Tbsp. sugar

3 Tbsp. oil for browning meat

Rebekah knew what she was doing when she prepared this meal—it was good enough to steal a father's blessing.

Place the lamb in a glass or earthenware bowl. Add onions and garlic. Combine remaining ingredients, except oil, in a saucepan and bring to a full boil. Pour over lamb and refrigerate 12–24 hours. Remove lamb from liquid; pat dry with paper towels. Put oil in a heavy pan and brown meat on all sides. Add liquid and cover. Let simmer over low heat for about 2 hours, or until tender.

Yield: 6–8 servings

Source: "Rebekah's 'Tasty Dish' ": adaptation used by permission of Whitaker House (www.whitaker house.com), as found in Frank L. and Jean McKibbin, *Cookbook of Foods from Bible Days*, copyright © 1971 by Whitaker House. All rights reserved.

Venison Stew

2 lb. venison for stewing	1 tsp. pepper
½ cup olive oil	6 juniper berries, crushed
1 onion, chopped	1 bay leaf
1 whole head of garlic, minced	1 tsp. zaatar
1 tsp. flour	½ tsp. sumac
1 rutabaga, peeled and diced	1 fennel bulb
6 carrots, diced	3 Tbsp. butter
2 cups pitted dates, chopped	1 tsp. light brown sugar
2 cups dry white wine	3 Tbsp. flat leaf parsley
½ tsp. salt	

Cut the venison into 1″ cubes. Heat the oil in a large electric frying pan and sear the meat well on all sides. Mince the onion and garlic in a food processor and add to the meat, cooking until the onion starts to appear translucent. Stir in the flour, then the rutabaga, carrots, and dates. Add the wine, salt, pepper, juniper berries, bay leaf, zaatar, and sumac. Cover and simmer for about 2 hours, or until the meat is very tender.

Cut the fennel into thin slices and sauté in butter with a bit of brown sugar for about three minutes; chop the parsley. When meat is cooked, remove bay leaf and lightly stir in caramelized fennel and parsley just before serving.

Yield: 12 servings

Mouthwatering Date and Walnut Bread

1 oz. yeast
¾ cup lukewarm water
½ cup warm white grape juice
4½ cups flour
1 tsp. salt
1 cup dates, finely chopped
1 cup black walnuts, finely chopped
olive oil

Preheat oven to 500°F.

Dissolve yeast in a mixture of water and white grape juice. Sift in the flour and salt. Add dates and walnuts. Mix well and knead in a large bowl for just a short time, then remove

This simple walnut and date bread combines sweetness with crunchiness for a moist and tasty treat.

to a flat surface that has been generously sprinkled with flour. Let stand for 2–3 minutes. Cut dough into 10 fairly equal groupings. Using the palm of your hand, flatten each ball till about 4″ in diameter, but no more than ¼″ in thickness. Cover a large cutting board with wax paper, and place a drop or two of olive oil under each flat cake, arranging them so that they are about ½″ apart. Place a clean dish towel over the cakes and set them aside, allowing them to rise to about ½″ or more in thickness. Bake for 5–6 minutes, or until lightly browned.

Yield: 10 cakes

❧ *Jacob's Green Bean Salad*

1½ lb. green beans

2 cloves garlic, minced

juice of one lemon

3 Tbsp. olive oil

a handful of fresh parsley

1 tsp. ground cumin

½ tsp. salt

½ tsp. black pepper

3 medium-sized fresh tomatoes, chopped

1 cucumber, scored and diced

3 spring onions

Crispy and tart, this green bean salad is a fresh alternative to long-baked vegetable dishes.

Steam green beans for just a few minutes until slightly crispy. Allow to cool. Push the garlic cloves through a press into a small bowl and mix with lemon juice and 2 Tbsp. of olive oil; pour over green beans. Chop the parsley to a very fine consistency and combine with remaining spices and 1 Tbsp. olive oil. Pour mixture over tomatoes, cucumber, and onions. Add to bean mixture and refrigerate. Toss before serving.

Yield: 4–6 servings

❧ *Edam Cheese and Seedless Grapes*

In the chapters prior to Genesis 27, we learn that Esau was also called "Edom," meaning "red." Hence Edam, the goat's milk cheese, very popular in Northern Africa and throughout Europe, is most often found in a large ball that has been sealed in a deep red wax. It can be purchased in almost any food store, and accompanied by seedless grapes, green or purple, makes an excellent appetizer, dessert, or accompaniment for any biblical meal.

Cheese and grapes were a typical dessert option for people of biblical times.

🎵 The Ultimate Deception

It is said that this recipe is a favorite of every Middle Eastern bride as she tries to impress her in-laws on their first dinner visit: the final product looks showy but is really quite easy to make. Try it and see for yourself how your guests ooh and aah!

6 eggs, separated

1 tsp. vanilla extract

1 Tbsp. olive oil

1 tsp. baking powder

¼ tsp. salt

flour

1 cup shortening

1 cup canola oil

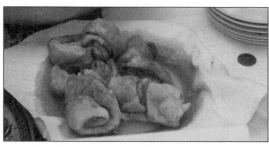

This recipe, known as The Ultimate Deception, is a favorite of every Middle Eastern bride trying to impress her in-laws on their first dinner visit.

Beat the egg whites until they are stiff and form peaks. Combine the egg yolks with the whites and beat again. Add vanilla, olive oil, baking powder, and salt to the egg mixture. Begin adding flour until a soft dough forms. Mold the dough into two balls, place in a covered bowl, and let stand for 1 hour. Take each ball and spread out as thin as possible. Cut the dough into 1″-wide strips. Heat the shortening and the canola oil in a deep pan. Take a fork and wrap a dough strip around the tines. Keep turning the fork in the oil so as to brown the curl on all sides. Be careful to stop when the curl is a light, golden brown. Repeat the process until all the strips are done. Place each curl on an absorbent paper towel after cooking to remove all the excess oil. Drizzle with sugary-lemon syrup and serve; or sprinkle with confectioners' sugar for a dessert that's a bit lighter.

Sugary-Lemon Syrup

2 cups sugar

½ cup lemon juice

1 cup water

Combine sugar, lemon juice, and water in a small pan and allow to boil for about 30 minutes or so. Remove from heat and slowly drizzle over the dessert.

Yield: 8–12 servings

NOTES

1. Ilse U. Köhler-Rollefson, "Animals," in *Harper's Bible Dictionary*, ed. Paul J. Achtemeier et al. (San Francisco: Harper & Row, 1985), 31.

2. George B. Eager, in "Bread" (*International Standard Bible Encyclopedia*, www.studylight .org/enc/isb), writes, "In the East bread is primary, other articles of food merely accessory; while in the West meat and other things chiefly constitute the meal, and bread is merely

secondary. Accordingly 'bread' in the Old Testament, from Genesis 3:19 onward, stands for food in general. Moreover in ancient times, as now, most probably, when the peasant, carpenter, blacksmith or mason left home for the day's work, or when the muleteer or messenger set out on a journey, he wrapped other articles of food, if there were any, in the thin loaves of bread, and thus kept them ready for his use as needed. Often the thin, glutinous loaf, puffed out with air, is seen today, opened on one side and used so as to form a natural pouch, in which meat, cheese, raisins and olives are enclosed to be eaten with the bread. The loaf of bread is thus made to include everything and, for this reason also, it may fitly be spoken of as synonymous with food in general."

3. Wade Cox, "Wine in the Bible (No. 188)," *Christian Churches of God*, www.ccg.org/english/s/p188.html

4. Charles L. Souvay, "Plants in the Bible," in *The Catholic Encyclopedia*, ed. Kevin Knight (www.newadvent.org, 2003), from *The Catholic Encyclopedia*, vol. XXII (New York: Robert Appleton Company, 1911).

5. Robert Jamieson, A. R. Fausset, and David Brown, *A Commentary, Critical and Explanatory, on the Whole Bible* (New York: George H. Doran, 1921), chap. 27, nn. 13–17.

6. Kitty Morse, *A Biblical Feast: Foods from the Holy Land* (Berkeley, Calif.: Ten Speed Press, 1998), 7.

Joseph Dines with His Brothers

4

THE TEXT

11 Their father Israel gave in. "If it has to be, it has to be. But do this: stuff your packs with the finest products from the land you can find and take them to the man as gifts— some balm and honey, some spices and perfumes, some pistachios and almonds.

12 "And take plenty of money— pay back double what was returned to your sacks; that might have been a mistake.

13 "Take your brother and get going. Go back to the man."

"Gum, balm and myrrh, honey, and nuts—all are packed into the saddle bags of the asses, loaded for the long journey southward."

. . . .

31 Then Joseph washed his face, got a grip on himself, and said, "Let's eat."

32 Joseph was served at his private table, the brothers off by themselves and the Egyptians off by themselves (Egyptians won't eat at the same table with Hebrews; it's repulsive to them).

33 The brothers were seated facing Joseph, arranged in order of their age, from the oldest to the youngest. They looked at one another wide-eyed, wondering what would happen next.

34 When the brothers' plates were served from Joseph's table, Benjamin's plate came piled high, far more so than his brothers. And so the brothers feasted with Joseph, drinking freely.

Genesis 43:11–13, 31–34, The Message

THE HISTORY

As recounted in Chapter 3, Jacob fled Esau's wrath and took refuge with their Uncle Laban in Haran. On the way, he had a vision of a ladder extending from earth to heaven; angels were gliding up and down the ladder when God appeared, to renew the covenant made with Abraham and to promise that the land of Canaan would belong to Jacob's descendants. Jacob called the place *Beth-el,* which means "house of God."

As soon as Jacob reached Haran, he fell in love with Rachel, Laban's second daughter. To gain his uncle's permission to marry her, Jacob agreed to indenture himself to the household as a shepherd for seven years. Although Jacob had played the role of deceiver with his brother, Laban proved more adept at the game of trickery. At the end of Jacob's period of service, Laban brought Leah, his first daughter, disguised as Rachel, to the bridal chamber, tricking his nephew into marrying her and forcing him into another seven years of servitude in order to marry Rachel. A week later he was permitted to marry Rachel, and Jacob began his second seven-year term with two wives. After the period of indenture was completed, he continued to work for Laban for several more years. They agreed on dividing the herds of sheep and goats, Jacob taking only those animals that were spotted or speckled; now it was Jacob's turn to best his uncle, and he did so by somehow causing the strongest animals to bear speckled and spotted offspring. In the meantime, Jacob's family increased in number: he accepted two concubines, Bilhah and Zilpah, and they and his two wives eventually bore him twelve sons and one daughter. Their names were Reuben, Simeon, Levi, Judah, Zebulun, Issachar, Dan, Gad, Asher, Naphtali, Joseph, Benjamin, and Dinah. Jacob favored Joseph because he was Rachel's first son.

After more than twenty years, Jacob decided that it was time to leave Haran and return to the land of his birth. So he assembled his family and his flocks and departed his father-in-law's house in secret. When he was not far from his destination, he received word that Esau and four hundred of his men were coming to meet him. Fearfully dispatching gifts to his brother, and in an act of cowardice sending his flocks, wives, and children to cross the Jabbok River to meet Esau ahead of him, Jacob made plans to flee—but in the night an angel came to wrestle with him, preventing him from leaving. Jacob finally bested the angel at daybreak, refusing to let the angel depart until he had received a blessing. The angel blessed Jacob with a new name, Israel (*Yisrael*), which means "the one who wrestled with God," "the one who overpowered God," or "God's champion." That day, Jacob reconciled with Esau, though the brothers did not remain together. Jacob and his family continued on to Shechem, where Dinah's abduction (or elopement) so angered her brothers that they destroyed the city and massacred the inhabitants. Finding himself in Beth-el again, Jacob experienced another direct encounter with God, who confirmed him in his new name and repeated the promise to give the land of Canaan to his descendants. Afterward, Jacob and his entourage went to Hebron.

In the ensuing years Joseph began to earn his brothers' enmity because he was Jacob's favorite: Jacob had indicated this by presenting Joseph with a "coat of many colors," a richly ornamented robe that symbolized the father's passing on of his inheritance to the son who would become the head of the household. In presenting such a robe to Joseph, Jacob indicated his intention to disregard long-standing tradition. Joseph was younger than all the brothers save one, and his elevation over his elders greatly angered them. Nevertheless, he naively persisted in telling them of his dreams, in which everyone, including all his older brothers, bowed down before him. Finally, Simeon and the other young men could stomach Joseph's arrogance no longer: they sold him into slavery, to a band of Ishmaelites, and told their father that a wild animal had killed Joseph. Jacob grieved his favored son and took solace in the childhood of Benjamin, his youngest.

Meanwhile, the Ishmaelites took Joseph, who was but seventeen years old, to Egypt, where he became a slave of Potiphar, captain of Pharaoh's guard. Joseph proved himself capable and was finally promoted to head of the servants, but he was imprisoned when he rebuffed the seductions of Potiphar's wife and she accused him of rape. The head jailer soon put Joseph in charge of the other prisoners, who eventually discovered Joseph's ability to interpret their dreams. The dreams of one, the royal cupbearer, predicted his reinstatement to his post, but that servant forgot all about his promise to help Joseph until, some two years later, Pharaoh had a strange dream that none of his advisors could decipher. Finally remembering his promise, the cupbearer brought Joseph to Pharaoh's attention. According to Joseph's interpretation, Pharaoh's dream predicted seven years of abundance followed by seven years of famine. Impressed, Pharaoh appointed Joseph chief steward of Egypt and ordered him to store up surplus grain against the coming years of want. During these years of abundance, Joseph married Asenath, a priest's daughter, was accepted as a member of the priestly class, and had two sons, Manasseh and Ephraim. After Pharaoh, Joseph was perhaps the most powerful man in Egypt—the grand vizier—all this by the time he was thirty.

Famine soon struck the region, and people from far and wide came to Egypt to buy food. In Pharaoh's name, Joseph took their money, their livestock, their land, and finally their very persons—all came to belong to Pharaoh. Some archaeological evidence indicates that this would have taken place about 1600 B.C.E., though some scholars place the date of Joseph's rise to prominence in Egypt as early as 1800 B.C.E. Still others question whether the story of Joseph in Egypt has any historical veracity.

BIBLICAL PASSAGE NOTES

The story of Joseph and his coat of many colors is well known to most Bible readers. It is a classic tale of sibling rivalry and jealousy, a recurrent and favorite theme in the scriptures. By this point in the book of Genesis (chapter 43), Joseph encounters his brothers the day they show up in Pharaoh's court to purchase grain; they, on the other hand, do not recognize Joseph. He soon learns that there is a brother younger than he who is staying at home with Jacob while the remaining ten brothers are on their pilgrimage for food. Desirous to reacquaint himself with the youngest of his clan, Joseph sends his brothers back to their father, demanding that the youngest present himself lest all end up in prison for spying on Egypt. Simeon, one of the eldest brothers, is held as a ransom until the remaining fraternity return with the youngest, "a lad" called Benjamin.

When the brothers return to Jacob and tell him what they have learned and experienced, he is grieved and crestfallen. One son, Simeon, is now in an Egyptian jail; a second son, Joseph, had been kidnapped and is presumed dead (that's what the brothers had told their father, though they know better); and now a third, the darling of Jacob's brood, is to be taken from his household. It was more than a father could bear.

It is here that we pick up the story. Jacob, realizing that there is no other good choice, relents and lets Benjamin go, both to get food and to redeem his brother in prison. The wise old man, Jacob, knows not to send them once again to Egypt empty-handed. He instructs his sons to carry some of the "best fruits of the land" to the grand vizier's court, the delicacies and spices that had been traded with the Ishmaelites (cf. Genesis 37:25), such as gum, balm and myrrh, honey, and nuts—and all are packed into the saddlebags of the asses, loaded for the long journey southward. Jacob understands the type of man he is dealing with in Egypt, and his gifts are meant to impress and show respect for the esteemed position of the high court official. He is leaving nothing to chance, and along with the food he sends back double the money that had been secreted by Joseph's servants into the packs of his brothers when they left Egypt. Double the money, double the gifts, double the effort means double the chances he will see his sons again. In the end, he gets more than he bargains for or could ever have expected.

When the ten brothers arrive once again in Egypt, Joseph is ready for them. He has instructed the palace steward to set the stage for a meal at which Joseph will reveal his true identity. But the sight of his brothers, this time with Benjamin in tow, is more than Joseph can emotionally handle. He is forced to leave the room, weeping in combined emotions of joy, mixed with sadness at his betrayal, tempered by his own dreamlike visions that God's guidance is behind all that has happened, as well as all that is about to take place.

Getting a grip on himself, Joseph returns to the banquet room and sits to eat. The servants attend to Joseph separately, as befits his station; next the brothers, humble shepherd visitors, but aliens in the land, nonetheless; finally, the rest of the Egyptian court who have little tolerance for usurping neighbors looking for a handout. Still, the text records that all eat and drink well, and are "merry with Joseph."

The hospitality of the meal serves as an icebreaker and lays the groundwork for the big surprise that Joseph later reveals to his siblings and their father: Joseph is alive, well, and wealthy, and despite all, he forgives them and loves them, because he sees God's hand in all that has happened. He discerns that he had been chosen by God to be the savior of his brothers and their people, having been sent ahead long before to pave the way to their salvation from hunger and starvation. Joseph understands that he is the right man in the right place at the right time to fulfill what he believes to be God's plan for the people of God, in keeping with the covenant God had made with Noah centuries before.

The Menu

Eesh Baladi (Egyptian Caraway Seed Bread)

Ful Medames and Scrambled Eggs

Coat of Jacob Salad

Fried Sole in Pistachio Crust

Bamya (Egyptian Meat and Okra Stew)

Marinated Duck with Juniper and Almond Sauce

Goat's Milk and Pomegranate Syrup Torte

Asbusa (Egyptian cookies)

Tiger Nut Sweets

Fresh Lemon Balm on Ice

Egyptian Beers and Wines

The Preparation

It is clear that Joseph loved his brothers, and despite his harsh treatment of them at times (perhaps so as to not tip his hand until he determined whether they were finally trustworthy), he did lavish upon them a great meal in his own palatial setting. Such an important feast would have required planning and preparation, and perhaps a little innovation. The menu? We can't be sure, but one supposes that wheat, if in such abundance and obviously highly prized, would appear in some form or another at the table. (The KJV calls the grain "corn," but corn was unknown in the Middle East and is a product of the Americas, where Native Americans grew it as *maize*. Barley, or some other grain such as wheat, is what the text intends the reader to understand.) It would probably have been impolite not to serve a portion of the gifts rendered from the brothers' homeland: the balm from Gilead (in Hebrew, *tsori*), in this instance a kind of pistachio oil from the mastic tree;[1] honey (in Hebrew, *debash*), the kind that was cultivated from bees; spices (in Hebrew, *nekoth*) of the rarest kind, especially the sweet-smelling sort; pistachios (in Hebrew, *botnim*) and almonds (in Hebrew, *shaqed*). If they ate and drank freely, there was certainly some sort of wine on hand. And a typical Egyptian meal fit for a grand vizier would undoubtedly have featured fish from the Nile, radishes, garlic, cucumbers, melons, dates, and other dried fruits, all presented in abundance (Benjamin's portion was five times that of his brothers) and fine style, well prepared, lovely to look at, tasty to shepherd and royal official alike.

THE RECIPES

❧ Eesh Baladi *(Egyptian Caraway Seed Bread)*

2 tsp. dry yeast

1 cup warm water

2½ cups whole wheat flour

1 tsp. salt

1 cup caraway seeds

fresh honey

Dissolve the yeast in the warm water. Mix the flour and salt together and slowly add it to the yeast. Add the caraway seeds. Work the mixture into a dough and knead for several minutes. Cover the dough with a damp cloth and let it rise in a warm place for 1–1½ hours.

Preheat oven to 350°F.

Divide the dough into 8 equal portions and roll into balls. Press into flat, round shapes. Place on a greased baking sheet and bake for about 20 minutes, or until barely golden.

Drizzle with fresh honey and serve warm.

Yield: 8 servings

Many cooks will serve *Eesh Baladi* (Egyptian caraway seed bread) with honey, but it is also very tasty when eaten plain.

❧ Ful Medames *and Scrambled Eggs*

1½ lb. dried fava beans	3 cloves garlic, crushed
6 cups fresh water	3 small onions, finely chopped

½ cup parsley, very finely chopped

1 green pepper, finely chopped

1 Tbsp. red pepper flakes

6 eggs, scrambled

Soak the beans for 12 hours, or overnight if possible. Drain; cover with fresh water in a large saucepan. Bring to a quick boil, then reduce the heat and simmer for about 1 hour. (Add water if necessary.)

Drain once again. In a large bowl, add the beans, garlic, onions, parsley, green pepper, red pepper, and mash. Served with scrambled eggs, either mixed in or as a side dish.

Yield: 6 servings

The broad bean, also known as the fava bean (*ful medames*), was widely cultivated in Egypt during biblical times, and the ancient Egyptians stocked the tombs of the dead with dried favas to provision life in the hereafter. Alone, fava beans can be a bit bland, but this combination of favas and scrambled eggs is quite tasty.

🍂 Coat of Jacob Salad

¼ lb. dandelion greens

1 medium cucumber, pared and diced

2 medium tomatoes, diced

4 green onions, sliced

½ cup cheddar cheese, shredded

½ cup ripe olives, cut in half

dressing of olive oil and lemon juice

freshly ground pepper

Wash dandelion greens in several waters. Remove damaged leaves and flower buds. If leaves are long, cut into 2″ pieces. Combine with remaining ingredients. Pour dressing made from olive oil and lemon juice over salad generously. Toss lightly and serve with freshly ground pepper.

Yield: 4 servings

Among the ancient Israelites, a father presented his cloak to the son, usually the firstborn, chosen to become the leader of the household. But when Jacob gave a rich cloak to Joseph, the youngest son save one, the older brothers felt slighted—and sought revenge. The scriptures indicate that Jacob's cloak was multicolored, and the ingredients in this Coat of Jacob Salad reflect all the colors of the rainbow.

Source: "Coat of Jacob Salad": adaptation used by permission of Whitaker House (www.whitakerhouse .com), as found in Frank L. and Jean McKibbin, *Cookbook of Foods from Bible Days*, copyright © 1971 by Whitaker House. All rights reserved.

❧ Fried Sole in Pistachio Crust

8 pieces of lotus root, thinly sliced

flour

½ cup butter

1 Tbsp. ginger root, minced

3 Tbsp. olive oil

6 ripe tomatoes, diced

1 cup fresh bean sprouts

4 scallions, sliced

1 cup pistachios, finely chopped

1 cup fresh bread crumbs

1 tsp. salt

2 tsp. black pepper

1 Tbsp. dried tarragon

4 sole fillets

½ cup flour

4 eggs, well beaten (for a wash)

a pint or two of cherry tomatoes, halved

lime juice

The Nile provided a wide variety of foodstuffs to both the ancient Egyptians and their Israelite slaves. This sole recipe draws upon such variety, combining lotus root with fish, as well as pistachios, tomatoes, bean sprouts, and scallions, for a mouthwatering dish.

Preheat oven to 350°F.

Roll the lotus root in flour and fry it in butter until crispy. Remove from pan and let drain on a paper towel, then cut it into small pieces. Set aside. In another frying pan, sauté the ginger root in a bit of olive oil for a few minutes, then add the lotus root, tomatoes, bean sprouts, and scallions, stirring frequently to prevent burning.

Mix the pistachios, bread crumbs, salt, pepper, and tarragon together in a small bowl. Cover each fillet of sole on both sides with flour, dip in an egg wash, then coat with the nut mixture. Place in a large baking dish so that the fillets are touching but not overlapping. Bake for 30–35 minutes. Remove from the oven.

Spread the tomato mixture evenly across a long and wide serving platter, surrounding it with halved cherry tomatoes placed around the rim edge. Remove the fish from the baking dish and place it in the center of the platter. Squeeze a bit of lime juice over the fish, and serve hot.

Yield: 12–16 servings

Bamya (Egyptian Meat and Okra Stew)

3 lb. fresh okra

1½ cups red wine or Balsamic vinegar

6 Tbsp. unsalted butter

2 onions, finely chopped

2 cloves garlic, minced

2 lb. stewing lamb or beef, cut into cubes

1 tsp. ground cumin

1 tsp. ground coriander

1 cup tomatoes, peeled and chopped

4 Tbsp. tomato paste

1 cup beef stock

large handful of mint leaves, freshly chopped

salt and freshly ground pepper

3 Tbsp. olive oil

Many food historians believe that the peoples of ancient Egypt grew okra and used it in their cooking. *Bamya*, a stew made from either lamb or beef, has a very distinctive taste and texture thanks to its okra base.

Preheat oven to 325°F.

Trim the tops of the okra and soak it in red wine or Balsamic vinegar for about 30 minutes.

Melt the butter in a large frying pan over medium-high heat. Sauté the onions and garlic until tender, about 10 minutes. Add the meat a bit at a time, frying the cubes until browned on all sides. Transfer the meat to a large, deep baking dish, leaving the onion, garlic, and meat juices. Heat this mixture, stirring well; then add to it the cumin, coriander, tomatoes, tomato paste, beef stock, and mint. When very hot, pour over the meat and season with a bit of salt and pepper. Cover and bake until all the liquid is absorbed, about 1½ hours.

Heat the olive oil in a frying pan. Sauté the wine-soaked okra over a low heat for about 3–5 minutes, stirring occasionally until it is light brown. Remove the stew from the oven and arrange the okra in a spoke pattern over the stew. Re-cover the dish and return it to the oven. Bake for approximately 35 minutes more. Add a little beef stock if the mixture seems too dry. Serve immediately.

Yield: 8–12 servings

Marinated Duck with Juniper and Almond Sauce

1 cup Grand Marnier

½ cup almond paste

3 cloves garlic, crushed

1 cup fresh chives

2 Tbsp. fresh tarragon leaves

1 tsp. fresh lemon thyme leaves

½ cup gin

6 juniper berries, crushed

1 tsp. ground cloves

4 bay leaves, crushed

½ cup slivered almonds

1 cup raspberry (or Balsamic) vinegar

2 lb. lean duck meat, sliced thin

2 cups wild rice

½ cup capers

Ducks were abundant along the Nile, and ancient Egyptian cooks developed a variety of ways to tenderize and flavor duck. Combining the bitter taste of juniper berries with the sour taste of vinegar, the sweet taste of Grand Marnier, and the nutty taste of almonds, the marinade in this recipe gives the duck a really spectacular flavor.

In a small saucepan, heat the Grand Marnier and the almond paste until they make a thick sauce, stirring frequently to prevent burning. Lower the heat and add the garlic, chives, tarragon, and thyme. Simmer for about 1 minute. Add the gin and juniper berries and stir quickly. Remove from the flame. Place the cloves, bay leaves, and almonds in a plastic bag and shake to mix; add to the vinegar. Lump the duck meat in a large bowl with a lid and pour the vinegar mixture over it. Pour the sauce evenly over the duck and marinate for at least 3 hours, or overnight if possible.

Preheat the oven to 275°F. Cook the duck slowly for 2½–3 hours. For the last 15 minutes of cooking, increase the oven temperature to 350°F. Serve in a soup tureen, and spoon over wild rice mixed with fresh capers. (Remove the bay leaf prior to serving.)

Yield: 6–8 servings

❦ *Goat's Milk and Pomegranate Syrup Torte*

2 cups all purpose flour

1 tsp. baking powder

¼ cup light olive oil

¼ cup sunflower oil

½ cup beer

1½ cups creamy goat cheese (or sheep's milk cheese)

⅓ cup pomegranate juice

1 tsp. vanilla extract

½ tsp. ground mastic

½ tsp. ground allspice

2 eggs

ground nutmeg

Preheat oven to 375°F.

In a large bowl combine the flour with the baking powder. Add the oils and beer and mix briefly by hand into a soft, oily dough. (If it becomes too soft to handle, add a bit more flour to your hands and knead again.) Work the dough mixture into a ball; cover and set aside for 10 minutes or so.

Take the dough and flatten it with both hands. Place in a baking pan with a removable bottom and press it evenly against the bottom surface as well as up the sides. Cover with aluminum foil and bake for 15 minutes. Uncover the pan, prick the dough all over with a fork, and bake for 15–20 minutes more. (The crust should look slightly browned.) Remove from the oven and allow to cool completely.

This torte, made from goat's milk and pomegranate syrup, can be served as part of the meal's appetizer course, or as a dessert.

In the meantime, combine the cheese, pomegranate juice, vanilla extract, mastic, and allspice in a blender until smooth. Add the eggs and blend again. Pour into the prepared crust and even out the surface with an icing spatula or flat spoon. Bake for approximately 30 minutes. While still warm, sprinkle with a bit of ground nutmeg.

Let cool before serving.

Yield: 8–12 servings

Asbusa (Egyptian cookies)

2½ cups sugar

2 lb. cream of wheat

¾ lb. butter

16 oz. plain yogurt

water as needed

slivered almond halves

Preheat oven to 375°F.

Bring all ingredients to room temperature. In a large bowl, mix the sugar and cream of wheat. Add butter; mix by hand, rubbing the butter, sugar, and cream of wheat between your palms for 10 minutes or more until the mixture is very well blended.

Asbusa, otherwise known as Egyptian cookies, are a flavorful dessert with a sweet, grainy texture.

Fold the yogurt into the dough and knead by hand until the dough feels smooth. (If it feels dry, add water 1 Tbsp. at a time so when you hold it in your hands it feels like pie dough.)

Butter a 13″ x 9″ pan and pat the dough into the pan with your hand. With a sharp knife slice the dough in 2″ squares or into diamond shapes. Press one almond half onto the surface of each piece. Bake for 30–40 minutes or until golden brown.

Yield: 12–16 servings

❦ *Tiger Nut Sweets*

1 cup fresh dates, pits removed

¼ cup water

1 tsp. ground cinnamon

½ cup walnuts, chopped

1½ cups honey

1 cup almonds, finely ground

Blend the dates in a bit of water. Add cinnamon and chopped walnuts, and roll into balls. (If too dry, add a little more water.) Dip each ball in a bowl of honey and roll around a bit, then remove with a spoon and roll once again, this time in the almonds. Place on a cookie sheet lined with waxed paper until ready to serve. (Refrigerate if not serving immediately. If they seem too sticky to handle when serving, roll them in a bit of powdered sugar.)

Yield: 24 balls

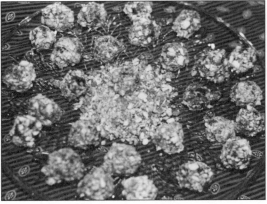

Also known as tiger balls, Tiger Nut Sweets contain two different types of nuts (walnuts and almonds) and two sources of sweetness (dates and honey), rolled together into a confection that will satisfy even the sweetest sweet tooth.

❦ *Fresh Lemon Balm on Ice*

Gather sprigs of lemon balm and orange mint (if available; if not, black mint or spearmint are good). Using the whole sprigs, wring them and crush them between your hands, then toss them into a pitcher of water mixed with 1 drop of rose petal water or almond extract. Serve over ice.

❦ *Egyptian Beers and Wines*

The brewing of beer originated in Egypt, so it is no surprise that all sorts of beers can be found in modern-day Egypt. In the United States, some are available from local importers. If you can find them, try a Stella (either the light or premium) lager, or perhaps a Sakara Seven Stars lager. They're on the heavy side of beer drinking, but flavorful.

As for wines, Egyptians have been drinking wine for thousand of years, though it is only recently that Egyptian wineries are starting to make an impact on the export market. The usual house wine for most Egyptian restaurants and hotel bars is Obelisk; some critics have recommended Omar Khayyam (they say it is "falafel-flavored") or Cru des Ptolomés (which has a reputation for being a bit on the vinegary side). If it is available, a Chateau Grand Marquis is supposed to have a good flavor for a red wine. Travel magazine writers have not liked most of the white or rosé wines, but of course, like everything else in life, it's a matter of personal taste.

NOTES

1. Patricia L. Crawford, "Balm," in *Harper's Bible Dictionary*, 90–91.

❧ 5 ❧

A Passover Meal

THE TEXT

1 The LORD said to Moses and Aaron in Egypt,

2 "This month is to be for you the first month, the first month of your year.

3 "Tell the whole community of Israel that on the tenth day of this month each man is to take a lamb for his family, one for each household.

4 "If any household is too small for a whole lamb, they must share one with their nearest neighbor, having taken into account the number of people there are. You are to determine the amount of lamb needed in accordance with what each person will eat.

5 "The animals you choose must be year-old males without defect, and you may take them from the sheep or the goats.

6 "Take care of them until the fourteenth day of the month, when all the people of the community of Israel must slaughter them at twilight.

7 "Then they are to take some of the blood and put it on the sides and tops of the door-frames of the houses where they eat the lambs.

8 "That same night they are to eat the meat roasted over the fire, along with bitter herbs, and bread made without yeast.

9 "Do not eat the meat raw or cooked in water, but roast it over the fire—head, legs and inner parts.

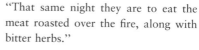

"That same night they are to eat the meat roasted over the fire, along with bitter herbs."

10 "Do not leave any of it till morning; if some is left till morning, you must burn it.

11 "This is how you are to eat it: with your cloak tucked into your belt, your sandals on your feet and your staff in your hand. Eat it in haste; it is the LORD's Passover."

Exodus 12:1–11, New International Version—United Kingdom

THE HISTORY

The figure of Moses presents a particular dilemma for historians. While the patriarchs Abraham, Isaac, and Jacob (Israel) are generally held (except by biblical literalists) to be symbolic personages of ancient Jewish mythology, there is much less agreement about who Moses might have been, or whether he even existed. Certainly, there are no extrabiblical accounts of the life of Moses nor of the enslavement of the ancient Hebrews in Egypt or their Exodus (escape from Egypt and forty-year wandering in the desert). Some scholars contend that the story was fabricated in the 7th century B.C.E. by scribes hired by King Josiah to explain his (and his subjects') monotheism. Other scholars assert that the Egyptians themselves may have destroyed any records of Moses and the Exodus, as the events portray a failure that the Egyptians would not have wanted to become part of their legacy.

If Moses were indeed a historical person, there are several hypotheses about who he might have been and when he might have lived.

First, there is the belief that Moses was indeed a Hebrew, the son of the Levite Amram and his wife, Jochebed (Yocheved), as recounted in the Bible's book of Exodus. His family would have been descendants of the sons of Jacob, who immigrated to Egypt during the great seven-year famine because one son, Joseph, had known the future through dream interpretation and had been in a position in Egypt to store up vast quantities of food to prepare for the catastrophe. Proponents of this theory date the life of Moses to the 16th century B.C.E., at the end of the Egyptian Hyksos era.

Second, there is the theory that Moses was an Egyptian prince who was a contemporary disciple of Akhenaten, an Egyptian Pharaoh of the 14th century B.C.E. Known as Amenhotep IV when he came to power, Akhenaten almost immediately set about simplifying Egyptian religious beliefs. He declared the obscure Egyptian sun-god, Aten (Aton), to be the Supreme God—then, a few years later, to be the One God, establishing state-sanctioned monotheism. Some scholars believe that Moses developed his devotion to the One God under Akhenaten's tutorship, and it is generally accepted that *Moses* is an Egyptian name meaning "son"—perhaps the symbolic son of Akhenaten or an adaptation of "sun" to "son." A few scholars even assert that Moses and Akhenaten were the same person, though there are few similarities between the religion of the ancient Israelites and Atenism, and there are many similarities between the Hebrew faith and other Semitic religions.

Third is the belief that Moses was Ramose (Ra-Moses), the Crown Prince of Egypt who disappeared from Egyptian records in the early 15th century B.C.E. Fourth is that Moses was indeed a Hebrew but had access to the court of Ramses II in the 13th century B.C.E. Finally, there is speculation that Moses was a renegade Egyptian priest who led a leper colony out of oppression.

If we follow the biblical narrative, Moses was born at a time when Pharaoh (perhaps Ramses II) became fearful that his slaves would become too powerful and consequently ordered all Hebrew boy babies killed. Jochebed hid Moses upon his birth, but after a few months she placed him in a basket and set him adrift on the Nile. Pharaoh's daughter found the baby and adopted him, allowing Moses' sister, Miriam, to take the child to Jochebed to nurse. It was Pharaoh's daughter who coined the name *Moses,* which means "to draw out"—a double entendre, as Moses was drawn out of the Nile, but he was also to draw the Israelites out of bondage. Moses grew up in the royal household, but he seems to have been a curious young man—he went out to the construction sites to observe the working of the slaves, for example. One day, he witnessed an Egyptian overseer mistreating a Hebrew slave; Moses killed the overseer and then hid the body. When he went to the construction sites another time, he stopped a brawl between two Israelites, and they taunted him about his murderous temper. Knowing that his crime had been discovered by Pharaoh, and that the penalty was death, Moses fled across the Sinai desert to Midian. There he married Zipporah, daughter of the Midianite priest Jethro, and settled into the life of a shepherd; in due course Zipporah bore a son, Gershom.

After many years (the Bible indicates forty, which is Bible code for a very long time), Moses happened to be pasturing his flocks near Mount Horeb when he observed a bush that seemed to be on fire without being consumed. When he approached, God spoke to Moses out of the bush and charged him with going to Pharaoh to persuade Egypt to free the Israelites. Diffidently, Moses returned to Egypt, enlisted the aid of his older brother, Aaron, as spokesman, and went to Pharaoh. To help convince the ruler of Egypt, God sent ten plagues to blight the land: locusts, gnats, frogs, hail, rivers of blood, days of darkness, and so forth. Finally, God sent the angel of death to kill all male firstborn of Egypt—both children and livestock—but spared from this plague the Israelites who had placed the blood of a newly slaughtered lamb on their doorposts. Archaeologists and most biblical scholars doubt that events happened in just the way they are depicted in the Bible, but certainly the story could be based on actual happenings. For example, the ancient world was sometimes afflicted with plagues of locusts or frogs, and the Bible narrative could simply be a symbolic extrapolation from natural occurrences. Afterward, the Egyptians forced the Israelites to leave, despising them for bringing such destruction upon Egypt. But Pharaoh seems to have had a change of heart—or else succumbed to his desire for revenge—and chased after the slaves to bring them back. Another interpretation is that Pharaoh finally allowed the Israelites to depart on a short pilgrimage into the desert to worship God, and that he only pursued them when they failed to return because they had become "lost."

BIBLICAL PASSAGE NOTES

This passage, without a doubt, is probably the most famous, if not the most sacred text of the Jewish scriptures. It recounts the words that God spoke to Moses and Aaron while they were still in Egypt regarding the last night the Israelites were to spend there prior to their exodus into the wilderness and the forty-year journey that led eventually to the Promised Land. "It is the LORD's Passover," the passage concludes, and we are led to think, if we read nowhere else, that the celebration and meals surrounding it get their name and rituals from God's action of passing over the houses of the Hebrews, sparing their lives and those of their firstborn, as God visits the last and most punitive of plagues on a stubborn Pharaoh and his people.

However, the rituals of Passover are extremely complex, interwoven as they are with three (at least) distinct, early sociocultic observances: a festival to celebrate the Exodus, the feast of the Unleavened Bread, and the Dedication of the Firstborn.[1] The Passover meal, which is in a state of constant change and reinterpretation, contains fragments of all three celebrations, and its religious and cultural significance has been greatly altered over time. Despite attempts to transfer its celebration to the Temple as a part of worship[2] (a move by the priestly authorities that they could not ultimately sustain), it has remained and is chiefly a community (and therefore a family) meal.

Next year in Jerusalem!

THE MENU

Horseradish Deviled Eggs

Haroset à la Greque

Matzoh Ball Soup

Pesach Black Bread *served alongside* Roast Lamb with Rosemary

Borscht (Beet Soup)

Russet Mashed Potato Casserole

Chilled Asparagus with Raspberry-Almond Vinaigrette

Spinach Salad with "Bitter Herbs"

Passover Rhubarb-Orange Cobbler with Lemon Sorbet

Coconut Macaroons

Kosher Red Wine

Our menu for this meal presents a variety of ways, from many Jewish communities, by which the Passover feast is celebrated.

THE PREPARATION

Currently, Passover is an eight-day religious holiday (seven days in Israel) that has both historical and agricultural components. The longstanding tradition of recounting and reliving the Passover meal (during the first two nights of the festival) in a ceremonial dinner known as the *Seder* (Hebrew for "order") is found in many versions of the *Haggadah* (a book/guide of "Retelling"), with each Jewish community in Israel and scattered throughout the diaspora celebrating in its own unique way. In some communities, it is forbidden to eat rice and vegetables during Passover; in others, the eating of rice and vegetables is highly celebrated. Regardless, the basic ceremony that accompanies the meal, though particularly formulaic, is nonetheless fluid and has adapted greatly to local needs and customs and, not surprisingly, to what is available at market.

As the Seder meal is notably and purposely symbolic, at the table one will surely find wine (to celebrate and toast God's deliverance and the redemption of God's people); *matzoh* (the bread without yeast, because in the Exodus there was no time to let the bread rise); *maror* (one or more bitter herbs representing the harsh experience of slavery in Egypt); *haroset* (a sweet paste made of fruit, wine, and nuts that recalls the mortar set between the bricks the slaves were forced to make in constructing the buildings of the Egyptians); *karpas* (a green vegetable symbolizing spring or the second chance of a new life); *betzah* (a roasted egg, suggestive of the festival sacrifice); and *zeroah* (a roasted shank bone [or the neck bone of an animal], symbol of the paschal sacrifice and proof that God's command was obeyed). Depending on the community remembrance, there might also be *chazeret* (lettuce to put with the matzoh in commemoration of Rabbi Hillel's[3] celebration of Passover); *mei melach* (salt water, or some bitter liquid [vinegar, lime juice, lemon juice], to recall the bitter tears of the enslaved Hebrew people and/or the waters that claimed the lives of the Egyptians as the waves of the Sea of Reeds came over them); and *tzafun* ("that which is hidden" is finally redeemed or uncovered, so there is joy and sweetness, i.e., dessert).

It should be noted that the Seder is a twofold meal, beginning with a ritual portion, then completed by serving a full dinner.[4] (Some families do a bit of interweaving, so that the children are more likely to behave and the guests don't faint from hunger.) In many places, there are two separate Seders held on successive days. However, the primary focus is on the symbolic meal and the reading of the ceremony in the *Haggadah;* any recipes used in subsequent dinners have one foot in the symbolic camp, while making adjustments for flavor, abundance, and quality in the culinary camp. In other words, the first meal is to feed one spiritually; the second meal, building on the nature of the first, is meant to please the palates of those present (some say "body *and* soul").

What we present below are recipes that, while keeping in mind the ritual, are more concerned with the full dinner presentation. We recommend that the reader explore the many *haggadot* available in bookstores and libraries so as to understand the variety of ways in which the Passover feast can be celebrated. For those looking for a "standard" second portion of the meal, we offer the following international menu.

THE RECIPES

❧ *Horseradish Deviled Eggs*

6 eggs

3 Tbsp. mayonnaise

⅛ tsp. Worcestershire sauce

2 Tbsp. red onion, minced

1 tsp. dry mustard

1 Tbsp. dill pickle, minced

2 tsp. fresh parsley, finely chopped

¼ tsp. salt

2 Tbsp. white horseradish

Old Bay seasoning

6 pimento-stuffed olives, sliced in half
   lengthwise

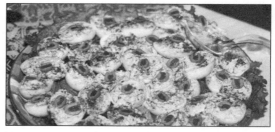

True to its name, this appetizer of Horseradish Deviled Eggs is spicy and piques the taste buds at the start of a satisfying Seder meal.

Hard boil the eggs in water and a bit of vinegar (about 8–10 minutes after water boils). Run under cold water for about 5 minutes, then peel. Slice the eggs in half lengthwise and remove the yolks. Mash the yolks and add mayonnaise and Worcestershire sauce. Stir in onion, mustard, pickle, parsley, salt, and horseradish.

Arrange the cooked egg whites on a platter, or egg plate if available. Scoop a generous portion of the yolk mixture into each white, and sprinkle with Old Bay seasoning. Place an olive half on top of each egg. Best if served cold.

Yield: 6 servings

Haroset à la Greque

1 apple, finely chopped

1 cup of dates, finely chopped

½ cup almonds, ground

¾ cup walnuts, ground

2 tsp. cinnamon

a bit of lemon peel, grated

1 cup black currants, chopped (or 1 cup of currant jam)

a pinch of powdered red brick

sweet red wine

Of all the recipes we've seen for *haroset*, this one intrigued us the most.

Combine all ingredients. Add wine until it is like a paste. Cover, but do not refrigerate. Serve as a side dish to the main meal.

Yield: 8–12 servings

Matzoh Ball Soup

3 eggs, separated

3 Tbsp. olive oil

2 Tbsp. seltzer water

1½ cups matzoh meal

1 Tbsp. fresh dill, chopped

1 Tbsp. fresh parsley, chopped

1 Tbsp. fresh thyme leaves

1 scallion, minced

½ tsp. salt

⅛ tsp. ground black pepper

9 cups canned chicken stock

2 cloves garlic, cut and pressed

1 carrot, peeled and shredded

2 stalks celery, thinly sliced

1 large onion, studded with three cloves

1 bay leaf

a bit of oil and water

In a blender, combine egg yolks, olive oil, and seltzer water. In a separate bowl, beat the egg whites until stiff. Slowly pour in egg yolk mixture. Add the matzoh meal, dill, parsley, thyme, scallion, salt, and pepper. Refrigerate mixture for 45 minutes, or longer if time allows. Meanwhile, in a large saucepan, combine chicken stock, garlic, carrot, celery, onion with cloves, and bay leaf, then bring to a rapid boil. Reduce heat; cover and simmer.

Wet hands with a bit of oil or water and form small balls out of the matzoh mixture. (Do not make them too large, since they expand greatly in cooking.) If the mixture seems too wet, add

Matzoh ball soup is said to be the "very soul" of Jewish cooking.

more matzoh meal. Gently lower balls into the simmering stock. Cover and simmer once again, this time for 30–45 minutes. Do not uncover the pot while cooking. Remove bay leaf and clove-studded onion, and serve hot.

Yield: 6 servings

Pesach Black Bread

1 cup warm water	2 (¼ oz.) envelopes active dry yeast
⅓ cup dark corn syrup	2 tsp. scallion, minced
1 Tbsp. brown sugar	4½ cups dark rye flour, or as needed
3 Tbsp. carob powder	½ cup oat bran
1 Tbsp. caraway seed	2 tsp. salt
½ tsp. fennel seed	

In a medium bowl, stir together the warm water, corn syrup, dry ingredients, and scallion. Sprinkle the yeast over the top, and let stand until foamy, about 5 minutes.

Add 2 cups of the rye flour and the oat bran to the yeast mixture, and beat until smooth. Stir in the salt. Set bowl in a warm place, and cover with a cloth or towel. Let rise for 30 minutes.

Stir in more flour, ½ cup at a time, until the dough is stiff. Turn the dough out onto a floured surface and knead in more flour by hand as needed to form a stiff but slightly sticky dough. You may use less or more flour. Form dough into a ball. Clean the mixing bowl, and lightly grease it. Place the dough in the bowl and cover with a towel. Place in a warm spot to rise until doubled. This may take as long as 2 hours.

Turn the risen dough out onto a floured surface, and press out the air bubbles. Roll dough into a loaf, and place into a greased 9″ x 5″ loaf pan. Cover the pan with plastic wrap, and let rise in a warm place until doubled, about 1 hour.

Preheat oven to 350°F.

Remove plastic wrap from loaf pan. Bake for 30–35 minutes in the preheated oven, or until the loaf sounds hollow when tapped on the bottom. Bread will not brown very much.

Yield: 1 large loaf of bread

Source: Recipe provided by www.Allrecipes.com Recipe submitted by Alexandra Romanov.

🐑 *Roast Lamb with Rosemary*

1 leg of lamb, 5–7 lb.

3 cloves garlic, mashed

salt and pepper

½ cup butter

¼ cup fresh rosemary leaves

½ cup celery leaves, shredded

⅓ cup green pepper, cubed

4 small sprigs rosemary

1 cup mint jelly

¼ cup orange juice

fresh mint leaves (optional)

Leg of lamb covered with fresh mint is a tasty Passover dish.

To get the most flavor out of a good leg of lamb, start the process with the lamb at room temperature.

Preheat oven to 375°F. Rub the meat all over with the mashed garlic; sprinkle well with salt and pepper. Place on a rack in a large roasting pan. Pour the butter over the lamb and drizzle with fresh rosemary leaves; surround with celery leaves and green peppers. Place entire sprigs of rosemary on top of the other greenery. Cook for about 1–1½ hours, until tender. (At this temperature, the meat would most likely be rare. One can use a meat thermometer: 145°F for rare, 160°F–170°F for medium. Do not overcook.) Remove from oven and allow to cool for about 10 minutes prior to serving.

Mix the mint jelly and the orange juice in a small pitcher and pour over lamb while cooling. Cover with fresh mint when serving, if desired.

Yield: 8–12 servings

🥣 *Borscht (Beet Soup)*

2–2½ lb. beets, peeled and grated

water

2 potatoes, peeled and diced

3 small onions, diced

¼ cup cider vinegar

2 tsp. brown sugar

2 tsp. salt

½ tsp. garlic pepper

4 eggs

½ cup chopped fresh parsley

Place beets into a large pot and add enough water to cover. Stir in potatoes and onions. Bring to a boil, then lower the flame and simmer (approximately 45 minutes). Add vinegar, brown sugar, salt, and pepper.

Beat eggs well in a small bowl. With a ladle, spoon a bit of the borscht into the eggs. Repeat ladling seven or eight times, stirring constantly, so as not to curdle the eggs. Pour the egg/borscht mixture into the pot, stirring all the while.

Serve sprinkled with parsley, either warm or cold.

Yield: 10 servings

No Passover meal is complete without borscht. This earthy soup is a standard among Russian Jews.

❧ *Russet Mashed Potato Casserole*

2 lb. baking potatoes, washed but unpeeled

2 tsp. salt

8 cups water

¾ cup mayonnaise

1 Tbsp. white horseradish

3 small onions, chopped

2 cloves garlic, mashed

½ tsp. sumac

1 carrot, diced and cooked until tender

1 cup frozen green peas

⅓ cup fresh cilantro

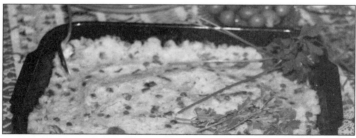

Not usually associated with Middle Eastern cooking, the potatoes in this casserole demonstrate how Jewish communities have adapted their Passover meals to what's available at the local marketplace.

Boil the potatoes with the salt in a large pot until tender, about 20–25 minutes. Drain the water and mash the potatoes in the pot with a potato masher. Add mayonnaise, horseradish, onions, garlic, and sumac, and stir with a wooden spoon until thoroughly mixed.

Place the carrot and frozen peas in a microwave-safe dish and microwave on high for about 4 minutes. Remove, drain off any water, and add to the potatoes.

Preheat oven to 400°F. Transfer all to a 9″ baking pan, and cook for about 20 minutes until tops of potatoes are golden brown. Garnish with cilantro before serving.

Yield: 8 servings

❦ *Chilled Asparagus with Raspberry-Almond Vinaigrette*

2–3 lb. asparagus

2 cups water

½ cup fresh basil leaves, chopped

½ cup white vinegar

1 clove garlic, mashed

1 tsp. dried mustard

20–25 fresh raspberries (do not use frozen)

¾ cup olive oil (or almond oil, if available)

½ tsp. salt

1 tsp. black pepper

½ cup toasted almonds

raspberries

Colorful and tangy, Chilled Asparagus with Raspberry-Almond Vinaigrette can be prepared in advance and served well chilled to enhance its flavor.

Buy the thinnest stalks of asparagus available at market. Break off the lowest part of the root end and discard the roots; wash the stalks in cold water. Combine water and chopped basil in a large pot. Using an inserted steamer, cook asparagus until al dente (still green, but beginning to soften—about 5 minutes). Place in a large glass dish, arranging stalks side by side, layered if necessary.

In a small food processor, blend the vinegar, garlic, mustard, raspberries, oil, salt, and pepper. Transfer to a large mixing cup, and stir almonds in by hand. Pour over asparagus, garnish with whole raspberries, and refrigerate, covered with foil or plastic wrap, for at least 2 hours before serving.

Yield: 6–8 servings

❦ *Spinach Salad with "Bitter Herbs"*

1 package fresh spinach

2 endive (leaves only)

1 head Boston lettuce

1 head red cabbage, shredded

1 bunch arugula

1 bunch radicchio

1 handful watercress, chopped

½ cup fresh basil

¼ cup fresh oregano

4 eggs, hard-boiled

2 cups walnut oil/berry vinaigrette

Though no one really knows which were the "bitter herbs" mentioned in the Exodus story, this salad covers all the possibilities.

Wash all the greens and toss into a large salad bowl. Crumble the hard-boiled eggs over the salad, and serve with a walnut oil/berry vinaigrette.

Yield: 8–12 servings

Passover Rhubarb-Orange Cobbler with Lemon Sorbet

Crust

1 cup flour

1 cup matzoh meal

⅔ cup heavy cream

½ cup light brown sugar

¼ cup butter, melted

1 Tbsp. baking powder

1 cup walnuts, finely chopped

½ tsp. mace

Topping

¾ cup granulated sugar

6 Tbsp. cornstarch

½ tsp. cinnamon

½ cup water

1 Tbsp. butter

½ tsp. vanilla extract

8 cups navel orange flesh, chopped and drained

4 cups rhubarb, diced

Garnish

lemon sorbet

fresh mint leaves

Preheat oven to 350°F.

Combine all the crust ingredients in a large bowl. Line the bottom of a square baking pan with the mix. Any that is left over, set aside to use with the topping.

Place all topping ingredients (except rhubarb) in a blender and mix well. Pour into a saucepan, add the rhubarb, and bring to a boil. Cook for 1 minute longer, stirring constantly. Pour over the crumb layer in the pan. Top with any leftover crumb mixture. Bake for 1 hour, until cobbler is bubbling. Best if presented warm or right from the oven. Serve in small bowls and top with lemon sorbet and a fresh mint leaf.

Yield: 8 servings

Coconut Macaroons

4 egg whites

¼ tsp. cream of tartar

5 cups sweetened flake coconut

½ cup granulated sugar

dash salt

1 Tbsp. almond extract

Preheat oven to 400°F. In a bowl, beat the egg whites with the cream of tartar until stiff. Add all other ingredients with a spatula. Drop heaping teaspoonfuls of mix onto a heavily greased cookie sheet. (Some cooks use aluminum foil to line the trays.) The macaroons will spread a bit, so do not place too close to one another. Bake for about 12 minutes, or until coconut starts to brown. Remove to a plate and allow to cool. Refrigerate or serve at room temperature.

Yield: 3 dozen cookies

For a dessert that combines both "joy and sweetness," nothing is tastier than freshly baked coconut macaroons.

🎕 *Kosher Red Wine*

For this particular holiday celebration, a sweet kosher red wine for the table would be a good choice.

Of course, no Passover meal is complete without a good kosher wine.

NOTES

1. See J. Coert Rylaarsdam on exegesis and J. Edgar Park on exposition, "The Book of Exodus," in *The Interpreter's Bible: A Commentary in Twelve Volumes*, Vol. 1 (New York: Abingdon-Cokesbury Press, 1952), 915ff.

2. Once the Second Temple was destroyed by the Romans in 70 C.E., the Passover celebration found its place again where it had begun: at home.

3. Anita Diamant with Howard Cooper, *Living a Jewish Life: Jewish Traditions, Customs, and Values for Today's Families* (New York: HarperCollins, 1991), 225.

4. Ibid., 226.

⚬ 6 ⚬

By the Numbers

THE TEXT

1 Now the people set up a lament which was offensive to Yahweh's ears, and Yahweh heard it.

. . . .

4 The rabble who had joined the people were overcome by greed, and the sons of Israel themselves began to wail again, "Who will give us meat to eat?" they said.

5 "Think of the fish we used to eat free in Egypt, the cucumbers, melons, leeks, onions and garlic!

6 "Here we are wasting away, stripped of everything; there is nothing but manna for us to look at."

7 The manna was like coriander seed, and had the appearance of bdellium.

8 The people went around gathering it, and ground it in a mill or crushed it with a pestle; it was then cooked in a pot and made into pancakes.

9 It tasted like cake made with oil. When the dew fell on the camp at nighttime, the manna fell with it.

. . . .

"A wind came from Yahweh and it drove quails in from the sea. . . . The people were up all that day and night and all the next day collecting quails."

31 A wind came from Yahweh and it drove quails in from the sea and brought them down on the camp. They lay for a distance of a day's march either side of the camp, two cubits thick on the ground.

32 The people were up all that day and night and all the next day collecting quails.

Numbers 11:1, 4–9; 31–32a, The Jerusalem Bible

The History

According to the Pentateuch (the first five books of the Bible, generally accepted as canonical by Jews and Christians), Moses led an incredibly large group of Israelites out of Egypt and into the desert: the Book of Numbers indicates that the group included more than 600,000 men who were of the right age to serve as soldiers! If one also counts the women, children, and aged, the Israelites must have numbered well over one million persons. Unfortunately, there are few reliable extrabiblical sources to corroborate the narrative found in the scriptures, nor have archaeologists been able to unearth at this far-removed date evidence that would definitively prove the passage of such a large mass of people from Egypt through the Red Sea (a mistranslation of the Hebrew *Yam Suf,* which means "Sea of Reeds") and into the Wilderness of Sin.

To follow the scriptural narrative: God protected and guided the Israelites with a pillar of cloud by day and a pillar of fire by night, sending a strong wind to part the waters of the Sea of Reeds so that the Israelites could escape from the pursuing Egyptian army. When they had reached the other side, God allowed the water to close over the Egyptians, drowning them. (In actuality, the sea may have been a marshy expanse that would not have impeded pedestrians but would have bogged down horse-drawn chariots.) Moses then led the Israelites to Mount Sinai, where on behalf of his people he received the tablets of the Covenant (commonly known as the Ten Commandments) from God, indicating God's intention to keep the covenant that God had made with Abraham, Isaac, and Jacob. Upon descending from the mountain, Moses found that his brother, Aaron, had allowed the people to worship a golden calf; enraged, Moses broke the law tablets that he had received from God and called upon the faithful of the tribe of Levi to slay those who had worshipped the idol. Because of their idolatry, God turned against the Israelites and sent a plague to punish them. Climbing the mountain again to speak with God, Moses attempted to atone for the sins of the people, and God gave Moses two new tablets to renew the covenant. When Moses returned to the people this time, his appearance was transfigured; thereafter, he was compelled to wear a veil, lest the Israelites die of fright. Under Moses' instructions, the people constructed an elaborate gilded ark to house the tablets and a tent to protect the ark. At some point God instructed the Israelites to enter Canaan, which was identified to them as the Promised Land, but when they refused to advance (their spies had said that the Canaanites were too powerful), God sentenced all of them to wander in the wilderness until the next generation had replaced the elder one. They did, however, manage to conquer the lands of the Amorites and of Bashan. Moses also transgressed one of God's commands, and for this he was forbidden from entering the Promised Land himself; tradition indicates that he spent the rest of his life conversing with God and writing the history of his people. When he died on Mount Nebo at the age of

120 (a propitious age according to Jewish tradition), Joshua, his top general, assumed leadership of the Israelites and assembled them to march west across the Jordan River into the Promised Land.

What does archaeology say about this story? The evidence is sketchy, but there are some indications that the biblical narrative has its basis in actual events. For example, an ancient Egyptian medical document known as the Brooklyn Papyrus (because it is owned by the Brooklyn Museum), dating from the 17th century B.C.E., is believed by some scholars to include slave names that are the same as some Israelite names found in the Bible. At the other end of the story, an Egyptian inscription known as the Merneptah Stele (dating from 1210 B.C.E.) is thought by some scholars to speak respectfully of a people known as Israel dwelling in Canaan. At best, the archaeological evidence would seem to suggest that the exodus of the Hebrews from Egypt occurred sometime in the 16th century B.C.E., after the descendants of Jacob had been in Egypt for a little more than 200 years, and may be identical with the expulsion of the Hyksos during the reign of Ahmose (1570–1550 B.C.E.). (Some scholars, however, place the date of the Exodus in the 13th century B.C.E.) By the 13th century B.C.E. the Hebrews (called *Hapiru*) had conquered Canaan and consolidated into a nation of twelve tribes known as Israel. But scholars have yet to agree on any irrefutable evidence, and the debates over the reliability of the artifacts and the interpretation of their meaning, not to mention the efforts to translate and interpret the biblical passages themselves, have often become quite emotional. This is perhaps understandable, when the history of a faith is at stake.

BIBLICAL PASSAGE NOTES

The book of Numbers is so named in English because a portion of the biblical tome deals with the numbering, or counting, of the Israelites, in the telling of the epic about how they came to be known as "the chosen people." The book's Hebrew title, "In the Desert," is perhaps more appropriate, as the majority of the book is the saga of a wandering people who have left Egypt and are on their way to a promised land. During this journey they test God often, and God in turn tests their allegiance. Sometimes the complaints to God are for basic needs: water and food. In chapter 11, the voice of the people is raised in anger: they are tired of manna, and they want meat! At least in Egypt there was meat and fish (they remind God), and lots of good fruits and vegetables, too! "Ah, we remember the good old days with great fondness," they seem to say, having forgotten that they were slaves in Egypt, and now murmuring against God as they trample on their new-found gift of freedom.

True, they had dust in their mouths, and it made them ungrateful. Even though the Israelites were a nomadic group of tribes who kept and nurtured animals that could provide them with meat, what they seemed to have wanted was *variety*, and they wanted it garnished with spices! Without the garnishes, they felt empty; they lacked the strength to continue (what was the point?); their souls were dried up, like the wilderness in which they were to wander for forty long years.

The people whose story is recounted in the book of Numbers might not have eaten as well as the meal shown here, but they would certainly have recalled the great variety of tastes they were missing, having left Egypt to wander in the wilderness.

THE MENU

Israeli Watermelon Soup with Ginger and Mint

Manna

Date-Manna Bread

Broiled Marinated Quail

Oven-Baked Perch with Tahini

Braised Rolled Leeks Stuffed with Cucumber Sauce

Caramelized Onions with Eggs

Seventh-Heaven Baklava

THE PREPARATION

It appears that however unpleasant it was in Egypt, the food was apparently good there, if not memorable. There were scores of species of fish, for instance:

puffers, tetras, catfish, tilapia, carp, perch, minnows, squeakers, elephant fish, and many more swimming in the Nile, all for the having, and free! Cucumbers and melons, both of which are rich in water, were widely cultivated in Egypt as they grew well in the silt runoff from the nutrient-rich Nile. The cucumbers (in Hebrew, *qishshuim,* literally "gourd") mentioned here are not the garden variety we are used to seeing in Western markets. What is being described here are probably muskmelons or chate melons (an unsweet variety), and the melons (in Hebrew, *abattichim*) were most likely cantaloupes, casabas, or honeydew. Watermelon was also grown in Egypt from the earliest times, their seeds having been found in the tombs of the pharaohs. The people also remembered their taste for leeks (in Hebrew, *chatsir,* which literally means any type of grass, including hay); onions (in Hebrew, *betsel*); and garlic (in Hebrew, *shum*); but they were apparently unable to cultivate these vegetables until much later in their history, as these Hebrew words (*abattichim, betsel, shum*) do not appear again in the scriptures.

Still, there was always manna to keep their stomachs filled. Just what manna was has been the topic of thousands of historical, archaeological, and anthropological articles over the years. The biblical scholar F. S. Bodenheimer has theorized that manna was a kind of honeydew secretion of two types of insects that feed on the sap of the *tamarisk,* or salt-cedar bushes, that are native to the wilderness area mentioned in the Bible.[1] Or perhaps, as others have suggested, it was either a dried form of algae or drought-desiccated and wind-dispersed lichen.[2] The Israelite wanderers describe it as a kind of white substance, not unlike coriander seed, and sticky like *bdellium,* a resinous gum. It was boiled in pots or ground up so that it could be baked or made into cakes. It was most likely very bland, and a steady diet of mainly manna made the complainants long for the spices and sweetness of their former lives in servitude.

God does respond to their spates of unhappiness by sending quail (in Hebrew, *selaw*) from the sea inland (a story not unlike the experience of the Mormon pioneers at the Great Salt Lake). But the people's appetite is not sated, and they further complain—an action that angers God, who in turn complains to Moses about the greed of the tribes he is leading. When will they "possess the land of milk and honey as promised to them?" a growing angry mob wants to know. Whether it be happenstance or bad directions or God's stubborn insistence on teaching them to rely on Divine Providence, they still had many miles and years to travel.

THE RECIPES

✥ *Israeli Watermelon Soup with Ginger and Mint*

8 cups seedless watermelon

1 mango, diced

6 Tbsp. lime juice

¼ fresh spearmint, chopped

2 Tbsp. confectioners' sugar

⅓ cup gin

1 Tbsp. orange blossom water

1 piece fresh ginger root, sliced into large pieces

mint sprigs

Believe it or not, it's the ginger that gives this watermelon soup its unique flavor.

In a blender, mix all ingredients except the ginger and mint sprigs. Add the ginger slices and chill the soup several hours. Remove the ginger, and serve the soup garnished with mint sprigs.

Yield: 8 servings

✥ *Manna*

For better or worse, the original recipe for manna has been misplaced. To capture at least the basic flavor of manna, one might care to try the following pancakes.

½ lb. cake-quality matzoh flour, sifted

2 tsp. dried coriander leaves

1 cup boiling water

1 Tbsp. sesame oil

2 Tbsp. honey

Resift the flour together with the coriander. Place the flour in a bowl and in the center make a well. Into this pour the boiling water and oil. Mix into a dough and then knead on a well-floured board until smooth and elastic. Divide the dough into 12 equal portions. Roll out a portion of the dough into a 4″ circle and brush with the sesame oil. Roll a second portion and cover the first with this. Roll the combined circles to make a 6″ pancake sandwich. Continue the process until all of the dough has been used and 6 pancake sandwiches are ready. Heat a heavy skillet, without oil, and in this fry the sandwiched pancakes one at a time, turning once so that both sides are cooked. The skillet should be kept moving constantly to prevent the pancakes from sticking, and cooking should be done over a moderate flame. When all of the pancakes have been cooked, separate the sandwiched pancakes. Spread one side of each pancake lightly with honey and fold each single pancake in half and then in half again. Serve at once or cover with a lightly dampened cloth and set aside to keep warm until ready to serve.

Yield: 12 pancakes

Source: Adapted from a recipe by Daniel Rogov at Strat's Place: www.stratsplace.com/rogov/israel/manna_breakfast.html Reprinted with permission from Daniel Rogov.

❧ Date-Manna Bread

For this recipe, use organic wheat. Much of our wheat is now treated with the herbicide Roundup to "ripen it quickly." This kills most of the seeds and they will not sprout. Put 4 cups of organic wheat in a plastic ice cream pail that has had holes punched in the lid. A large jar would work as well. Soak the wheat for a few minutes; then invert the container to drain most of the water. Repeat this several times as necessary. When the sprouts are ½ to ¾ the length of the grains of wheat, they are ready. In a warm house, it is possible to start the process before supper, repeat the soaking before going to bed and then again the next morning; the wheat will usually be ready that evening. If it is ready too soon, put it in the refrigerator until you can use it.

2 cups sprouted organic wheat	1 cup raisins
flour as needed	¼ tsp. cloves
½ lb. dates	¼ tsp. cinnamon

Preheat oven to 300°F.

Place the sprouted wheat in a food processor and whir it until it is ground up and pasty. Add flour until the mixture is doughy. Fold in the dates, raisins, and spices and process a little more to mix. Form into small loaves or one larger loaf. Bake for about 2½ hours.

Yield: 12 servings

Source: Adapted from Barb Beck, "Date-Manna Bread recipe," FatFree.com: The Low Fat Vegetarian Recipe Archive, www.fatfree.com/recipes/breads-quick/date-manna-bread Date-Manna Bread recipe reprinted by permission of www.fatfree.com

❧ Broiled Marinated Quail

6 quail

½ cup brandy (or cognac)

¼ cup vegetable oil

2 Tbsp. white horseradish

1 Tbsp. Balsamic vinegar

3 cloves garlic, crushed

2 Tbsp. light brown sugar

1½ tsp. five-spice powder

2½ tsp. paprika

½ tsp. dried thyme

½ tsp. sea salt

½ tsp. black pepper

wild rice

We consider quail a delicacy, but the Israelites were said to have had their fill of it while in the desert.

Cut the quail in halves with poultry shears. Rinse thoroughly. In a small bowl, mix the brandy, vegetable oil, horseradish, vinegar, garlic, brown sugar, and five-spice powder. Put the quail in a large plastic bowl with a lid (or use two bowls, if needed). Pour the brandy marinade over the quail; cover and refrigerate 4–8 hours, turning the bowl(s) upside down and shaking every so often.

When well-marinated, discard the liquid and pat the quail dry. Lightly brush them with olive oil. Mix the paprika, thyme, salt, and pepper in a small bowl, then sprinkle over the quail. Cook the birds breast-side down in the broiler for 15–20 minutes, turning once or until crisp and well browned. Serve on a bed of wild rice.

Yield: 8–12 servings

Oven-Baked Perch with Tahini

8 perch fillets

2 Spanish onions

3 cloves garlic, minced

½ cup pine nuts

5 Tbsp. olive oil

¼ cup water

3 Tbsp. tahini

2 Tbsp. lemon juice

½ tsp. salt

¼ tsp. paprika

¼ cup red currants

watercress

cherry tomatoes

6 eggs, hard-boiled

"Think of the fish we used to eat free in Egypt," lamented the Israelites. Undoubtedly, they were remembering fine meals of flavorful perch from the Nile.

Preheat oven to 400°F.

Rinse the fillets in cold water and pat them dry. Score the skin of each fish; then place it in a shallow, lightly greased pan with the skin-side down. Dice the onions and fry them with the garlic and pine nuts in olive oil until lightly browned. Stir in the water, tahini, lemon juice, salt, and paprika till it forms a pasty mix. Reduce the heat and add the currants.

Spoon the mixture over the fish. Bake for 15–20 minutes. Remove to a large platter carefully, as it may be flaky. Garnish with watercress, and surround with cherry tomatoes and crumbled hard-boiled eggs.

Yield: 8 servings

❧ Braised Rolled Leeks Stuffed with Cucumber Sauce

2 small cucumbers, peeled and chopped
　　into cubes

8 leeks

3 cloves garlic, minced

6 sprigs fresh dill

1 cup ricotta curds

plain pie crust, cut into ½″ strips

2 Tbsp. butter, melted

dried mustard

dried red pepper

Braised rolled leeks stuffed with cucumber sauce combines two of the foods that the Israelites pined for while they were wandering in the desert.

Preheat oven to 375°F. Cut one cucumber in half; dice one half into very small pieces and set aside. Wash the leeks well and cut in half from top to bottom. Cut off the top leaves and remove all roots. Parboil for 10 minutes and drain. In a blender or food processor, mix the 1½ remaining cucumbers, garlic, and dill; carefully drain off the top layer of juice. Add the ricotta and blend until smooth.

Lay out two pie crust strips in a buttered baking dish for each leek and place the leek diagonally along them. Make a well in every leek, then pour a small amount of the cucumber mixture into the depression. Drop in some of the diced cucumber that was set aside, then carefully lift up the pie crust ends and wrap them like a loose blanket around each stalk. Sprinkle with a dash of dried mustard mixed with red pepper. Bake for 20–30 minutes until leeks are tender.

Pour any remaining cucumber mix into a small bowl with a spoon in it and place it in the center of a large serving platter as a dip. Arrange the leeks around the bowl and sprinkle them with bits of diced cold cucumber.

Yield: 8–12 servings

❧ Caramelized Onions with Eggs

4 large red onions

2 yellow peppers

4 Tbsp. cooking oil

water

1 tsp. Balsamic vinegar

½ tsp. ground nutmeg

¼ tsp. ground mace

¼ tsp. ground cloves

½ tsp. ground black pepper

½ tsp. garlic salt

1 tsp. honey

8 eggs

fresh chopped coriander (cilantro)

Peel the onions and slice them very thin. Chop the peppers into tiny bits. Heat the oil in a heavy skillet or electric frying pan and add the onions and peppers. Cook over the lowest heat possible, stirring every so often so that they do not burn. After about 15 minutes, add a bit of water and continue cooking, then once again add water after 10 more minutes. When the onions are light brown and somewhat crispy and the peppers are quite soft, sprinkle with vinegar, spices, and honey and mix thoroughly. Make 8 depressions in the mixture and break an egg into each. With a fork lightly scramble each egg, and top with a pinch of fresh coriander. Serve while hot.

With all those quail, there must have been some extra eggs to be had. Caramelized onions with eggs has been popular in the Middle East for centuries.

Yield: 8–12 servings

 Seventh-Heaven Baklava

In connection with a celebration of the themes of this biblical passage, "Sephardic women take pride in baking a seven-layer Shavuot cake called 'Siete Cielos' (Seven Heavens), representing the seven celestial spheres the Torah traversed until it arrived on Mount Sinai. Fashioned in seven circular rising tiers, it is decorated with symbols such as a Star of David, the rod of Moses, the two tablets, manna, Jacob's ladder, and the Ark. Others top the cake with a seven-rung ladder to recall Moses ascending Mount Sinai.

Once you have a bite of this honey-glazed dessert, you'll understand why it is called "Seventh Heaven."

"Similar elaborate 'Sinai' pastries allude to the mountain. A large cake or bread with raisins, known as 'pashtudan' or 'floden' baked for Shavuot was also called 'Sinai'. Some Sephardic women bake 'baklava,' a sweet cake of nuts, sugar and honey."[3]

It has been impossible to locate a recipe for Siete Cielos cake, but here are the instructions for making a great baklava.

½ lb. unsalted butter, melted

1 lb. filo pastry (about 24 paper-thin sheets)

3 cups pistachios, chopped

½ cup sugar

1 Tbsp. cinnamon

¼ tsp. ground cloves

½ tsp. rose water

Syrup

1 cup water

2 cups sugar

2 Tbsp. fresh lemon juice

¼ cup honey

Grease a large baking dish with butter. Spread the filo sheets in the pan, brushing each layer with butter. (Keep the sheets of filo covered with a damp dish towel as you are working so they do not dry out.) When half the sheets are in the dish, combine the chopped pistachios with sugar, cinnamon, cloves, and rose water; spread the mixture over the filo base you have created. Place the remaining filo sheets on top of the nut mixture, buttering and laying out each sheet as before. (Make sure to butter the top sheet as well.) Cover and refrigerate for about ½ hour so that the butter has time to set; this will make the baklava easier to cut.

Preheat the oven to 350°F.

Using a very sharp knife, cut all the way through the pastry, creating about 36 diamond-shaped pieces. Bake for 30 minutes; then raise the heat to about 400°F and bake for 15 minutes more. The pastry should look puffed and slightly browned. Remove from the oven.

As the pastry is cooking, prepare the syrup. Boil all the ingredients (except the honey) till it forms a light-colored glaze, about 20 minutes. Add the honey. Let cool, and spoon over the pastry as it comes out of the oven.

When the baklava has cooled down, recut the diamonds. Serve hot or cold.

Yield: 16–20 servings

NOTES

1. F. S. Bodenheimer, "The Manna of Sinai," *The Biblical Archaeologist* 10 (1947): 2–6.

2. Kitty Morse, *A Biblical Feast: Foods from the Holy Land* (Berkeley, Calif.: Ten Speed Press, 1998), 7. In the first chapter of her book, Morse discusses the work of noted biblical botanists Harold and Alma Moldenke regarding manna.

3. "Shavouth: Holiday Laws and Customs," www.jewish-holiday.com/shav65laws.html

⋙ *7* ⋘

The Reapers' Meal

THE TEXT

14 At mealtime Boaz said to Ruth, "Come over here. Have some bread and dip it in the wine vinegar." When she sat down with the harvesters, he offered her some roasted grain. She ate all she wanted and had some left over.

15 As she got up to glean, Boaz gave orders to his men, "Even if she gathers among the sheaves, don't embarrass her.

16 "Rather, pull out some stalks for her from the bundles and leave them for her to pick up, and don't rebuke her."

Ruth 2:14–16, New International Version—
United Kingdom

"As Ruth got up to glean, Boaz gave orders to his men, 'Even if she gathers among the sheaves, don't embarrass her. Rather, pull out some stalks for her from the bundles and leave them for her to pick up.'"

THE HISTORY

Ruth was a Moabitess, a non-Jewish native from a country located between Edom and Ammon, on the eastern side of the Dead Sea, in what is modern-day Jordan. She and her sister, Orpah, married Israelite men who during a time of famine went with their parents to settle in Moab; the men died very early in their marriages. Their mother, a widow named Naomi, decided to return to Bethlehem, and she entreated her daughters-in-law to return to their own families. Orpah relented; but Ruth insisted that she not be separated yet again from loved ones, begging her mother-in-law to allow that they travel on together: "Where you go I will go," Ruth said to Naomi. "And where you stay I will stay. Your people will be my people and your God my God." Naomi agreed.

When the two widows arrived in Bethlehem, Ruth (whose name derives from an ancient Syrian word that means "woman companion" or "friend")[1] had to find a way to set up a life for herself (women could not inherit property; because she had no children, there were not many options open to her). With the help of Naomi, she secured a place in the grain fields owned by a relative of her dead husband, a kind man by the name of Boaz (Hebrew for "fleet; strength"). Impressed by her loyalties, despite the hardships they had imposed, Boaz invited Ruth to glean the barley fields as an act of charity, and he gave her shelter, food, and extra attention. In the end, they were married (after some legal maneuvering), and Ruth had a son, Obed, who was the father of Jesse, who in turn was the father of King David.

BIBLICAL PASSAGE NOTES

The Book of Ruth, from which this text is taken, is one of the few books in the Bible named for a woman. It is an important book for several reasons. First, it shows that at various times throughout its history, Israel did tolerate, and was quite friendly to, marriage outside of its strict laws. Ruth is also an important figure because it is through her lineage that St. Matthew traces the genealogy of Jesus back to Abraham through her great-grandson David, demonstrating that Jesus was both a righteous heir of the Covenant and of royal stock, worthy to be called a "king." And there are other reasons the book is seen to be one of the real jewels of the Bible. It is a simple tale, beautifully told; some feminists hold it in high regard for its portrayal of Naomi and Ruth as strong, resolute women, surviving against great odds. Historically speaking, it gives us a glimpse of the daily agricultural life of Israel at the time of the Judges, before the monarchy established by Saul, David, Solomon, and their heirs. And it shows the intricate workings of Jewish family law regarding the custom of Levirate marriage.[2]

THE MENU

Braided Challah with Poppy Seeds and Lemon

Field and Orchard Barley Soup

Trout Méditerranée

Wheatberry, Yellow Squash, and Cantaloupe Salad

Gleaner's Artichoke and Cheese Casserole

Shawandar Bil Leban (Beets with Yogurt and Mint)

Thyme-Poached Apricots and Figs in White Wine

Friendship Cake

The Preparation

In the three verses that we have here lifted out of the story of Ruth, we encounter her at a noontime meal. She was invited by Boaz to partake of the reapers' lunch, which is very unusual on several fronts. First, Jews did not routinely sit down with Gentiles for meals; though hospitality did dictate that one should offer food to strangers,[3] there were proscriptions against eating at the same table with those outside of the Jewish faith. Second, Jewish men did not sit at table with women; women might serve the meal, but rarely if ever was it served to them. Boaz was proving himself to be a man of unique sensitivities.

Ruth was told to dip her bread in wine vinegar (in Hebrew, *chomets*), a sour concoction often made from unripe grapes, which commentators tell us was a typical reapers' repast. (Bread [in Hebrew, *lechem*], as used here, is a broad term, meaning not only some grain product, but food in general [sustenance], whatever form it might take.) Boaz also offered her roasted grain (the KJV says "parched corn," though corn as we know it did not exist in the Middle East at that time).

Again, we learn a useful tidbit here about the cooking preparations of the biblical era. According to author Daniel Cutler, "raw ears of grain could be made more palatable by roasting or 'parching' them."

> The heat also breaks down the starches and makes the cereal more digestible. Parching was accomplished in two ways. One was simply to hold the stalks in a flame for a few moments. This was an especially convenient meal in the fields and probably constituted the lunch Ruth and Boaz shared during the barley harvest.[4]

The meal was apparently sufficiently filling, and gratefully eaten. Ruth even had grain to spare. And to boot, she was allowed to go back to the fields and glean more, a further generosity. Boaz went so far as to give his men instructions to drop some of the fruits of their hard work on the ground so that Ruth might pick them up without having to go and cut the barley in the field herself. They were probably willing to do so, in exchange for some favor or another from Ruth; but Boaz strongly advised them not to harass her, to let her be. In other words, the boss has his eye on her, so treat her well, if you know what is good for you!

But what of these "sheaves" Ruth was collecting? Just what is a sheaf? In modern parlance, a sheaf is a long leaf of some grain, such as wheat or barley. The Hebrew word is *omer*, which is also an ancient measure, being one-tenth of an *ephah* (see Appendix A). The biblical text reveals yet another bit of historical knowledge, namely that barley was so precious in ancient times that it was measured and used as collateral in trade.

So Ruth ended the day with a bounty much greater than she could have anticipated. She rushed back to Naomi to share her good fortune, and together they discussed what such providence could possibly mean. Naomi, wise in years, intuited Boaz' interest, and sent Ruth back at night with a mission, i.e., to let Boaz know of Ruth's availability. The plan worked, and Boaz made Ruth his bride, in a marriage in which, we suspect, her "salad days" were finally over.

The story of Ruth and Boaz in the Jewish tradition is closely linked to the festival of Shavuot, as it takes place during the time of the harvest. With this in mind, many of the recipes that follow are those used during the celebration of Shavuot.

THE RECIPES

❧ Braided Challah with Poppy Seeds and Lemon

In that the bread offering is one of the few biblical rites for Shavuot, a special emphasis is placed on the making and eating of challah. Usually, each family prepares two loaves. Here's an excellent recipe to start the meal off on the right foot.

2 packages dried yeast	2 cups warm milk
1 cup sugar	5 cups sifted flour
¼ cup lukewarm water	2 tsp. salt
½ tsp. saffron	1 egg yolk
2 eggs	4 tsp. poppy seeds
1 Tbsp. olive oil	1 tsp. lemon juice

Combine the yeast, 2 tsp. of sugar, water, and saffron. Let stand 5–7 minutes.

Mix the eggs, oil, and milk in a large bowl. Slowly stir in the yeast mixture. Sift the flour, add salt, and combine with other ingredients in bowl. Knead on a floured surface until smooth and elastic, about 10 minutes or so. Grease a separate large bowl, and place the dough inside, working it so that it is covered with a thin, oily glaze all over. Cover with a towel, set in a warm place, and let rise for 1 hour, or until about doubled in bulk.

Preheat oven to 375°F.

Turn the dough onto a floured board and divide it into three equal parts. Punch down and knead again. Using extra flour on your hands, roll the dough into six strips of even length. Braid 2 sets of 3 braids together (for 2 loaves) and place them on separate greased baking sheets. Brush the loaves with a bit of egg yolk and sprinkle with poppy seeds and ½ tsp. lemon juice each.

Bake for 30–35 minutes or until lightly browned. (Each loaf should sound hollow when tapped.) Cool on wire racks.

For a little variety, you can add cinnamon or dried cranberries (or both) to the egg/milk mixture when making the dough. It's really quite good.

Yield: 10–12 servings

❧ Field and Orchard Barley Soup

1 cup barley

3 Tbsp. butter

3 cups vegetable stock (or other)

1 cup apple cider

½ cup onions, chopped

3 cloves garlic, minced

1 tsp. dried thyme

¼ tsp. dried marjoram

1 bay leaf

½ lb. mushrooms

butter or oil

salt and pepper

Combine the barley and the butter in a heavy soup pot. Add the stock and the cider; then stir in the onions, garlic, dried spices, and bay leaf. Cover and simmer for about an hour. Stir occasionally to prevent sticking. (It may be necessary to add a bit of water at times if the mixture is getting too thick.) Sauté the mushrooms in a bit of butter or oil, then stir into the soup. Salt and pepper to taste.

Yield: 8–10 servings

❧ Trout Méditerranée

8 trout fillets

½ cup butter, melted

lemon pepper

1 large tomato, sliced

1 cup fresh basil leaves

8 sprigs fresh oregano

½ cup feta cheese, crumbled

1 cup pine nuts

1½ cups scallions, diced

Preheat the oven to 375°F.

Rinse the fish well. Place the fillets in an oven-proof dish. Pour a bit of butter over each fillet; then sprinkle with lemon pepper. Place a tomato slice, some basil leaves, and a small sprig of oregano on one portion of the fillet, then fold the fillet over on itself. Top each fillet with 1 Tbsp. of feta cheese. Hold in place with a toothpick if the stuffing is too high. Grind the pine nuts in a food processor or blender and sprinkle over the fillets. Surround the fish with diced scallions. Bake for 35–40 minutes or until fish flakes when tested with a fork.

Yield: 8 servings

❧ Wheatberry, Yellow Squash, and Cantaloupe Salad

2 cups wheatberries

2–2½ cups watercress

3–4 yellow squash

2–3 cups cantaloupe, seeded

¼ cup fresh lemon juice

¼ cup walnut oil

2 tsp. spicy mustard

2 garlic cloves, crushed

salt and fresh ground pepper to taste

crushed mint

Soak wheatberries overnight in water that is at least 2″ above the level of the berries. Drain well. Line a large bowl with watercress and place the wheatberries in the middle, forming a large mound. Grate the unpeeled squash over the berries. With a melon baller, scoop out the cantaloupe and drop the balls around the edge of the mound.

Whisk together the lemon juice, walnut oil, and mustard. Stir in garlic that has been forced through a press. Add salt and pepper. Pour over the contents of the bowl. Add a sprig or two of crushed mint to the top of the mound. Serve cold or at room temperature.

Yield: 8 servings

Gleaner's Artichoke and Cheese Casserole

8 fresh artichokes	6 cloves garlic, minced
2 cups tap water	6 eggs
⅓ cup cider vinegar	3 cups firm goat's milk cheese
¼ cup fresh tarragon	cayenne pepper
lemon water	4 cherry tomatoes
½ cup Spanish onions, chopped	water
3 Tbsp. pine nuts	¼ cup lemon juice

Wash the artichokes and cut them off at the base of the stem. In a large pot, combine water, cider vinegar, and tarragon. Place artichokes in a steamer or colander basket above the liquid and steam for about ½ hour.

Preheat oven to 350°F.

Remove the leaves from the chokes and scoop out the "meat" at the bottom of each leaf with a sharp knife, placing it in some lemon water to keep it fresh. When all the leaves have been removed, slice off the membrane, making sure to scoop out any remaining fibers (they're a nuisance!). With a sharp knife, hollow out the artichoke shell, place the heart in a large bowl, and mash. When all the hearts of the chokes have been removed and mashed, add the onions, pine nuts, and garlic, and stir well. Using an electric mixer, beat in the eggs and the cheese; then add the meat of the leaves as well. Stuff each shell with the artichoke/egg/cheese mixture to the brim; sprinkle with a bit of cayenne pepper, and place a halved cherry tomato, cut-side down, on top of each choke.

Arrange in a large baking dish with just a small amount of water mixed with ¼ cup lemon juice. Bake for about 30 minutes. Serve piping hot.

Yield: 8 servings

Shawandar Bil Leban (Beets with Yogurt and Mint)

8 beets	2 cups plain yogurt
4 cups cold water	¼ cup sour cream
2 cloves whole garlic	salt and pepper to taste
1 red onion, chopped	¼ cup fresh mint, chopped

Trim the beets of their greens and place them in a saucepan; cover with cold water and add garlic. Bring water to a boil; reduce heat and simmer until the beets are barely tender. Drain under cold water, reserving the stock; discard garlic, and remove the beet skins. Let cool to the touch. Cut beets into fourths and place in a serving dish. Sprinkle with chopped onion. Beat the yogurt and sour cream till smooth. Add 2–3 tsp. of the beet stock into the mixture; then pour in all the remaining stock. Flavor with bit of salt and pepper, and top with fresh mint. Cover and refrigerate for at least 1 hour before serving.

Yield: 8–12 servings

Thyme-Poached Apricots and Figs in White Wine

1½ cups white dessert wine	½ lb. figs, stemmed
2 Tbsp. honey	2 cups dried apricots
¼ tsp. vanilla extract	ricotta curds
juice of ½ lime	sprigs of lemon balm
½ tsp. fresh thyme	

In a saucepan, bring the wine, honey, vanilla, lime juice, and thyme to a boil. Stir and simmer over medium heat for about 3 minutes. Add the figs and apricots, reduce to low heat, and cook about 10–12 minutes, or until the figs are very soft. Place a bit of the fruit in long-stemmed glasses and pour some of the wine/honey syrup over them. Serve warm or chilled, with a dollop of ricotta curds on top, and a sprig of lemon balm for decoration.

Yield: 6–8 servings

Friendship Cake

Because the relationship between Ruth and Naomi is often seen as the prototype of an ideal friendship, we thought we'd end this chapter with the following recipe. It takes 10 days, but it's worth it!

Yeast Mixture

1 package yeast

1 cup warm water

Do not use a mixer. Do not refrigerate. Use the same teacup throughout and a very large bowl.

Use the cup to make up the yeast mixture. When mixture is ready (i.e., frothing), pour it into the bowl and proceed:

Day 1: Add 1 cup of granulated sugar and 1 cup of plain flour to the yeast mix. Do not stir.

Day 2: Stir well. Add 1 cup of milk.

Days 3 & 4: Do nothing!

Day 5: Same as Day 1.

Day 6: Same as Day 2.

Days 7, 8, & 9: Do nothing!

Day 10: Stir well. Remove 3 cupfuls and give to 2 friends with a copy of this recipe! Set one aside for your own use—this will be the base for your next Friendship Cake.

On day 10, preheat oven to 325°F. Add the following ingredients, in order:

Cake

1 cup sugar	2 cups plain flour
½ tsp. salt	⅔ cup corn oil (or similar)
2 tsp. vanilla extract	1 cup walnuts, chopped
2 heaping tsp. cinnamon	½ cup raisins
2 heaping tsp. baking powder	½ cup maraschino cherries
1 or 2 cooking apples (peeled, cored, and chopped)	confectioners' sugar
2 eggs	

Mix well. Put mixture into a large roasting pan. Sprinkle top with confectioners' sugar. Bake for 1–1½ hours. Let cool before serving.

Yield: 8–12 servings

Source: Adapted from *The Scots Independent Newspaper Online—The Flag in the Wind*, www.scotsindependent .org/features/food/german_cake.htm Friendship & Scripture Cake recipes reprinted by permission of Alastair McIntyre KTJ, FAS Scot. (www.scotsindependent.org).

NOTES

1. Other scholars think the name means "satiation," though it does not seem to fit the story.

2. The Levirate marriage law obligated the brother (or closest male relative) of a man who died without a son to marry the wife who survived. As Ruth was not a Jew, she was not bound by the law, but she submits to its tenets anyway as further respect for her adopted people and for Boaz' position in the community.

3. In Leviticus 23:22, God mandates, "When you reap the harvest of your land, do not reap to the very edges of your field or gather the gleanings of your harvest. Leave them for the poor and the alien. I am the LORD your God."

4. Daniel S. Cutler, *The Bible Cookbook: Lore of Food in Biblical Times Plus Modern Adaptations of Ancient Recipes* (New York: William Morrow, 1985), 136.

✌ 8 ✍

Abigail Cooks to Appease

The Text

14 ...One of the young shepherds told Abigail, Nabal's wife, what had happened: "David sent messengers from the backcountry to salute our master, but he tore into them with insults.

15 "Yet these men treated us very well. They took nothing from us and didn't take advantage of us all the time we were in the fields.

16 "They formed a wall around us, protecting us day and night all the time we were out tending the sheep.

17 "Do something quickly because big trouble is ahead for our master and all of us. Nobody can talk to him. He's impossible—a real brute!"

18 Abigail flew into action. She took two hundred loaves of bread, two skins of wine, five sheep dressed out and ready for cooking, a bushel of roasted grain, a hundred raisin cakes, and two hundred fig cakes, and she had it all loaded on some donkeys.

19 Then she said to her young servants, "Go ahead and pave the way for me [with David]. I'm right behind you."

20 As she was riding her donkey, descending into a ravine, David and his men were descending from the other end, so they met there on the road.

21 David had just said, "That sure was a waste, guarding everything this man had out in the wild so that nothing he had was lost—and now he rewards me with insults. A real slap in the face!

Abigail gathered up extravagant amounts of food, along with some of the most valued products of the land, especially cakes of dried figs, so that she might appease David.

22 "May God do his worst to me if Nabal and every cur in his misbegotten brood isn't dead meat by morning!"

23 As soon as Abigail saw David, she got off her donkey and fell on her knees at his feet, her face to the ground in homage, saying, "My master, let me take the blame! Let me speak to you. Listen to what I have to say. Don't dwell on what that brute Nabal did."

I Samuel 25:14–25a, The Message

THE HISTORY

As noted in Chapter 7, Ruth and Boaz were David's great-grandparents. But what had been happening in Israel during the intervening years, and how had David come to be the leader of a small army?

When Joshua led the Israelites into the Promised Land (Canaan), perhaps in the 13th century B.C.E., the tribes were still governed by their own elders. These leaders came to be called judges, chosen because of their knowledge of the Law and their ability to resolve conflicts among the members of the community. They also served as military and spiritual leaders, mobilizing the people to confront external enemies and teaching the community how to worship God and live according to the Covenant. Joshua (Moses' top general) is sometimes identified as the first judge. Some scholars count fifteen judges; others, sixteen—the history of this period (13th–9th centuries B.C.E.) being very uncertain. Among the more important judges were Deborah, Gideon, and Samson.

Near the end of the reign of the judges, probably in the 12th century B.C.E., God raised up a young prophet, Samuel. As he grew in wisdom and stature before God and the people, Samuel attempted to appoint his sons as judges to succeed him, but because of their corruption, and because of continued threats of foreign invasion, the elders of the twelve tribes of Israel demanded that God have Samuel appoint a king to rule over the united kingdom. The prospect enraged Samuel, but God stepped in and indicated that Samuel should anoint Saul ben Kish, of the tribe of Benjamin, as the first king. Under Saul's leadership, the Israelites vanquished their enemies, among whom were the Ammonites and the Amalekites. However, Saul disobeyed God's command to destroy every Amalekite—man, woman, and child, as well as all the livestock—sparing the life of Agag, the Amalekite king, as well as the prize sheep and cattle. Therefore, God rejected Saul as king over Israel and told Samuel to anoint another king. In due course, God guided Samuel to the house of Jesse and identified David, the youngest son, as the next king. Samuel anointed David, a shepherd, in secret; ironically, David was soon summoned to play the lyre for Saul, to help ease the king's troubled spirit. Dividing his time between his own home and that of Saul, David also brought provisions to his brothers as they continued to engage the Philistines in battle. It was during one of these forays that David succeeded in striking down

Goliath, the champion Philistine warrior, with a stone and a slingshot, securing his reputation as an accomplished warrior.

As David's star rose, Saul's enmity toward the younger man increased. David's covenant with Saul's son Jonathan exacerbated the hard feelings, as Jonathan conspired to protect David against the king's plots. At one point, Saul attempted to have David done in, sending him into battle against one hundred Philistine soldiers; when David returned unharmed, having dispatched all the Philistines, Saul gave his daughter Michal in marriage to David, even though the two men had previously agreed that the elder daughter, Merab, would be David's prize for victory in that battle. Observing how the people adored David, Saul became obsessed with getting rid of the young man. As the conflict between the two grew more desperate and dangerous, David began to gather an army of loyal supporters.

BIBLICAL PASSAGE NOTES

Abigail (Hebrew for "source or cause of delight"), undoubtedly one of the most astute and politically savvy women of the Bible (and considered to be one of the seven female prophets of the Hebrew scriptures), is portrayed in this short but important story as the clever wife of a gluttonous lout, a man known as Nabal (in Hebrew, "fool"). Nabal was a wealthy landowner who owned more than 3,000 sheep. At the end of the sheep-shearing season, it was customary to celebrate with a great feast set out for all those who had worked hard to bring the year to a successful end. It was expected, therefore, that Nabal would regale his men, as well as any others who had been kind enough to help in some way during the year, both as a token of thanksgiving to God and as an act of goodwill toward the neighbors. When David (in Hebrew, "beloved") and his army approached their neighbor's home to collect what was owed them for the protection they had offered for Nabal's flocks and shepherds during the year, Nabal insulted David by refusing to offer proper hospitality, even when David reminded him of what was expected. Instead, Nabal continued to feast with his friends and cronies, seemingly oblivious to the dangerous faux pas he was committing. Tipped off by a loyal servant that David was on his way and that her husband was paying no mind to the formidable encroaching army, Abigail set out to head off the ruin and possible destruction of her family and all of its holdings. Nabal had earlier summarily ignored David's request for bread, wine, and meat for him and his men (verse 11), an imprudent and disrespectful act by the standards of the time. But Abigail seemed to know just what this tension-filled moment required. Acting swiftly, she gathered up extravagant amounts of food, along with some of the most valued products of the land, so that she might appease David and at the same moment atone for her husband's insolence by the abundance of the fine gifts she loaded onto her pack mules.

THE MENU

Raisin Challah Bread

Lamb with Figs and Red Wine

Sautéed Lamb with Walnuts and Pomegranate Juice

Baked Sheep's Milk Cheese and Fresh Dates

Roasted Grain with Yams and Turnips

Wheatberry and White Bean Salad

Tabbouleh

Abigail's Lentil Dish

Pressed Fig Cake

Raisin Cake

Apricots Abigail (a fritter)

Carmel Cabernet Sauvignon or Merlot

THE PREPARATION

All that Nabal had denied, Abigail provided and then some. The items on the shopping list of goods that Abigail gave David, though seemingly random, are in order of importance to the story. First on the list are the items that Nabal denied David and his men in verse 11, beginning with two hundred loaves of bread. That much bread could not have been prepared in the moment, so one may wonder where it came from. The suggestion, of course, is that it had been prepared for the feast that Nabal was holding with his entourage; and the fact that they had not yet needed it or called for it made Nabal's refusal to David not merely inhospitable; with so much at hand, his rudeness smacked of greed. The Hebrew word used for bread (*lechem*) is also the generic term for "food"; therefore, whatever was prepared, if it were not bread, it must have been quite a lot of some standard staple known to this particular community.

Or perhaps not. "Two hundred" (in Hebrew, *resh*) is understood numerologically to mean "in the beginning." So as bread is at the beginning of the list, the two hundred might just be a modifier to indicate what was most important, or what was to be first on Abigail's list.

Following the bread, we are told that two skins of wine (in Hebrew, *yayin*, literally "what is pressed out") were sent to David. The King James Version (KJV) of this text says that Abigail packed two "bottles" (in Hebrew, *nebel*); yet it hardly seems likely that she would have provided just *two bottles* of refreshment to wash down so much food, and with so many men to be served. Not to mention that *bottles*, in common parlance, seems to indicate some sort of glass container. Although glass has its origins in the Middle East or North Africa, it is unlikely that it was being used to store wine anywhere in Israel at this point in time. *Nebel* can also mean "vessel," "flagon," or "pitcher," so the idea of two *large skins* as vessels for the wine, especially in a community that raised sheep and goats, makes much more sense. It is also interesting to note that the Hebrew root for this wine container, *nbl,* is the same root for the name of Abigail's husband, Nabal (perhaps indicating that too much wine makes one foolish?). All in all, it appears that however much wine was sent, David and his men were satisfied by the portions.

Next on the list of gifts to David and his men are "five sheep dressed out and ready for cooking." Once again, the butchering could not have been done on the spur of the moment, so these sheep must have been provisions that Nabal had set apart for his own meal, already cooked and seasoned ("dressed") so that at best, come meal time, they might have had to be cut or warmed by the fire. But why *five* sheep? Is there a symbolic meaning here, as above with two hundred and with two? Perhaps there is. Five in Hebrew numerology represents strength and severity. It can also represent peace, wholeness, or appeasement. Perhaps Abigail chose five finely prepared and tasty sheep, knowing that David would understand her intentions as she humbly asked his pardon for her husband's insolence.

Not content to provide only what had once been denied by Nabal, Abigail went beyond what might have been considered an adequate recompense and sent grains and fruits as further ingratiation. Some Bible translations speak of "five *seahs* (or *ephahs*) of parched corn."[1] Because it follows as it does the five sheep on her list of giving, perhaps David might have understood her generosity as "what was required, and to further underscore our desire for peace, then five of grain, also." (What Abigail took from Nabal's storehouse was most likely roasted barley [in Hebrew, *qali*], or some other dark grain.) And just how much is five *seahs* or *ephahs*? A *seah* is a biblical measure, three of which equal one *ephah.* One *ephah* in modern-day units is about three-fifths of a bushel (see Appendix A). The Message translation above of "a bushel" is probably a good compromise understanding of the amount Abigail packed; once cooked, as the grain expanded, a bushel could feed a small army with sufficiency.

To accompany the grain, Abigail gathered one hundred raisin cakes. Some translations say, "one *omer* of raisins" (an *omer* is one-tenth of an *ephah*), but whether that translates into one hundred cakes is anyone's guess. The understanding of biblical weights and measures requires a lot of conjecture. However, suffice it to say that Abigail did put together many bunches or clusters of dried fruits native to the region, both dried grapes and dried figs. "Cakes" as it is used here does not mean a baked good, but merely indicates a large pressed mound of dried goods. And why one hundred? One hundred (in Hebrew, *qof*) signifies holiness, and is a reminder of the one hundred daily blessings. Perhaps Abigail was also trying to flatter David by sending along blessings as well with all the ingredients of the meal.

Finally, we are told that David also received two hundred fig cakes, and here the list of the bounty ends. Like the dates, these fig cakes were dried groupings of figs, held together in mounds or cakes by the sweet juices that as they dry become very sticky. As the list begins, so it ends with two hundred. Abigail understood her offering and what it would mean to the man she sent it to: peace, humility, blessings, atonement, and subservience before a man of great stature. In the end, her unique political insights paid off: when her husband Nabal later died (of an apparent stroke), David sent for her, and she took her place of honor as one of his wives of important stature.

Most of us will never have to cook for four hundred people, so we have reduced the recipes to what might suffice for a meal served to just ten or twelve friends and family in celebration and in thanksgiving for all the goodwill that is engendered by hospitality to one's neighbors.

THE RECIPES

🍇 Raisin Challah Bread

Challah is a traditional Jewish bread often baked and served for Rosh Hashanah. It has been linked with the story of Abigail and David (especially for Ashkenazi Jews) as the bread of atonement, which is the theme of another Jewish feast day, Yom Kippur. Its rich and light flavor makes it a perfect accompaniment to a menu of lamb, fruit, and wine, just like the one that Abigail prepared for David and his men.

2 packages dry yeast	7 Tbsp. vegetable oil
⅛ tsp. saffron threads	4½–5 cups all-purpose flour
⅔ cup warm water	1½ cups raisins
¼ cup golden honey	1 egg yolk, beaten
¼ cup granulated white sugar	1 tsp. sugar
2 tsp. salt	1 tsp. water
5 eggs	

In a large mixing bowl stir together the yeast, saffron threads, and water. Let the mixture stand 5–10 minutes to allow yeast to swell and dissolve. (It should look a bit foamy.)

Quickly and with a firm hand stir in the honey, sugar, and salt. (Do not use a bread maker or hand mixer for this recipe.) Add the eggs and oil, and then enough flour (about 4 cups) so that the dough turns into a workable mass that is not too sticky. Turn out the dough onto a floured board and knead by hand for about 10 minutes, adding more flour if necessary so that the batter is elastic but not gooey.

Allow the dough to sit on the board for about 10 minutes, then work the raisins in little by little, folding or kneading them into the dough so that they are well assimilated (and not just sitting on top of the dough). Place the dough into a large greased bowl and cover with plastic wrap, then place a damp clean dish towel over the bowl, and set it aside in a warm place to allow the bread to rise. This should take about 45 minutes to 1½ hours. When the bread mixture has nearly doubled in size, proceed to the next step.

Preheat oven to 375°F.

Divide the dough in thirds. Shape each section into a long, snakelike rope, thicker on one end than the other (about 12″ in length, each). Connect the 3 coils at the slimmer ends, then wrap the entire length into a loose spiral, tucking the thicker ends back into the coil to form a large, rounded braid.

Place on a greased baking sheet, and glaze the bread with an egg yolk mixture (yolk, sugar, and water); place in the center of the oven for about 30–35 minutes, or until golden brown. Let loaf cool thoroughly before slicing.

Yield: 10–12 servings

Lamb with Figs and Red Wine

3 medium onions, chopped	2 tsp. ground coriander
3 cloves garlic, minced	2 tsp. ground cumin
3 Tbsp. vegetable oil	¼ tsp. cinnamon
3 lb. boneless leg of lamb, cubed	¼ tsp. ground ginger
1 cup chicken stock	¼ tsp. cayenne pepper
1½ cups dry red wine (not cooking sherry)	½ tsp. salt
¼ cup Balsamic vinegar	1 cup dried figs, cut into quarters
2 bay leaves	1 Tbsp. brown sugar
2 tsp. dried mustard	bed of hot rice

In an electric frying pan, brown the onions and garlic in vegetable oil until golden brown. Add the lamb and cook at a high temperature until the meat is well seared, being careful that the mixture does not burn. Stir in the chicken stock, wine, vinegar, bay leaves, dried spices, and salt, and bring to a boil. Place the cover on the frying pan and simmer until lamb is almost tender, about 1 hour.

Add figs and brown sugar, cover and continue cooking for about 20 minutes, or until lamb is tender. Bring to a final boil so that the lamb has a brown sugar glaze, and serve hot over a bed of rice.

Yield: 8–10 servings

Sautéed Lamb with Walnuts and Pomegranate Juice

3 Spanish onions, chopped	1 cup walnuts, finely chopped
½ cup olive oil	3 cups pomegranate juice
2½–3 lb. lamb, ground	dash or two of salt
3 cups tepid tap water	2 tsp. rice flour
½ cup fresh parsley	1–2 tsp. white refined sugar (optional)
3 cups fresh mint	rice
2 cloves garlic, chopped	handful of fresh mint sprigs

Fry the onions in a large pan of olive oil until slightly browned. Add the lamb and cook until all the meat has turned color; then add water. Bring the mixture to a boil. Turning down the heat, allow to simmer for 25–30 minutes, occasionally adding more water if the ingredients in the pan start to look a bit dry.

Wash the fresh herbs and peel the garlic cloves; chop them all into small pieces either by hand or in a food processor. Siphon off a bit of the liquid from the lamb and onion mixture, and in a separate pan, fry the herbs and garlic for just a few minutes; strain and add them to the meat.

Pour in the walnuts, pomegranate juice, and a dash or two of salt, and bring the dish to a slow boil. Place the rice flour in a cup of cold water and stir till it dissolves, then add it just a moment or two before the end of cooking.

Take a quick taste. If the sauce seems a bit sour, add a teaspoon or two of sugar.

Serve over white rice surrounded by sprigs of fresh mint.

Yield: 8–10 servings

Baked Sheep's Milk Cheese and Fresh Dates

Preheat oven to 350°F.

Place a mound of a creamy sheep's milk cheese in a small loaf pan, and spread a teaspoon of honey over the surface. Bake for 45 minutes. Scoop out onto a large dish and surround with fresh dates for dipping and eating!

Roasted Grain with Yams and Turnips

1 cup whole hull-less barley	1 garlic clove, pressed
½ tsp. salt	½ tsp. thyme
3½ cups cold water	½ tsp. dried crushed mint
1 large Spanish onion	¼ tsp. black pepper
2 large turnips, peeled	sliced green pepper rings and halved cherry tomatoes (optional)
3 medium cucumbers	
4 medium-sized yams	2 sliced hard-boiled eggs with paprika sprinkling (optional)
1 cup okra	
3 Tbsp. butter	

In a large pan, place the barley and salt in water and bring to a boil. Reduce the heat and simmer with lid slightly askew for about 45 minutes.

Slice the onion, turnips, cucumbers, and yams into small strips. Place them in a steamer with the okra and cook for about 20 minutes until they are nearly soft enough to mash. Drain and remove the vegetables to a large bowl and pour the cooked barley over them.

In a microwave or a small pot, combine the butter, garlic, and dried herbs and gently heat. Pour the mixture over the barley and vegetables and toss. Serve with sliced green pepper rings and halved cherry tomatoes, or sliced hard-boiled eggs sprinkled with paprika for a great presentation.

Yield: 6–8 servings

❧ Wheatberry and White Bean Salad

1 cup wheatberries	½ cup plum tomatoes, diced
4 cups water	¼ cup fresh basil, chopped
1 cup white or navy beans	vinaigrette
½ cup fresh chives	fresh spinach and variegated arugula
½ cup zucchini (or yellow) squash, chopped	

In a large pot, cook the wheatberries in 2 cups of water (this may take up to 45 minutes), then drain. At the same time, cook the beans in 2 cups of water (this may take up to 25–30 minutes) until they are al dente; then drain. Combine the wheatberries and beans in a large bowl, and make a cover layer with the chives, zucchini, tomatoes, and basil. *Do not mix.*

Prepare a vinaigrette as follows. Fill a mixing cup halfway with olive oil; add another ¼ cup of cider vinegar. Mix in two tablespoons of a spicy mustard (Dijon or some other), a dash of salt, and a dash of pepper. Force three small garlic cloves through a press. Beat vigorously with a fork for about 1 minute; then pour vinaigrette over the wheatberry and bean dish. Once again, *do not mix.*

Cover with plastic wrap and allow to chill for several hours. Just before serving, toss the salad, and pour it out onto a large platter of fresh spinach and variegated arugula for serving.

Yield: 8–12 servings

❧ Tabbouleh

¾ cup bulgur wheat	2 cups parsley, finely chopped
1 cup Spanish onion, minced	2 cups scallions, finely chopped
1 tsp. allspice	4 ripe tomatoes, finely chopped
¼ tsp. ground cumin	½ cup fresh black mint, chopped
½ tsp. salt	½ cup lemon juice
1 cup chickpeas, finely chopped	½ cup olive oil
1 cup cucumber, chopped	fresh grapevine leaves or endive
1 tsp. ground black pepper	

Soak the wheat in just enough very hot to boiling water (leaving about ½″ above the surface of the wheat) in a covered pot for about ½ hour. Pour the grain into a colander and allow to drain, stirring a bit with a fork to help fluff up the kernels.

Combine all the remaining ingredients (except the lemon juice, olive oil, and greens) in a large bowl, and fold in the wheat, stirring gently. Cover and refrigerate for at least 1 hour.

Prior to serving, dress the salad with lemon juice and olive oil. Serve on a bed of fresh grapevine leaves or endive, which can be used to scoop up the mix.

Yield: 8 servings

❧ *Abigail's Lentil Dish*

1 cup dried lentils	3 Tbsp. oil
3 cups water	1 cup cooked rice
1 bay leaf	¼ tsp. mace
3 sprigs parsley	salt and pepper
1 onion, chopped	1½ cups tomato sauce

Wash the lentils and soak in water for about an hour; do not drain. Add bay leaf and parsley and cook until tender—about 1 hour. Meanwhile, brown the onion in the heated oil; then add the remaining ingredients with the exception of the sauce. Heat through, and serve with sauce in a side dish.

Yield: 8 servings

Source: Adapted from Marian Maeve O'Brien, *The Bible Cookbook* (St. Louis: Bethany Press, 1958), 204.

> *Though the cakes of figs and raisins that Abigail took to David were mere mounds of dried fruit (not cakes made from flour, in this instance), tradition has long overlooked the true meaning of the word, and one can find hundreds of recipes for fig and raisin cakes that refer to or cite the biblical text above. So who are we to argue? After all, what's a good meal without dessert?*
> *Here are two traditional recipes to help complete our Abigailian menu.*

❧ *Pressed Fig Cake*

1 cup sweet butter	1½ cups dried figs
2 cups honey	2 Tbsp. vinegar
4 eggs	1 tsp. cinnamon
2 cups milk	3 Tbsp. water
6 cups whole wheat pastry flour	

Preheat oven to 400°F.

Cream butter with 1 cup of honey. Add eggs, milk, and most of the flour, then mix well to make a dough. Dust the dough with flour and put in a very cold place for 20 minutes.

Grind the figs and mix with the remainder of the honey, the vinegar, and the cinnamon. Pour the water and the filling mixture into a pot, simmer for 15 minutes, then let cool.

With oiled hands, evenly spread half the dough into a 9″ x 12″ buttered baking dish, spread the filling over, then cover with the rest of the dough. Bake for 15 minutes, or until golden brown.

Yield: 8–12 servings

Source: Pressed Fig Cake recipe reprinted with permission of Dr. Tibor S. Rodin, as found in *King Solomon's Feast: Culinary Delights from the Cuisine of Biblical Israel* by Cuia and Tibor S. Rodin (self-published: 1994).

❧ Raisin Cake

1½ cups raisins

2 cups water

1 cup white granulated sugar

1 tsp. Balsamic vinegar

¾ cup butter

3 eggs

2 tsp. vanilla extract

1½ cups oatmeal

1 tsp. baking soda

½ tsp. salt

1½ cups all-purpose flour

2 tsp. ground cinnamon

1½ tsp. ground allspice

1 tsp. ground nutmeg

2 tsp. baking powder

½ cup chopped walnuts

whipped cream or vanilla butter cream frosting

Preheat oven to 350°F. Lightly grease a 10″ tube pan or a 10″ square pan.

In a large pot, boil the raisins in enough water to cover (about 2 cups). Add the sugar and vinegar and stir. Set aside and let cool for about 10–12 minutes. To the same pot, add the butter, eggs, vanilla, and all the remaining dry ingredients. Mix well, then pour batter into pan. Bake for 35–45 minutes, or until tester comes out clean. Serve with whipped cream or a vanilla butter cream frosting.

Yield: 8–12 servings

❧ Apricots Abigail (a fritter)

2 eggs, separated

⅔ cup milk or water

1 Tbsp. lemon juice

1 Tbsp. butter, melted

1 cup flour, sifted

¼ tsp. salt

2 Tbsp. granulated white sugar

1 large can apricots, drained and halved

confectioners' sugar (optional)

butter and syrup (optional)

Beat egg yolks and add milk or water, lemon juice, and butter. Resift flour with salt and sugar and add to yolks, stirring well. Beat egg whites with a dash of salt until stiff, then fold into the batter. Dip apricots in the batter and sauté in butter until delicately browned, turning just once. Drain on paper towels and serve hot. May be sprinkled with powdered sugar or served hot with butter and syrup.

Yield: 6–8 servings

Source: "Apricots Abigail": adaptation used by permission of Whitaker House (www.whitakerhouse .com), as found in Frank L. and Jean McKibbin, *Cookbook of Foods from Bible Days*, copyright © 1971 by Whitaker House. All rights reserved.

❧ *Carmel Cabernet Sauvignon or Merlot*

For this meal, try a bottle or two of Israeli red wines from the Carmel region, home of Abigail and Nabal, of which there are usually 4–5 fine choices available from your wine merchant.

NOTES

1. See the discussion regarding "corn" in the Preparation section of Chapter 1.

❧ 9 ❧

King David's Nuptials

THE TEXT

39b Then David sent word to Abigail, asking her to become his wife.

40 His servants went to Carmel and said to Abigail, "David has sent us to you to take you to become his wife."

41 She bowed down with her face to the ground and said, "Here is your maidservant, ready to serve you and wash the feet of my master's servants."

42 Abigail quickly got on a donkey and, attended by her five maids, went with David's messengers and became his wife.

I Samuel 25:39b–42, New International Version

A jug of olive oil was representative of the feast of kings, as the ancient Hebrews believed that olive oil was capable of restoring health and adding longevity.

THE HISTORY

As related in Chapter 8, King Saul had become extremely jealous of David's success in battle, his popularity among the people, and his special relationship with God, to the point that Saul actually tried to murder David with a spear while the young man was playing music. David, aided by his wife Michal and Saul's son Jonathan, managed to elude Saul's men and to gather a large band of supporters. Even though he was a fugitive, David cornered Saul on two different occasions, but each time David spared the king's life. Saul and three of his sons, including Jonathan, finally met their end during another battle with the Philistines, Saul committing suicide instead of allowing the enemy to kill him. Afterward, David went to Hebron and became king of Judah; he was but thirty years old. A war between the House of Saul and the House of David ensued, and after seven years of fighting David's forces prevailed; he was then anointed king of Israel as well. Historians date the unification of Judah and Israel to the 11th century B.C.E.

David reigned for about thirty-three years as ruler of the united kingdom. During that time he was able to subdue the Philistines and conquer the rest of Canaan. Historians also credit David with having provided strong spiritual leadership to a fractious group of tribal families who were easily tempted to abandon the Covenant in favor of the religious practices of the native peoples. He made Jerusalem the capital of the new nation of Israel because that city was and still is considered to be sacred to God: within its boundaries is Mount Moriah, the place where Abraham was supposed to have gone to sacrifice Isaac and the place where Jacob was believed to have had his vision of a ladder ascending to heaven. To this holy spot David brought the Ark of the Covenant with the Tablets of the Ten Commandments, and there he is believed to have composed many of the works found in the book of Psalms.

Before and during his reign as king, David took at least eight wives, a number of concubines, and had at least twenty children, including a son, Daniel, with Abigail; a son, Absalom, and a daughter, Tamar, with Maachah; and a son, Solomon, with Bathsheba. It was Solomon, known for his wisdom, who succeeded to the throne when David died, and it was he who built the great Temple at Jerusalem.

BIBLICAL PASSAGE NOTES

The Bible does not provide us with any words about the preparations for David's marriages, but there seems to be a long history associated with a wedding feast in the House of David. The imagery is seen over and over again in the Song of Songs, where some scholars and a longstanding tradition identify the male protagonist, the lover, as Solomon, David's son and successor. In addition, the parable of the wedding feast in the Christian gospels (Matthew 22:1–14, Luke 14:15–24) is rooted in a Jewish understanding of the marriage of a great king. The stories surrounding David were undoubtedly on the minds of the gospel writers as they related the teachings of Jesus, who himself was said to be a descendant of David.

THE MENU

Solomon's Flat Bread

Zaatar Bread

Israeli Salad

Hummus with Olive Oil and Pine Nuts

Onion Salad with Sumac and Capers

Mulukhiya (Middle Eastern Chicken and Greens Soup)

Kufta (Ground Lamb with Potatoes and Tomatoes) *or Sabenekh* (Lamb Chops and Spinach) with Rice

Makluba (Lamb Steaks with Cauliflower and Apricots)

Princely Beans in Tomato Sauce *or Fasooleyah Khodra Bi Zeit* (Arabian Beans and Sun-dried Tomatoes)

Bathsheba's Crispy Baked Potatoes with Rosemary

Red Wine, Creamy Cheese, and Concord Grapes

King David's Chocolate-Covered Coconut Macaroons

King David's Wedding Cake

A feast fit for a king and his bride, this meal will sate an entire retinue of family and friends.

THE PREPARATION

What would a feast for such a great king look like? In modern-day Israel, one will come across more than a few sites pitching "King David's Feast" (such as *Genesis Land* just outside of Jerusalem) to the tourist trade; and many of the cookbooks of the last seventy years have a recipe or two that imagine some glorious confection worthy of the Jerusalem court. We've attempted a fair cross section of both offerings, while adding in a few recipes we think would make an 11th-century B.C.E. royal meal complete. If you're going to try the whole menu at one sitting, make sure you have left yourself a lot of preparation time and that you've invited lots of friends and family with hearty appetites!

THE RECIPES

❦ *Solomon's Flat Bread*

1½ cups whole wheat flour

⅓ cup fine cornmeal

1 Tbsp. olive oil

1½ tsp. salt

½ cup lentils, cooked

1 Tbsp. millet, ground into powder

1½ cups water

1 tsp. onion powder

½ cup sesame seeds

Preheat oven to 350°F.

Combine flour, cornmeal, olive oil, salt, lentils, millet, and water to make a dough mixture, and flatten onto an oiled baking sheet. Sprinkle with onion powder and sesame seeds. Bake 20 minutes or so. For a crispier cracker, leave in oven an extra 10 minutes.

Yield: 6 servings

One of the few breads to incorporate lentils in the dough, Solomon's Flat Bread is great when served with hummus or some other dip.

❦ *Zaatar Bread*

Basic frozen pie crust

5 Tbsp. zaatar

5 Tbsp. of extra virgin olive oil

Preheat oven to 400°F.

Roll out basic pie mixture to form 2 flat oval loaves around ¾″ thick and let stand covered with a cloth for half an hour. Make a paste with the zaatar and oil and lightly coat the top of each loaf before baking for 10 minutes.

Yield: 6–8 servings

Quick and easy, Zaatar Bread nevertheless has a taste of the exotic.

❧ Israeli Salad

3 cucumbers	1 green pepper
3 tomatoes	3 scallions
½ cup radishes	¾ tsp. salt
¼ cup fresh parsley	½ tsp. celery seed
olive oil	½ tsp. zaatar
lemon juice	

Chop the cucumbers, tomatoes, pepper, scallions, radishes, and parsley into small pieces and combine. Just prior to serving, season lightly with olive oil, lemon juice, salt, celery seed, and zaatar, then toss. Serve cold or at room temperature.

Yield: 8 servings

❧ Hummus with Olive Oil and Pine Nuts

¼ lb. chickpeas, soaked for a few
    hours

½ cup fresh lemon juice

3 Tbsp. tahini

2 garlic cloves, crushed

½ tsp. salt

1 Tbsp. olive oil

1 tsp. paprika

½ tsp. ground cumin

a few sprigs of parsley, finely
    chopped

1 cup pine nuts, sautéed

½ cup plain yogurt

You can buy hummus already prepared at most grocery stores, but try making it yourself with this recipe.

Drain the chickpeas and simmer in fresh water for about 1 hour or until tender. Save the cooking water.

Process the chickpeas in a blender (or food processor) with the lemon juice, tahini, garlic, salt, and a small bit of the cooking liquid to obtain a soft, creamy paste. Transfer to a large bowl. Mix in the olive oil, paprika, cumin, a little chopped parsley, pine nuts, and the yogurt. Cover and chill for at least ½ hour and serve cold on hot bread. Makes a wonderful appetizer!

Yield: 6–8 servings

❧ Onion Salad with Sumac and Capers

4 Spanish onions
½ cup capers
1 tsp. ground sumac

salt and black pepper
2 Tbsp. olive oil

Slice the onions very thin and place them in a bowl. Add the capers. Sprinkle with sumac and add salt and pepper to taste. Cover with olive oil and let stand for 1 hour or so before serving.

Yield: 6–8 servings

❧ Mulukhiya (Middle Eastern Chicken and Greens Soup)

2 frozen packets (1 lb. each) *mulukhiya*
1 onion, cut in half
½ tsp. salt
bay leaf
4–5 cardamom grains
6 large boneless chicken breasts
olive oil
15–20 garlic cloves, crushed
1 Tbsp. dried coriander
1 Tbsp. lemon juice

Place the frozen packets of *mulukhiya* into a pot of boiling water. Stir until completely thawed.

In a separate pot, boil the onion, salt, and bay leaf; toss in cardamom tied in a muslin bag; then add chicken and cook until tender. Remove chicken, cut into small strips, and fry in olive oil.

Many Middle Eastern cooks are "graded" on their ability to make a good *mulukhiya*. The key is to make sure not to overcook; otherwise, the leaves will sink to the bottom and the soup becomes dull and heavy.

Throw out the bagged cardamom, as it has done its job. Mash the onion and throw it back into the soup, bringing it to a fast boil.

Add the now-thawed *mulukhiya* and simmer for about 5 minutes. *Do not overcook,* as this will make all the leaves sink to the bottom of the pot; it is essential that they remain floating at or near the top.

Mix together the crushed garlic and the dried coriander and fry it in olive oil until it is golden brown. Add to the boiling *mulukhiya* and simmer for 2 minutes. Stir in lemon juice.

Serve in bowls while piping hot.

Yield: 8 servings

❦ Kufta (Ground Lamb with Potatoes and Tomatoes)

¾ cup fresh parsley

1 large onion

4 cloves garlic

2 lb. lamb, ground

1 tsp. salt

½ tsp. allspice

1 tsp. black pepper

½ tsp. garlic powder

3–4 red potatoes, peeled, thinly sliced

3–4 beefsteak tomatoes, thinly sliced

dash of garlic salt or onion salt

Chop the parsley in a blender or small food processor until fine. Place in a large mixing bowl. Next chop the onion and garlic into small pieces, again in the food processor or blender, until they too are of a fine consistency. Add the onion/garlic mixture to the parsley and mix in the ground lamb, salt, and all dried spices. Knead with the fingers, as if one were making hamburger patties, until well mixed.

Lightly pack the meat mixture into the bottom of a large baking pan, turn the oven to broil, and quickly bake until the top of the meat is browned. Remove from the oven and set aside for a few moments. Using the peeled and sliced potatoes, create a layer across the meat, and top with a layer of sliced tomatoes. Sprinkle with a dash of garlic salt or onion salt.

Reset the oven to 425°F. Cover the pan with aluminum foil and bake for about 45 minutes to 1 hour.

Serve from the pan.

Yield: 8 servings

❦ Sabenekh (Lamb Chops and Spinach) with Rice

4 Tbsp. olive oil

¼ cup pine nuts (plus extra for decoration)

1 onion, chopped

6 lamb chops or 6 small fillet mignons

¼ tsp. sumac

¼ tsp. paprika

¼ tsp. dried thyme

¼ tsp. sage

salt and pepper

3 cloves garlic, crushed

1 Tbsp. ground coriander

1 cup fresh coriander, chopped

1 lb. fresh spinach, washed and roughly
  chopped

If you're looking for a nice variation on the presentation of lamb chops, this recipe for *Sabenekh* with Rice will fit the bill.

1 cup water or beef stock

3 Tbsp. lemon juice

basmati rice

Heat 2 Tbsp. olive oil in a pan and fry the pine nuts until browned. Remove with a slotted spoon, allowing the olive oil to drain back into pan. Add onions to same pan; fry until lightly browned, then fold in meat, half the dried spices, and a pinch of salt and pepper; continue frying until the meat is well cooked. Heat the remaining oil in a separate pan. Add garlic and ground coriander, stirring for 1 minute. Next place half of the meat into the mixture along with the fresh coriander and spinach. Cover and simmer on low heat until the spinach begins to release its juice. Add water (or stock), along with lemon juice, remaining spices, and a pinch more of salt and pepper. Cook on low heat for ½ hour. Serve with basmati rice, sprinkled with the rest of the meat broth. Decorate with pine nuts.

Yield: 6–8 servings

❦ Makluba *(Lamb Steaks with Cauliflower and Apricots)*

Makluba *means "upside down."*

1 large cooking onion, chopped

6 cloves garlic, chopped

olive oil for frying

6 large lamb steaks

8–12 cups water

salt and pepper to taste

1 tsp. ground cardamom

2 heads cauliflower

3–4 cups uncooked basmati rice

1 large tomato

½ cup pine nuts, browned

1 lb. dried apricots

Many cultures have developed "upside-down" dishes, and *makluba* is an especially attractive rice dish made more special by the addition of a garnish of nuts and apricots.

In a deep cooking pot with lid, sauté onion and garlic with a small amount of olive oil till limp and clear. Add meat and water, plus salt, pepper, and cardamom. Simmer meat until it is tender and the broth is richly flavored (about 45 minutes). While that is cooking, cut cauliflower into small and manageable florets. Fry florets in olive oil till thoroughly cooked and browned on all sides. Drain cooked florets on a plate covered with a paper towel to help remove as much oil as possible.

When meat, broth, and cauliflower are done, remove meat and broth from the cooking pot (or use another deep pot). Layer uncooked rice, meat, and cauliflower, one on top of the next, creating two or three 3-part layers. Place another layer of rice on top. Slice tomato into thin pieces and place the slices around on top of the rice. Season with a bit more salt and pepper. Pour the broth over the entire casserole. Add a bit more water so that the rice will cook well. Put a tight lid on the pot and let ingredients steam until rice is cooked and virtually all the liquid is absorbed.

Upturn the pot of *makluba* onto a large platter. Garnish with browned pine nuts, surrounded by dried apricots.

Yield: About 6–8 servings

❧ Princely Beans in Tomato Sauce

½ cup olive oil

4 spring onions (use entire onion), minced

2 small cloves garlic, minced

2 lb. green beans

1 lb. large tomatoes, chopped

1 cup water

2 tsp. minced mint

salt and pepper to taste

1 large carrot, shredded

sprig of mint

Green beans with mint: it's hard to imagine a tastier combination.

Heat the olive oil over medium heat in a large skillet or saucepan. Add the onions and garlic; then sauté till just slightly limber. Cut both ends off the green beans, divide in halves, and sauté for approximately 5 minutes. Add tomatoes, then water, and finally the remaining ingredients. Bring the entire mixture to a boil. Lower heat; cover and simmer for about 30–40 minutes. Serve piping hot. Just prior to serving, top with uncooked shredded carrot, mounded in the middle, with a sprig of mint as a flag.

Yield: 6 servings

❧ Fasooleyah Khodra Bi Zeit *(Arabian Beans and Sun-dried Tomatoes)*

1 lb. green beans

3 small onions, chopped

2 small garlic cloves, minced

½ tsp. allspice

½ cup olive oil

2 cups sun-dried tomatoes, finely chopped

2 cups water

1 tsp. salt

½ tsp. black pepper

one mound cooked basmati rice

handful of finely chopped sun-dried tomatoes

Wash and drain beans, cutting off both ends. Slice lengthwise, exposing the pod. Fry the onions, garlic, and allspice in oil until lightly browned. Toss in beans and quickly stir-fry (about 2 minutes). Add tomatoes, water, salt, and pepper. Simmer on low heat for about 40 minutes. Hollow out a mound of rice; place beans in center, and top with sun-dried tomatoes.

Yield: 6 healthy servings

❧ Bathsheba's Crispy Baked Potatoes with Rosemary

8 small new potatoes, quartered

4 Tbsp. extra-virgin olive oil

1 long sprig fresh rosemary, finely chopped

salt and pepper to taste

a sprinkle or two of Balsamic vinegar

radicchio leaves as needed

With starch, spice, and sweetness, Bathsheba's Crispy Baked Potatoes with Rosemary has all the makings of a great potato dish.

Preheat oven to 400°F.

Place potatoes, olive oil, and rosemary in large bowl; put a dinner plate over the bowl and toss, shaking up and down a few times until well-mixed. Arrange potatoes on large baking sheet. Sprinkle with salt and pepper; bake, turning occasionally, about 45 minutes, or until golden brown. Before serving, baste with Balsamic vinegar and place on a bed of radicchio for a fine presentation.

Yield: 8 servings

❧ *Red Wine, Creamy Cheese, and Concord Grapes*

There are some red wines known by the name Carmel "King David" (muscat, almog, concord, etc.), but they tend to be very sweet. Still, they do complete the picture for a Davidic meal. However, for the more discerning diner, try a nice dry red wine from the Kidron Valley vineyards, available from most importers in major cities. Serve with a fresh creamy goat's or sheep's milk cheese and grapes for decoration.

❧ *King David's Chocolate-Covered Coconut Macaroons*

3½ cups unsweetened shredded coconut

¼ cup matzoh cake meal

1¼ cups granulated sugar

2 large eggs, separated, plus 1 egg white

6 oz. imported bittersweet chocolate

¼ cup water

1 tsp. almond extract

Cover 2 baking sheets with parchment paper. Preheat oven to 325°F.

In bowl, mix together coconut, matzoh cake meal, and 1 cup of the sugar. Add eggs and extra egg white and mix with fingers until well blended. Gently shape about 2 tablespoons dough into a pyramid and set on prepared baking sheet. Repeat with remaining dough, leaving about 2″ between cookies. Bake for about 25 minutes or until golden on top. Cool completely.

In saucepan, melt chocolate with the water, almond extract, and remaining ¼ cup sugar. Bring to boil; then simmer slowly for a few minutes until mixture starts to thicken. Cool slightly. Holding each macaroon with 2 fingers, dip half the cookie into the chocolate so that it is half black and half white. Allow to dry for a few seconds while tilted over a dish, then place on wax paper. Repeat with remaining cookies. Cool completely.

Yield: 16 macaroons

Source: King David's Chocolate-Covered Coconut Macaroons recipe reprinted by permission of Recipe Gold Mine (www.recipegoldmine.com).

King David's Wedding Cake

1 large can sliced pineapple with syrup

water, as needed

¼ cup butter

1 cup dark brown sugar

1 package white cake mix

¼ cup nonfat dry milk

No nuptial meal is complete without a wedding cake. Though King David himself might not have had this exact version, tradition holds this rich confection as fit for a king.

Preheat oven to 375°F.

Drain the syrup from the pineapple; add enough water to make 1⅛ cups liquid. In a 10″ skillet that can go into the oven, melt the butter; remove from heat and sprinkle with the brown sugar. Arrange slices of pineapple on the sugar. Let stand. Choose a white cake mix that calls for milk on the package; turn this into a 2-quart bowl and mix in the nonfat dry milk. Add ⅔ cup of the pineapple syrup; beat hard 2 minutes. Add ⅓ cup syrup and beat hard 1 minute. Pour batter over the pineapple in the skillet; bake 45–50 minutes or until the cake pulls away from the sides of the pan. Remove from the oven; let the cake stand 5 minutes, then turn out.

If you use an iron skillet, reduce the heat to 350°F and bake for 5–10 minutes longer.

This is a good basic recipe usable with any fruit such as peaches, pears, cherries, and apricots. Serve with whipped topping.

Whipped Topping

½ cup instant nonfat dry milk

½ cup ice cold water

3 Tbsp. lemon juice

3 Tbsp. sugar

Place the milk into a 1-quart bowl. Add the ice water and beat with a rotary beater at high speed until the mixture stands in peaks—about 2 minutes. Pour in the lemon juice, beat again, and then gradually add the sugar. This is better if it chills for about 30 minutes. Makes about 2½ cups.

Yield: 8–12 servings

❧ 10 ❧

The Lovers in the Garden

THE TEXT

4:12 A garden inclosed is my sister, my spouse; a spring shut up, a fountain sealed.

4:13 Thy plants are an orchard of pomegranates, with pleasant fruits; camphire with spikenard,

4:14 Spikenard and saffron; calamus and cinnamon, with all trees of frankincense; myrrh and aloes, with all the chief spices:

4:15 A fountain of gardens, a well of living waters, and streams from Lebanon.

. . . .

5:1 I am come into my garden, my sister, my spouse; I have gathered my myrrh with my spice; I have eaten my honeycomb with my honey; I have drunk my wine with my milk: eat, O friends; drink, yea, drink abundantly, O beloved.

"Let us get up early to the vineyards; let us see if the vine flourish, whether the tender grape appear."

. . . .

7:11 Come my beloved, let us go forth into the field; let us lodge in the villages.

7:12 Let us get up early to the vineyards; let us see if the vine flourish, whether the tender grape appear, and the pomegranates bud forth; there I will give thee my loves.

7:13 The mandrakes give a smell, and at our gates are all manner of pleasant fruits, new and old, which I have laid up for thee, O my beloved.

Song of Songs 4:12–15; 5:1; 7:11–13, King James Version

THE HISTORY

The Song of Songs is one of the books attributed to King Solomon, who succeeded his father, King David, as ruler of a united Israel. Solomon was the son of David and Bathsheba, whom David had taken as wife under less-than-honorable circumstances. Nevertheless, Solomon, and through him all of Israel, was blessed by God. Under Solomon's forty-year reign (some scholars date it to the 10th century B.C.E.; others, to the 9th or 8th), Israel remained at peace with all of its neighbors. Consequently, concerns turned from warfare and the consolidation of power to other matters. The people of Israel constructed the Temple at Jerusalem and made it the center of religious life for all the people. Commerce flourished, and the city became a hub of international trade; visitors came from all nations to wonder at the wealth of Israel, including the Queen of Sheba, who journeyed from Ethiopia (or Yemen), according to tradition. They also came to absorb the erudition of the Hebrew court, as Solomon had become legendary for extraordinary wisdom in his own lifetime. Though there is no conclusive evidence, rabbinical tradition attributes the books of Proverbs, Ecclesiastes, and Wisdom to Solomon's own hand.

Unfortunately, the golden age would not last. To forge political alliances and maintain the peace, Solomon took seven hundred wives; he also had three hundred concubines, and untold numbers of children. With such a large family, it is understandable that one person, no matter how wise a leader, could not be in touch with everything each member of the household did, said, thought, or believed; and since so many of his wives had not been raised according to the Covenant, a larger portion of his family began to revert to their former religious rituals. The Israelites considered these foreign practices to be idolatrous and blamed the king for allowing them to take place under his own roof. As Solomon's reign wore on, criticism of his neglect of family affairs began to fracture the unity of the Israelites, and finally the situation became so untenable that God pronounced judgment on Solomon: the kingdom would be divided, and Solomon's heir would rule over only a tiny portion of the nation. Upon Solomon's death, severe tensions developed between the northern and southern portions, and within a few years ten of the original tribes of Israel had split off to form a northern kingdom.

BIBLICAL PASSAGE NOTES

These passages, taken from the Song of Songs (also known as the Song of Solomon), reveal one more instance of the way food is used in the scriptures, and its importance to people of the biblical era. Throughout the Song of Songs, the physical features and attributes of the lovers at the center of this epic poem are described with extensive use of plant and animal imagery. Whether one interprets the verses as allegorical or takes them at face value, the reader is treated to a veritable archaeological index of the flora and fauna of the Solomonic era.

The main characters of the Song of Songs are a man and a woman, and in quotable poetic language they repeatedly extol their love for each other, perhaps as a kind of courtship dance leading up to marriage, or, as many interpreters believe, in lyrics of devotion and commitment in the midst of the seven days of the marriage ceremony itself.

THE MENU

Fragrant Oils (to set the mood)

Shepherd's (Bedouin) Bread with Fresh Olives and Camel's Milk Cheese

Ezo Gelin (Wedding Soup)

Spiced Baked Fish

Pounded Chicken Breasts with Pomegranates and Walnuts

Solomon's Rainbow of Vegetables

Arroz de Bodas (Sephardic Wedding Rice)

Pleasant Fruits in Cinnamon Spice Syrup

Lovers' Saffron Cake

Fine Israeli Red Wine

THE PREPARATION

In the first poetic proclamation above (4:12ff.), it is the man who is speaking. Some scholars claim that the speaker is King Solomon himself; others believe it is a humble lovesick shepherd who, like Romeo, attempts to seduce his Juliet through flattery and an accounting of his great deeds so that he might earn a place at her side. His true love is a veritable orchard of pomegranates (in Hebrew, *rimmon*)—a fruit that is fleshy, whose juice is refreshing—an ancient symbol of fertility and eternal life. She is likened to pleasant fruits (from the Hebrew, *meged*, i.e., "precious") and is the essence of camphire (in Hebrew, *kopher*, a shrub like privet) and spikenard (in Hebrew, *nerd*, i.e., "nard"); hence we are given to understand that she was possessed of a spicy sweet fragrance. Continuing the metaphor, the lover describes "the plants" of his spouse's "garden" (that is to say, her finest attributes) as reminiscent of saffron (in Hebrew, *karkom*, i.e., "crocus"), calamus (in Hebrew, *qaneh*, i.e., a "reed" or "cane"), and cinnamon (in Hebrew, *qinnamon*)—inferring that she tastes sweet in so many ways. Finally, he alludes that she is to him like frankincense (in Hebrew, *lebonah*), myrrh (in Hebrew, *mor*), and aloe (in Hebrew, *ahaloth*)—sensual, fragrant, and healing. His love, his spouse, the woman who inspires his poetry, is *all these things*, and more.

His spouse's presentation of herself is fully satisfying to him—all the spices gathered in one person—and he is joyous, like a man who has his cake and can eat it too. He is blessed with the richness that personifies Israel (milk and honey from the comb; sweet wine). In celebration, he entreats his friends to eat and drink and love as he has been fortunate to do.

In chapter 7, it is the woman who speaks. She pleads with her lover to go with her to the vineyards and fields to partake of their goodness: tender grapes (in Hebrew, *semadar,* i.e., "tender flower, the bulb"), pomegranates, mandrakes[1] (in Hebrew, *dudai,* also known as "love apples"), and all manner of pleasant fruits. Perhaps because the man views her as a garden of delights, she in response styles herself as a vineyard of love. Or one can understand her invitation literally as one of eager anticipation to consummate their union. This can be seen in her comparison of their love to "fruit stored over the door": in the ancient Near East, fruit was often stored on a transom shelf above the door, hidden high up and away so that it might become ripe and tasty. In effect, she appears to be telling him that she is storing up all her love for him, and that it is his alone to enjoy.

All told, these verses from the Song of Songs are a kind of love allegory expressed through the imagery of eating and drinking at a wedding feast: the couple, having tasted the sweets of each other's goodness, find themselves drunk—intoxicated by the sheer physical love they are now sharing. The man has found his perfect mate and is living out what the author of the Book of Proverbs meant when he wrote, "Find joy with the wife you married in your youth, fair as a hind, graceful as a fawn. Let hers be the company you keep, hers the breasts that ever fill you with delight, hers the love that ever holds you captive" (5:19, JB).

The feast in the Song of Songs, whether real or imagined, was seen in the ancient Near East as the prototype of the love feast for couples getting married. Even today, readings from the Song of Songs are used at Jewish and Christian weddings. Though the text provides no specific menu for the bride planning the day itself, we're sure that at least some of the ingredients mentioned in the above verses made their way onto the matrimonial dinner table. Here is our version, with recipes, of what a bride and groom, using the themes from the Song of Songs, might expect.

THE RECIPES

❧ *Fragrant Oils (to set the mood)*

The setting and ambiance of a meal is very important to the dining experience. For this meal, try making an oil composed of some of the plants mentioned in the Song of Songs. The recipe is simple, and will help set the mood for a romantic dinner.

½ oz. benzoin	½ oz. galangal
½ oz. cinnamon	½ oz. frankincense

1 oz. myrrh

3 drops honey

3 drops lotus oil

1 drop rose oil

a pinch of powdered orris root

Mix all ingredients well, and heat or burn in a low dish next to a candle to help carry the scent throughout the room.

❧ *Shepherd's (Bedouin) Bread with Fresh Olives and Camel's Milk Cheese*

½ cup olive oil

1 oz. dry baker's yeast

1 Tbsp. honey

1–1¼ cups tepid water

3½ cups flour

2 tsp. salt

fresh olives

camel's milk cheese

Because of their peripatetic life, Bedouin shepherds would have eaten foods that were easily prepared. Though simple, this combination of bread, olives, and cheese makes a delicious appetizer.

Dissolve yeast and honey in tepid water, and let sit for a bit. Mix in the flour and salt. Knead the dough on a floured board. Cut dough into 8 pieces and shape into rounds. Roll or flatten with hands until 5″ across and ¼″ thick. Put on lightly greased cookie sheets, cover with a clean, damp towel, and allow to rise in a warm place for 1–2 hours. (They should be about ½″– ¾″ thick.)

Preheat oven to 500°F. Bake for 12–15 minutes. Serve surrounded by fresh olives and camel's milk cheese.

Yield: 8–12 servings

❧ *Ezo Gelin (Wedding Soup)*

1½ cups dried red lentils

6 cups chicken stock

2 cups water

1 large Spanish onion, finely chopped

3 cloves garlic, minced and pressed

½ cup bulgur wheat

2 Tbsp. tomato paste

1 tsp. ground coriander

1 medium tomato, peeled and finely chopped

6 Tbsp. butter

½ tsp. salt

1 tsp. paprika

½ tsp. cayenne pepper

1 Tbsp. lemon juice

½ cup fresh mint leaves

Put the lentils in cold water and soak for 1 hour; then drain. Combine lentils, stock, water, onion, garlic, bulgur, tomato paste, coriander, tomato, 2 Tbsp. butter, and salt in a large saucepan. Cook on very low heat for about 30–35 minutes, stirring occasionally, until soup appears soft and creamy.

Just before serving, stir the paprika and cayenne with the lemon juice into the soup. Let soup simmer for 5 minutes longer. Using the microwave, melt 4 Tbsp. butter in a measuring cup; crumble the fresh mint between your fingers and rub between the palms of your hands. Stir mint into the butter, and drizzle the mixture over the soup when serving.

This recipe for *Ezo Gelin* includes both lentils and bulgur wheat, two common grains that were included in the soup for the wedding meal because of their importance as dietary staples.

Yield: 8 servings

Spiced Baked Fish

½ tsp. cumin

½ tsp. coriander

½ tsp. caraway seeds

½ tsp. dried dill

½ tsp. tarragon

½ tsp. cayenne pepper

½ tsp. sumac

½ tsp. salt

3 cloves garlic, minced

1 large onion, chopped very fine

4 tomatoes, chopped into small pieces

6 red or gray mullet fillets

½ cup white wine vinegar

1 cup Bloody Mary mix

Although the peoples of the Bible would not have had access to Bloody Mary mix, they would have been quick to use cumin, coriander, caraway, dill, tarragon, cayenne pepper, salt, garlic, onion, and sumac to make a dish such as this spiced baked fish.

Preheat oven to 400°F.

Mix all the spices in a small mortar and grind with a pestle until they are reduced to a powder. Combine the garlic, onion, and tomatoes in a bowl, and spoon half of the mixture across the bottom of a large, greased baking dish. Arrange the fillets close to one another on top of the mixture.

Measure out the vinegar, and stir the powdered spices into it. Pour over the fish and let stand for 10 minutes or so. Place the remaining tomato mixture on top of the fish, then cover as much as possible with Bloody Mary mix.

Bake for 20–25 minutes.

Yield: 6 servings

Pounded Chicken Breasts with Pomegranates and Walnuts

2 cups walnuts, finely chopped

1 Tbsp. garlic powder

¼ cup walnut oil

1 cup diced onions

3 Tbsp. butter

2 Tbsp. ketchup

12 boneless chicken breasts, pounded thin

2 Tbsp. fresh lemon juice

3 cups water

1 Tbsp. light brown sugar

1 cup fresh pomegranate juice

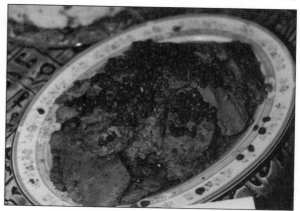

Within the tomb of Tutankhamun, pharaoh of ancient Egypt, dating from about 1350 B.C.E., is found a painting of a chicken, indicating that chickens were a valued domestic livestock during biblical times, though they were probably available only to the wealthy or on special occasions such as wedding feasts. This photo shows our version of Pounded Chicken Breasts with Pomegranates and Walnuts.

Mix the walnuts and garlic powder by shaking in a plastic bag; then add to the oil and sauté in an electric frying pan for 5–10 minutes. Scoop out the nuts and reserve. Using the same pan, sauté the onions in butter, then add ketchup and cook for about 2 minutes, stirring well. Lower the cooking temperature and return the nuts to the frying pan, cooking for approximately 5 minutes (taking great care not to burn them).

Push everything to the side of the pan and arrange chicken pieces in the center. Place some of the nut mixture on top and around the chicken.

In a blender, mix the lemon juice, water, sugar, and pomegranate juice. Pour over the chicken and cook for about 20 minutes, until breasts are browned and easy to cut.

Yield: 6–12 servings, depending on size of chicken breasts

Solomon's Rainbow of Vegetables

5 summer squash, diced

2 stalks celery, chopped

8 plum tomatoes, chopped

1 package frozen lima beans (or 1 can fava beans)

1 red onion, minced

1 orange pepper, chopped

1 cup pomegranate juice

2 cloves garlic, pressed

1 tsp. salt

½ tsp. chili pepper

3 cups white rice

handful of fresh chervil or cicely (myrrh)

Preheat oven to 375°F.

With red, green, yellow, and orange vegetables, Solomon's Rainbow of Vegetables is a reflection of the vast richness over which the king ruled.

Combine all vegetables into a large bowl and toss. Pour pomegranate juice into a glass and press garlic into it; stir with a fork until well mixed. Grease a large baking pan and arrange vegetables in it, creating a rainbow of colors. Pour pomegranate/garlic juice over vegetables; add salt and pepper. Bake for 35–40 minutes. Remove from oven; pour into a large bowl and mix with rice and chervil. Form into balls using an ice cream scoop. Serve piping hot.

Yield: 8–12 servings

Arroz de Bodas *(Sephardic Wedding Rice)*

4 cups water

4 cups chicken stock

¼ tsp. butter or oil

1 tsp. salt

4 cups basmati rice

10 scallions, chopped

1 tsp. turmeric

1 cup green seedless grapes

½ cup pine nuts, toasted

mint leaves

The presentation of *Arroz de Bodas* (Sephardic Wedding Rice) is key, and guests at King Solomon's wedding feast would have been delighted by this "sculptured" dish.

Pour water and stock into a large cooking pot with a lid; add butter and salt and bring to a boil. Add rice, scallions, and turmeric. Turn heat to very low and cover, leaving a crack for the steam to escape. After 5 minutes, stir the rice to make sure nothing is sticking to the bottom or sides. Re-cover (except for the crack for the steam) and cook for 8–10 minutes, or until fluffy when stirred with a fork.

Cut the grapes into quarters and heat them in the microwave for 2–3 minutes. Mix with the pine nuts and stir into the rice. Scoop the rice mixture into a large, greased, round gelatin mold and pack it tight. Prior to serving, invert the mold onto a large platter and decorate with mint leaves.

Yield: 12–16 servings

❧ Pleasant Fruits in Cinnamon Spice Syrup

½ cantaloupe

½ muskmelon

½ cup pear nectar

½ cup white grape juice

¼ cup brown sugar

1 tsp. freshly ground nutmeg

¼ cup Balsamic vinegar

¼ cup fresh mint leaves

⅛ tsp. almond extract

3 cinnamon sticks

¼ cup freshly squeezed lime juice

Using a melon baller, carve out bite-sized portions of seeded cantaloupe and muskmelon, then place in a large Pyrex serving dish with a lid. Combine the remaining ingredients (except lime juice) in a saucepan and bring to a quick boil; turn down heat and simmer for about 5 minutes. Pour liquid over the melons. Squeeze lime juice over the fruit and refrigerate for about 3 hours before serving. Serve in chilled parfait cups.

Yield: 8–12 servings

❧ Lovers' Saffron Cake

½ cup water

¼ tsp. saffron strands

1 cup sugar

½ cup butter

2 eggs

2 cups flour

¼ cup buttermilk

1 tsp. baking soda

1 tsp. baking powder

¼ tsp. nutmeg

½ cup raisins

½ cup red currants

1 tsp. lemon extract

2 Tbsp. powdered sugar

Saffron, perhaps the most expensive spice ever cultivated, certainly makes Lovers' Saffron Cake a wedding confection fit for King Solomon and his bride—or for any wedding couple beginning married life.

Place water in a measuring cup and heat in a microwave for about 2 minutes, till it boils. Add the saffron strands and allow the mixture to sit overnight, so that in the morning the water is a nice yellow color.

The next day, preheat oven to 350°F.

In a large bowl, mix together all the ingredients except for the raisins, currants, extract, and powdered sugar. When a smooth consistency, add the fruits and lemon extract. Pour into a large greased cake pan and bake for 40–45 minutes. Allow to cool on a baking rack. Sprinkle lightly with powdered sugar before serving.

Yield: 8–10 servings

❧ *Fine Israeli Red Wine*

At a Middle-Eastern style wedding or for the celebration of any fine occasion, only the best red wine that Israel has to offer will do. With this meal, try a red from the Golan Heights Winery: a *Cabernet Sauvignon, Elrom Vineyard, Yarden*, 2001; or a *Merlot, Ortal Vineyard, Yarden*, 2001. Alternately, a *Castel Vineyard, Grand Vin Castel*, 2001 is very nice, as is the *Margalit Vineyard, Cabernet Sauvignon, Special Reserve*, 2002. You won't be disappointed with any of these fine choices.

NOTES

1. In the ancient Near East, mandrakes were a symbol of erotic love because they were thought to have the properties of an aphrodisiac. They were often used as a fertility drug.

11

Elisha Cooks Masterfully at Gilgal

THE TEXT

38 Elisha went back down to Gilgal. There was a famine there. While he was consulting with the guild of prophets, he told his servant, "Put a large pot on the fire and cook up some stew for the prophets."

39 One of the men went out into the field to get some herbs; he came across a wild vine and picked gourds from it, filling his gunnysack. He brought them back, sliced them up, and put them in the stew, even though no one knew what kind of plant it was.

"Put a large pot on the fire and cook up some stew for the prophets."

40 The stew was then served up for the men to eat. They started to eat, and then exclaimed, "Death in the pot, O man of God! Death in the pot!" Nobody could eat it.

41 Elisha ordered, "Get me some meal." Then he sprinkled it into the stew pot. "Now serve it up to the men," he said. They ate it, and it was just fine—nothing wrong with that stew!

42 One day a man arrived from Baal Shalishah. He brought the man of God twenty loaves of fresh baked bread from the early harvest, along with a few apples from the orchard. Elisha said, "Pass it around to the people to eat."

43 His servant said, "For a hundred men? There's not nearly enough!" Elisha said, "Just go ahead and do it. God says there's plenty."

44 And sure enough, there was. He passed around what he had—they not only ate, but had leftovers.

II Kings 4:38–44, The Message

THE HISTORY

As related in Chapters 7, 8, and 9, the twelve Israelite tribes united under King Saul to form the Kingdom of Israel sometime around 1050 B.C.E. After the kingdom grew into an empire under King David (the second king) and experienced a period of peace under King Solomon (the third king), severe tensions developed between the northern and southern portions of the state. By 920 B.C.E. the kingdom had fallen apart: ten tribes split off as the Kingdom of Israel in the north, under King Jeroboam (Solomon's overseer), and two tribes remained as the Kingdom of Judah in the south, with Jerusalem as the capital under King Rehoboam (Solomon's son). Strife and warfare between the two kingdoms continued for a long time; and though the northern kingdom was larger, it suffered from excessive internal divisions and was geographically more vulnerable to invaders, spies, and traitors.

Into this political stew, during the reign of King Joram (also known as Jehoram; 851–842 B.C.E.), the ninth king of Israel, a prophet by the name of Elisha (Hebrew for "God is salvation") rose to prominence. Born into a farming family, Elisha had no political aspirations, but one day while he was plowing, the great prophet Elijah came and covered the farmer with his cloak—an indication, as we have seen from the story of Joseph's "coat of many colors," that Elijah intended to pass on a double portion of his legacy (spirit) to Elisha. Some scholars contend that the anointing took place during the reign of King Ahab (875–853 B.C.E.), when Elijah had become active in Israel, but the actual date of the anointing (if indeed it did actually occur) has been lost to history.

Sometime during the reign of King Joram, Elijah seems to have gone into retirement, perhaps on Mount Carmel. At some unrecorded date he sought Elisha at Gilgal, and the two proceeded to Bethel and Jericho, crossed the Jordan River, and came to Gilead. Tradition states that Elijah was taken up to the heavens in a blazing chariot, his cloak falling back to the ground to settle on Elisha.

Previously, Elisha seems to have been resident with a school of prophets in Gilgal, but after Elijah's ascension, Elisha became a wandering prophet, purifying a water spring in Jericho, cursing a group of young men in Bethel, raising from the dead a wealthy benefactress' only son in Shunem, and even traveling to Damascus to anoint a new Syrian king. Along the way, Elisha cured Naaman of leprosy, multiplied twenty barley loaves into food sufficient for one hundred men, was said to have caused the rainfall that prevented the army of Joram from dying of thirst, and was believed to have performed many other miracles on behalf of the people he encountered. He also seems to have functioned as a sort of political advisor to the kings of Israel, helping to defeat the Moabites, to prevent disaster at the hands of the Syrians, and to prophesy Israel's victories in battle.

Elisha is believed to have died sometime during the reign of Joash (also known as Jehoash; 797–781 B.C.E.), the 12th king of Israel, though this is not much more than speculation based upon the narrative found in the scriptures. The scriptures also recount that a year after Elisha's death, the body of a dead man was thrown into Elisha's grave; upon touching Elisha's bones, the dead man was revived and stood up.

BIBLICAL PASSAGE NOTES

In the story above, Elisha has returned to Gilgal (Hebrew for "circle [of stones?]"), probably the present-day village of Khirbet 'Alyata, about seven miles north of Bethel. At that time, a famine had struck the city, and the prophets' guild (circle, perhaps) were present, apparently to divine what could be done to help the people who were in need of food. Would God intervene? Was God angry at the people or at the king of Israel for his apostasy? Should the people suffer for the deeds of their king? These were just a few of the questions that must have been going through the minds of the king's subjects as they gathered to discuss their options at Elisha's meal.

THE MENU

Apple and Barley Cake

Fried Cucumbers

Celery and Fennel Casserole

Field Herbs with Corn

Seethed Gilgal Stew

Barley-Apricot Salad with Roasted Hazelnuts

Dried Fig, Date, and Raisin Cakes with Nuts and Cheese

THE PREPARATION

Elisha, aware of the hunger of the prophets who had gathered, instructs his servant to put a pot on the fire and make some pottage. (According to some scholars, this pot was a big cauldron like those found in Egyptian kitchens, with legs that stood over the fire in the floor. A "seethed" pottage, like the one made here, consisted of meat cut into small pieces, mixed with rice or meal and vegetables.)[1] One of the men goes into a nearby field and gathers some greens (in

Hebrew, *orah*, or "shiny herbs") and wild gourds (in Hebrew, *paqquoth*), from which he makes a stew. Apparently unfamiliar with the flora of the area, the forager picks fruit from a vine and cuts it up for stew in a mixture that was so dreadful and bitter no one could eat it! Just what was so awful?

Apparently, what the unsuspecting cook had picked to serve for dinner was colocynth, or wild cucumber, as it is known in places near the Dead Sea, where it still can be found today. Other names for this viny gourd are "bitter apple," "egusi," or "vine of Sodom." It is an extremely acrid fruit about the size of a lemon, yellowish-green in color, with a spongy texture. Its seeds, however, are quite edible, nutty-flavored, and rich in fat and protein. The fruit, picked fresh from the field and sliced open in bits, would have ruined any stew. In fact, it is said that when consumed in large quantities, the colocynth can be fatal. In small portions, it is a quite effective laxative, so the prophets undoubtedly were pretty sick to their stomachs, feeling quite rapidly like "death warmed over" ("Death in the pot, O man of God!" they clamored).

Elisha commands that he be given some "meal" (in Hebrew, *qemach,* often translated as "flour"), and according to the story, its addition remedies the bitter taste of the stew. It's difficult to believe that any amount of flour would actually have rendered the pottage edible. The storyteller is more eager to present Elisha's handiwork as one of a series of minor miracles meant to glorify the subject of the tale. But this is the stuff of legends.

In what seems at first to be an unrelated story, a man arrives at the prophets' camp, having come from Baal Shalishah. He brings with him from the first fruits of the harvest twenty loaves of barley bread, and some other things to eat.[2] (The version above says "apples from the orchard"; the KJV tells us "full ears of corn in the husk thereof," both incorrect, as neither apples nor corn existed in the Middle East during this period. The Hebrew word of the text, *karmel,* means "garden land," or "grain." If what the servant brought was *the best of Carmel,* the land of Abigail, it was more likely apricots, as we learned in our earlier discussion of I Samuel 25.) Elisha instructs that the food be shared with all those present, though such a small amount would hardly feed one hundred hungry men. But in a move not unlike the feeding of the 5,000 people by Jesus in the Gospel of John,[3] the provisions are passed out and there is plenty left over. In this passage, as in the one prior to it, the storyteller is eager for us to envision Elisha as a miracle worker, not necessarily of grand proportions (though his later works are accomplished on a greater scale), but as a man of the people with an astute level of compassion—a true leader! The redactors of II Kings present in Elisha a type of folk hero, what in Yiddish is known as a *mensch,* with the qualities the Jewish people later came to expect of the Messiah. Hence, in Christian writings, when Jesus asks his disciples, "Who do the crowds say I am?" they answer (perhaps with the above text in mind), "John the Baptist; others Elijah; and others say one of the ancient prophets [Elisha?] come back to life" (Luke 9:19, JB).

THE RECIPES

❧ *Apple and Barley Cake*

2½ cups barley flour

2 tsp. baking powder

a dash salt

2 eggs

2 apples, pared and chopped

¼ cup whipping cream

¼ cup honey

Preheat oven to 400°F.

  Sift together the barley flour, baking powder, and salt. Beat eggs lightly with a fork. Combine with apples, cream, and honey, and add to dry ingredients; mix well. Pour batter into cake or loaf pan and bake for 20–25 minutes. Cut into squares while warm.

Yield: 12 squares

❧ *Fried Cucumbers*

6 medium-sized cucumbers

2 eggs, beaten

1 cup goat's milk

1 cup cornmeal

1 tsp. garlic powder

1 tsp. black pepper

1 cup sunflower oil

Peel the cucumbers and slice lengthwise. In a large bowl, beat together the eggs and goat's milk. In a separate bowl, combine the cornmeal, garlic powder, and pepper. Dip each cucumber slice in the egg batter, then transfer to the cornmeal mixture and completely cover on both sides. Fry in large pan using sunflower oil, about 4–5 minutes on each side, being careful not to burn the delicate slices.

Yield: 8–12 servings

❧ *Celery and Fennel Casserole*

4 fennel bulbs

3 bunches celery stalks

8 Tbsp. olive oil

½ cup flour

1 tsp. salt

½ tsp. black pepper

1 cup milk

1 cup soft bread crumbs

½ cup butter, melted

caraway seeds

Preheat oven to 350°F.

  Cut fennel bulbs into small pieces; do likewise with the celery stalks. Sauté fennel and celery in olive oil; add flour, salt, and pepper. Pour in milk and stir constantly, until thickened. Transfer to a baking pan. Pour bread crumbs over vegetables and drizzle with melted butter. Bake for 35–40 minutes. Sprinkle with caraway seeds prior to serving.

Yield: 6–8 servings

❧ Field Herbs with Corn

12 ears fresh corn	⅛ tsp. pepper
16–20 cups water, as needed	¼ tsp. marjoram
½ cup flavored vinegar	¼ tsp. dill
½ cup lemon juice	¼ tsp. parsley
1 tsp. salt	1 bay leaf
2 cloves garlic, minced	sumac

Shuck and clean corn. Place water in a large pot. Add all other ingredients except corn and sumac and bring to a boil. Add corn, and bring to a boil a second time. Remove and sprinkle with sumac before serving.

Yield: 12 servings

❧ Seethed Gilgal Stew

1 can beef stock	½ cup raisins
2 carrots, sliced	1 tsp. ground cinnamon
1 butternut squash, peeled, seeded, and chopped	½ tsp. mace
1 red onion, diced	½ tsp. salt
6 cloves garlic, minced	½ tsp. paprika
1 can garbanzo beans, drained	¼ tsp. ground coriander
1 can stewed tomatoes	1 bay leaf

Place all ingredients in a large crock pot, and cook on low for 4–5 hours. Remove bay leaf before serving.

Yield: 8 hearty servings

❧ Barley-Apricot Salad with Roasted Hazelnuts

2 whole scallions, chopped	1 tsp. salt
1 cup dried apricots, chopped	1 Tbsp. olive oil
½ cup roasted hazelnuts, chopped	2 tsp. honey
¼ cup fresh parsley, chopped	1 cup plain yogurt
½ tsp. cinnamon	1 tsp. fresh thyme
3½ cups vegetable broth	½ cup raisin or berry vinegar
½ cup orange or cranberry juice	⅛ tsp. ground fresh nutmeg
2 cups barley	

In a large bowl, combine scallions, apricots, hazelnuts, parsley, and cinnamon, and set aside.

Mix the broth and the juice in a medium saucepan and bring to a boil. Add the barley, salt, and oil, and boil again. Reduce heat, and simmer, partially covered, for about 25 minutes. Keeping cover on, remove from heat and allow to cool. Once cool, fold in the scallion and apricot mixture and toss.

Whisk together the honey and the yogurt, and fold in the thyme and vinegar to make a sweet dressing. Scoop the barley mixture into a large bowl, add the scallion-apricot-hazelnut mixture in the center, and pour the dressing over all. Sprinkle with fresh ground nutmeg and serve.

Yield: 8 servings

Dried Fig, Date, and Raisin Cakes with Nuts and Cheese

Gather a grouping of dried figs, dates, and raisins and place on a serving board for easy pickings. For a little spice, add garlic-roasted pistachios or sugared walnuts. Use all these dried fruits to surround a large piece or two of cheese. Everyone is sure to find something they'll like.

NOTES

1. See Robert Jamieson, A. R. Fausset, and David Brown, *A Commentary, Critical and Explanatory, on the Whole Bible* (New York: George H. Doran, 1921) at www.ccel.org/j/jfb/jfb/JFB12.htm#Chapter

2. Here the author of II Kings is making a political statement, in effect stating that a nation with an apostate king and priests do not deserve the portion of the first fruits normally reserved for them under Deuteronomic Law (Deuteronomy 18:4); the faithful servants of God (in this instance, the prophets) would now receive them. Hence, the traveler seeks out Elisha, and makes the proper offering.

3. The feeding of the five thousand "men" is recounted in all four gospels in some form or another; however, only the Gospel of John relates the details regarding "loaves of barley."

12

Dinner with the Governor

THE TEXT

14 From the time King Artaxerxes appointed me as their governor in the land of Judah—from the twentieth to the thirty-second year of his reign, twelve years—neither I nor my brothers used the governor's food allowance.

15 Governors who had preceded me had oppressed the people by taxing them forty shekels of silver (about a pound) a day for food and wine while their underlings bullied the people unmercifully. But out of my love for God I did none of that.

16 I had work to do; I worked on this wall. All my men were on the job to do the work. We didn't have time to line our own pockets.

17 I fed one hundred and fifty Jews and officials at my table in addition to those who showed up from the surrounding nations.

"One ox, six choice sheep, and some chickens were prepared for me daily."

18 One ox, six choice sheep, and some chickens were prepared for me daily, and every ten days a large supply of wine was delivered. Even so, I didn't use the food allowance provided for the governor—the people had it hard enough as it was.

19 Remember in my favor, O my God,
Everything I've done for these people.

Nehemiah 5:14–19, adapted from The Message

The History

Nehemiah, royal cupbearer to the Persian king, was born to the tribe of Judah and may have been a native of Jerusalem. At that time (5th century B.C.E.), Judah was a province of the Persian Empire. The history of how this came to pass is complicated. As related in Chapter 11, the united kingdom of Israel had split into two states, Israel in the north and Judah in the south, in the 10th century B.C.E. Both kingdoms were able to maintain their autonomy, despite the conflicts they had with each other, because their neighbors were relatively weak. But in the 8th century B.C.E. the Assyrians conquered Israel and deported many Israelites into captivity. At the beginning of the 6th century B.C.E. the Babylonians, having destroyed the Assyrian empire, took control of Judah. The Babylonians razed the Temple at Jerusalem and carried away the Ark of the Covenant (which disappears from history at this time), essentially severing the living connection between the Jews and God. Nebuchadnezzar II, the Babylonian king, ordered the deportation of most of Judah's people to Babylon. This period of exile, when the Jews were enslaved in Assyria or Babylon or were forced to flee to Egypt or other lands, is known as the *First Diaspora,* or Dispersion. In the mid-6th century B.C.E. the Persian Empire, under King Cyrus the Great, conquered Babylonia and most of western Asia, including all of Israel. Cyrus permitted a number of Jews to return to Jerusalem, and under the leadership of Sheshbazzar, they began to build the Second Temple.

When Artaxerxes I became king of Persia in the 5th century B.C.E., he granted Nehemiah's request to return to Jerusalem in order to help in the rebuilding of the city. Beginning in 446 B.C.E., Nehemiah governed Jerusalem for about thirteen years, restoring the traditional religious observances and continuing the reforms begun by Ezra, his predecessor. When Nehemiah returned to Persia, however, Jerusalem quickly fell back into corruption and idolatry. At this point the prophet Malachi began to exhort the Jews to return to the Law, and Nehemiah rushed back to Jerusalem after an absence of only two years, shocked at the quick decline in the moral state of his people and determined to bring them back to God. He was able to maintain public order and worship and remained in his post as governor until his death in about 413 B.C.E. Afterward, Judah became a part of Syria, under the administration of the high priest.

Biblical Passage Notes

One of the major figures of the postexilic period of the ancient history of the Jewish people, Nehemiah made a name for himself as the rebuilder of the wall surrounding the city of Jerusalem. When we first encounter Nehemiah in the book that bears his name, he is an officer in the court of Artaxerxes when he learns that the Jews of his homeland are suffering under a great oppression and that the city wall and the entrance gates of his beloved Jerusalem have been almost totally destroyed. Nehemiah commences a period of mourning and fasting that does not go unnoticed by the king, who later gives Nehemiah a royal commission with all the proper credentials to journey to Jerusalem so that he might bring his people whatever help they needed. With a royal decree in his pocket allowing him to requisition the materials necessary to restore the wall, the fortress, and the Temple at Jerusalem, he accomplishes the task in a relatively short time despite the efforts of many others to halt his work. In his role as governor, Nehemiah also institutes needed social reforms, particularly with respect to the oppression of the poor by the rich. It is his actions on behalf of the less fortunate that frame the biblical passage pertinent to the seemingly extravagant meal described in verses 17–18 above.

Nehemiah invited the local leaders and visiting emissaries (with their retinues) from surrounding countries to his table for dinner as a gesture of goodwill and hospitality in an effort to demonstrate what he believed were the qualities of leadership that others should follow. As governor, he had the right to use public funds garnered from extra taxes levied on the common folk so that he might entertain the dignitaries at his table. Instead, he used his own financial resources, and as part of his effort at social reform, set the example so that other officials might follow his lead. In this instance, Nehemiah was carrying out a common biblical and theological understanding of what God required: to provide hospitality, not only to one's own circle of family and friends, but to others as well, including the stranger; to invite the rich and the poor to sit down at the table; to provide a meal from one's own bounty; to prepare an ample feast; and to present it as a thanksgiving for all that God has provided. Nehemiah was viewed as a righteous man and a faithful servant of God through these actions, and his good deeds are set forth in the Hebrew scriptures as the prototype for everyone to emulate.

THE MENU

Rosemary Pita Bread

Ezra's Ox Meat with Rice and Greens

Artaxerxes' Ox Pan

Persian Lamb Stew with Sweet Fruits

Spiced Lamb à la Garden and Grove

Musakhan (Chicken and Onion Bread)

Circassian Chicken (*Cerkez Tavugu*)

Roast Quail with Apricots and Pecans

Artichokes in Lemon Sauce

Almond Soup

Spinach and Lentil Soup

Lebanese Mint, Egg, and Onion Omelet

Orange Peel and Almonded Curds

Governor's Cake

THE PREPARATION

The Hebrew text indicates that a large portion of meat, poultry, and wine—enough for as many as five hundred people, perhaps—was set aside daily for Nehemiah in his role as governor; if he used the provisions at all, it was not to entertain his friends and guests. Instead he prepared elaborate dinners from the funds of his own pocket, which resulted in meals much better than the diners at his table were expecting. The proportions set out in this chapter were customary for a man of his position (compare Solomon's food list in I Kings 4:22ff.). For example, in the 19th century C.E., the bey (a ruler of comparable power to the position Nehemiah held) of Tunis was known to receive as his daily entitlement twelve sheep, along with fish, fowls, soups, oranges, eggs, onions, boiled rice, and other goods. When the bey dined, his nobles dined with him; after they were finished, the servants sat down; and when they were finished, the poor took what was left over. By looking at both examples, we can begin to piece together a fuller picture of what it was like to eat a meal at the gubernatorial palace.

The chickens that are mentioned in verse 17 might be a flight of imagination (excuse the pun); though the breeding of chickens was widespread in Israel at the beginning of the Christian era, the poultry or fowl that Nehemiah served to his guests might just as well have been quail (which were well known and considered a fine meal), or perhaps partridge, dove, or sparrow, all of which were apparently in abundance in Israel and the surrounding area. We'll hedge our bets and provide a recipe for both chicken and quail, and leave the more enterprising cook to find the best ways to prepare partridges and doves, should one's palate have a hankering for smaller fowl (we've deemed sparrows to be off limits).

But what of the wine? The Hebrew word used here is *yayin,* a nondescriptive, generalized term for any type of red wine. It was apparently laid in stock by the servants every ten days or so, according to need but within the parameters of entitlement. At dinner it was served in abundance.

When cooking this meal, one has to use a bit of common sense and a lot of ingenuity. There are not many kitchens these days that feature the cooking of oxen. "Oxtails" are enjoying somewhat of a revival among top chefs and are a tasty menu item; yet unlike the days of old when there was truth in advertising, and oxtails were just that—the tails of oxen—today they are simply the tails of beef cattle of both genders. In some parts of the world (Norway, Madagascar) recipes using real oxen are still popular fare; but most of us are going to have to settle for what the butcher in our area can provide. Even at that, there is only one tail per animal available to the butcher, so you might have to put in a special order ahead of time if oxtails are on your menu. But if one can find ox meat for any of the recipes that follow, all the better for the cook and the lucky diner who has been invited for supper.

THE RECIPES

✌ *Rosemary Pita Bread*

2 cups warm water

1 Tbsp. granulated sugar

1 packet yeast

1½ tsp. salt

2–3 sprigs fresh rosemary

5½ cups all-purpose or bread flour, unsifted

3 Tbsp. olive oil

Heat the warm water and the sugar in a small saucepan, stirring until the sugar dissolves; do not let boil. Pour into a large bowl. Slowly add the yeast, stirring just a bit. Let stand for 5–7 minutes. Tear apart the rosemary and cut the leaves into very fine, small parts; do not

This bread is so delicious, served alongside a fresh goat cheese, that your guests will be tempted to make it a meal in itself.

use the stem, as it will leave too strong a taste in the bread. Add the salt, rosemary, and 4 cups of flour to the mixture, and as it starts to thicken, slowly add the remaining flour. Continue stirring until the dough pulls away from the sides of the bowl. (If the mixture seems too sticky, just add a little more flour until it starts to hold together well; if it seems too dry, add a little more water.)

Knead well for about 5–7 minutes. Put a little olive oil on the palms of the hands and smooth all over the dough to help prevent crusting. Place dough mixture into a greased bowl; cover with a wet towel, and set it aside for about ½ hour. The dough should rise to double its size.

Preheat oven to 500°F. (With this sort of bread, the hotter the oven, the better.) Divide the dough in half; then form into 12 balls. Roll out each ball into a 6″ circle, about 1/16″ thick, on a generously floured table or countertop. Bake on ungreased cookie sheets for 5–8 minutes or until lightly browned. Make sure there are no creases in the dough and that the pitas are lying flat on the cookie sheet.

When finished cooking, place pitas in a paper lunch bag with a damp towel and seal. Let cool completely before serving.

Yield: 8–12 servings

🎋 *Ezra's Ox Meat with Rice and Greens*

2 lb. chopped ox meat (or beef or steak)

2 Tbsp. sunflower oil

1 onion, finely chopped

3 cloves garlic, finely chopped

½ cup galangal (or ginger root), sliced

¼ tsp. turmeric

½ cup fresh spinach

½ cup fresh watercress

½ cup arugula

½ cup borage

2 beefsteak tomatoes, chopped in bits

1½ cups water

salt and pepper to taste

2 cups basmati rice

sprigs of fresh oregano

Some say the prophet was a vegetarian, but had he coveted a meat dish, Ezra's Ox Meat with Rice and Greens surely would have been one of his favorites.

Brown the chopped meat in a large pot with the sunflower oil; slowly add the onion, garlic, galangal, and turmeric. Let simmer about 5 minutes. Cut the greens into thin strips and stir into the pot along with the tomatoes, 1 cup of water, and a bit of salt and pepper. Bring to a boil, then lower to a medium heat and continue cooking for 10–15 minutes. Add ½ cup more water, then cover the pot and let cook at low-to-medium heat for approximately 15–20 minutes. Serve over a bed of basmati rice surrounded by leaves of fresh oregano.

Yield: 4–6 servings

🎋 *Artaxerxes' Ox Pan*

1–2 cups white flour	2 Tbsp. water
2 tsp. salt	1 large onion, coarsely chopped
1 tsp. black pepper	1 Tbsp. mustard
3 lb. ox meat (or beef or steak)	1 cup tomatoes, finely chopped
sesame seed oil	cabbage leaves (or lettuce)
¼ cup chopped mint	paprika

Preheat oven to 350°F.

Mix flour, salt, and pepper in a large bowl. Cut the meat into cubes and roll them in the flour mixture. Braise the meat in a large frying pan that is covered with a thin layer of sesame seed oil; when well browned, place aside in a large oven-proof casserole dish lined with the fresh mint. Add the water to the gravy in the pan, bring to a quick boil, and pour over the cooked beef. Add a bit more sesame oil to the pan and sauté the onion. When lightly browned, scoop it

out of the pan with a slotted spoon and distribute evenly over the beef. Bake for 1 hour. Prior to serving, stir the mustard and a cup of freshly diced tomatoes through the cooked casserole. Remove from dish and place on a bed of cabbage (or lettuce) and sprinkle with paprika.
Yield: 8–12 servings

Persian Lamb Stew with Sweet Fruits

2 tsp. ground nutmeg	6 cloves garlic, finely chopped
1 tsp. salt	2 sticks cinnamon
1 tsp. ground ginger	¼ tsp. ground cloves
¾ tsp. ground black pepper	¼ cup unsalted butter (or margarine)
½ tsp. ground mace	1 cup seedless white raisins
½ tsp. ground allspice	½ cup pine nuts (or crushed black walnuts)
¼ tsp. ground cinnamon	½ cup dates (or dried apricots), chopped
¼ tsp. crushed saffron	½ cup honey
3 cups water	couscous (or yellow rice)
3–4 lb. boneless lamb, cut into 1″ cubes	two bunches seedless Concord grapes
1 Spanish onion, minced	

Combine the nutmeg, salt, ginger, pepper, mace, allspice, cinnamon, saffron, and 1 cup water in a large pot, stirring until dried spices are partially dissolved. Add lamb cubes, the remaining water, onion, garlic, cinnamon, cloves, and butter, and cook on a low flame, partially covered, until lamb has lost a lot of its toughness and can be cut through with a sharp knife (approximately 1–1½ hours). Fold in raisins, pine nuts, dates, and honey; then simmer, partially covered, for about ½ hour longer, or until meat is very tender. Remove pot lid and cook over medium heat, being careful that the mixture does not burn, until stew begins to get thicker, about 15 minutes or so. Serve over couscous or yellow rice on a platter surrounded by seedless Concord grapes.
Yield: 8–10 servings

Spiced Lamb à la Garden and Grove

4 onions, diced	2 chicken bouillon cubes
6 large green peppers, cut in quarters	4 limes, cut in halves
6 Tbsp. butter (or margarine)	4 tsp. cardamom
2 lb. lamb, ground	4 cinnamon sticks
¼ cup fresh lemon thyme leaves	1 tsp. zaatar
1½ lb. tomatoes, diced	3 cups cooked rice
4 cloves garlic, minced	½ cup seedless raisins
1 tsp. salt	½ cup slivered almonds
1 cup water	a pinch of dried lemon thyme

In a large skillet, sauté the onions and peppers in butter over medium heat until brown, taking care not to let them burn. Add the lamb, lemon thyme, tomatoes, garlic, salt, and 1 cup water in which the bouillon cubes have been dissolved. Simmer over a low-to-medium heat until the lamb is tender (about 1–1½ hours). Add the limes, cardamom, cinnamon, and zaatar and bring to a boil.

Preheat oven to 350°F.

Remove from heat and stir in the rice, raisins, and slivered almonds. Pour into an ovenproof casserole dish and cook for 30 minutes or so until heated thoroughly. Sprinkle a small amount of dried lemon thyme over meat just prior to serving.

Yield: 8–10 servings

One can see why the governor would have served his royal guests such an elegant lamb dish; it has all the best of garden and grove.

Musakhan (Chicken and Onion Bread)

8 chicken breasts, boned	3 Tbsp. ground sumac
2 cups olive oil	⅛ tsp. ground cinnamon
salt and pepper to taste	⅛ tsp. ground nutmeg
juice of one lemon	½ tsp. cayenne pepper
½ cup water	1 cup pine nuts
6 bunches scallions, finely chopped	any type of flat bread (e.g., Mountain *Lavash* or Syrian *Saj* bread), cut in halves
2 cloves garlic, crushed	
1 tsp. saffron	

Preheat oven to 400°F.

Rinse the chicken, pat dry, and rub with olive oil. Sprinkle with salt and pepper, and place in an ovenproof dish; pour the lemon juice and water over the chicken and set aside. In a frying pan, sauté the scallions and the garlic for about 20 minutes, or until golden brown (do not let them burn). Add 1 cup or so of the scallion/garlic mixture to the chicken, and bake for 30 minutes, turning the breasts occasionally.

Strain the remaining scallions with a large slotted spoon and remove to a separate bowl; retain the oil. Add to the scallions the saffron, sumac, cinnamon, nutmeg, and pepper, and give the mixture a good stir. Next brown the pine nuts in the remaining oil until soft and toasty. With a slotted spoon, remove the pine nuts and fold them into the scallion mixture, again taking care to save the oil for later use. Remove the chicken from the oven and generously spoon the spiced scallion/pine nut concoction on and around the chicken. Return the breasts to the oven and cook for 30 more minutes or so, until the chicken is done.

Cut the flat bread into halves and soak in the oil from the scallions for the remainder of the time it takes to cook the chicken. Remove the chicken from the oven and switch to the broil setting. Place the bread portions on a cookie sheet covered by a piece of chicken and the baked scallions. Broil for about 5–7 minutes. Serve piping hot.

Yield: 8 hearty servings

Circassian Chicken (Cerkez Tavuğu)

4 boneless chicken breasts	salt and pepper to taste
1 onion, finely chopped	1 lb. shelled walnuts, finely chopped
2–3 cups water, as needed	6 cups fresh bread crumbs
½ cup lemon juice	1 Tbsp. paprika
1 cup fresh cilantro	small jar of pimentos
1 cup fresh parsley, chopped	

Wash the chicken thoroughly in cold water and place it in a large frying pan with the onion. Cover with water, lemon juice, cilantro, and parsley, and bring to a boil. Place a lid over the pan and simmer at low heat until the chicken is tender, about 30 minutes. Remove the chicken, cut into small pieces, and sprinkle with salt and pepper to taste. Keep the chicken stock with the herbs for use later.

Turn the oven dial to the broiler setting. Mix the walnuts, bread crumbs, and paprika in a blender. (To get a thorough mix, add the bread crumbs a little at a time so as not to choke the blender blades.) Place these dry ingredients in a large bowl and slowly add the reserved chicken stock (without the herbs this time—liquid only) to the mixture, stirring by hand until all has been used and the consistency is like that of a thick soup.

Put the chicken pieces in an oblong ovenproof dish that will fit in the broiler and cover with all of the stock sauce. Sprinkle with paprika so that the dish is completely covered. Broil for 5–10 minutes (do not let it burn). Just prior to serving, garnish with red pimentos.

Yield: 6 servings

Roast Quail with Apricots and Pecans

1 lb. ground meat sausage (any kind)	1 cup celery, chopped
1 cup all-purpose flour	½ cup spring onions, chopped
⅓ cup light brown sugar	4 ripe apricots, chopped (without pits)
1½ tsp. baking powder	6 Tbsp. Balsamic vinegar
1 cup buttermilk	6 semi-boneless quail
2 eggs	salt and pepper to taste
1 cup flavored bread crumbs	handful of paprika
2 sprigs fresh thyme, cut in pieces	1 tsp. ground dried ginger
1 cup chopped, roasted pecans	flour coating
1 carrot, peeled and diced	

1 cup sunflower oil

½ tsp. salt

¼ tsp. pepper

chopped parsley

cherry tomatoes

Preheat oven to 325°F.

This roast quail dish is so rich, with buttermilk and sausage, that you may feel as if you're gaining weight just from cooking it.

Fry the sausage and set it aside; reserve the drippings. Mix the flour, brown sugar, baking powder, buttermilk, eggs, bread crumbs, thyme, and sausage drippings together, along with half of the pecans, carrots, celery, and onions, and spoon into a small loaf pan. Bake for about 50 minutes. Let cool completely.

Place a few large spoonfuls of the baked bread crumb mixture in a large bowl, and mix it well, mashing if necessary, with the sausage, the apricots, and the remaining pecans. Add half the Balsamic vinegar and stir well.

Wash the quail thoroughly and pat dry, inside and out. Season the inside of each quail cavity with salt and pepper; then stuff a few spoonfuls of the bread crumb mixture inside each bird. Season the outside of the bird with a little paprika mixed with ginger and tie the legs together with some twine or unflavored dental floss.

Mix a handful of flour, salt, and pepper in a bowl as a coating for each quail and see to it that they are well covered on both sides. Heat the sunflower oil in a large skillet and sear the quail, turning occasionally, until the entire bird has a golden tinge to its skin. Remove the quail from the skillet and transfer to a large, deep, ovenproof pan. Add the remaining vinegar to the pan drippings and bring to a boil; then spoon over the quail. Raise the oven temperature to 350°F and bake for 45 minutes to 1 hour. Serve over the remaining baked bread crumb mixture, surrounded by chopped parsley and cherry tomatoes.

Yield: 6 hearty servings

❧ *Artichokes in Lemon Sauce*

4 cups water

juice of one lemon

2 cloves fresh garlic, peeled and minced

6 fresh artichokes

radicchio or variegated arugula

vinaigrette dressing or butter dip

Pour the water into a large saucepan and put in place a basket or standing strainer/sieve. Add lemon juice and garlic to the water. Cut the stems off the chokes and with scissors or a sharp knife cut the upper part of the

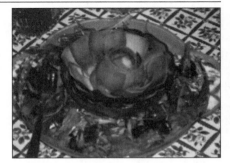

Artichokes in Lemon Sauce is very simple, but the presentation is sure to please everyone at the table.

leaves straight across (they tend to be spiny and prickly, so it's best to remove them before cooking or eating), leaving a flat top. Place the artichokes in the strainer, partially cover the pot, and cook for about 30–35 minutes at a medium-to-high heat. (Do not overcook, or they become mushy.) Remove from pot and arrange on a large platter surrounded by radicchio or variegated arugula. Serve with a vinaigrette dressing or a warm butter dip.

Yield: 6 servings

❧ Almond Soup

1 small onion, grated	salt and pepper to taste
2 cloves garlic, peeled and crushed	⅓ cup almonds, ground
2 cups clear chicken broth	3 Tbsp. extra-virgin olive oil
2 cups water	2 hard-boiled egg yolks
¼ tsp. coarsely crumbled saffron threads	4 scallions, finely chopped
⅛ tsp. lemon peel, grated	6 Tbsp. fresh yogurt
½ tsp. ground cumin	

Combine onion, garlic, broth, and water. Add the lemon peel, herbs, and spices; bring to a boil, then lower the heat and simmer.

Sauté almonds in olive oil in a large skillet until golden brown (about 4 minutes). Remove from pan with a slotted spoon and drain on a paper towel. Scoop almonds into a small bowl and crumble egg yolks over them.

Toss almond/egg mix and scallions into broth. Simmer for 10 minutes and serve with a dollop of fresh yogurt on top.

Yield: 6 servings

❧ Spinach and Lentil Soup

2 cups brown lentils	1 lb. fresh spinach
2 bay leaves	1 tsp. ground cumin
4 cups water	2 Tbsp. fresh coriander
½ cup olive oil	2 Tbsp. fresh lemon juice
1 large onion, finely chopped	salt and pepper to taste
2 cloves garlic, peeled and crushed	2 tsp. flavored vinegar

Cook lentils and bay leaves with 3 cups of water in a large pot and bring to a boil; reduce heat and simmer, covered, for about 35–45 minutes, or until lentils are soft enough to mash with a fork. In a large skillet, heat olive oil and sauté the onion together with the garlic for about 5 minutes. With a slotted spoon, transfer the cooked onions and garlic to the lentil mixture; stir in the spinach, cumin, coriander, lemon juice, a bit of salt and pepper, and 1 cup water. Stir briskly and simmer for about 15–20 minutes, adding more water if needed. Just before serving, sprinkle a few teaspoons of flavored vinegar (lemon thyme is nice) into broth. Serve piping hot.

Yield: 6 servings

❧ *Lebanese Mint, Egg, and Onion Omelet*

6 eggs

½ cup light cream

1 Tbsp. flour

a dash or two of paprika

salt and pepper to taste

1 cup olive oil

½ each red, green, and yellow peppers, finely chopped

1 medium onion, finely chopped

½ tsp. sumac

4 sprigs fresh mint (leaves only), chopped

Leave it to the Lebanese to create one of the best omelets you'll ever eat.

Preheat oven to 350°F.

Crack the eggs into a bowl and beat them by hand until light in color. Slowly stir in the cream, flour, paprika, salt, and pepper; set aside. Heat a large skillet and fry the peppers, onion, and sumac in olive oil until the ingredients are soft and somewhat mushy. Line a small but deep ovenproof pan with the peppers and onion mixture, and pour the egg combination over it. With a sharp knife on a hard cutting board, gather the mint leaves together and cut them finely, then chop them into small pieces. Mash with a mortar and pestle or in a small bowl using the handle end of a table knife. Stir half of the mint into the omelet fixings; sprinkle the rest on top. Cook for 15–20 minutes or until the surface is just beginning to brown.

Yield: 4 servings

❧ *Orange Peel and Almonded Curds*

4 Tbsp. finely chopped orange peel

2 cups whole-milk cheese curds (ricotta or some other)

¼ tsp. Madagascar bourbon vanilla

2 tsp. white refined sugar

⅓ cup red currants

½ cup slivered toasted almonds

This rich but light dessert of orange peel and almonded curds can even be served as an appetizer, depending on the type of curds used.

Place a glass or metal bowl in the refrigerator for 1 hour. After 45 minutes, peel an orange, and chop the rind by hand or in a blender at a high speed. Or, if preferred, use prepared candied orange peel (available from most Middle Eastern grocers). In a blender or food processor, whir the orange peel, curds, and vanilla until you have a smooth, creamy texture, like that of heavy whipped cream. Add the sugar and mix again. Pour the mixture into the prepared cold bowl and fold in the currants and all but a handful of the almonds. Stir well and refrigerate, or serve immediately in individual dishes, garnishing each with a few almonds to top off the presentation.

Yield: 6 servings

Governor's Cake

Cake

2 cups sugar

1½ cups all-purpose flour

1 cup cocoa

1 tsp. baking powder

1 Tbsp. plus ½ tsp. baking soda

1 cup buttermilk

3 eggs

1 stick butter, melted

1 cup brewed coffee

Hold onto your horses! Governor's Cake contains more than 2,700 calories per serving, and we're not kidding.

Preheat oven to 350°F.

Sift all dry ingredients together. Mix buttermilk and eggs in a medium bowl. Combine melted butter and coffee in another bowl. Mix all ingredients together in a large bowl. Divide batter between two 10″ pans lined with parchment and sprayed with non-stick cooking spray. Bake both for 1 hour.

Hard Ganache

1 cup milk

1 cup heavy whipping cream

1½ lb. semisweet chocolate bits, melted*

Heat milk and cream to just short of boiling in a saucepan. Remove from heat and mix in chocolate. Set aside to cool.

Chocolate Mousse

½ lb. plus 1 oz. (1 square) bittersweet baker's chocolate*

7 large egg yolks

7 Tbsp. sugar

1½ cups plus 2 Tbsp. heavy whipping cream

Melt chocolate in double boiler. Turn off heat and keep warm. Put egg yolks and sugar in mixing bowl and mix at high speed. Add two tablespoons heavy whipping cream, mixing slightly. Separately whip 1½ cups whipping cream to soft peaks. Place chocolate in a large bowl and quickly add egg mix. Fold in thoroughly, using a spatula. Add whipped cream and continue folding. Cool for 8 hours in refrigerator.

Spread chocolate mousse between the two cake layers, then cover cake with the rest of the mousse, making sure it is totally smooth. Refrigerate until exterior is firm, about 1 hour, then frost top of cake with hard ganache. Serve at room temperature.

Yield: 10 servings

*Do not substitute chocolate bars or other processed chocolate for the baker's chocolate or chocolate bits as they will cause the ganache and mousse to fail.

Source: Governor's Cake recipe. Reprinted by permission of J. Fife Symington III. As originally published in *The Arizona Republic* (September 4, 2004).

13

Esther Saves Her People

The Text

1 That same day King Xerxes gave Queen
Esther the estate of Haman, archenemy of
the Jews. And Mordecai came before the
king because Esther had explained their
relationship.

2 The king took off his signet ring, which he
had taken back from Haman, and gave it
to Mordecai. Esther appointed Mordecai
over Haman's estate.

3 Then Esther again spoke to the king, falling
at his feet, begging with tears to counter
the evil of Haman the Agagite and revoke
the plan that he had plotted against the
Jews.

The traditional foods of Purim include *hamentaschen*
(literally, "Haman's pockets"), a triangular fruit-
filled cookie said to emulate the shape of Haman's
three-cornered hat.

4 The king extended his gold scepter to Esther. She got to her feet and stood
before the king.

5 She said, "If it please the king and he regards me with favor and thinks
this is right, and if he has any affection for me at all, let an order be written
that cancels the bulletins authorizing the plan of Haman son of Hamme-
datha the Agagite to annihilate the Jews in all the king's provinces.

6 "How can I stand to see this catastrophe wipe out my people? How can I
bear to stand by and watch the massacre of my own relatives?"

7 King Xerxes said to Queen Esther and Mordecai the Jew: "I've given
Haman's estate to Esther and he's been hanged on the gallows because he
attacked the Jews.

8 "So go ahead now and write whatever you decide on behalf of the Jews; then seal it with the signet ring." (An order written in the king's name and sealed with his signet ring is irrevocable.)

9 So the king's secretaries were brought in on the twenty-third day of the third month, the month of Sivan, and the order regarding the Jews was written word for word as Mordecai dictated and was addressed to the satraps, governors, and officials of the provinces from India to Ethiopia, 127 provinces in all, to each province in its own script and each people in their own language, including the Jews in their script and language.

10 He wrote under the name of King Xerxes and sealed the order with the royal signet ring; he sent out the bulletins by couriers on horseback, riding the fastest royal steeds bred from the royal stud.

11 The king's order authorized the Jews in every city to arm and defend themselves to the death, killing anyone who threatened them or their women and children, and confiscating for themselves anything owned by their enemies.

12 The day set for this in all King Xerxes' provinces was the thirteenth day of the twelfth month, the month of Adar.

13 The order was posted in public places in each province so everyone could read it, authorizing the Jews to be prepared on that day to avenge themselves on their enemies.

14 The couriers, fired up by the king's order, raced off on their royal horses. At the same time, the order was posted in the palace complex of Susa.

15 Mordecai walked out of the king's presence wearing a royal robe of violet and white, a huge gold crown, and a purple cape of fine linen. The city of Susa exploded with joy.

16 For Jews it was all sunshine and laughter: they celebrated, they were honored.

17 It was that way all over the country, in every province, every city when the king's bulletin was posted: the Jews took to the streets in celebration, cheering, and feasting. Not only that, but many non-Jews became Jews—now it was dangerous not to be a Jew!

Esther 8:1–17, The Message

THE HISTORY

In 539 B.C.E. King Cyrus II (also known as Cyrus the Great) of Persia conquered Babylon and issued what has come to be known as the Cyrus Cylinder, a declaration that the Persians would destroy neither the Babylonians nor their culture. He also decreed that the peoples exiled under the Babylonians could return to their homelands. While the document did not mention the Jews specifically, the policy allowed many Jews (some scholars say 42,000) to go back to Jerusalem; many more (perhaps up to 1 million) remained in Persia, for the Persians were tolerant of all religious practices (though many Persians had adopted Zoroastrianism), including the Jews' observance of the Law and worship of God. Upon reaching Jerusalem, the returning refugees began rebuilding the Temple, and immediately ran into conflict with the Samaritans of the area, who did not hold the Temple as the center of religious life and did not want to lose their privileged position in society. Threatening rebellion, the Samaritans petitioned Cyrus for a stop-work order on the Temple, which he granted.

Previously, Cyrus had united the Persian kingdoms in 559 B.C.E. and had defeated the Medean Empire in 550 B.C.E. and annexed Lydia. Cyrus died (probably in battle) about 530 B.C.E., and rule passed to his son, Cambyses II, who conquered Egypt. Cambyses' reign was short, and in 521 B.C.E. power passed to his relative, Darius (Dariush) I. After quashing a number of rebellions and consolidating power, Darius married Atossa, a daughter of Cyrus the Great. Darius reformed the legal code and the military while extending the empire as far north as the Caucasus. Governing such an enormous area proved unwieldy, so he divided the empire into twenty semiautonomous provinces (called satrapies) and appointed a satrap to administer each one. He also had a canal excavated to join the Nile River to the Red Sea and had a new capital built at Persepolis. Under Darius, Persia became a mighty economic power, trading as far west as Sicily and Carthage and as far east as the Indus River. When he died in 485 B.C.E., his son Xerxes I came to the throne. Like his father, who suffered defeat at the Battle of Marathon, Xerxes tried to invade Greece but was unsuccessful; afterward, the empire fell into a state of unrest, and Xerxes was murdered in 465 B.C.E., at which point Artaxerxes I became king. He ruled until 424 B.C.E., succeeded by his son Xerxes II, who was assassinated after only forty-five days in office. Xerxes' half-brother Ochus seized the throne and took the name Darius II; he died in 404 B.C.E., and Artaxerxes II came to power.

Scholars are quite divided about how the narrative related in the Book of Esther fits into the historical chronology, or even if the narrative is actually historic or purely allegoric. Some claim that Ahasuerus (also known as Achashverosh) may be the same ruler otherwise known as Xerxes I; others, that he may have been Artaxerxes II. A number of scholars also claim that the reason Darius II allowed the Jews to recommence reconstruction of the Jerusalem Temple was that he was the son of Esther and Xerxes I. As there are no extrabiblical accounts of a Queen Esther of Persia, the historicity of the narrative remains a subject of contention, particularly since the story continues to serve as the basis for the Jewish folk holiday of Purim.

BIBLICAL PASSAGE NOTES

The Book of Esther (in Hebrew, *Hadassah,* meaning "myrrh") is an oddity (or some would say, a rarity) in the canon of Jewish scriptures for several reasons. First, it is one of only two books named after women (Ruth being the other); second, it is one of the only books in the Bible not to mention God (although there seems to be a vague reference in the text to an entity that will save the people, if it is not Esther); third, the story it tells of the deliverance of the Jewish people from near certain annihilation thanks to the political savvy of a Jewish woman married to a foreign king demonstrates once again (as in the case of Ruth) Israel's tolerance and adaptiveness to marriage "outside of the tribe" in certain eras of its long history. Though some scholars believe the story takes place during the reign of Xerxes (also called Ahasuerus, King of Persia, in the 6th century B.C.E.), most scholars date the writing of the book to the 4th century B.C.E., about the time of the death of Alexander the Great.

As a result of this remarkable story, the Jewish people added another feast day to their already celebratory calendar, one of the most joyous of all Jewish holidays known as Purim (Hebrew for "lots"). In the biblical selection above, Queen Esther has foiled Haman, the evil advisor to the king, and all his plans to eradicate her uncle, Mordecai, and the Jewish people as well. At the advice of her uncle, Esther had never revealed to the king her true ethnic identity, and taking a gamble that he loved her enough to grant her wishes despite her background, she saves her countrymen and -women and vanquishes their scheming foes. Hence Esther is celebrated as a savior of the people, and Purim is both her feast and theirs.

Esther's skillful maneuvering within the court of the Persian king centers around two banquets by which she carries out her plan to unveil Haman's evil plotting and to demonstrate how his jealousy and prejudices will cause his undoing. We are never told exactly what was served at either of these meals, although one can imagine that a dinner with the King of Persia would not have been a simple affair. Perhaps as a continuance of the spirit of Esther's banquets, Purim celebrations center on a meal—a meal that over time has developed its own protocol. The holiday is preceded by a minor fast to commemorate Esther's three days of eschewing food prior to approaching the king with her supplications. On the main day of Purim itself (usually sometime around the end of February), the book of Esther (called the *megillah*, or "scroll") is read, either in its entirety or in some shortened form. It is customary for the listening audience to boo, hiss, stamp their feet, and rattle *graggers* (noisemakers or clackers) at the mention of Haman's name: the purpose is to "blot out the name of Haman," just as he had tried to blot out the lives and the spirit of the Jewish people.

The Talmud instructs that everyone should "eat, drink and be merry" to the point where the difference between "cursed be Haman" and "blessed be Mordecai" cannot be distinguished. But revelry is not the only focus: the festival places a great emphasis on gifts to charity, the "sending out of portions" of food and drink. Purim celebrations also often include plays and beauty contests that tend to have a carnival-like atmosphere. For these reasons, Purim is greatly anticipated and widely celebrated among all Jews, though in a unique way within each community.

The Menu

Chocolate Chip Challah
Creamy Artichoke Soup
Traditional Potato Latkes
Sweet and Sour Sea Bass
Herb-basted Turkey Breast
Vegetable Cholent
Lemon Poppy Seed Cake
Hamentaschen
Red Wine

The Preparation

The traditional foods of Purim include *hamentaschen* (literally, "Haman's pockets"), a triangular fruit-filled cookie said to emulate the shape of Haman's three-cornered hat; latkes (potato pancakes); vegetarian fare (tradition holds that Esther kept kosher by eating beans and peas while living in the Persian capital of Susa); poppy seeds (a symbol of Esther's fasting), and other seeds as well; *kreplach* (ground meat wrapped in dough, much in the same way and shape as *hamentaschen*); braided challah (as a remembrance of the rope that hung Haman); *folares* (in the Sephardic tradition, pastry dough wrapped around hard-boiled eggs); fish (baked in vinegar, raisins, and spices); turkey; and of course, wine for the drinking portion. All are served at a festive meal, held late in the afternoon, called the *Seudah*. It is usually celebrated with family and friends, with a menu not unlike what follows.

The Recipes

❧ *Chocolate Chip Challah*

2 cups potato flour
½ tsp. salt
2 Tbsp. sugar
1½ tsp. yeast
½ cup warm water

2 tsp. vanilla extract
3 Tbsp. corn oil
2 eggs
1 cup semi-sweet chocolate chips

Preheat oven to 350°F.

In a bread machine, mix together all ingredients according to the manufacturer's instructions. After the first rising, remove dough.

Turn dough out onto a lightly floured work surface. Divide into thirds, and make three long ropes. Braid ropes and finish off (pinch together) at ends. Cover with a damp cloth, and allow to rise again. Place on a large greased cookie sheet, and bake for 40–45 minutes until well browned. Cool for at least 10 minutes before serving or slicing.

Yield: 1 large loaf

❧ Creamy Artichoke Soup

3 cans artichoke hearts

cayenne pepper

3 Tbsp. butter

2 cloves garlic, minced

½ cup white rice (uncooked)

2 cans unsalted chicken broth

1 tsp. salt

1 pint light cream

fresh dill

handful of pimentos

If you take care to simmer this creamy artichoke soup but not allow it to boil, your guests will rave that it's one of the most delicious soups they've ever tasted.

Drain artichokes and place on a large cutting board. Sprinkle with a bit of cayenne pepper and cut into quarters. Melt butter in electric frying pan, and sauté chokes for about 5–7 minutes, stirring constantly. Add garlic, rice, and half the broth. Cover and simmer for 20 minutes or so.

Transfer the artichoke mixture a few spoonfuls at a time to a blender and purée until smooth, pouring what has been puréed each time into a large saucepan until all are done. Add remaining broth and salt; then stir in cream. Simmer for 5–7 minutes (do not allow to boil), stirring all the while to make sure the soup does not burn.

Serve in bouillon cups, garnished with fresh dill and pimentos.

Yield: 6–8 servings

❧ Traditional Potato Latkes

6 potatoes	¼ tsp. garlic powder
2 onions	1 tsp. salt
2 eggs	½ tsp. cayenne pepper
1 tsp. lemon juice	¾ cup olive oil
¼ cup matzoh meal	applesauce or sour cream

Peel and grate potatoes, placing in cold water as you go to prevent darkening. Strip onions and grate them also. Transfer potatoes and onions to a colander and press out any excess moisture.

In a separate bowl, combine eggs, lemon juice, matzoh meal, garlic powder, salt, and cayenne; add potatoes and onions, and mix well. (If the mixture is too wet, add a bit of flour or matzoh meal.) Heat the olive oil in a large frying pan. Drop a heaping spoonful of the mixture into the oil and press down with a spatula to flatten. Fry until brown and crispy on the edges, cooking each side for about 3 minutes. Drain on paper towels placed on a large platter and keep warm until serving. Present with applesauce or sour cream on the side.

For a nontraditional approach, substitute yams for potatoes and serve with melted marshmallows—it's a whole different experience!

Yield: 12 servings

These latkes are more full-bodied than the traditional potato pancakes; for a batter with finer consistency, you can try blending instead of grating the potatoes and onions.

❀ Sweet and Sour Sea Bass

4 lb. sea bass fillets

4 onions, diced

1 tsp. garlic salt

⅔ cup slivered almonds

½ cup raisins

¾ cup dried apricots, chopped

½ cup sundried tomatoes, chopped

¾ cup sweet white wine or vermouth

1 can flat beer

3 Tbsp. soy sauce

3 Tbsp. orange marmalade

½ tsp. ground ginger

½ tsp. zaatar

¼ tsp. ground black pepper

¼ tsp. ground sumac

Sweet and Sour Sea Bass has a wonderful mélange of tastes, from sweet apricots to crunchy pistachios to tart marmalade.

½ tsp. salt

watercress

ground pistachio nuts

Preheat oven to 325°F.

Wash the fish thoroughly and score with a sharp knife. Place in a well-greased 9″ Pyrex baking dish. Slice each fillet in half like a sandwich, yet not cutting all the way through, so as to create a kind of pocket. Set aside. In a large frying pan, sauté the onions and garlic salt until golden. Add the almonds, raisins, apricots, sundried tomatoes, and white wine; cook on low heat for about 5–7 minutes, stirring constantly. Spoon mixture inside and around the fish.

In a mixing cup, stir together the beer, soy sauce, marmalade, and ginger. Add remaining spices and pour over fish. Bake for about 50–55 minutes, or until fish is flaky when poked with a fork. Serve on a bed of watercress sprinkled with ground pistachio nuts.

Yield: 8–12 servings

Herb-basted Turkey Breast

1 large turkey breast

2 bay leaves

½ stick butter

1 cup apple cider

2 garlic cloves, minced

2 tsp. onion salt

1 tsp. dried thyme

1 tsp. black pepper

1 tsp. dried sage

1 tsp. dried sumac

½ tsp. dried oregano

½ tsp. dried basil

whole cranberries or crab apple jelly

Preheat oven to 350°F.

There are many ways to roast a turkey, but this recipe contains a mix of spices that will set the palate tingling.

Wash the turkey breast and pat dry; then place in a shallow roasting pan (breast side up) on top of two sheets of aluminum foil placed perpendicular to each other so that the pan is completely covered and there is enough foil left to lift the bird from the pan when holding all ends. Slip a bay leaf under the breast at the north and south of the bird.

Melt the butter and pour it over the breast. Mix the apple cider and garlic in a small measuring cup and pour evenly over the bird. Combine the spices and dried herbs in a small bowl, mix thoroughly, and then sprinkle them over the turkey as well.

Bake uncovered for 2½–3 hours, basting the turkey occasionally from its own juices. Let stand for 10 minutes before slicing. Serve with whole cranberries or crab apple jelly on the side.

Yield: 6–8 servings

Vegetable Cholent

2 cups frozen lima beans	1 cup fresh broccoli, diced
2 cans red kidney beans	1 cup fresh cauliflower, chopped
4 new potatoes, diced	2 bell peppers, chopped
3 fresh tomatoes, sliced	4 cloves garlic, minced
3 onions, diced	3 Tbsp. sunflower oil
1 cup pearl barley	2 tsp. cornstarch

1 tsp. kosher salt

½ tsp. cayenne

1 tsp. sage

½ tsp. cumin

¼ tsp. ginger

6 cups water

feta cheese (optional)

Such a simple dish, this vegetable *cholent* could be a hearty meal unto itself.

Preheat oven to 350°F.

Place all ingredients in a large baking pan, mix thoroughly, and cover well. Bake for 3–4 hours. Serve piping hot, sprinkled with feta cheese if desired.

Yield: 8–12 servings

Lemon Poppy Seed Cake

4 egg yolks

6 Tbsp. butter

⅓ cup granulated sugar

⅓ cup confectioners' sugar

1¼ cups all-purpose flour

2¼ tsp. baking powder

⅛ tsp. salt

¼ cup poppy seeds

½ cup cashews, ground

1 cup plain yogurt

2 tsp. lemon peel, grated

2 Tbsp. fresh lemon juice

1 tsp. Madagascar bourbon vanilla extract

½ tsp. lemon extract

1 cup Cointreau (optional)

This lemon poppy seed loaf is a creamy, rich cake with a special punch for hardy souls.

Preheat oven to 350°F.

Beat egg yolks until light in color. In a separate bowl, cream butter and sugars; add yolks and mix well. Sift together the flour, baking powder, and salt, then stir in poppy seeds and cashews; add to egg/butter/sugar mixture.

In a large mixing cup, beat the yogurt with a fork until loose; then add lemon peel, lemon juice, and extracts. Fold into cake mixture.

Pour batter into well-greased and floured loaf pan. Bake for 50–55 minutes, or until tester comes out clean.

If desired, soak with Cointreau and allow to stand overnight (in refrigerator) before serving. Serve cold or at room temperature.

Yield: 6–8 servings

Hamentaschen

⅔ cup butter

½ cup sugar

2 eggs

½ tsp. vanilla extract

¼ cup orange juice (without pulp)

1 cup white flour

1 cup wheat flour

2 tsp. baking powder

⅛ tsp. salt

various preserves or pie fillings

Blend butter, sugar, eggs, and vanilla extract. Slowly add orange juice and mix well. Combine with dry ingredients and form into a large ball. Refrigerate batter overnight, or for at least a few hours.

Use cherry, apricot, strawberry, or other preserves as filling for these *hamentaschen*; don't be afraid to experiment.

Preheat oven to 375°F. Roll out dough as thin as possible on a well-floured board. Cut into 3″ or 4″ circles using a glass, and put a dollop of your favorite filling (perhaps prune butter or apricot) in the middle of each. Fold up the sides to make a triangle and squeeze the corners tightly so that just a smidgen of the filling is visible. Bake on an ungreased cookie sheet for about 10–12 minutes, or until golden brown. Let cool for about 5 minutes before removing them to a plate for serving.

Yield: 2–3 dozen cookies

Red Wine

For Purim, choose a young, fruity wine that is light but flavorful. Or try a Syrah, processed from what was originally a Persian grape. Even better, perhaps your international wine merchant has something to recommend from Iran (formerly Persia) itself.

14

A Meal in the Wilderness

THE TEXT

1 While Jesus was living in the Galilean hills, John, called "the Baptizer," was preaching in the desert country of Judea.

2 His message was simple and austere, like his desert surroundings: "Change your life. God's kingdom is here."

. . . .

4 John dressed in a camel-hair habit tied at the waist by a leather strap. He lived on a diet of locusts and wild field honey.

5 People poured out of Jerusalem, Judea and the Jordanian countryside to hear and see him in action.

6 There at the Jordan River those who came to confess their sins were baptized into a changed life.

Matthew 3:1–2; 4–6, The Message

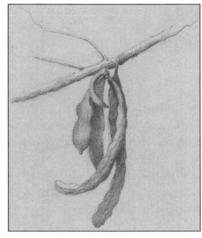

A very common belief is that the "locust" of the biblical text refers not to the insect, but to the locust tree, the most dominant in all the terrain, planted and nurtured for its shade as well as for its very desirable fruit, the carob.

THE HISTORY

In 63 B.C.E. General Pompey (Gnaeus Pompeius Magnus) captured Jerusalem (some scholars indicate that he was invited in to settle a dispute between the crown princes), and the Kingdom of Judea became a client kingdom of the Roman Republic, with Hyrcanus, son of the Hasmonean Queen Alexandra, serving as prince, high priest, and puppet ruler for the Romans. Antipater became the first Roman procurator of Judea sometime around 49 B.C.E., but when he died in 44 B.C.E. his son Herod took over, becoming governor in 41 B.C.E. and ruler in 37 B.C.E. He would come to be known as Herod the Great, for he was a capable administrator who set about rebuilding Jerusalem, including the Temple complex; but he was also known for his cruelty and ruthlessness; he murdered many family members and rabbis in order to protect his power, to promote the Hellenic (Greek) way of life, and to remain in favor with Rome. Yet Judea prospered economically, for it was located on the important trade routes and was itself agriculturally fruitful, and the Romans did not much interfere in Herod's affairs. In fact, the Romans even exempted the Jews from observing the Roman religion; but for the privilege of being allowed to follow the Law, the Jews were made to pay a heavy tax. Nevertheless, Herod had put the Sadducees, a group of wealthy Jews who supported Roman rule, in charge of the Temple, appointed his own high priest, and hand-picked the members of the Sanhedrin, the rabbinical court. His actions caused resentment among the Pharisees, who resisted Hellenization and generally had the support of the common people of Judea. In addition, there were the Zealots and the Sicarii, who agitated for open revolution against the Romans, and dozens of other sects and factions. When Herod died in 4 or 2 B.C.E., the kingdom had become so fractious that it split into three pieces, each governed by one of Herod's sons: Herod Archelaus, Herod Antipas, and Herod Philip. Some time around 6 C.E. the Roman Emperor Caesar Augustus dismissed Archelaus for incompetence and combined Judea with Samaria and Edom (Idumea) into the Roman province of Iudaea (Judea), administered by a prefect or procurator who reported directly to the emperor. This was the political climate into which John the Baptist and Jesus of Nazareth were born and raised.

In the 1st century C.E., Flavius Josephus, a Jewish historian, wrote a twenty-one-volume *apologia* called *Antiquities of the Jews*. Bringing his work to the public in 93 C.E., Josephus (as he is known today) intended to provide an explanation of Jewish history, laws, and customs in the wake of the destruction of the Temple in 70 C.E. and the expulsion of the Jews from Judea. By outlining the stories of the patriarchs, he was also arguing in support of the many contributions that the Jewish people had made to civilization.

This source is not without controversy. Josephus himself had fought in the rebellion against Rome but afterward had cooperated with Roman authorities to the extent that he had been made a Roman citizen and been given land in Judea and a pension. As a result, many scholars have branded Josephus a traitor and informer and have refused to consider *Antiquities of the Jews* as anything but propaganda and an attempt at historic self-rehabilitation, for he took pains to include a defense of his cooperation with Rome. Other scholars, however, argue that he was an important bridge-builder between cultures, himself remaining a Jew who observed the Law yet explaining for non-Jews how Jewish and Graeco-Roman philosophies could exist compatibly.

Antiquities of the Jews does include an account of the man known as John the Baptist:

> Now some of the Jews thought that the destruction of Herod's army came from God, and that very justly, as a punishment of what he did against John, that was called the Baptist: for Herod slew him.... Now when [many] others came in crowds about him, for they were very greatly moved [or pleased] by hearing his words, Herod, who feared lest the great influence John had over the people might put it into his power and inclination to raise a rebellion, (for they seemed ready to do any thing he should advise), thought it best, by putting him to death, to prevent any mischief he might cause, and not bring himself into difficulties, by sparing a man who might make him repent of it when it would be too late. Accordingly he was sent a prisoner, out of Herod's suspicious temper, to Macherus, the castle I before mentioned, and was there put to death.[1]

This account generally corresponds to the biblical story, though some of the details (such as the reason for John's assassination) differ. There is also a section of the work that offers an account of the life of Jesus:

> Now there was about this time Jesus, a wise man, if it be lawful to call him a man; for he was a doer of wonderful works, a teacher of such men as receive the truth with pleasure. He drew over to him both many of the Jews and many of the Gentiles. He was [the] Christ. And when Pilate, at the suggestion of the principal men amongst us, had condemned him to the cross, those that loved him at the first did not forsake him; for he appeared to them alive again the third day; as the divine prophets had foretold these and ten thousand other wonderful things concerning him. And the tribe of Christians, so named from him, are not extinct at this day.[2]

This section has come to be called the *Testimonium Flavianum*. Many scholars have difficulty accepting the authenticity of these sections that have a particularly Christian flavor. Extant copies seem to have been based on early Christian sources and not to have been transmitted accurately through history. The consensus among modern scholars is that Josephus did write something about John the Baptist and about Jesus of Nazareth but that the text has been corrupted to a significant degree by copyists' interpolations, additions, and errors. A minority of scholars continue to completely reject the authenticity of the *Testimonium Flavianum* and many other portions of Josephus' work.

Nevertheless, whether there is extrabiblical corroboration or not, the biblical stories of John the Baptist and, especially, of Jesus of Nazareth have changed the course of history and continue to influence the way many people live their lives.

Biblical Passage Notes

Other than the parents of Jesus, John the Baptist, whom tradition names as the son of the Virgin Mary's cousin, Elizabeth, is perhaps the best-known member of Jesus' family in the scriptures. Like Jesus, he was a descendant of Aaron on both sides, a member of the priestly tribe known as the Levites. His name is derived from Hebrew and means "the Lord is gracious." Tradition says that he was born in the hill country of Judea, in a town known today as Ein Karem, in Israel.

The scriptures tell us next to nothing of his early life, and by the time he appears in the gospels as a grown man, he has taken on the mantle of a prophet, wandering in the wilderness, eating off the land, and uttering apocalyptic pronouncements that often place him at odds with the religious leaders of his day. When he dares to criticize King Herod Antipas for an adulterous and incestuous marriage, he is sent to prison and eventually murdered in fulfillment of a cruel and vengeful promise (see Matthew 14:7–11).

In the passage cited above, we encounter John in the "desert country of Judea." It was a barren, often brutally dry place, inhabited in biblical times by wild animals and nomads, some of whom, like John the Baptist, were ascetics searching for wisdom and solace away from the crowds of the larger cities and towns of southern Israel. It appears that John might have been Nazir, and like his ancestor, Samson, subjected by vow to certain abstinences. Nazirites are Jewish men who refrain from cutting their hair, abstain from wine and meat, have no contact with the dead, and are known to be celibate—vows taken usually for only a short time (see Numbers 6). These characteristics may help to explain John's appearance and diet. His clothing evoked visions of Elijah, another ancestor and Nazir. In fact, those who first encountered John asked if *he were* Elijah, as it was the expectation and hope of the day that Elijah himself would return and restore the fortunes of the Jewish people. In John the Baptizer—prophetically calling the people to repentance, acting like a hermit, living in the wilderness—many saw the realm of God, i.e., the end days when judgment would be laid upon those who did not believe in God, to be at hand. If John were neither Elijah nor the Messiah, he surely spoke as if he were. But John, prophet that he was, pushed all this aside, and is quoted as saying that there was yet one to come who would be even greater than he, whose sandal he would not even be worthy to untie. Just a few biblical verses after this proclamation, Jesus, his cousin, appears at the river to be baptized, and it becomes clear from then on that the mantle of Elijah, the ascetical camel-garb symbol that John wore with authority, would soon be passed to Jesus. Very quickly John's role in the story decreases, and as quickly, Jesus' ascendancy increases.

John the Baptist would have really enjoyed a good, hearty bread with many of the foodstuffs from the land he traveled, such as this loaf made with raisins, rosemary, and camel's milk yogurt. It's a great taste if you're tired of carob and honey!

THE MENU

Judean Desert Salad with Hot Honey Dressing

Honey, Mint, and Cucumber Salad

Honey-roasted Lamb with Couscous

Marinated Bass

Wilderness Squash

Wings of Life Bread

Salome's Honey-Carob Brownies

Zachariah's Temple Loaf

Elizabeth's Carob Cake

Christening (Baptismal) Cake

Chorba El Jourad (Locust Soup)

THE PREPARATION

There is much to learn in this cameo appearance of the great New Testament prophet. The mere fact that the Matthean text mentions the eating habits of John the Baptist should be a clue to us of their importance, both to history and to John's character; it is not merely passing commentary. The writer of the Gospel of Matthew informs us that "John lived on a diet of locusts and wild field honey." The Greek word for locust, *akris,* is used four times in the New Testament and seems to refer to the class of insect known as *Orthoptera,* or "straight-winged." By Mosaic law they were reckoned "clean," so John could not have been accused of doing anything illegal by claiming them for food. And we do know that dried locusts were a rather common staple of many ancient Near Eastern communities, most particularly the Essenes, a religious sect of which many scholars believe John was a member. To this day, locusts are prepared as food in the Middle East and Africa in various ways: sometimes they are pounded and mixed with flour and water to be baked into cakes; other cooks boil, roast, or stew them in butter for eating. Dried and salted locusts have long been part of the diet of many nomadic tribes.

Still, biblical scholars, anthropologists, and other scientists have reached no consensus as to whether these foods could have sustained the Baptist in the wilderness. A very common belief, which we have adapted here for our purposes, is that the "locust" of the biblical text refers not to the insect, but to the *locust tree* (in Greek, *keration*), a plant species that is widespread in Israel. In many areas, including the Judean desert, the locust tree is the most dominant in all the terrain, planted and nurtured for its shade as well as for its very desirable fruit, the *carob*.

Given its ubiquity, and its connection to the Judean wilderness of the Baptist, it may be no surprise that the carob fruit is known throughout the Middle East as *St. John's Bread*. It has been dried and used as a food for cattle, people, and most especially swine (see the story of the Prodigal Son in Luke 15:16), and as many as eight hundred pounds of seed pods can be harvested yearly from a single tree. Carob has a long and distinguished history dating back to the ancients who accorded it such high respect that the weight of its seeds are most likely the original measure for what is today a goldsmith's *karat*.

Supposing (for the sake of argument) that John the Baptist was dining on carob fruit, and not locusts, as the King James Version insists, what new understanding might this bring to the interpretation of the text? Because carob powder can be used in place of cocoa at levels up to 50 percent, and it has a natural sugar content of up to 48 percent, one might begin to understand the somewhat manic and strange appearance attributed to John in the iconography of biblical art. Eating a lot of carob as a regular diet could have your hair standing on end by sunset! And although John might not have been aware of all the benefits of carob, he probably had some idea that it provided a lot of nutrients, and it was a good, all-around substitute for whatever else was lacking in his daily food regimen. "Carob contains as much vitamin B1 as asparagus or strawberries, the same amount of niacin as lima beans, lentils or peas, and more vitamin A than eggplant, asparagus and beets. It is also high in vitamin B2, calcium, magnesium and iron."[3] All of which is to say that though scholars might not be able to agree on whether locusts could sustain the Baptist in the wilderness, surely *locust tree fruit*, aka "carob," would do the trick!

And what of honey (in Greek, *meli*)? The word itself is used only four times in all of the New Testament, in contrast to the nearly fifty times we encounter it in the Hebrew scriptures (in Hebrew, *debhash*). The Promised Land where the Israelites finally settled was known as a land "flowing with milk and honey," which gives us some idea of the high esteem it too was given by our biblical forebears. Yet it was rare enough to be considered somewhat of a luxury, typifying sumptuous dining and finery of preparation. In the translation used for this chapter, "wild field honey" is the type stored by bees in rocks or in trees. Particularly in the wilderness of Judea, honey bees were known to build their hives in the crevices of rocks and in rotting lumber. The honey, oozing from between the stone formations or out of a log, gave it the appearance of *flowing* (hence the coining of the phrase), and some biblical commentators think that this is what the wandering Israelites encountered in the desert, naming it *manna*, remarking how sticky and sweet it was, like "food of the gods." John the Baptist undoubtedly came across lots of honey in his travels; and because it was an excellent source of nutrition and was a curative for many ailments (including stomach upset), it provided a good balance to his other dietary choices.

John's fashion sense—he was "dressed in a camel hair habit tied at the waist by a leather strap"—gives us some insight about the animals he came in contact with as he went preaching from one location to another. Obviously, he was aware of the generous uses for all parts of the camel: skin for clothing and liquid storage, milk for cheeses and other dairy needs, meat to complement vegetarian choices. Perhaps the leather was from the hide of a camel; or it might have been fashioned from the tough skin of some other domesticated animal (a steer, ox, lamb, or goat). Wherever his clothing products came from, it is clear that he was familiar with more than just the products of the land.

Keeping his appearance and his food opportunities in mind, we have included recipes that encompass a whole range of possibilities, including whatever fish John might have encountered at the Jordan River, baptizing and fishing for converts and all else his wide prophetic net might bring to shore.

The Recipes

Judean Desert Salad with Hot Honey Dressing

1 head lettuce

4 oz. camel's milk curds*

2 oz. sundried tomatoes, sliced

6 Tbsp. white wine vinegar

9 Tbsp. olive oil

2 Tbsp. clear honey

1 cup shallots, finely chopped

1 red chili, diced

¼ cup green olives, chopped

3 cloves garlic, crushed

½ tsp. black pepper

½ tsp. sea salt

Living in the desert would not have been conducive to the preparation of elaborate dishes with exotic ingredients. This hot honey salad relies upon foods that would have been readily available or easily preserved.

Place the lettuce, curds, and sundried tomatoes in a bowl. Mix the remaining ingredients in a medium-sized jar. Just before serving, place lid on, screw tight, and shake vigorously for about 30 seconds. Pour over salad and serve.

Yield: 8 servings

*Camel's milk products can be found in most Mediterranean markets or through vegetarian grocers like Mrs. Green's Market or Whole Foods.

✵ Honey, Mint, and Cucumber Salad

4 whole cucumbers, thickly sliced

8 sprigs of mint, finely chopped

8 Tbsp. clear honey

1 large container of plain kefir (camel's milk or some other milk)

juice of 2 limes

A honey, mint, and cucumber salad such as this would have been extremely refreshing to a parched desert wanderer.

Prior to cutting the cucumbers, take a salad fork and score the rind, making thick indentations. Slice the cucumber into fairly thick slices (the scoring will give them a variegated, fancy look), and throw them into a large bowl with the mint. Mix together the honey and the kefir, and pour over the cucumber/mint combination. If you are not going to serve the salad right away, refrigerate. Just prior to serving, squeeze the juice of 2 limes over the salad.

Yield: 8 servings

✵ Honey-roasted Lamb with Couscous

1 large package of couscous

¾ cup boiling water

2 lb. lamb, trimmed of fat and cubed*

olive or sunflower oil

1 tsp. turmeric

1 tsp. allspice

½ tsp. ground cloves

4 Tbsp. honey

2 cups fresh chives, diced

4 cloves garlic, crushed

1 tsp. black pepper

½ tsp. salt

½ cup dried cranberries or craisins

juice and rind of 1 lemon

small bunch fresh parsley, chopped

Preheat oven to 450°F.

In a large bowl, mix the couscous with boiling water and wait for about 10 minutes. Whisk with a fork, cover, and set aside. (If the mixture seems dry, add a bit of hot water, 1 Tbsp. at a time, until it appears fluffier.)

Place lamb cubes into a large frying pan and brown, brushing them with olive or sunflower oil while constantly turning over the cubes. Sprinkle on turmeric, allspice, and ground cloves and continue to cook on a low temperature for about 10 minutes, all the while brushing the cubes with oil. Slowly pour the honey over the meat, increase the temperature, and cook for about 5 minutes, making sure that the meat is done but not burned.

The scriptures may not indicate that John the Baptist ate lamb but does relate John's announcement of the coming of the "Lamb of God." This photo shows our honey-roasted lamb with couscous.

Remove the lamb and set aside in a large, covered serving bowl. Sauté the chives, garlic, pepper, and salt in the juice remnants (if very little juice remains, add a bit of hot water and 1 tsp. oil and continue) and cook for 5–7 minutes on a moderate heat. Stir in the dried cranberries (or craisins) and the lemon juice and rind; then mix in the couscous.

Pour the couscous mixture over the lamb and toss in the chopped parsley. Turn out onto a large cake platter and serve.

Yield: 8 servings

*Ask your butcher to trim the fat from the lamb before cubing.

❧ *Marinated Bass**

2 Tbsp. wild honey

2 Tbsp. raspberry vinegar

2 Tbsp. dried mustard

½ can flat beer

8 bass fillets

a bit of olive oil

½ cup fresh tarragon, chopped

fresh cherry tomatoes, halved

Combine the honey, vinegar, mustard, and beer in a large measuring cup to create a marinade. Lay the fillets in a flat, shallow pan and pour mixture over fish. Cover with tarragon, seal with plastic wrap, and refrigerate for several hours or overnight.

Honey, raspberry vinegar, mustard, and beer combine for an amazingly zestful marinade for this fish dish.

Brush a charcoal or gas grill grate with a bit of olive oil. Grill the fish, basting frequently with the marinade while turning. Serve on a platter surrounded by fresh cherry tomatoes for an attractive presentation.

Yield: 8 servings

*If bass is not available, mackerel or trout or some other large fish will suffice.

❧ Wilderness Squash

6 acorn squash*

¼ cup honey

¼ cup pistachios, chopped

½ cup dried apricots, chopped

2 Tbsp. butter

2 Spanish onions, chopped

¼ tsp. Angostura bitters (or Balsamic vinegar)

Cut the acorn squash into cubes and place into a large ovenproof dish with a lid. Add all the remaining ingredients, cover, and cook for 10 minutes (exactly) in a microwave at medium to high. Serve immediately. (Careful—it'll be *very* hot!)

Yield: 10–12 servings

A modern take on an old idea, this recipe for honey and spiced squash relies on the microwave for quick and easy preparation.

 *For those who are thinking about substituting a different type of squash, like zucchini, for instance—don't. It will taste awful!

❧ Wings of Life Bread

8 oz. dried apricots

3 or 4 very ripe bananas

8 oz. seedless raisins

6 oz. black walnuts, roughly chopped

9 cups brown bread flour

2 cups white bread flour

1 tsp. sea salt

1 Tbsp. baking soda

4 Tbsp. melted butter

4 Tbsp. honey

20 oz. kefir or natural yogurt

With apricots, bananas, raisins, and walnuts, not to mention the yogurt, Wings of Life Bread is a healthy meal on its own.

Preheat oven to 400°F.

Start by cooking the apricots in as little water as possible. When soft, drain off and save the cooking liquid to mash the bananas in. Add the raisins and walnuts to the cooked apricots and reserve. Grease three loaf tins. In a big bowl mix the flours together with the salt and soda and stir in the butter and honey, then the bananas blended in the cooking liquid; add the apricot/raisin/walnut mix and work the dough quickly. Add the kefir slowly so that you end up with a dough just moist and homogeneous. Quickly divide the dough into three parts and put it in the prepared tins. Bake for 30 minutes, then a further 20 minutes or so at 300°F. Do not let it burn; when it sounds hollow it is ready. Leave to cool outside the tins at room temperature.

Yield: 10–12 servings

Source: Adapted from a recipe by Maria Fremlin at http://maria.fremlin.de/recipes/wings.html

Salome's Honey-Carob Brownies

¾ cup flour	½ cup carob powder
1 tsp. baking powder	1 cup bee honey
¼ tsp. salt	2 eggs
¼ tsp. mace	½ cup fresh brewed coffee
¼ cup oatmeal	½ cup pistachios, chopped
⅔ cup butter	1 tsp. almond extract

Preheat oven to 300°F.

Sift together the flour, baking powder, salt, and mace. Stir in oatmeal. Melt the butter in a small pan over low heat. Add carob powder and honey and blend well, removing from heat. In a mixing bowl, beat the eggs and gradually add the carob mixture. Add the coffee, pistachios, and almond extract and mix well. Pour into an oiled 8″ square pan and bake for about 35 minutes, or until done.

Yield: 2 dozen brownies

Zachariah's Temple Loaf

2½ cups whole wheat flour	½ stick butter, softened
1 cup white flour	1 cup kefir (or buttermilk or yogurt)
½ cup rolled oats	1 cup seedless raisins, chopped
1 tsp. baking soda	6 sprigs fresh rosemary, leaves only
½ tsp. salt	

Preheat oven to 425°F.

Mix all dry ingredients in a large bowl. Rub in the butter with your fingertips. Slowly add the kefir (or buttermilk or yogurt) and the raisins and chopped rosemary until a nice kneading consistency is achieved. If you overdo it, then add more oats or flour. You must not knead this dough.

Quickly make two round loaves. Put them on an oiled tray and with the back of a long knife mark lines across the tops. Divide each loaf into 6 sections. Bake for 20–30 minutes until moist but firm.

Yield: 6–8 servings

❧ Elizabeth's Carob Cake

½ cup butter, melted

½ cup honey

½ cup blackstrap molasses

2 eggs

1 tsp. baking soda

½ tsp. baking powder

⅓ cup carob powder

2 cups whole wheat flour

½ tsp. nutmeg

¾ cup hot water

½ cup dates, chopped

½ cup dried figs

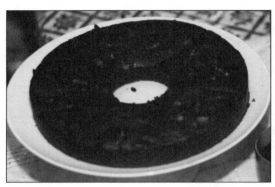

Go easy on this carob cake with carob frosting: it has enough zip to it to make your hair stand on end.

Preheat oven to 375°F.

Beat the butter, honey, and molasses. Add the eggs and beat again. Sift the dry ingredients into the bowl, mixing with ¼ cup of water until all water is added. Stir in the dates and figs. Pour into a lightly greased baking pan. Bake for about 45 minutes, or until the cake easily separates from the sides of the pan.

Carob Frosting

4 Tbsp. butter

⅓ cup sweetened condensed milk

⅓ cup carob powder

¼ cup honey

3 egg whites

4 Tbsp. whipping cream

1 tsp. vanilla extract

½ tsp. anise extract

Cream the butter, milk, and carob powder. Add the honey. Beat the egg whites until stiff. In a separate bowl, whip the cream until it peaks. Add both to the carob mixture. Fold in vanilla and anise extracts and stir until smooth. Ice once cake is fully cooled.

Yield: 10–12 servings

❧ Christening (Baptismal) Cake

¾ lb. butter

4 cups sugar

8 eggs, separated

4 cups flour

1 Tbsp. baking powder

2 tsp. nutmeg

1 tsp. allspice

1 cup rum

1 cup pecans, chopped

½ lb. raisins

½ tsp. cream of tartar

Preheat oven to 300°F.

Cream the butter and sugar together until the texture is a smooth paste. Separate the eggs and beat the yolks until a very light color, then fold into the butter/sugar mixture and blend thoroughly. Sift the dry ingredients (except the cream of tartar) together and add alternately with the rum. Stir the pecans and raisins in by hand.

Beat the egg whites with the cream of tartar until stiff; then add to the cake mixture. Pour into a well-greased cake pan and bake for 4 (yes, 4!) hours.

Yield: 8–10 servings

Chorba El Jourad *(Locust Soup)*

And, if you must . . .

12–24 locusts	12 slices bread
1 qt. water	butter
nutmeg, to taste	rice or dumplings, as desired
pepper, to taste	

Trim the small forelegs and the skinny part of the hind legs of the locusts. Pull the heads off and discard. Season the meat with nutmeg and black pepper; then plunge into boiling water for a few minutes.

Strain the locusts, keeping the broth. Pound the cooked locusts along with pieces of bread fried in butter and make a well-mixed paste.

Return the bread/locust paste to the stock, simmer for about 10 minutes or so; then serve piping hot with rice or dumplings.

Yield: 12 servings

Source: Adapted from Calvin W. Schwabe, *Unmentionable Cuisine* (Charlottesville: University of Virginia Press, 1979). Reprinted with permission of the University of Virginia Press.

NOTES

1. Flavius Josephus, *Antiquities of the Jews*, Book XVIII, Chapter 5:2, trans. William Whiston, www.ccel.org/j/josephus/JOSEPHUS.HTM

2. Ibid., Book XVIII, Chapter 3:3.

3. See the article "Did John the Baptist Eat Carob Tree Fruits or Bugs?" at www.geocities.com/Athens/Parthenon/3664/locusts.html

15

The Prodigal Son Returns

THE TEXT

11 ...There was a certain man who had two
    sons;

12 And the younger of them said to his father,
    Father, give me the part of the property that
    falls to me. And he divided the estate be-
    tween them.

13 And not many days after that, the younger
    son gathered up all that he had and jour-
    neyed into a distant country, and there he
    wasted his fortune in reckless and loose
    [from restraint] living.

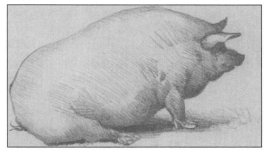

"And he would gladly have fed on and filled his
belly with the carob pods that the hogs were eating."

14 And when he had spent all he had, a mighty famine came upon that country,
    and he began to fall behind and be in want.

15 So he went and glued himself upon one of the citizens of that country,
    who sent him into his fields to feed hogs.

16 And he would gladly have fed on and filled his belly with the carob pods
    that the hogs were eating, but they could not satisfy his hunger, and nobody
    gave him anything better.

17 Then when he came to himself, he said, How many hired servants of my
    father have enough food, and even food to spare, but I am dying here of
    hunger!

18 I will get up and go to my father, and I will say to him, Father, I have
    sinned against heaven and in your sight.

19 I am no longer worthy to be called your son; just make me like one of
    your hired servants.

20 So he got up and came to his own father. But while he was still a long way off, his father saw him and was moved with pity and tenderness for him; and he ran and embraced him and kissed him fervently.

21 And the son said to him, Father, I have sinned against heaven and in your sight; I no longer deserve to be recognized as a son of yours!

22 But the father said to his bond servants, Bring quickly the festive robe of honor and put it on him; and give him a ring for his hand and sandals for his feet.

23 And bring out that wheat-fattened calf and kill it; and let us revel and feast and be happy and make merry,

24 Because this my son was dead and is alive again; he was lost and is found! And they began to revel and feast and make merry.

25 But his older son was in the field; and as he returned and came near the house, he heard music and dancing.

26 And having called one of the servant boys to him, he began to ask what this meant.

27 And he said to him, Your brother has come, and your father has killed that wheat-fattened calf, because he has received him back safe and well.

28 But the elder brother was angry with deep-seated wrath and resolved not to go in. Then his father came out and began to plead with him.

29 But he answered his father, Look! These many years I have served you, and I have never disobeyed your command. Yet you never gave me so much as a little kid, that I might revel and feast and be happy and make merry with my friends;

30 But when this son of yours arrived, who has devoured your estate with immoral women, you have killed for him that wheat-fattened calf!

31 And the father said to him, Son, you are always with me, and all that is mine is yours.

32 But it was fitting to make merry, to revel and feast and rejoice, for this brother of yours was dead and is alive again! He was lost and is found!

Luke 15:11–32, Amplified Bible

THE HISTORY

As recounted in Chapter 14, the writings of Josephus (*Antiquities of the Jews*) are among those cited as extrabiblical corroboration of the life of Jesus of Nazareth. What are the other sources of the information that many people have come to accept as historical truth?

Foremost are the texts found in the New Testament of the Christian Bible, both the gospel accounts and the epistles. Four gospels have been accepted as canonical: those of Matthew, Mark, Luke, and John. The first three are termed the synoptic gospels because they generally tell the same narrative, though the details vary considerably. The following is the scholarly consensus about when the gospels were written.

- the Gospel of Mark was written 68–73 C.E.
- the Gospel of Matthew was written sometime between 70 and 100 C.E.
- the Gospel of Luke (and the Acts of the Apostles) was written 80–100 C.E.
- the Gospel of John was written between 90 and 110 C.E.[1]

These four gospels would all have been written years after the crucifixion of Jesus of Nazareth, which most scholars now date to sometime between 26 and 36 C.E., the years of Pontius Pilate's term as governor of Judea. Scriptures experts now generally hold that all the gospels were based on oral tradition—stories passed on by word of mouth—as well as on a hypothetical Q document and, perhaps, on the Gospel of Thomas, and that the actual editors, or redactors, of these canonical gospels were not the apostles whose names were co-opted to lend authenticity to the accounts. The consensus is that all the gospels were written in Greek, the common language of that part of the Roman Empire, though some scholars assert that the Gospel of Matthew was originally written in Aramaic, the language spoken by some 1st-century Jews.

The earliest extant and reliable texts referring to Jesus are the epistles attributed to Paul. Born Saul, Paul was a native of Tarsus (in present-day Turkey), a member of the tribe of Benjamin and of the Pharisee sect, yet also a Roman citizen, and a rabbi who became a persecutor and murderer of those Jews who called themselves Christians (followers of Christ, the risen Jesus). Paul never met Jesus of Nazareth, yet on the road to Damascus, where Paul was traveling to conduct another punishment of Christians for defying the Law, he experienced a profound vision that turned his life upside down and made him a believer in Christ. Thereafter, he journeyed throughout the Roman world, receiving additional revelations from Christ, spreading what he called the good news, and founding many Christian churches. Before he was executed in Rome, Paul had written many letters to the churches he had established, offering them advice and criticisms and support. Scholars now generally believe that Paul himself composed the following letters: Romans, I Corinthians, II Corinthians, Galatians, Philippians, I Thessalonians, and Philemon, with I Thessalonians probably the earliest, composed about 51 C.E. The other letters traditionally attributed to Paul's pen are now considered to have been written by believers who usurped Paul's name to give authority to their writings.

Other books have also been accepted into the New Testament canon; these include the remaining Pseudo-Pauline letters, the epistles of James, Peter, John, I and II Timothy, and Jude, and the Revelation to John. Again, these were most probably not written by the cited apostles but, rather, by members of their communities.

Additional gospels and documents exist; these have not been accepted into the canon of the New Testament, and their authenticity is subject to interpretation, yet according to some scholars they provide important information and interpretations about the life of Jesus, not to mention data about life in 1st-century Judea. Called New Testament Apocrypha (Pseudepigrapha), these include the Gospel of Pseudo-Matthew (also known as the Birth of Mary and Infancy of the Savior), the Protoevangelium of James (also called the Gospel of James), the Infancy Gospel of Thomas, the Life of John the Baptist, the History of Joseph the Carpenter, the Nativity of Mary, the Gospel of the Hebrews, the Gospel of the Nazarenes, the Gospel of Philip, the Gospel of Peter, the Gospel of Nicodemus (also known as the Acts of Pilate), the Gospel of Mary Magdalene (also called the Gospel of Mary), the Acts of Peter, the Acts of John, the Epistle of Barnabas, the Apocalypse of Stephen (also known as the Revelation of Stephen), and numerous others.

A few secular sources also mentioned the Christian sect, such as a letter of Pliny the Younger to Emperor Trajan, dated to 112 C.E., and passages in Tacitus' *Annals* of 116 C.E.

Given the uncertain authenticity of the vast majority of these documents, a handful of scholars have posited the theory that the Jesus described in the New Testament never existed in the flesh but came to life only in the mythological and imaginative realm. While plausible, this conjecture does not fully account for the disciples' fearless emergence from Jerusalem after Pentecost, nor for Paul's profound conversion to Christianity and evangelization in the name of Christ. Perhaps humankind will never know what the man named Jesus actually did or said, but the accounts of his deeds and sayings, whether authentic or not, add up to a story that most people admire for its interior "truth," its brilliant incorporation of diverse cultural and historical elements, and its inspiring message of hope for the downtrodden and outcast of society.

BIBLICAL PASSAGE NOTES

Of all the writings of the Christian New Testament, the tale of the return of the prodigal son is one of the most famous parables spoken by Jesus. It is part of a three-part discourse in the Gospel of Luke, used to demonstrate the way in which God loves all people and will go to any lengths to welcome back those who have been separated from God by sinful living and deeds. The story is unique to this gospel, but the sibling rivalry and the jealousy between brothers makes the tale a universal one.

It begins with what could only have been seen by 1st-century believers as a horrific rejection. The youngest son comes to his father and asks for his inheritance. In Middle Eastern culture, this was nothing short of rude and ungrateful; it was as if to say, "Father, I wish you were dead, but since you are not, I want what you have now, instead of having to wait till you die in order to get it." The older son is equally guilty in his silence. He does not speak up, letting the younger brother get away with his insolence. He therefore accepts his own share of the estate by not arguing for a reconciliation between his younger brother's wishes and his father's well-being. Under the laws of inheritance in Israel, the younger son walks away with one-third of the wealth, the older with two-thirds.

Having given in to his impetuous sons, where does that leave the ever-generous father? He apparently continues to live on the land of his children's inheritance, managing it as a caretaker, in essence, till the day comes when he will die. His older son, who could have pressed for his father's removal, to his credit leaves well enough alone[2]—that is, until his squandering vagabond of a brother returns and asks for help.

The cause then of the increased enmity between the brothers is the father's preparation of a great feast when the younger, having gone through all his inheritance, returns. The older brother wants to know why such wasteful behavior should be rewarded. The father responds in a way that could not have satisfied the older brother, but, the story leads us to believe, these are the actions of a loving parent (and by extension, the ways of God), whether we understand them or not.

THE MENU

Poor Lad's Loaf

Veal Kebabs

Honey-baked Goat with Mint Sauce

Heifer Fondue

Fresh Mallow with Pomegranate Vinaigrette

Grilled Corn on the Cob

Fresh Kefir Yogurt with Concord Grapes

Figs in Chamomile Tea and Cream

Carob Cake for Two Sons

THE PREPARATION

At the core of the older son's hurt is the father's extravagance in calling for the wheat-fatted (in Greek, *siteutos*) calf (in Greek, *moschos,* or "young calf") to be killed and served for dinner. The killing of this animal is not just a daily food necessity. Killing the fatted calf was the kind of action one reserved for only the most important of guests, for example, if the governor or the president were coming by for dinner. Hence the older brother was understandably angry. He had never been given even a measly skinny goat (the text says "kid," in Greek *eriphos*)[3] to share in revelry with his friends.

But this being a parable (a rabbinic teaching tool), there is a lesson to be learned. The loving father does not wish that any of his children be so reduced to hunger that they would beg for what "farmers" were feeding to the pigs. This was the absolute worst thing a Jewish father could have wished on anyone! True, it was a time of famine, and the son decided to seek employment rather than return home. Still, becoming a swineherd was the most abhorrent job a Jew would ever accept. A Talmudic proverb of the day reprimanded, "Cursed is the man who tends swine." But the younger son came to envy those very pigs who were feasting on carob husks (some translations say it was corn cobs the swine were eating,[4] yet that is a modern interpolation into the text, as corn was native to the Americas and would not have been known to the peoples of the Bible). And having the job of swineherd did not entitle the younger son to room and board. In fact, the text says that though the pig slop was right in front of him, as a hired servant he was not in a position where he could help himself; and to make matters worse, no one would even give him a bit of it. He was, to be sure, in terrible straits.

The younger son comes to his senses and reasons that his father's hired men "have enough food (some translations say "enough bread"),[5] and even food to spare." Should his father's hired servants have more than he, a foreigner's hired hand? If he goes back to his father (he reasons), at the very least he'd be fed what *those* servants were eating.

So he returns. His father sees him from far away and begins the preparations. The younger son never even gets to use his entire rehearsed speech. The father calls for the festive robe of honor (like the coat of many colors Jacob gives to Joseph); he calls for sandals for his barefoot (i.e., poor) child, and a ring for his hand, in symbolic recognition that they are united once again, and that regardless of what has transpired, the younger man retains his place and favor as a son.

The fatted calf is killed (one translation says "the grain-fed heifer is roasted"),[6] the table for the feast is set, and all are rejoicing when the older son returns to reproach his father for having loved so extravagantly. Tipped off by one of the townspeople as to what has transpired ("Your brother has returned, and your father has killed that wheat-fatted calf"),[7] the older son is beside himself with anger, remorse, jealousy—a whole range of emotions.

There is a secondary reality that must have struck him at this point: his father had begun the celebration without him. Not only was he left out of the proceedings once again, but as everyone knew, it was the responsibility of the eldest son to play host at a father's banquet. It is the eldest son who is to see to the seating of the guests, the serving of the meal—all the festivities surrounding the dinner. Not only was he not there to do so, he had not been informed about the meal, and even worse, he had not been invited! And upon discovering that the meal is in honor of his younger brother, he won't even go in to the feast. His father has to leave the meal, and not unlike the approach to welcome the younger son home, goes out to welcome the older son to take a seat at the table. The elder son refuses. He is hurt; his brother is a lout; his father is an insensitive and unjust parent.

But the father's love will not allow distinctions between the good deeds of one child and the irresponsible deeds of another (although at this point it's hard to know which is which and who is who!). In the end, he loves them both—perhaps not equally (depending on which son is speaking), but fully.

The early church used this story not only to demonstrate the magnanimous love of God but as a way of further describing the banquet feast that awaits believers, even those lately repentant. It leveled the playing field, so to speak, which was particularly important to the Lucan church, composed mostly of Gentiles, who had not been included under the original covenant with Noah by which the Israelites became the chosen people of God. This tale helped to demonstrate (among other things) that through Jesus, the love and promises of God were now extended to all who came to God, even those formerly excluded or thought to be unworthy. This was good news for some, sad news for others; but it was to be the "new way," the "Path," that set the tone for an emerging and ever-growing movement within 1st-century Judaism soon to take on the name of "Christianity."

THE RECIPES

Poor Lad's Loaf

1½ cups barley flour

½ tsp. salt

1½ tsp. baking powder

2 Tbsp. brown sugar

1 egg

½ cup milk

2 Tbsp. butter, melted

Preheat oven to 425°F.

Sift flour, salt, and baking powder together. Add sugar. Mix egg and milk and stir well. Add butter. Combine both mixtures. Turn out on a floured board. Roll and pat into a flat circle about ½″ thick. Place in buttered 9″ pie plate. Bake for 15 minutes. Serve hot with honey.

Yield: 4 servings

Barley, one of the first plants cultivated for food, does not respond to yeast, so it was perhaps the most common grain used in making unleavened bread. Using barley flour, this bread recipe would have been followed by those families that could not afford to buy yeast—hence the name, Poor Lad's Loaf.

Source: "Poor Lad's Loaf": adaptation used by permission of Whitaker House (www.whitakerhouse.com), as found in Frank L. and Jean McKibbin, *Cookbook of Foods from Bible Days*, copyright © 1971 by Whitaker House. All rights reserved.

❧ Veal Kebabs

1 cup pine nuts

¼ cup dried tarragon

1 cup olive oil

6 veal fillets, pounded thin

2 cups dried apricots

4 onions, cut in large pieces

2 cups canned pears

1 dozen plum tomatoes, quartered

bed of rice

Mix the pine nuts and tarragon in a blender or food processor with the olive oil to form a thick paste. Cut the veal fillets into thirds in long, slender slices, and roll. On kebab skewer, place a rolled veal fillet, followed by two apricots, followed by a piece of onion, a piece of pear, and finally a tomato quarter. Baste with the pine nut paste. Cook over a charcoal fire, turning frequently, until well browned on all sides. Serve over a bed of rice.

Yield: 8–12 servings

❧ Honey-baked Goat with Mint Sauce

4 lb. goat, cubed

12 cups water

1 cup onions, finely chopped

1 tsp. garlic pepper

1 cup olive oil

2 cups green peppers, diced

1 cup honey

1 cup dry white wine or vermouth

2 Tbsp. lemon juice

1 tsp. salt

2 cups fresh mint

¼ cup sugar

¼ cup grenadine liqueur

¼ cup water

couscous or some other grain

fresh mint

Preheat oven to 350°F.

Parboil the goat in water until tender; drain and set aside. In an electric frying pan, heat the onions and garlic pepper in olive oil. Add the goat and peppers; simmer on low for about 20 minutes. With a slotted spoon, remove all ingredients from the frying pan and transfer to a large baking dish. Pour on honey, wine, and lemon juice, then add a bit of salt. Bake for 40–45 minutes.

Meanwhile, mix the fresh mint, sugar, grenadine, and water in a blender. Ten minutes before removing the goat from the oven, pour the mint sauce on top of the meat.

Serve over couscous or some other grain and garnish with fresh mint.

Yield: 8–12 servings

❧ Heifer Fondue

3 lb. boneless beef sirloin or tenderloin

1 cup red wine

1 Tbsp. honey

1 Tbsp. mustard

1 Tbsp. garlic powder

3 cups peanut or sesame oil

Cut the beef into small cubes and trim off all the fat.

In a small saucepan, heat the red wine, honey, mustard, and garlic powder, and bring to a quick boil. Pour into a heated bowl and place in the middle of a large platter.

Fill a fondue pot with peanut or sesame oil and heat slowly over a moderate flame. When the oil begins to boil, place a beef cube on a fork or skewer into the pot, and cook for 1–2 minutes. (This can be done with 6–8 forks at a time.) Place the cooked meat on a platter surrounding the sauce, and allow guests to help themselves, using forks or toothpicks for dipping and eating.

Yield: Enough for a large crowd

❧ *Fresh Mallow with Pomegranate Vinaigrette*

6 eggs	½ cup white vinegar
2 lb. fresh mallow (or spinach)	3 cloves garlic
1 cup scallions, chopped	1 tsp. dried mustard
6 plum tomatoes, chopped	½ tsp. salt
½ cup black olives, chopped	¾ tsp. black pepper
½ cup pomegranate juice	

Hard-boil eggs and set aside. Rinse the mallow (or spinach) and allow to drain in a colander. In a large bowl, mix the scallions, tomatoes, and olives. Add the mallow. Remove shells from eggs, slice, and place on top of greens.

In a large mixing cup, combine the pomegranate juice, vinegar, garlic, mustard, salt, and pepper. Whisk with a fork, and pour over salad as a dressing. Refrigerate covered to serve later, or place on the table for immediate enjoyment.

Yield: 8–12 servings

❧ *Grilled Corn on the Cob*

12 ears of corn	½ cup dried tarragon
2 cups butter, melted	1 tsp. salt
2 cups chives, minced	3 Tbsp. garlic pepper
½ cup dried dill	1 tsp. chili powder

Remove husks and silk from the corn and place each ear on a piece of aluminum foil. Mix the butter with all the other ingredients, and spoon a bit onto each ear of corn. Wrap and bake on the grill, turning frequently until done (about 20 minutes).

Yield: 12 servings

❧ *Fresh Kefir Yogurt with Concord Grapes*

2 lb. seedless Concord grapes	½ cup almonds, toasted
1 lb. kefir yogurt	½ cup lime juice

Wash the grapes and remove from vine, then place in a large bowl. Pour kefir over grapes, and add toasted almonds on top. Sprinkle with a bit of lime juice. (Do not toss until serving). Serve cold.

Yield: 6–8 servings

Figs in Chamomile Tea and Cream

4 cups chamomile tea	½ lb. confectioners' sugar
3 Tbsp. honey	1 tsp. lemon juice
1 lb. dried figs	ground nutmeg
6 egg whites	

In a saucepan, bring tea and honey to a boil. Add figs and simmer for 1 hour or so. Remove from heat and let cool; then place in serving dishes or parfait glasses. In a separate bowl, beat egg whites until stiff, and add sugar and lemon. Spoon egg mixture over the figs, sprinkling a dash of fresh nutmeg on top.

Yield: 8 servings

Carob Cake for Two Sons

1½ cups flour	2 egg yolks
2 cups sugar	2 tsp. baking powder
¾ cup milk	1 tsp. vanilla
5 Tbsp. cooking oil	1 tsp. salt
2 tsp. vinegar	6 Tbsp. carob powder

Preheat oven to 350°F. Grease and flour a large cake pan.

Mix all the ingredients in a large bowl. Pour into a pan. Bake for 1 hour. Serve warm.

Yield: 8 servings

NOTES

1. Raymond E. Brown, *An Introduction to the New Testament* (New York: Doubleday, 1996), 7, 127, 172, 226, 334.

2. For an excellent discussion of the Middle Eastern customs that are part of the subtext for this story, see Ron Grieb, *Understanding God's Love: A Study of the Misunderstanding and Misrepresentation of God* (Casco, Mich.: Christian Traditions Publishing, 1999), as found at www.domestic-church.com/CONTENT.DCC/20000501/ARTICLES/gods_love_review

3. It is perhaps noteworthy that these words, *moschos* and *eriphos,* are not used anywhere else in the New Testament. To our way of thinking, this underscores both the uniqueness of this story and the rarity of the action taken by the father. It is not only the older son who finds his father's actions untenable; the hearer of the story likewise sympathizes with the

older brother. True, we would all like to believe we are worthy to have the fatted calf killed *on our behalf,* but most likely not at the expense of losing any of *our inheritance.*

4. "He was so hungry he would have eaten the corncobs in the pig slop, but no one would give him any" (Luke 15:17, The Message).

5. "And coming to himself, he said, How many hired servants of my father's have abundance of bread, and I perish here by famine" (Luke 15:17, Darby Translation). The King James Version uses "bread" also. The Greek word is *artos,* which means "bread," or "loaf of wheat."

6. "Then get a grain-fed heifer and roast it" (Luke 15:23a, The Message).

7. The Message translation reads, "Your brother came home. Your father has ordered a feast—*barbecued beef!*" As strange as this might sound, it is probably not too far from the truth. As we saw in Chapter 1, the only way to quickly cook a fatted calf would be to make top slices, cut the beef into small pieces (kebabs), and cook them on a stick over a hot flame.

16

Jesus Dines with the Pharisee

THE TEXT

37 As he spake, a certain Pharisee besought him to dine with him: and he went in, and sat down to meat.
38 And when the Pharisee saw it, he marveled that he had not first washed before dinner.
39 And the Lord said unto him, Now do ye Pharisees make clean the outside of the cup and the platter; but your inward part is full of ravening and wickedness.
40 Ye fools, did not he that made that which is without make that which is within also?
41 But rather give alms of such things as ye have; and behold, all things are clean unto you.
42 But woe unto you, Pharisees! For ye tithe mint and rue and all manner of herbs, and pass over judgment and the love of God: these ought ye to have done, and not to leave the other undone.

Luke 11:37–42, King James Version

"But woe unto you, Pharisees! For ye tithe mint and rue and all manner of herbs."

THE HISTORY

The most successful military commander of the ancient world was Alexander the Great (Alexander III of Macedonia). After unifying the Greek city-states under Macedonian control, he took his armies forth and conquered a vast region stretching from Greece in the north, Egypt in the west, and Persia and the Punjab in the east. However, when he died in 323 B.C.E., he left no recognized heir, and the empire he had forged began to disintegrate. In 312 B.C.E. Seleucus, one of

Alexander's generals, established control over the eastern reaches of Alexander's holdings from Babylon, the center of power, to the Mediterranean coast. This was the foundation of the Seleucid Empire, which brought Hellenistic influences to Persians, Medes, Jews, and Indians alike.

But the empire proved to be too large, and the people resisted Hellenization; it was not long before the outer reaches began to break away. By the time of King Antiochus IV Epiphanes, who reigned from 175 to 163 B.C.E., aggressive efforts to de-Judaize the Jewish populace of the empire led to a breaking point. In about 167 B.C.E. Mattathias (of the tribe of Levi) and his sons Judah "Maccabee" (the Hammer), Eleazar, Yohanan, Yonaton, and Shimon led a successful uprising against the Seleucid overlords in Judea. Though fighting would continue for twenty-five years, in about 164 B.C.E. the Maccabees (for so they became known) were able to retake Jerusalem; they cleansed the Temple of foreign influences (including the sacrificing of pigs) and reestablished Jewish worship there. In 139 B.C.E. Shimon (the only surviving son) became both High Priest and Leader, establishing the Hasmonean line of succession in Judea. The memory of the purification of the Temple gave rise to the Jewish festival of Hanukkah (Chanukah).

At the end of the conflict with the Seleucids, the Jews had become divided into three different parties. The first were the Essenes, a group of ascetical mystics who lived in isolation in the desert. The second were the Sadducees, the priests and Jewish aristocracy; though they were religiously conservative, following a strict and inflexible interpretation of the written Torah, they were socially liberal, having embraced Hellenistic cultural practices. The Temple was the center of worship for the Sadducees; indeed, it was the only place where true worship could occur. The third group were the Pharisees, who believed in both a written and an oral Torah, both of which Jews were bound to follow and both of which the rabbis were empowered to interpret. In general, the Pharisees highly valued education but were opposed to Hellenism and to the Hasmonean usurpation of the Priesthood. These party divisions persisted even after Rome conquered Judea, though Roman conquest led to the rise of the Zealots and Sicarii, revolutionaries whose sole goal was the overthrow of Roman imperialism.

From the beginnings of the Hasmonean Empire until the Roman destruction of the Second Temple in 70 C.E., the Pharisees and the Sadducees bitterly opposed each other. The conflicts were manifold: the Sadducees promoted the interests of the wealthy and tended to favor hierarchy, while the Pharisees showed concern for the common people and tended to favor more participatory religious practices; the Sadducees followed Greek social customs, while the Pharisees attempted to preserve Jewish traditions; the Sadducees put the Temple first and tended to restrict religion to the Temple grounds, while the Pharisees put the word of God before everything and tended to sanctify the everyday world; and the Sadducees adhered to the letter of the Law, while the Pharisees believed that the Law was a living, changing force. The Pharisees also believed in the importance of ritual washing before all meals and in the resurrection of the dead at the end of time.

The New Testament scriptures present a very critical picture of the Pharisees and Sadducees. The new Jewish sect known as "Christians" emphasized God's love and forgiveness for all people, including society's outcasts. The Sadducees were presented as people of privilege who hoarded everything, including God's grace, for their own select group; and the Pharisees were presented as being obsessed with purification rites, to the exclusion of anyone who did not correctly perform their rituals. On the other hand, some scholars have posited that Jesus was himself a Pharisee, and that his efforts to include all persons in God's beloved community echoed the Pharisees' emphasis of participatory religion. Indeed, many of the teachings of Jesus as related in the gospels are consistent with the philosophies of the Pharisees of his day, including one of the most well known, whose name was Paul.

BIBLICAL PASSAGE NOTES

Throughout the New Testament gospel writings, Jesus is often in a war of words and deeds with the Pharisees, a group of religious Jews that had their own interpretation of how to live a life that was true to the practice of Judaism, to which they were utterly devoted. They embraced a lifestyle that placed great emphasis on, among other things, Sabbath observances and food tithes (a tithe is a tenth of what one earns). To some, and most certainly to the gospel writers, they were hardnosed and stubborn legalists; to many of their fellow Jews, they were men greatly to be admired, as they were learned in Jewish law and often hailed from some of the finest families in Jerusalem that were politically connected to both the most revered of religious authorities and, often, to Rome itself.

In this passage, Jesus has been invited to dine with one of the Pharisees, an amazing offer considering that the Pharisees rarely, if ever, would have thought to dine with someone outside their own circle. To have received such an esteemed invitation, either Jesus was a Pharisee himself (a view held by many scholars today), or he impressed them so by his knowledge of the scriptures and his interpretation of the Law that curiosity allowed internal rules to be set aside for at least one meal.

Jesus had barely entered the house when he is admonished for not having washed his hands, for it was a common practice of observant Jews to purify their hands prior to eating. The thought process was that impure hands made food impure; eating impure food made the body impure; eating a meal (a sacred act before God) with an impure body was an insult to God.

Undoubtedly, those who first heard this story would have responded with an "Oh, no!" thanking God, no doubt, that such a guest had not been invited to their home! Why? Because the interaction between Jesus and the Pharisee presented an uncomfortable conundrum. True, Jesus did not wash; but the lack of hospitality on the part of his host, who had apparently not offered a towel or water, was an incredible social faux pas. And in a further breach of manners, the host had the bad sense to insult his guest by pointing out the error; even worse, he made the observation *after* Jesus had already reclined to dine.

Jesus' previous experience with the Pharisees and their rituals fueled his anger at the host; having been dealt with impolitely, Jesus takes off the kid gloves and charges into the fight, calling the Pharisee and all his brothers in the faith (in essence) miserable hypocrites. Then Jesus goes on to tell them the how and the why. First, he imputes, they are more concerned with the outward appearances of inanimate objects than they are with the inner feelings of the people around them. Second, they fail to see that God made all things, and it is wrong, therefore, to give a greater importance to one thing over another, as all things are of God. And finally, Jesus criticizes the Pharisees for putting aside a portion of what they have earned as a sacrifice in honor of God, yet all the while being judgmental of others in a way that dishonors God. It is a strong condemnation, and it could not have made for a very pleasant meal!

It appears that the host was either even more intrigued by the dressing down or totally embarrassed; in either case, Jesus apparently stays for the meal, to which other Pharisees and scribes have also been invited. From this moment, perhaps between bites (?), Jesus denounces the practices of the religious elite, to the point that when he finally leaves, they press him more, hoping that he will say something by which they can charge him with speaking blasphemously.

Despite the rancor, this is not his last invitation to sit down with the Pharisees. In chapter 14 (v. 1ff.), Jesus accepts the invitation to sup with the Chief Pharisee; and as others begin once again to criticize Jesus' actions during the meal, the author of Luke finally lays down what was understood to be the rules of a good host (v. 12ff.); he tells them the parable of the Great Banquet, a metaphor for his understanding of how life would be if we all comprehended the love of God.

THE MENU

Onion Board (Pletzels)

Pickled Herring

Tuna Baked in Pistachios and Dill

Minted Veal with Yellow Summer Squash

Cucumbers and Onions with Rue and Mustard Dressing

Jerusalem Cheese and Honey Pie

Fruit Platter of Fresh Grapes, Dried Dates, and Figs

Nicodemus' Anise Cookies
Red Wine

The Preparation

It is apparent that Jesus did a lot of his teaching at mealtime, particularly if it were one of the main meals of the day. Just what was a meal with the Pharisees like? What did they dine on?

The Pharisees bought food only from those who tithed; they also tithed the food they bought. The Lucan biblical text reports that the Pharisees were tithers of mint (in Greek, *heduosmon*), rue (in Greek, *peganon*), and all types of garden herbs (in Greek, *lachanon*), so these must have been in their kitchens and store-rooms, and used often in their cooking. The parallel text in the Gospel of Matthew substitutes anise (in Greek, *anethon*) in place of rue, and other translations of the same text claim that dill was tithed, which in effect was the more likely scenario. In this instance we can get just a glimpse of how greatly translations of the Bible vary!

According to the British Broadcasting Corporation (BBC), people in 1st-century Palestine ate a fairly straightforward diet of cereals, gruel, olives, dates, and figs. In addition, lots of wine was consumed.[1]

Verse 37 states that "he sat down to meat," a strange phrase in Greek (*anapipto*), used only here and nowhere else in the Bible. *To sit down to meat* apparently means to fall back or down, but has nothing to do with *meat* as such. The phrase implies that he reclined to eat his meal, which was the cultural norm for men at meals in that era.

If not meat, then what? Probably fish, as they were near the sea, and it would not be difficult to see how Jesus might have come to know some of the Pharisees through the business dealings of his disciples, many of whom were fishermen.

It is likely that this meal was not the principal meal of the day, but one of the earlier meals. We infer this because of the guests that were present: being the Sabbath, certainly the lawyers and other religious leaders would have been at their own homes if it were the time of day for the main meal ("dinner") of a holy day.

In that one of the favorite foods of Palestinian Jews of Jesus' day was "young meat," the menu for the Pharisee's meal would likely have included goat, lamb, or veal.[2] (Neither beef nor fowl were cooked very often.) And certainly there was bread, and lots of it. Due to the belief that it was the staff of life, no religious man would dare to have entertained guests without it.

Marian Maeve O'Brien, in *The Bible Cookbook*, claims "that actual meals served in biblical times *have* been preserved for us,"[3] and she goes so far as to present an outline of the typical midday meal for a middle-class family in Jerusalem in the 1st century. It includes, among other things, locusts, onions, and grapes.[4] She does not cite her source, but it would not be unreasonable to assume that at least part of the menu has historical merit. Another food author, Kitty Morse, in *A Biblical Feast: Foods from the Holy Land*,[5] writes that she believes a 1st-century supper usually started with something pickled in brine or vinegar, which would have stimulated the appetite. This was followed by a stew or some pottage that been thickened by grain and enhanced with lots of garden vegetables and herbs.[6] To this menu, other scholars would add a milk dish into which people dipped their bread, and honey, eggs, cheeses, cucumbers, lentils, beans, and peas.[7]

Perhaps we'll never be sure just what was served at the meal Jesus shared with the Pharisee. But we can be certain of one thing: it was prepared with care, according to cleanliness rituals as understood by the Pharisees. So, it was probably a well-presented meal with frugal portions, yet not overly stingy so as to not appear inhospitable.

THE RECIPES

❧ Onion Board (Pletzels)

4–5 cups whole wheat flour

2 packages dry yeast

2 Tbsp. honey

2 eggs, beaten

1 tsp. salt

2 cups warm water

4 cups onions, chopped

¾ cup vegetable oil

1 tsp. salt

1 tsp. paprika

2 Tbsp. poppy seeds

This onion bread has a tangy taste that goes well with a sweet sheep's milk cheese.

Combine 2 cups of flour with yeast, honey, eggs, and salt in a large bowl; add water and beat with a hand mixer for about 2 minutes. Gradually add more and more flour by hand so that the dough is workable enough to knead. Pour out onto a floured surface and work dough until smooth and somewhat elastic. (Add more flour or water until you get it just right.) Place in a well-oiled bowl, cover with a damp towel, and set aside for 30 minutes.

Punch the dough down and divide into four parts. Grease four pie pans and spread with dough. Using a brush or a paper towel, coat surfaces of dough in each pan with a bit of oil. Cover with plastic wrap and refrigerate for 4–12 hours (the longer, the better!).

When ready to bake, preheat oven to 375°F. Sauté the onions in vegetable oil until golden. Remove from heat and add salt, paprika, and poppy seeds. Spread over dough and bake for 25–30 minutes, until lightly browned. Serve fresh out of the oven, or wrap in a clean towel or cloth napkin until serving.

Note: Tastes great with a spread of sheep's milk cheese!

Yield: 8–12 servings

Pickled Herring

4 jars herring fillets

¼ cup fresh dill, chopped

1 tsp. ground allspice

2 bay leaves

2½ Tbsp. lemon juice

½ cup Spanish onions, chopped

3 Tbsp. distilled white vinegar

1 tsp. ground black pepper

¼ cup vegetable oil

2 Tbsp. brown sugar

Allowing enough time for aging is vital when making pickled herring.

Drain the herring fillets and rinse well; transfer to a mixing bowl. In a small pot, combine the remaining ingredients and bring to a boil. Allow to cool. Pour the mix over the herrings. Cover and refrigerate for at least 3 hours (if you have the time, 2–3 days is even better) prior to serving.

Yield: 6–8 servings

Tuna Baked in Pistachios and Dill

½ cup pistachios, shelled

¼ cup fresh dill

1 cup green olives, chopped

2 cloves garlic

6 coriander seeds

2 tsp. whole mustard seeds

1 tsp. caraway seeds

Preheat oven to 400°F.

1 tsp. lime juice

1 cup dry white wine (or vermouth)

6 tuna fillets

2 bunches whole radishes

18–20 radish slices

handful of fresh dill

Radishes, dill, and mustard add sharpness and tang to this tuna dish.

In a blender, mix the pistachios, dill, olives, garlic, all the seeds, lime juice, and white wine. Rinse the tuna fillets and place them in a large baking dish side by side. Pour the pistachio sauce over the tuna, and cook for about 20 minutes or so, or until the tuna flakes when poked with a fork.

Wash the radishes and their greens thoroughly, taking care to remove all dirt, especially from the bulbs themselves. Shake to dry. On a large serving dish or platter, arrange radish greens with whole radishes still attached around the perimeter, the greens facing the middle. Place the tuna on top of the greens to serve (do not use the sauce—discard it), and top each fillet with 3 small pieces of cut radish, sprinkled with a smattering of fresh dill. Serve cold or hot with a spicy garnish.

Spicy Garnish

1 large dill pickle, cut in slices

½ cup mayonnaise

1 Tbsp. Old Bay seasoning

Process pickle in a blender on high speed until well chopped; pour out juice. Add mayo and seasoning, and blend once again. Pour over fish or serve on the side.

Yield: 6 servings

❧ Minted Veal with Yellow Summer Squash

4 large onions, chopped	6 coriander seeds, crushed
3 cloves garlic, minced	1 tsp. ground mace
6 Tbsp. olive oil	⅛ tsp. ground cloves
8 veal loin chops	1 Tbsp. lime juice
¾–1 cup water, as needed	6 cherry tomatoes, halved
1 Tbsp. flour	6 sprigs fresh mint leaves, chopped
1 tsp. ground white pepper	8 yellow summer squash
2 tsp. sumac	1 Tbsp. Balsamic vinegar

2 cups beef stock

mound of basmati rice

sprigs of mint for garnish

In a large electric frying pan, sauté the onions and garlic in the oil until slightly golden. Add the veal portions and cook in batches until brown on all sides. Remove the veal and set aside. Stir in the water, flour, and pepper and bring to a quick boil. Blend in all the other spices while cooking on a low heat. Add the lime juice, tomatoes, and mint; replace the veal, cover, and simmer for about 30 minutes, or until veal is very tender.

Although veal may not be as popular today, it was a prized delicacy among the well-to-do of 1st-century Judea.

In the meantime, cut the squash into eighths or twelfths. Place in a large, covered ovenproof dish along with the vinegar and beef stock and heat in the microwave on high for 10 minutes. Spoon the squash and vinegar stock over the veal and serve on a large bed of basmati rice surrounded by fresh mint.

Yield: 8 servings

Cucumbers and Onions with Rue and Mustard Dressing

6 large cucumbers

3 large sweet onions

2 tsp. ground mustard

¼ tsp. cumin

½ tsp. rue*

¼ cup pine nuts

2 tsp. honey

½ cup cider vinegar

3 garlic cloves

Use rue sparingly in this cucumber and onion salad; parsley may be substituted if desired.

Peel the cucumbers and slice into long strips. Place in a steel bowl. Chop the onions into small pieces and add them to the cucumbers. In a small food processor, grind the mustard, cumin, rue, and pine nuts. Place them into a mixing cup and add honey and vinegar. Peel and press 3 garlic cloves into the mixture. Pour over the cucumbers and onions; cover. Refrigerate for at least 1 hour, and serve cold.

Yield: 6–8 servings

*Rue has been known to have an adverse effect on some diners; parsley can be substituted if one wishes, although the results are a bit different in taste.

❧ Jerusalem Cheese and Honey Pie

1 lb. creamy sheep's or goat's milk cheese (at room temperature)

¼ cup honey, slightly warmed

6 Tbsp. sugar

3 eggs, lightly beaten

1 tsp. vanilla extract

ground cinnamon

1 9″ pie crust

powdered sugar topping

fresh berries of the season

Preheat oven to 350°F.

Top off this honey cheese pie with blueberries, raspberries, blackberries, strawberries, peaches, cherries, or any other seasonal fruit.

Combine cheese with honey and mix well. Add the sugar, eggs, and vanilla, and toss in a bit of cinnamon. Bake in a pie crust (frozen or fresh) for 30–35 minutes. Best served warm.

Just prior to serving, sprinkle with a touch of cinnamon mixed with powdered sugar. Top with berries of the season.

Yield: 8 servings

❧ Fruit Platter of Fresh Grapes, Dried Dates, and Figs

On a large platter of mint leaves and lemon balm, place bunches of fresh grapes in the center and surround with dried dates and figs. Cut lemon and lime wedges and place in a pile at either side as an individual garnish for the discerning diner.

Grapes, dates, and figs make a sweet yet refreshing finish to a fine meal.

✻ *Nicodemus' Anise Cookies*

1 cup butter

1 cup granulated sugar

1 cup light brown sugar

3 eggs

¼ cup milk

¼ tsp. baking soda

½ tsp. salt

1 tsp. baking powder

3 Tbsp. molasses

2 tsp. anise extract

4 cups flour

1 cup pecans, finely chopped

buttercream frosting laced with anisette
   liqueur (optional)

The anise in these cookies adds a warm, inviting flavor to an old standard.

Mix all ingredients, one after the other, as listed. Refrigerate for 4–12 hours (or overnight is best).

Preheat oven to 375°F.

Roll dough out onto a large floured board using a rolling pin. Shape into small logs, and cut about ¼″ thick. Bake for 10–12 minutes.

If desired, ice with buttercream frosting laced with a bit of anisette.

Yield: 6–8 dozen cookies

✻ *Red Wine*

For this meal, try a good red kosher wine, perhaps from Carmel Mizrachi Wineries or Tishbi Wineries, both of Israel.

Notes

1. See the article at www.bbc.co.uk/religion/programmes/mary/evidence/8.shtml
2. See the commentary at http://truthinheart.com/EarlyOberlinCD/CD/edersheim/IV.CHAPTERXIITH.htm
3. Marian Maeve O'Brien, *The Bible Cookbook* (St. Louis: Bethany Press, 1958), 25.
4. Ibid.
5. Kitty Morse, *A Biblical Feast: Foods from the Holy Land* (Berkeley, Calif.: Ten Speed Press, 1998), 8.
6. Ibid.
7. Cf. http://truthinheart.com/EarlyOberlinCD/CD/edersheim/IV.CHAPTERXIITH.htm

17

The Wedding Feast at Cana

THE TEXT

1 Three days later there was a wedding in the village of Cana in Galilee. Jesus' mother was there.

2 Jesus and his disciples were guests also.

3 When they started running low on wine at the wedding banquet, Jesus' mother told him, "They're just about out of wine."

4 Jesus said, "Is that any of our business, Mother—yours or mine? This isn't my time. Don't push me."

5 She went ahead anyway, telling the servants, "Whatever he tells you, do it."

6 Six stoneware water pots were there, used by the Jews for ritual washings. Each held twenty to thirty gallons.

7 Jesus ordered the servants, "Fill the pots with water." And they filled them to the brim.

8 "Now fill your pitchers and take them to the host," Jesus said, and they did.

9 When the host tasted the water that had become wine (he didn't know what had just happened but the servants, of course, knew), he called out to the bridegroom,

10 "Everybody I know begins with their finest wines and after the guests have had their fill brings in the cheap stuff. But you've saved the best till now!"

John 2:1–10, The Message

"Stoneware water pots were there, used by the Jews for ritual washings. Each held twenty to thirty gallons."

THE HISTORY

In Jewish tradition, marriage is held to be the ideal state, and all Jewish men and women are generally encouraged to marry. For the peoples of the Old Testament (particularly the Jewish Torah), polygyny was the most common form of marriage. Polygyny is defined as "the practice of having more than one wife or female mate at one time," and the scriptures provide many examples of polygyny: Abraham had both a wife and a concubine; Jacob had two wives and two concubines; King David had eight wives; King Solomon was said to have had seven hundred wives and three hundred concubines. Often a slave would become the wife or concubine of her master, and sometimes a childless wife would offer her serving girl to her husband in order to produce heirs. Although there was no legal limit and a man could have as many as he could afford to support, it was really only the very wealthy or powerful who had more than one or at most two wives or concubines.

The Jewish prophets, such as Hosea and Isaiah, seem to have been proponents of monogamy (having only one spouse or mate at a time), for they represent the Chosen People's relationship to God as that of a monogamous couple, and they portray God as a jealous husband of one beloved wife. By the time of the Roman conquest, monogamy was the norm among the Jews.

The stories of the patriarchs also reflect the practice of endogamy: marriage within a specific group. The marriages of both Isaac and Jacob are held as exemplars, for they went well out of their way to marry kinswomen. Marrying outside of the tribe was seen to cause grief and turmoil, as, for example, in the story of Esau. When the Israelites moved into Canaan, however, some of them intermarried with the Canaanite women, and the Israelite kings, such as David and Solomon, sealed foreign alliances through intermarriage. The proscription of marriage with someone outside the tribe was relaxed during the times of exile, though the prophets blamed intermarriage, among other transgressions, for the calamities that befell the Chosen People. In general, men were prohibited from marrying their immediate blood relatives (mothers, daughters, sisters, granddaughters), as well as aunts, stepmothers, mothers-in-law, sisters-in-law, and stepdaughters (those who had legally become the equivalent of blood relatives). As a result of endogamy, a high degree of social cohesion was maintained.

Another custom followed by the ancient Hebrews was that of Levirate marriage, according to which a man is obligated to marry the childless widow of his deceased brother and to beget children on behalf of that brother. There were two purposes for Levirate marriage: to prevent the dead brother's name from passing away, and to ensure the proper disposition of the dead brother's property. In both cases, the firstborn son of the widow was considered the rightful heir of the dead brother's estate. A widow whose brother-in-law was unwilling to marry her could publicly humiliate him by loosening his sandal and spitting in his face.

While the wife was considered to be the property of the husband, she was to be valued and well cared for. Many wives, such as Deborah, one of the judges of the tribes, held important positions in the community, and most wives were responsible for managing the affairs of the household. A wife was supposed to be obedient, and infidelity on her part was a sin carrying the penalty of death. While the strictures were not identical for husbands, they were encouraged to be faithful as well and to respect and honor their wives.

Before a marriage could occur, a betrothal had to be arranged. A betrothal required the consent of the woman's (or girl's) parents and the payment of a fee to the man's family (a dowry). Sometimes the woman would also receive gifts from her father or relatives. Betrothals could occur either months or years before the nuptials would be celebrated; in many cases, parents would arrange betrothals for their children not long after their births. Once betrothed, a woman was considered to be a wife in everything but name, and she was required to behave as a wife should. The marriage and nuptial feast were mere formalities allowing the consummation of the union, though the celebration, held in the house of the bridegroom, might continue for many days.

BIBLICAL PASSAGE NOTES

It's a dangerous task for the writer to attempt to comment on the wedding feast at Cana, as it is considered by many in the Christian tradition to exemplify the miracles of Jesus. Turning water into wine is not an everyday affair, and to our knowledge there are no recipes for doing so, neither in ancient cookbooks nor in the magical tomes of antiquity. Nor is there a lot of information in the Bible (or elsewhere) on matrimonial customs of the Galilean middle class in the 1st century. Perhaps the best we can do is to read between the lines and interpolate a scenario based upon later (and current) traditions in order to give us a fair idea of the type of feast Jesus and his disciples attended in Cana so long ago.

The exact location of Cana is uncertain. Latin and Orthodox churches point to a modern-day site known as Keft Kenna, about four miles northeast of Nazareth. However, most scholars agree that the more likely spot is at the ancient village of Khirbet Qana on a hill about nine miles to the north of Nazareth. Who the party was that was getting married and the name of the host are not part of the biblical narrative, but as Nathanael of Cana is mentioned just a few verses earlier (ch. 1:45ff.), some have supposed that the invitation to the wedding might have come through him.

THE MENU

Wedding Challah

Endive Salad with Olives and Clementines

Dolmas (Stuffed Grapevine Leaves)

Baked Sardines in Tahini Sauce

Roast Duck with Mulberries and Horseradish

Rack of Lamb with Spicy Mint Sauce

Sweet Millet Fruit Balls

Mary's Almond Cookies (*Mamool*)

Platter of Melon Balls, Raisins, Dates, and Candied Jordan Almonds

Galilean Red Wine

THE PREPARATION

The festivities probably began on the third day of the week as was the prevailing custom, and continued for another four. Reclining guests (men) ate on floor mats, consuming lots of food and wine between listening to music and dancing. Women congregated elsewhere and were not part of the main activities of the celebration, remaining "behind the scene." Mary and other female relatives of Jesus were apparently present—which, one tradition suggests, indicates that the bride was probably a close relation. According to the same source, the customs for that time required that there be a feast of roasted lamb and herbs, bread, and a lot of wine, which was used both for drinking and in the preparation of the foods.[1]

Just what other foods might have been at the myriad of tables set up for guests is uncertain. If it were a typical Palestinian wedding feast of the era, some writers, such as the authors of *The Good Book Cookbook,* have speculated that the feast would also have included, at the very least, olives, sardines, grapevine leaves, millet, dried apricots, dates, almonds, raisins, duckling, pomegranates, and rice.[2] Whatever was served, it was not in stingy portions.

When Jesus and his disciples arrive at the feast, it is apparently a few days into the celebration, as the wine is running short. This was a very serious matter; so Mary, who apparently had some role in the wedding celebration, approaches Jesus to see what can be done.[3] Just how it is accomplished is a matter between theologians and the faithful, but the biblical story reports that the water is changed into wine. What is particularly noteworthy is the abundance of wine that is delivered as a result of Jesus' actions: 120 gallons! (Or more, if you consider that the Jews typically diluted their wine seven parts [water] to one [wine].) The water into wine is really a most generous gesture and gift, which the early Christian Church came to interpret as a prototype of God's heavenly banquet reserved for believers.

The Recipes

✺ Wedding Challah

1–1½ cups warm water

2 eggs, beaten

⅓ cup honey

1 tsp. salt

1 cup red or black currants

½ cup slivered almonds

¼ cup extra-virgin olive oil

6¼ cups white flour

2 tsp. active dry yeast

1 egg yolk

pinch of salt

1 Tbsp. water

Before beginning, make sure all ingredients are at room temperature.

Put 1 cup water, eggs, honey, and oil in bread machine; then add all but the last three ingredients. Turn machine to "dough setting." (During the first kneading, add a bit more water if the dough is not elastic enough.) At the end of the cycle, punch down, knead briefly, and form into two loaves. Place in oiled bread pans, cover, and let rise until doubled in bulk.

Preheat oven to 350°F.

Whisk an egg yolk and a pinch of salt with 1 Tbsp. water in a measuring cup, and brush the loaves with this mixture. Bake for about 35 minutes or until golden.

Note: If you wish to have braided bread, stretch and roll each loaf into ropes; arrange side by side on a floured surface and intertwine. Bake on an oiled baking sheet instead of in the pan.

Yield: 8–12 servings

✺ Endive Salad with Olives and Clementines

4 cloves garlic, finely minced

⅓ cup olive oil

2 lb. endive, cut into bite-sized pieces

1 small head radicchio, shredded

½ cup chicken stock

¼ cup oil-cured olives, pitted and chopped

2 Tbsp. capers

toasted almonds

10 clementines

crumbled goat cheese

Mince the garlic cloves in a food processor; transfer to an electric frying pan and sauté in oil until golden. Add the endive and radicchio and continue to sauté for 5 minutes. Stir in the chicken stock, olives, and capers. Cover and simmer for 15 minutes, stirring frequently.

Peel the clementines and separate segments from inner membranes. Cover the inside base of a large bowl with clementines, and line them along its sides. Pour endive mixture into middle and sprinkle with almonds. Crumble a bit of goat cheese on top prior to serving. Serve cold or at room temperature.

Yield: 8–12 servings

❧ Dolmas (Stuffed Grapevine Leaves)

1 cup uncooked rice	½ tsp. mace
2 Tbsp. butter, melted	a dash of salt and pepper
1 lb. lamb, ground	50–60 grape leaves (canned), unstuffed
2 onions, diced	2 or 3 lamb chops
¼ cup pine nuts, ground	chopped garlic
½ tsp. cinnamon	¼ cup lemon juice

Pour cold water over the rice and drain. Place rice in a large bowl and add all of the remaining ingredients (except the grape leaves, lamb chops, garlic, and lemon juice). Mix well; set aside to be used as stuffing.

Remove the grape leaves from the can or jar and rinse. Unfold several leaves at a time onto a large plate and put 1 tsp. of the stuffing toward the center. Roll up the leaf as firmly as possible. (They should look like little cigars, about ½"–¾" thick.) Repeat this process until all leaves have been stuffed and rolled.

Place lamb chops in the bottom of a deep pot. Arrange the leaves in compact layers on top of the chops. Barely cover the leaves with boiling water. Weigh down the rolls with a heavy pottery plate to help keep them from moving or separating. Bring pot to a boil, then reduce the heat and simmer for about 45 minutes. Add chopped garlic and lemon juice at end of cooking. Remove and allow to cool. Serve at room temperature or chilled.

Yield: 50–60 bite-size appetizers (6–8 servings)

❧ Baked Sardines in Tahini Sauce

2 lb. sardines	½ cup water
½ cup olive oil	1 cup tahini
salt and pepper	1 cup onions, chopped
⅔ cup lemon juice	¼ cup parsley, chopped

Preheat oven to 350°F.

Wash the sardines and let them drain. Grease a large baking dish and cook the sardines about 40 minutes or so, uncovered, with a little olive oil, salt, and pepper spread over the surface of the fish.

While the fish is baking, add lemon juice and water to tahini, mixing well until you have a smooth sauce. Sauté chopped onion in olive oil. Drain and add to the sauce. Pour sesame sauce over fish and return to oven. Bake uncovered for about 15 minutes. Serve in the same dish, sprinkled with chopped parsley.

Yield: 8–10 servings

✣ Roast Duck with Mulberries and Horseradish

1 7–8 lb. duck	1 cup horseradish, grated
2 cloves garlic, minced	1 egg
2 tsp. salt	4 Tbsp. fresh bread crumbs
¼ tsp. pepper	2 Tbsp. brown sugar
1 pint mulberries (or some other berry)	crushed mulberries
6 fresh figs	

Preheat oven to 350°F.

Wash the duck thoroughly and pat dry. Place on a rack in a large roasting pan. Prick the skin all over with a fork (this will be repeated about every half hour during cooking). Rub the minced garlic all over the bird, then season with salt and pepper. Combine the mulberries, figs, horseradish, egg, and bread crumbs, then stuff the mixture into the duck's cavity. Sprinkle brown sugar on top of the duck and roast for 2½–3 hours, or until duck is tender. Pour off fat often during roasting.

About ½ hour before duck is fully cooked, pour crushed mulberries over surface of the duck. Just prior to serving, baste duck with mulberry and fat drippings.

Yield: 6–8 servings

✣ Rack of Lamb with Spicy Mint Sauce

2 racks of lamb	1 cup fresh mint leaves
½ cup olive oil	2 cups water
2 Tbsp. black pepper	3 Tbsp. Dijon mustard
6 cloves garlic, crushed	shredded fresh mint leaves
1 cup honey	

Preheat oven to 400°F.

Place lamb in a large roasting pan. In a food processor, combine the olive oil, black pepper, and garlic. Brush the racks with a light coating of this mixture and bake for about 30 minutes.

Mix the honey, mint leaves, and 1 cup water in a blender on low. Add whatever quantity of water might be necessary to make the mix pour like a thick gravy. Drop the mustard in and give it one quick whir. Slowly pour over racks of lamb so as to cover, and cook for an additional 10 minutes. Garnish with shredded fresh mint leaves when serving.

Yield: 8–12 servings

✣ Sweet Millet Fruit Balls

1 cup hulled millet seed	1 cup dried apricots, chopped fine
2 cups pear juice	⅓ cup lime juice
2 tsp. walnut oil	powdered sugar
2 cups pitted prunes, chopped fine	

Rinse the millet seed; place it in a saucepan with juice and oil, and simmer, covered, for about 20 minutes. Let stand for 20 minutes so that the seeds will open up. Allow to cool.

In a large bowl, mix prunes and apricots with lime juice. Add millet and form into small balls. Roll in powdered sugar, and place on a large cookie sheet lined with wax paper. Refrigerate until serving.

Yield: 24–30 fruit balls

Mary's Almond Cookies (Mamool)

4 cups flour	2 cups almonds, ground
1 lb. butter	¼ tsp. ground nutmeg
1 cup warm milk	⅛ tsp. ground cloves
1 tsp. almond extract	1 cup white granulated sugar
1 tsp. orange extract	1½ cups clarified butter
tap water	1 cup colored granulated sugar

Make dough of flour, butter, and milk. Knead for about 5 minutes. Add the extracts and a bit of tap water, and knead again until mixture is soft and easily shaped. Cover and let sit for an hour or two (or overnight if you have the time).

Preheat oven to 350°F.

Knead dough again, and form into small balls. Make a thumbprint hollow into each ball, and pinch up the sides to make a container shape. Fill with almonds that have been coated with nutmeg, cloves, sugar, and butter.

Place on a greased cookie sheet and decorate by making little impressions with the tines of a fork. Bake for about 20 minutes; do not allow to brown. Dust with colored sugar while still warm.

Yield: 3–4 dozen cookies

Platter of Melon Balls, Raisins, Dates, and Candied Jordan Almonds

Arrange a large cutting board with a low bowl of balled watermelon, muskmelon, and cantaloupe. Squeeze lemon juice over them to help keep them fresh. Surround by handfuls of dark and golden raisins, dried dates, and candied Jordan almonds.

Galilean Red Wine

For a wedding meal, one might try a kosher red from the Galilee region in Israel. Dalton Wineries is just one of many that produce Cabernet Sauvignon, Merlot, and a rich port wine, made with grapes grown in the hills near Cana and Nazareth. Check the Internet for a large list of wines from the area to help make your meal an "authentic experience."

NOTES

1. Edgar Cayce, *Edgar Cayce on Jesus and His Church* (New York: Warner Books, 1988), 75ff.

2. Naomi Goodman, Robert Marcus, and Susan Woolhandler, *The Good Book Cookbook* (Grand Rapids, Mich.: Fleming H. Revell, 1995), 88.

3. See George Carey's *Bible Study Notes: Life of Christ: John 2:1–11* at www.geocities.com/npford/loc18.html?20052 : "The law of reciprocity dictated how much food and wine were served. To provide a one-week feast exacted a tremendous toll upon the finances of the family hosting the festivities. One thing which helped them though was the realization that others hosting wedding festivities would reciprocate. Not to reciprocate in like manner would not only result in social embarrassment for the host but also in a lawsuit because he had failed to reciprocate appropriately." Therefore, when it appeared that there might not be enough wine to continue to serve the guests, there was a cause for great concern.

﹏ 18 ﹏

A Galilean Breakfast

THE TEXT

1 After this, Jesus appeared again to the disciples, this time at the
Tiberias Sea (the Sea of Galilee). This is how he did it:

2 Simon Peter, Thomas (nicknamed "Twin"), Nathanael from
Cana in Galilee, the brothers Zebedee, and two other disciples were
together.

3 Simon Peter announced, "I'm going fishing."
The rest of them replied, "We're going with you." They went out
and got in the boat. They caught nothing that night.

4 When the sun came up, Jesus was standing on the beach, but they
didn't recognize him.

5 Jesus spoke to them: "Good morning! Did you catch anything for
breakfast?"
They answered, "No."

6 He said, "Throw the net off the right side of the boat and see what
happens."
They did what he said. All of a sudden there were so many fish in it,
they weren't strong enough to pull it in.

7 Then the disciple Jesus loved said to Peter, "It's the Master!"
When Simon Peter realized that it was the Master, he threw on
some clothes, for he was stripped for work, and dove into the sea.

8 The other disciples came in by boat for they weren't far from land, a hundred
yards or so, pulling along the net full of fish.

9 When they got out of the boat, they saw a fire laid, with fish and bread
cooking on it.

10 Jesus said, "Bring some of the fish you've just caught."

"Jesus said, 'Bring some of the fish you've just caught.'"

11 Simon Peter joined them and pulled the net to shore—153 big fish! And even with all those fish, the net didn't rip.

12 Jesus said, "Breakfast is ready." Not one of the disciples dared ask, "Who are you?" They knew it was the Master.

13 Jesus then took the bread and gave it to them. He did the same with the fish.

14 This was now the third time Jesus had shown himself alive to the disciples since being raised from the dead.

John 21:1–14, The Message

THE HISTORY

In the ancient world, eating meat was such a rarity for most people that vegetarianism was essentially the major lifestyle—a lifestyle of necessity, not of choice. People of wealth would have been able to afford to eat meat, perhaps on a regular basis; for the rest, however, religious festivals or special occasions of hospitality may have provided the rare opportunity to add meat to the diet.

Fish, when available, did provide an important supplement to the diet of ancient peoples, so important, in fact, that Jerusalem had a marketplace called the Fish Gate (II Chronicles 33:14, Nehemiah 3:3; 12:39, and Zephaniah 1:10). Jewish dietary laws divided fish into clean and unclean food for consumption: those fish with scales and fins (that is, most fish) were considered clean (though eels were excluded, and shellfish were certainly prohibited [see Leviticus 11]). Fish, whether small or large, were consumed fresh or dried, salted or pickled, raw or cooked. The smallest fishes were thought to be particularly healthful, though the Jews seemed to have avoided young fish (other cultures did not). Often enough, fish were allowed to begin decomposing before being prepared for the table so as to achieve a distinctive taste. The eating of fish was also recommended during pregnancy. Fish brine was used as a seasoning, fish oil as a fuel, and fish skins as a writing surface; fish bones were fashioned into writing implements, hooks, needles, and hair ornaments.

The Jewish people employed several different methods of catching fish. First was the dragnet, which was thrown over the side of a boat and allowed to sink to the bottom, trapping the fish as the boat pulled the net through the water. Second were smaller nets and wicker baskets cast from a boat or from shore. Third were hook and line, thrown from the shore or from a boat. Harpoons (spears) were sometimes used, though probably less frequently than other methods of fishing.

The scriptures (particularly the New Testament) refer frequently to fishing—an indication of how important fishing was to the people of the 1st century. Many of Jesus' disciples made their living by fishing in the Sea of Galilee. In fact, Simon (Peter), Andrew, James, John, and other disciples who were fishermen must have been relatively well to do, for the scriptures seem to indicate that they were able to leave their boats and nets for long periods in order to follow after Jesus during his years of public ministry. Because the Sea of Galilee lies on the Via Maris, the ancient, heavily traveled trade road linking Egypt to the north and east, Galilean fishermen were readily able to trade their catches to traveling merchants, who would either consume the fish or pack them up for sale later. Perhaps it seems odd that Jesus, who was said to be a carpenter, would rely on fishermen to help spread his teachings, but he promised that they would be able to put their skills to good use, making them "fish for people" (Matthew 4:19 and Mark 1:17)—a phrase that has a double meaning, for they would proceed both to gather people and to "feed" those who hungered for the spiritual message they sought to impart.

BIBLICAL PASSAGE NOTES

To people living in the Western world, the concept of fish for breakfast might seem a bit unusual. Other than lox or perhaps a whitefish spread, or maybe a nice piece of salmon on a fresh bagel, fish is not usual morning menu fare. The current interest in sushi for almost any meal among many baby boomers notwithstanding, fish has traditionally been relegated in Western cultures to tuna fish salad for lunch, or fish sticks, fish and chips, or the likes of salmon steaks for dinner.

There does not seem to be any tradition, biblical or otherwise, that supports fish as a typical breakfast meal among the people of Jesus' day. The "anything" of verse 5 (in Greek, *prosfagion*) is an unusual word; it is used to describe a side dish to be eaten with bread, and in some contexts was the equivalent of meat or fish. That Jesus was preparing fish for the disciples to eat is probably more symbolic in nature than menu-related. (Fish was a symbol for early Christians, as the letters in the Greek word *ichthus* form an acrostic consisting of the first letters of an early confession of faith: *Jesus Christ, the Son of God.*) Yet taking the biblical passage at face value, this is what we know: the disciples were out fishing following the death and resurrection of Jesus when they spotted him on the nearby beach preparing a meal over a fire. As they returned to shore, he fed them with fish and bread, and it was by these actions that they were assured of who he was.

The meal took place at the Sea of Galilee, a large lake-like body of water that runs six miles wide and twelve miles long. It is fed by springs from three countries: Lebanon, Israel, and Syria, and today it provides nearly one-fourth of Israel's fresh-water supply. Israelis now refer to the Sea of Galilee as Yam Kinneret (the Gospel of John calls it the Sea of Tiberias, while the Gospel of Luke speaks of Lake Gennesaret). To this day, the Sea of Galilee supports a thriving fishing industry.

THE MENU

Grilled Mackerel on a Stick
Sweet Barbels

St. Peter's Fish with Parsley Sauce

Pistachio-Crusted Sunfish

Eggplant and Cheese Casserole (*Almodrote*)

Israeli Breakfast Salad

Manáish with Goat Cheese and Black Peppermint Tea

Campfire Cinnamon Coffee Cake

Galilean Sand Cake

THE PREPARATION

In this gospel account, the preparation of the fish by grilling, though seemingly primitive and foolproof, was actually neither. There was a technique involved that required some forethought and preparation. Perhaps Jesus knew of the tradition common among fishermen of cooking by *masguf* (roofing), a process whereby a fire is lit and the fish are hung on large sticks in an upright position at the edge of the flame, allowing them to roast slowly and without fear of burning. The result is a tender, tasty smoked fish; every part of the fish is used and consumed, head to tail. Or, as the biblical verse blandly reports, perhaps the fish were simply laid flat and cooked on a bed of coals.

The Sea of Galilee has had a reputation for good fishing since ancient times. What type of fish would Jesus and his disciples have eaten at daybreak on its shore? There are currently about eighteen different species that are known to inhabit the lake. Three of these types of fish were known in Jesus' day and sought after by fishermen: sardines, barbels, and musht. *Sardines* are endemic to the lake and are most likely the small fish mentioned in the Gospel of Matthew that Jesus used for the feeding of the five thousand. Today, when fishermen cast their nets at night in the Sea of Galilee during the height of the fishing season, tens of thousands of sardines are hauled in by morning. It is well known that these small fish, along with bread, were a staple among the local villagers of Galilee in the 1st century. *Barbels* are so called because of the barbs located at the corners of their mouths. They were very popular at feasts and for the Sabbath meals. Musht (*comb*) is more popularly known as "St. Peter's Fish." It has a long dorsal fin that looks like a comb and can grow to be 1½ feet long and weigh as much as 3½ pounds. During the winter, these tropical fish gather in the deeper shoals at the northern edge of the lake where there are warmer waters, created from the runoff of the springs from the hills of nearby Eremos. The congregation of large schools of musht allows for great fishing and nets filled to bursting. Perhaps it was here that Jesus, having spotted a multitude of fish, instructed Peter to cast his net, which allowed for the seemingly "miraculous" catch.

The Recipes

❧ *Grilled Mackerel on a Stick*

⅓ cup sunflower or sesame oil

juice of 3 limes

1 Tbsp. tarragon

1 tsp. salt

1 tsp. paprika

2 lb. fresh mackerel or sea bass, cut into 1"
    chunks

2 large onions, cut and separated into small
    wedges

12 small truffles

4 ripe tomatoes, cut into thirds

1 green pepper, cut in pieces

1 yellow pepper, cut in pieces

3 limes, cut in half

basmati rice and capers

lime juice

Concoct a spicy marinade of sesame oil, lime juice, tarragon, salt, and paprika. Place the fish chunks in a large dish and marinate in the refrigerator for at least 3 hours.

Skewer the fish, alternating with wedges of onion, tomato, truffle, and green and yellow pepper. Place over hot flame or coals, turning frequently, for about 6–8 minutes, being careful not to overcook the fish. Serve on a bed of basmati rice and capers, and sprinkle with lime juice squeezed by hand.

Yield: 8 servings

❧ *Sweet Barbels*

4 medium-sized barbels

½ pint port or sherry, or cooking wine

10 scallions, sliced

2 tsp. Balsamic or herb-flavored vinegar

a small bunch of fresh rosemary, lemon
    thyme, sage, and peppermint

½ cup fresh lemon juice

¼ tsp. sea salt

vegetables or bed of flavored bread crumbs

1 tsp. allspice

Plunge the barbels in cold water and let them sit for about 15 minutes. Next place the fish in a large pot of boiling salted water, cooking about 6–8 minutes. Remove the fish from the pot, taking care that they do not break into pieces. Pour out all but about one-third of the water in the pot and add the remaining ingredients (except the allspice) to the briny mixture. Do not allow the liquid to come to a boil; simmer slowly for about ½ hour.

Place a colander or large sieve over a second pot. Strain the soup, discarding the larger remnants of the herbs and spices. Carefully replace the fish into the mixture and heat gently, about 5–10 minutes, ensuring once again that the liquid does not come to a boil.

Remove fish from pot and serve with vegetables or on a bed of flavored bread crumbs; sprinkle with allspice.

Yield: 8 servings

❧ St. Peter's Fish with Parsley Sauce

In the Pacific regions or in small lakes in the United States, St. Peter's Fish are known by the name Tilapia *or, more often than not,* Sunfish. *This fish tends to absorb the flavor of the water it is raised in, so it is important to buy from a dependable market or grocer. But when prepared well it is a great crowd pleaser: firm, light, and slightly sweet without that oily or fishy aroma. It is best to prepare these fish by baking, broiling, steaming, or sautéing, making sure to avoid eating the skin, as it can leave a bitter taste.*

1 cup fresh parsley	3 Tbsp. flour
1 clove garlic, chopped	6 St. Peter's fish, bass, or trout, filleted
4 Tbsp. water	½ cup olive oil
juice of one lemon	3 Tbsp. onion, chopped
salt and pepper	

In a food processor, combine the parsley and the garlic with 2 Tbsp. of water and whir until the mixture is completely smooth. Thin the mixture with an additional 2 Tbsp. of water and mix well. Add the lemon juice and salt and pepper to taste. Set aside, covered.

On a flat plate combine about 2 Tbsp. flour with about ½ tsp. each of salt and pepper and mix well. Into this dip the fillets, coating well and shaking off the excess. In a large, heavy skillet, heat the oil and in this fry the fish until well browned on both sides. Transfer the fish to a preheated serving platter and set aside to keep warm.

Discard about half of the oil and in what remains sauté the onions until golden brown. Sprinkle in the remaining flour and over a low flame cook until the sauce is a light brown, stirring constantly. Add the parsley mixture and cook, continuing to stir, for 2–3 minutes longer. Pour the gravy over the fish and serve immediately.

Yield: 6 servings

Source: Recipe adapted from www.holiveoil.com/services.html

❧ Pistachio-Crusted Sunfish

2 cups pistachios (or almonds), finely chopped	4 eggs, well beaten
3 Tbsp. zaatar	1 stick butter, melted, or ½ cup sunflower
8 nice-sized sunfish	oil

Chop the nuts finely just short of a powder. (You can use a blender or a mini-food processor or do it the old-fashioned way, with a mallet in a sieved cloth). Place the nuts in a large bowl and quickly mix in the zaatar. Wash the fish in cold water; then dip them into the beaten eggs. Sprinkle the nut and zaatar mixture onto one side of the fish; then press it in to provide an ample coating. Fry the fish in melted butter or sunflower oil at a very high temperature, turning frequently so that they do not burn.

Yield: 8 servings

❧ *Eggplant and Cheese Casserole* (Almodrote)

4 eggplants

1 cup of creamy goat's milk cheese

1 cup of kashkaval or grated cheddar cheese

4 eggs, lightly beaten

¾ cup fresh bread crumbs or mashed potatoes

2 cloves garlic, minced

⅓ cup sunflower oil

½ tsp. salt

1 tsp. black pepper

shredded cheddar cheese

bits of fresh chopped parsley

Preheat the oven to 400°F and bake the eggplants whole on a large baking sheet for about 35–45 minutes. When they are cool enough to handle, peel them and discard the seed pockets. Squeeze out as much of the juice as possible and firmly mash with a wooden spoon.

In a separate bowl, mix the cheeses, bread crumbs, eggs, garlic, and 4 Tbsp. sunflower oil; then add the eggplant, stirring and mashing as you go along to make a lumpy paste. Fold out the mixture into a greased baking dish, and sprinkle with salt and pepper and a handful or two of shredded cheddar as a topping. Drizzle the remaining sunflower oil over the entire dish. Bake for approximately 50 minutes and serve hot, garnished with bits of fresh parsley.

Yield: 8 servings

❧ *Israeli Breakfast Salad*

2 large cucumbers, peeled and seeded

3 large ripe tomatoes

1 scallion

1 Tbsp. freshly squeezed lemon juice

2 Tbsp. olive oil

salt and pepper to taste

Chop cucumbers, tomatoes, and scallion very fine. Toss with dressing made with the rest of the ingredients. Chill and serve.

Yield: 4 servings

Source: Marian Maeve O'Brien, *The Bible Cookbook* (St. Louis: Bethany Press, 1958), 221.

❧ *Manáish with Goat Cheese and Black Peppermint Tea*

loaf of flat bread

½ cup (or more, if needed) olive oil

2 Tbsp. zaatar

2 Tbsp. sumac

goat cheese

black peppermint tea

Preheat oven to 300°F.

Cover a loaf of flat bread with olive oil. Sprinkle zaatar and sumac over the oil. Bake the bread for about 5 minutes or until lightly browned. Serve with a fresh, spreadable goat cheese and a pot of black peppermint tea.

Yield: 8–12 servings

❧ Campfire Cinnamon Coffee Cake

1 Tbsp. plus 2 tsp. prepared cinnamon-
    sugar

2 Tbsp. plus 2 tsp. butter or margarine

1 cup packaged biscuit mix

⅓ cup evaporated milk, undiluted

Mix together 5 tsp. of granulated white sugar with a small amount of cinnamon and set aside. Slice 2 Tbsp. butter into small pieces over the biscuit mix in a medium-sized bowl. Toss lightly with a fork until the butter is well-coated. Make a well in the center. Pour in the milk and 1 Tbsp. of the cinnamon-sugar mixture, stirring with a fork just until the mixture is moistened. Turn the dough into a lightly greased and floured 8" shiny, heavy skillet. With floured hands, pat down evenly into the skillet. Cook, covered, over a very low heat, about 12–15 minutes, or until a cake tester or wooden pick inserted in the center comes out clean. While still warm, spread 2 tsp. of butter or margarine over the cake. Sprinkle with 2 tsp. prepared cinnamon-sugar. Cut into quarters and serve warm.

Yield: 4 servings

Source: Campfire Cinnamon Coffee Cake recipe reprinted by permission of Razzle Dazzle Recipes (www.razzledazzlerecipes.com).

❧ Galilean Sand Cake

½ cup persimmons

1 cup sifted white flour

1 cup sifted cornstarch

2 tsp. baking powder

½ tsp. salt

1 cup butter or margarine, softened

1 cup granulated white sugar

2 Tbsp. Grand Marnier

8 eggs, separated

buttercream frosting with blanched almonds
    (optional)

Preheat the oven to 350°F.

Cook the persimmons in water until they boil and set aside; when cool, chop into small pieces. In a large bowl, sift together the flour, cornstarch, baking powder, and salt. In a separate large bowl, cream the butter, and slowly add the sugar until the mixture is light and airy. Mix in the persimmons and the Grand Marnier by hand; add the egg yolks one at a time, beating well after each. Continue beating, gradually adding in all the dry ingredients.

Beat the egg whites into peaks; gently fold into the batter. Turn into a greased 10″ funnel pan and bake for 45–50 minutes. Cool the cake in the pan on a rack for 5 minutes; then turn it out to cool on a large plate. Ice with a buttercream frosting mixed with blanched almonds, or serve as is.

Yield: 10–12 servings

❧ PART II ❧

The Lore of the Ingredients

Cross-references to other sections in Part II appear in **bold** type. Ingredients are listed alphabetically within each section.

Meats and Fish

Barbel

The barbel (*Barbus barbus*) is a slender, muscular, long-bodied (up to 35 inches and 15 pounds have been recorded) fish that is native to Europe, ranging as far north as Britain, as far south as Sicily, and as far east as Hungary. Some authorities assert that the barbel is also found in the Sea of Galilee. With a high dorsal fin, it has two pairs of sensory barbels (slender, whisker-like tactile organs) around its lips. These barbels give the fish its name, though other fish such as carp and catfish also have barbels. The fish is golden bronze on top, fading to a creamy white on the belly, with reddish-brown fins. Active mostly at dusk and during the night, the barbel is a bottom-living fish that prefers fast-flowing rivers and streams.

The barbel was a particularly popular eating fish during the early Renaissance era, though it used to be known as the pigfish, so named for the way it roots in riverbeds for food. It is less known now, except in Britain, which has angling societies dedicated exclusively to the barbel, as it is a strong fish that puts up a fierce fight when hooked.

Bass

"Bass" is the common name for a large number of both saltwater and freshwater fishes. These include the black sea bass (*Centropristis striata*), which ranges along the eastern coast of the United States; the giant sea bass (*Stereolepsis gigas*), which is native to the coast of California; the Chilean sea bass (*Dissostichus eleginoides*), which was previously known as the Patagonian toothfish; the largemouth bass (*Micropterus salmoides*), which inhabits North American rivers east of the Rocky Mountains; the smallmouth bass (*M. dolomieu*), which is also native to eastern North America; the striped bass (*Morone saxitilis*), which is sometimes called the rockfish and ranges along the eastern coast of the United States; and the Mediterranean sea bass (*Dicentrarchus labrax*), which is native to the Mediterranean Sea and the northeastern Atlantic Ocean but which also ventures into brackish lagoons. All of these bass are good game and fine food.

The Mediterranean sea bass is perhaps the oldest known, having been a favorite in the diet of the ancient Greeks. The ancient Romans referred to it as the "sea wolf," so known because of its voracity, and it is still called the sea wolf in French, Italian, and German. With firm, white flesh, it is a staple of Mediterranean cuisines. Often grilled or barbecued, it can also be baked, poached, broiled, sautéed, or steamed.

Sea bass is lower in cholesterol, fat, and calories than freshwater bass. As with most fish, bass is a good source of the B vitamins and vitamin D.

Beef

All domestic cattle (*Bos taurus*) are descended from *Bos primigenius*, the aurochs that prehistoric peoples painted onto cave walls. Cattle have long been domesticated and were known in ancient Egypt as early as 3500 B.C.E. and are often mentioned in the Bible, including the Ten Commandments (Exodus 20:10). The biblical patriarchs measured their wealth in numbers of cattle, and the consumption of beef often indicated special family celebrations. The same was true in ancient Greece, where cattle were so expensive that they were usually slaughtered only to create a special meal to honor dignitaries, heroes, or guests. Beef was the archetypal meat of medieval meals throughout Europe, and even when game was plentiful the inclusion of beef on the menu brought honor to guests and hosts alike. As beef became more affordable, the per capita consumption of beef in Europe continued to explode. By the 19th century, however, the per capita consumption of beef in the Americas surpassed that of Europe, and beef is today the most popular meat in the Americas. In fact, more beef is eaten than any other meat around the globe, despite the fact that religion forbids the eating of beef in India and among Hindu peoples (who consider the cow to be holy) and that it is generally too expensive in places like Japan. More than fifty breeds of cattle are now known throughout the world, and certain regions like Argentina, Australia, New Zealand, the United States, Canada, Europe, and even Japan are well known for the quality of their beef. Farmers have selectively bred cattle to increase their **milk** production, to improve their strength (so that they make better draft oxen), to make them more resistant to disease, to augment the amount of beef they carry, and to enhance the flavor of their meat.

Beef is a primary source of protein for many people. It is a good source of vitamin B12, calcium, sodium, and phosphorus. Beef has fallen out of favor among some groups because it tends to be high in cholesterol and fat; also, raising cattle requires an enormous expenditure of vegetable energy, and vegetarians say that it would be more healthful and energy efficient for people to raise and eat vegetables directly than to filter the energy through cattle.

The main cuts of beef include brisket (from the front part of the breast), chuck (from the shoulder, arm, and neck), flank (from just behind the belly), foreshank (from the forelegs), rib (from the ribs), round (from the rear hip section), short loin (from the loin area), short plate (from the rear of the breast), sirloin (from between the round and the short loin), and ground beef (from chuck, sirloin, or round). Each cut of beef may be prepared in particular ways, and around the world it has been roasted, broiled, stir-fried, marinated, tenderized, spiced, corned, salted, dried, and even boiled. Indeed, the ways of preparing and eating beef are limited only by the human imagination.

Given the long association between humans and cattle, it is not surprising that cows have taken on particular symbolic meanings. In the Chinese zodiac, people born in the year of the ox are said to be powerful and faithful, exhibiting good leadership traits and positive attitudes toward family and work. In America, a person who is very powerful is said to be "strong like a bull" or "strong as an ox."

Chicken

The domesticated chicken (*Gallus gallus*) is a descendant of wild Asian jungle fowl, first domesticated in India about 2000 B.C.E. for use in religious ceremonies and then for consumption. From India, domestication of the chicken spread to China and the Pacific islands and, by 1500 B.C.E., to central Europe. Chickens did not make their way to the eastern Mediterranean until about the 14th century B.C.E., and the earliest representation of a chicken was found in the tomb of Tutankhamun, pharaoh of ancient Egypt, dating from about 1350 B.C.E. Assyrian seals of the 8th century B.C.E. portray chickens, as does Corinthian pottery of the 7th century B.C.E., but there is no mention of chickens in the earliest translations of the Old Testament, though it is difficult to believe that the Israelites did not have domesticated chickens since their Egyptian neighbors did. The ancient Greeks and Romans ate lots of chicken **eggs** (but initially little chicken, as the birds were probably too tough and thin for good eating), and the Romans used chickens for auguries; but by the 2nd century B.C.E. the Romans were eating chicken, having learned from the Greeks on the island of Cos how to fatten poultry for the table. Chicken, especially capons (castrated roosters), were widely consumed in Europe during the Middle Ages. While Christopher Columbus probably introduced chickens to the Caribbean, they did not appear in North America until imported by the settlers of Jamestown and Plymouth in the 17th century. Today, chickens are raised almost everywhere in the world; of the domesticated animals, only the dog has a larger range. Chickens are the most common birds in the world, and their population tops the 25 billion mark.

Across the centuries, hundreds of varieties of chickens have been developed through selective breeding. Among the most common breeds are the Barred Rock, Barred Plymouth Rock, Cochin, Cornish, Leghorn, Red Cap, Rhode Island Red, Sussex, and Swiss Hen.

Chicken is an extremely versatile meat that can be broiled, fried, deep-fried, stir-fried, roasted, stewed, poached, steamed, and baked. It can also be used in soups and salads, can be added to pizzas, and is even processed into fast-food "chicken nuggets."

Compared with other meats, chicken is relatively low in cholesterol. It is low in fat unless eaten with the skin, and its dark meat has more fat and cholesterol than the light meat. Chicken provides vitamins B6 and B12, iron, magnesium, niacin, phosphorus, riboflavin, and zinc.

In recent years, animal-rights activists have protested the conditions under which most chickens are raised and have recommended that chickens not be raised in cages, pens, or coops but be allowed to range freely in large yards and scratch for their own food. This said, free-range chickens are no more nutritional than other chickens and are no less prone to salmonella contamination.

Given the long association between humans and chickens, it is not surprising that chickens have taken on certain symbolic meanings. In the Chinese zodiac, people born in the year of the rooster are said to be hard working and definite in their opinions.

Duck

"Duck" is the common name for a large number of birds, both wild and domesticated, of the *Anatidae* family (a family that also includes geese and swans). Mostly aquatic birds, ducks thrive in both salt- and fresh-water environments and can be classified into subfamilies as follows:

- Whistling ducks (*Dendrocygninae*)
- White-backed ducks (*Thalassorninae*)
- Freckled ducks (*Stictonettinae*)
- Shelducks, sheldgeese, and steamer ducks (*Tadorninae*)
- Dabbling and diving ducks (*Anatinae*), which include the wood ducks, widgeons, gadwalls, teals, pintails, mallards, shovelers, and mandarins
- Eiders, scoters, sawbills, and sea ducks (*Merginae*), which include harlequin ducks, goldeneyes, and mergansers
- Stiff-tail ducks (*Oxyurinae*), which include black-headed ducks

Ducks entered domestication relatively late, as wild ducks have been plentiful and easily hunted throughout human history—up until quite recently, anyway—and many people who enjoy eating duck prefer the taste of wild birds to that of domesticated ducks. The ancient Egyptians included duck in their diet long before they came to eat chicken, though these birds were probably wild. The Romans held ducks in net enclosures until they were needed for the table, but these again were probably captured in the wild. The ancient Chinese may have been the first to domesticate ducks—they were the first to artificially incubate duck eggs—though it might have been the Incas or the Aztecs who first accomplished this. Eating duck was popular in medieval and Renaissance Europe; duck was very inexpensive in Elizabethan England, but it is not certain that ducks were yet domesticated. In North America, ducks do not seem to have been domesticated until the end of the 19th century, when an entrepreneur imported several Peking ducks, the ancestors of millions of America's domestic ducks, now generally known as the white Pekin or Long Island duck.

Among the most flavorful ducks for the table are the gadwalls of England, the Rouens and Nantais of France, the Pekins of the United States, and the teals, mallards, pintails, widgeons, and canvasbacks internationally.

Duck is generally high in calories, fat, and cholesterol. It does provide significant amounts of vitamins B6 and B12, copper, vitamin E, iron, niacin, phosphorous, riboflavin, thiamin, and zinc. Duck may be roasted, broiled, and grilled or may be stuffed or marinated before cooking. As most of the duck fat resides in the skin, it should be removed before eating (but after cooking).

Duck eggs are also delicious, prepared as any other **eggs**, and ducks provide feathers and down for many domestic products.

Goat

Native to much of Eurasia and Africa, goats were among the first domesticated animals, probably coming under human care in the mountains of Iran as early as 8000 B.C.E. at about the same time as **sheep**. In the wild, goats thrive in difficult conditions, from arid scrublands to cold and rocky mountain regions, and it was easy for early nomadic herders to care for herds of goats. The recognized species of goats include:

- Wild goat (*Capra aegagrus*), of which the domestic goat is a subspecies (*C. aegagrus hircus*) and the Angora goat (from which mohair is taken) is a variety
- West Caucasian tur (*C. caucasia*)
- East Caucasian tur (*C. cylindricomis*)
- Cashmere goat (*C. hircus*)
- Markhor (*C. falconeri*), of which there are 4 subspecies
- Alpine ibex (*C. ibex*), of which the Nubian ibex and the Asiatic ibex are subspecies
- Spanish ibex (*C. pyrenaica*), of which the Pyrennean and Portuguese ibex are subspecies
- Walia ibex (*C. walie*)

From earliest times, even before domestication, humans hunted or trapped goats for their skins and meat. After domestication, people also began to milk the nanny (female) goats, using the **milk** as a beverage and as the base for cheeses and other milk products. Goat hair, such as that from cashmere and Angora goats, has been spun into thread or yarn and used to make sweaters, hats, gloves, and other items. Goat skins have been tanned and made into gloves and other clothes and have even been used as wine or water containers and as writing parchment. People still consume goat's milk and meat, though more commonly in the developing world than in the developed. Confusion sometimes results because some peoples refer to goat's meat as "mutton" or "lamb," words more frequently used for sheep's or **lamb**'s meat. Over the centuries, livestock herders have selectively bred varieties of goats for specific purposes: for their meat, their milk, their wool, and as pets.

Goat's meat, sometimes known as chevon, is thought by some to be like **veal** and by others like **venison**, though as with other animals, the age of the goat often determines the flavor and texture. Goat's meat is comparable to chicken in its fat and cholesterol content and is definitely healthier than mutton. People have been stewing, baking, grilling, barbecuing, mincing, canning, and stuffing goat's meat for millennia, and there is an incredible variety of recipes for goat's meat from the Middle East, Asia, and Africa. Certain cultures even consider goats' brains, livers, heads, and legs as delicacies. Because the meat can sometimes be tough, tenderizing and marinating can make it even more delectable.

Goat's milk has long been known to be more easily digested by humans than cow's milk, and infants usually do much better with goat's milk than cow's. The reason is that goat's milk has much smaller curd and lacks the protein agglutinin present in cow's milk. An average dairy doe (female) can produce about 6 pounds of milk per day. Goat's milk does not have an offensive flavor, though sometimes the scent from the billy goats can rub off on the nannies and taint the milk.

As with sheep, goats do not need to be killed in order to have their wool harvested but can be sheared, in the case of Angora goats, or combed, in the case of cashmeres. The cashmere goat has been selectively bred so that its coat consists of a higher proportion of the fine, soft fibers that grow close to the skin and a much lower proportion of guard hairs. The Angora goat has been bred to grow long, curling locks of mohair, with no guard hairs. Although a single goat produces less wool than a single sheep, goat's wool is warmer than sheep's and is not scratchy or allergenic.

Intelligent and curious, goats sometimes seem individualistic and do make lively pets, but they are also suitable herding animals. Contrary to myth, goats do not eat everything they encounter; they do tend to chew on almost anything, but they consume weeds and shrubs and almost any plant.

Because of their long association with human society, a large body of folklore has developed around goats. In Norse mythology, goats pulled the chariot of Thor, the god of thunder; though he would eat them at night, they reappeared each morning. The twelve-year Chinese zodiac features the goat (or sheep) as one of its annual symbolic animals; people born in the year of the goat are said to be creative, perfectionist, and introverted. In the Western zodiacal system, the sign of Capricorn is a goat with a fish's tail. Goats are frequently mentioned in the Bible (Genesis 15:9, 38:17; Numbers 15:27; etc.).

Interestingly, in the Middle Ages, Christians linked goats with the devil, believing that goats spoke lewd thoughts into the ears of saintly people, and the devil was often portrayed with the face of a goat, horns, and a "goatee." Black masses were thought to center on dark-colored goats, believed to be manifestations of Satan. Even today, some Christians believe the pentagram, the symbol of Wicca, depicts a goat's head and thus indicates (erroneously) a connection between Wicca and Satanism.

Herring

Herring include the two hundred or so species of the *Clupea* genus of fish. Most are native to the northern Atlantic Ocean, though some species inhabit the Baltic Sea. The most common are the Atlantic (or English) herring (*C. harengus*), which can reach a length of 18 inches and a weight of 1.5 pounds, and which are found from the northern limits of the Atlantic as far south as France and the Chesapeake Bay. The Pacific herring (*C. pallasi*) is common from Siberia to Japan and from Alaska to northern Mexico; some biologists consider the Pacific herring to be the same fish as the Atlantic species.

Prehistoric peoples of northern Europe fished for and ate herring either raw or cooked. Perhaps as early as the 3rd century B.C.E., herring began to be fermented, pickled, or otherwise cured for longer storage. Although herring does not air dry as well as cod, having too much oily fat, it does respond deliciously to smoking, and smoked herring became a luxury of the European diet by the 12th century C.E. and a staple of the diet of the poorer classes by the 13th. People also began salting herring to preserve it. Herring was perhaps the main product that led to the fortunes of the Hanseatic League, an alliance that monopolized trade in northern Europe and the Baltic region between the 13th and 17th centuries. The French were the first to grow wealthy on herring fishery, in the 12th century, followed by the Danes in the 13th–14th, the Dutch in the 15th, and the English in the 17th. Although the English continue to maintain a lead in herring fishing today, many fishery experts believe that herring has been overfished and may not be far behind cod in being nearly fished out.

Among the fishes, herring is relatively high in calories, fat, and cholesterol.

The ways of preparing herring for consumption have not changed much over the centuries. Pickled herring, very popular in Scandinavia, is made by cutting the fish into fillets and placing them in a solution of **vinegar, salt, sugar,** peppercorn, **bay leaves,** and raw **onions.** Some variations on herring preparation include the Dutch *maatjes* ("little girls") herring, which are made from immature herring cured lightly in sugar; the German *Bismarck* herring, which is pickled in vinegar with onions; English kippers (split or filleted herring) and bloaters (whole herring), which are salted and smoked cold; and German-Jewish *schmaltz* (fat) herring, which is served in sour **cream** sauce. Some cooks make rollmops from pickled herring, wrapping the fish around a piece of pickled **cucumber;** traditionally, rollmops were made of raw herring fillets encasing **shallots, capers,** and gherkins, then immersed in a solution of **wine vinegar, mustard** seed, and peppercorns. Herring can also be used to make soup, can be fermented to make the Swedish *surströmming,* and can be canned for much longer shelf life.

Lamb

"Lamb" is sometimes used to refer to the meat of both young sheep and young **goats,** but most often, "lamb" means the meat of young sheep; "mutton" is the word used for the meat of mature sheep. Domestic sheep (*Ovis aries*) are the most numerous mammalian livestock in the world, probably descended from the wild moufflon (sometimes called urial; *O. orientalis*) of south-central and southwestern Asia or from the European moufflon (*O. musimon*) of Sardinia, Corsica, and western Asia, especially Turkey and southern Iran; domestic sheep may also be a hybrid of these moufflons or a hybrid with other species. Domestication of sheep occurred so long ago (approximately 8000 B.C.E.) that there are no historic records, so scientists have been looking to the new science of DNA analysis to slowly piece together the lineage of the domestic sheep. Other species of sheep, such as the following, may also have contributed to the genetic makeup of the modern domestic sheep:

- Argali (*O. ammon*)
- Bighorn sheep (*O. Canadensis*)
- Thinhorn sheep (*O. dalli*)
- Snow sheep (*O. nivicola*)

Over the centuries, sheepherders have selectively bred their sheep for particular purposes, developing breeds that are sheared for their wool, breeds that are eaten, and breeds that provide both wool and meat. Among the breeds raised for their wool are the Merino, Rambouillet, and Lincoln. Those raised for meat include the Suffolk, Hampshire, Dorset, Columbia, and Texel. One dual-use breed is the Corriedale. Certain sheep are also raised for their **milk,** which serves as a beverage and as the raw material for **sheep's cheese** and **yogurt.** In general, raising sheep is a highly efficient endeavor, for a single sheep can return up to 400 percent on investment. Today, sheepherding is extremely important economically in Australia, New Zealand, Uruguay, and Sardinia and is significant economically in England, Wales, Ireland, and the United States.

Lamb's meat, from animals that are less than a year old, is generally considered a tender delicacy and appears frequently in recipes from the Mediterranean, the Middle East, and southern Asia. Lamb is very high in vitamin B12, iron, niacin, phosphorus, riboflavin, and zinc and provides significant amounts of vitamin B6, folacin, potassium, and thiamin. Generally high in calories and cholesterol, lamb is also high in protein. Mutton, which is much less available in the developed world than lamb, has a stronger flavor but can be tougher and fattier.

To prepare lamb for cooking, the fat should be trimmed off. Otherwise, there is no need for tenderizing, as the meat is naturally tender. Roasting, grilling, and broiling are favorite methods of cooking lamb, although poaching and braising or stewing are common. Lamb can also be used in soups and curries, and ground lamb sometimes substitutes for ground **beef** or **turkey**. Many different herbs and spices are used to add flavoring, as are marinades, depending on the cultural background of the cooks who prepare it.

Because of the sheep's long association with human society, a large body of folklore has developed around them. Sheepherding is important both historically and symbolically in Judaism and Christianity. Abraham, Jacob, Moses, and King David all worked as shepherds. The Jewish Passover meal features lamb as the main course, and the Jewish prophets tell of the wolf and the lamb lying together peacefully in the Promised Land (Isaiah 11:6). Christians refer to Christ as the Good Shepherd and as the sacrificial Lamb of God. Orthodox Christians prepare a meal of Paschal lamb for Easter. In the Chinese zodiac, the sheep (or goat) is associated with artistic and introverted personality traits. In the Western zodiacal system, the sign of Aries is a ram (male sheep).

Sheep are more intelligent than most would believe. Sheep do, however, possess strong flocking behavior. Such behavior benefits nonpredatory animals, as the strongest individuals force their way to the center of the flock and there find greater protection from predators.

Locust

The name "locust" refers to the swarming phase of grasshoppers of the *Acrididae* family. Briefly, short-horned grasshoppers are locusts when they form into large swarms and completely consume and destroy the vegetation of an area. There are several species, the most widespread being the desert locust (*Schistocerca gregaria*), which is native to northern Africa, the Middle East, and the Indian subcontinent. It migrates across vast distances and is most probably the locust species said to have swarmed across Egypt during the plagues that God sent to Pharaoh to convince the ruler of Egypt to let the Israelites go free (Exodus 10:4).

Many cultures around the world consider grasshoppers and other insects as delicacies of the palate. Grasshoppers can be washed and roasted until they are crispy. They can then be ground into **flour**, which is used in baking; cut into pieces; or eaten whole. Grasshoppers provide calcium, iron, and some protein.

Mackerel

As with many fishes, "mackerel" is the common name that can refer to a large number of species that live in all tropical and temperate oceans and bays. These include the Atlantic mackerel, Atlantic Spanish mackerel, blue mackerel, broad-barred king mackerel, chub mackerel, Australian spotted mackerel, double-lined mackerel, Indian mackerel, Indo-Pacific king mackerel, Island mackerel, Japanese-Spanish mackerel, king mackerel, Spanish mackerel, streaked Spanish mackerel, and spotted Spanish mackerel of the *Scombridae* family; the Atlantic horse mackerel, blue jack mackerel, Cape horse mackerel, Cunene horse mackerel, greenback horse mackerel, Japanese horse mackerel, Mediterranean horse mackerel, and jack mackerel of the *Trachuridae* family; the Okhostk Atka mackerel and Atka mackerel of the *Hexagrammidae* family; the black snake mackerel, blacksail snake mackerel, snake mackerel, violet snake mackerel, and white snake mackerel of the *Gempylidae* family; and additional species known simply as mackerel, such as bigeye scad, blue runner, butterfly kingfish, cero, and leatherjack.

The king mackerel (*Scomberomorus cavalla*) is the largest species, growing to a length of 5 feet or more. It inhabits the subtropical waters of the western Atlantic Ocean and the Gulf of Mexico and is silver-to-gray in color with green and purple iridescence. All mackerels are slim, cylindrical fish with razor-sharp teeth that feed on smaller fish and squid. They are prized for their tasty meat and their fighting ability and are important commercial and game fish.

Generally, mackerel is very high in calories and fat and high in cholesterol, potassium, phosphorous, and vitamins D and B12. It is an oily fish, with an outer layer of red meat and a lighter interior meat. Mackerel spoils very quickly, so shoppers must carefully select the freshest fish. Mackerel is usually poached, baked, or broiled, and a citrus or vinegar marinade helps temper the richness of its taste. It is also salted, smoked, canned, and frozen for longer shelf-life.

It is possible that the ocean-going peoples of the Bible were familiar with mackerel. Mackerel remains have been discovered in Stone Age archaeological sites (such as those at Site #3 in present-day Kuwait), and the ancient Romans prized a certain seasoning, *garum,* sometimes made from decomposing mackerel.

Mullet

There are two fish families that have come to be known as mullet: the red mullet, of the genus *Mullus,* and the gray mullet, of the genus *Mugil.* Some biologists consider the gray mullet to be the only true mullet; others refer to both families as mullets.

The red mullet family consists of about forty species, most of which are native to the Indo-Pacific tropics and subtropics, but two of which inhabit the Mediterranean. The most important of these latter, the striped mullet (*Mullus surmuletus*), also ranges into the Atlantic Ocean as far north as England. Both the ancient Greeks and Romans thought red mullet a fine fish: the Greeks dedicated it to Hecate, goddess of witchcraft and magic, but the Romans esteemed it so highly that it became a priceless commodity, and a single fish was known to sell for the same price as four yoke of oxen. Red mullet are generally considered much tastier than gray, with dry, firm, flaky flesh and a gamey taste.

The gray mullet family consists of about one hundred species, which inhabit most of the world's tropical and temperate waters. Remarkably, many gray mullet can move easily from salt to fresh water and back. Larger than the red, the gray mullet can reach 12 pounds in weight and is flavorful, with white, light flesh.

Mullet is delicious when baked, broiled, grilled, and sautéed. Among the fishes, it has a fair number of calories and a relatively high level of cholesterol.

Perch

The perch is a freshwater fish that is somewhat bony but quite prized for its delectable flavor. There are three species: the yellow perch (*Perca flavescens*), native to North America; the river or European perch (*P. fluviatilis*), which is found in Europe and northern Asia; and the Balkhash perch (*P. schrenkii*), which inhabits Lakes Balkhash and Alakol in Kazakhstan. Yellow perch can grow to 10 inches in length and can weigh up to 2 pounds, somewhat smaller than their relatives, which can reach lengths of 23 inches and weigh in at 5 pounds.

Humans have been fishing for and eating perch since prehistory, and both the Gauls and the ancient Romans highly esteemed the fish. In the Middle Ages, when feudal lords and monasteries owned the fishing rights to most inland waters, perch were not readily accessible to the general population in Europe, but when fishing became open again, common anglers avidly sought perch by line and by net. In North America, Native Americans took advantage of the availability of yellow perch, which are relatively easy to catch, because they travel in schools when young and become solitary only when they are older.

Perch have firm, flaky-white flesh that, compared with that of other fish, is low in calories but very high in cholesterol. Preparation includes sautéeing, baking, broiling, and poaching.

Quail

"Quail" is a collective name referring to a number of small- to mid-size birds, often in the Pheasant family, and are usually divided into Old World (Europe, the Middle East, and Asia) and New World (the Americas) quail. The common quail (*Coturnix coturnix*) is the best known of the Old World species, though there are at least another dozen related birds. In the Americas, the favorite is the northern bobwhite (*Colinus virginianus*), but another thirty-some species are also commonly referred to as quail.

In general, quail are not migratory birds, and they prefer to run from danger rather than fly away. Consequently, they do not have the dark meat associated with strong-flying birds but instead have large, white-fleshed muscles that have more flavor than those of barnyard birds. Nowadays, quail are not commonly found on the table but are much appreciated when they are, and quail **eggs** are prized as a delicacy and are often used in making sushi.

Quail are important in the story of the Israelites' escape from Egypt. As related in the book of Exodus (16:1–16), God sent quail in the evening and manna in the morning to keep the people from starving in the desert. The story told in the book of Numbers (11:4–34) is slightly different: although the quail appeared as promised, God became angry with the greed of the people and struck them with a deadly plague before they could even finish their meal.

Although the Israelites would not have known, there may be a natural explanation for why so many of them died while eating quail: the birds find the seeds of certain poisonous plants, such as hemlock, a delicious treat, and while the poison does not hurt the quail, it can remain in their tissues for a time and can be swiftly fatal to anyone who eats the flesh while it is still contaminated.

St. Peter's Fish

St. Peter's fish is usually known as tilapia, of which there are more than a dozen species. The species usually referred to as St. Peter's fish is *Tilapia galilaea,* which according to tradition is the fish Jesus used in the miracle of the loaves and fishes (Matthew 14:13–22; Mark 6:30–44; Luke 9:10–17; John 6:8–13). Other traditions hold that the miraculous draught of fishes referred to in the New Testament (John 21:6) is tilapia, which have a habit of gathering in immense schools in the early morning. Also known as the Wonder Fish (for biblical reasons) and the Nile perch (because the ancient Egyptians recorded tilapia aquaculture [fish farming]), St. Peter's fish have a long and important history in human cuisine and have been taken from their native African/Middle Eastern habitat and introduced around the world.

Vegetarians themselves, tilapia convert a greater proportion of their feed into growth than most other fish species and so grow very rapidly. Native to warm waters, they can thrive in salt, brackish, or fresh water and are very disease resistant. They also reproduce year-round.

Tilapia are a high source of protein with an excellent flavor.

A relative of St. Peter's fish, the Taiwan tilapia (a hybrid of the Mozambique [*T. mossambica*] and the Nile [*T. nilotica*] varieties), was the first fish sent into outer space, selected by NASA scientists because of the species' hardiness.

Sardine

"Sardine" is a name used to refer to any of a number of small oily fish, and the use of the name varies from region to region. Some people consider the European pilchard (*Sardina pilchardus*) to be the true sardine; others, the **herring**. Among those fishes also called sardines are the rainbow sardine (*Dussumieria acuta*) and slender rainbow sardine (*D. elopsoides*), the slender white sardine (*Escualosa elongata*) and white sardine (*E. thoracata*), the round sardinella (also known as the gilt sardine or Spanish sardine: *Sardinella aurita*), and the South American pilchard (also known as the Pacific sardine, the California sardine, the Chilean sardine, and the South African sardine: *Sardinops sagax*). In common usage, "sardines" are any fish that is available in tins.

Sausage

The word "sausage" refers to any mixture of ground-up meat and other animal parts, herbs, and spices, stuffed into a casing (often the intestines of animals) and preserved. The making of sausage perhaps dates from the time of ancient Sumeria

(3000 B.C.E.), and the *Odyssey* (c. 8th century B.C.E.) mentions a type of blood sausage. The Chinese were recording the making of sausage by the 6th century B.C.E., and sausage was a popular dish for the ancient Roman Lupercalia Festival. The early Roman Catholic Church banned the festival and made sausage-eating a sin, so Emperor Constantine (4th century C.E.) outlawed the making of sausages. Yet sausages never really disappeared, as they are an efficient way of preparing the edible but not necessarily attractive parts of animals.

In the United States, sausages are usually classified as cooked, cooked-smoked, fresh-smoked, fresh, or dry. Hot dogs, wieners, kielbasa, mortadella, braun-schweiger, pepperoni, and salami are all types of sausages. Today, cellulose, collagen, and even plastic are often used instead of intestinal casings.

Sea Bass

Sea basses are the saltwater varieties of the bass fishes. See **bass**.

Sole

As with many of the fishes, there is great confusion in the naming of the flatfishes, of which the soles are a family. Some people refer to flounders as soles, and vice versa. It may be simpler to refer to them all as flatfishes, with flounders and soles being of different families.

The flatfish constitute the order *Pleuronectiformes,* and their name comes from the Greek word for "side-swimmers," for that is just what they are: these fish have evolved to lie flat on the ocean bottom, hiding or sometimes burying themselves in the sand or debris. Some species lie on their left side, some on their right, and others are not particular. During development, the eye on the "bottom" side migrates to the other side so that both eyes are located on the "top" side of the mature fish; simultaneously, the mouth distorts itself so that most of its opening ends up on the "bottom" side. Many of the flatfishes can change color to blend in with their environment. Among the more than four hundred species of flatfish are such important food fishes as turbot, plaice, halibut, the Dover sole, and, of course, flounder and other types of sole. In general, the soles belong to the suborder *Soleoidei* (the families are *Soleidae, Achiridae,* and *Cynoglossidae*), and the flounders to the suborder *Pleuronectoidei* (the families are *Citharidae, Scophthalmidae, Bothidae, Pleuronectidae, Paralichthyidae, Achiropsettidae,* and *Samaridae*).

Flounders live in the oceans of northern Europe and eastern North America and along the coasts of the northern Pacific Ocean. The common flounder is *Platichthys flesus.* Other types of flounder include the summer flounder (also called fluke: *Platichthys dentatus*), the winter flounder (also called blackback, rusty brown, or red-spotted flounder: *Pseudopleuronectes americanus*), the yellowtail flounder (also called rusty dab: *Limanda ferruginea*), the dab (or sand dab: *Hippoglossoides platessoides*), the dusky olive southern flounder (*Paralichthys lethostigmus*), the Gulf flounder (*Platichthys albiguttus*), the gray sole (*Glytocephalus cynoglossus*), and the naked sole (*Gymnarchirus williamsoni*). Growing to about 15 inches in length, flounder feed on mussels, insects, and the spawn of other fish. Extremely low in fat and calories, though average in cholesterol, flounder can be broiled, sautéed, stuffed, baked, or steamed. Sometimes flounder is sold mistakenly as lemon sole, gray sole, petrale sole, rex sole, or Dover sole.

True soles inhabit both salt and fresh water, eating small crustaceans and other invertebrates. The true Dover sole is *Solea solea*.

Halibuts (of the genus *Hippoglossus*), which are native to the northern Pacific and northern Atlantic Oceans, are among the largest of the flatfishes and can often reach lengths of 8 feet and weights of 500 pounds, though specimens of 12 feet and 700 pounds have been caught; they feed on octopi, crabs, salmon, and lampreys. In the Pacific, *H. stenolepis* is a common halibut. Halibut fillets are delicious poached, baked, broiled, or sautéed. Among the fishes, halibut are about average in their caloric and cholesterol content but are low in fat.

Plaice (*Pleuronectes platessa*) are fish of the North and Irish Seas. The preferred fish for making fish and chips, they are often classed with the flounders.

If one is confused about what to use when a recipe calls for sole (or flounder, halibut, turbot, or plaice), take heart: the tastes of all of these fish are very similar, mild to bland in general, with the ability to pick up the flavors of the foods with which they are cooked.

Sunfish

"Sunfish" is the common name for a very large number of unrelated fishes. There are the ocean sunfish (*Mola mola*), a pelagic (oceangoing) fish, the largest bony fish in the world; the moonfishes (order *Perciformes*), which include about 40 percent of all fish; the common sunfishes of the *Lepomis* genus, which are fresh-water fishes; and the opah, of the *Lampris* genus. The opah are the sunfish thought to have possibly been part of the diet of certain oceangoing peoples of the Bible.

The opah—which are also known as kingfish, Jerusalem haddock, and moonfish (yes, it is confusing)—are oceangoing and occur in two species: *L. guttatus*, which may grow to a length of 6 feet or more and reach 200 pounds; and *L. immaculatus*, which is smaller, reaching about 3 feet in length. The smaller opah resides in the southern hemisphere; the larger ranges around the world's major oceans, primarily in the northern hemisphere, and the Mediterranean.

Opah are thin and disc-shaped fish with a steely blue body grading to lighter blue on the belly, with white spots on the sides and reddish fins. Generally solitary, they feed on deep-ocean squid and smaller fish. In turn, they are eaten by great white and mako sharks.

Opah is often prepared for sashimi (a type of sushi). It is also baked, broiled, poached, steamed, and smoked and has a moderate, pleasant flavor.

Trout

"Trout" is the common name for a number of species of freshwater fish of the Salmon family. These include the Adriatic, brown, Marmorata, flathead, ohrid, and sevan trout of the *Salmo* genus; the Apache, cutthroat, Gila, golden, and rainbow trout of the *Oncorhynchus* genus; and the brook, bull, Dolly Varden, lake, and silver trout of the *Salvelinus* genus. Trout inhabit cool, clear streams and lakes and are native to North America, Europe, and northern Asia. They have been introduced to Australia and other regions. Trout may have been known to the peoples of the Bible as they are present today in the Hermon River; the ancient Romans probably encountered trout in Gaul, the Germanic lands, and the British Isles. Of course, trout were an important staple of the Native North American peoples. Some trout spend their adult lives in the ocean and return to their birth streams to spawn (lay eggs) and die. Because of heavy recreational fishing, trout are now often raised in farms and released into the most popular fishing streams.

Trout can vary from 1 foot to 3 feet in length, and the largest can weigh up to 60 pounds. They are somewhat bony but very tasty, and recreational anglers highly prize trout because of the fierce fight they exhibit. Fly fishing is the preferred method of trout fishing for recreational anglers.

Trout can be relatively high in calories and cholesterol. They are very rich in vitamin B12 and contain large amounts of niacin, phosphorous, vitamin B6, and sodium. Often broiled, they are also tasty when poached, steamed, and smoked.

Tuna

As with many fish, the name "tuna" is the common name for a number of species of large saltwater fish. In general, tuna are fast-swimming fish; to help them achieve their speed, their blood has the capacity to carry more oxygen than that of other fish, and this capacity gives tuna its pink flesh (the flesh of most ocean fish is white). Some larger tuna species can increase their blood temperature above that of the surrounding water through fast swimming, and a few tuna species are even warm-blooded; but they do prefer colder waters. Tuna also need to swim to survive, to keep their blood oxygenated by moving large amounts of water past their gills; some tuna can even achieve speeds of 45 miles per hour.

The most common species of tuna are:

- Bluefin, which includes northern bluefin (*Thunnus thynnus*), southern bluefin (*T. maccoyii*), and Pacific bluefin (*T. orientalis*). The northern bluefin is native to the Atlantic Ocean and Mediterranean Sea and is often found in the Black Sea. It is a very important food fish and is also cultivated off the coast of Japan for sushi. It can reach 6 feet or more in length and 1,100 pounds in weight; the largest ever recorded was 1,500 pounds. These fish can live up to thirty years; they don't start to reproduce until five years of age and don't reach full reproductive maturity until they are thirteen or fourteen years old. The fastest swimmers, bluefin tuna have the reddest flesh and are sometimes referred to as the red tuna. Overfishing has endangered the populations of bluefin tunas as smaller and younger fish are being taken and fewer are reaching reproductive maturity.
- Yellowfin (*T. albacares*). This tuna can weigh up to 45 pounds and is often called the light-meat tuna.

- Albacore (also known as the long-finned albacore, the white tuna, and the germon: *T. alalunga*). This tuna inhabits both the Pacific and Atlantic Oceans. Albacore can reach lengths of 4 feet and weights of 65 pounds. It is the only tuna that can be labeled as white meat.
- Bigeye
- Longtail (*T. tonggol*)

Other fish that are also called "tuna" include:

- Skipjack tuna (*Katsuwonus pelamis*), which is also a light-meat tuna and grows to 3 feet and 15 pounds. It prefers open ocean and rarely enters the Mediterranean.
- Slender tuna (*Allothunnus fallai*)
- Bullet tuna (*Auxis rochei rochei*)
- Frigate tuna (*Auxis thazard thazard*)
- Kawakawa (also known as little tuna or mackerel tuna: *Euthynnus affinis*)
- Little tunny (also known as little tuna: *E. alletteratus*), which has markings on its back that look like writing—thus its binomial. It can grow to 3 feet in length.
- Butterfly kingfish (also known as butterfly tuna: *Gasterochisma melampus*)
- Dogtooth tuna (*Gymnosarda unicolor*)

Humans have been catching and eating tuna since prehistoric times, and tuna bones have been found in European archaeological sites dating from before the Iron Age (c. 4000 B.C.E.). The ancient Greeks honored tuna and dedicated it to Artemis, the goddess of the hunt. Both the wealthy and the poor ate tuna, the former having flavored it with spices and herbs, the latter having purchased it salted, as it was the least expensive fish available. The Greeks also preserved tuna in oil, as modern canneries often do today. Tuna was a favorite of the ancient Romans, for whom the fish's fermented intestines were used to make a delectable seasoning called *garum* (which could also be made from mackerel). During the Middle Ages, herring and cod supplanted tuna in the common diet, and consumption of tuna remained below that of herring and cod until quite recently, when the fisheries of the latter began to give out and tuna began to fill the increasing demand for fish.

In general, tuna is high in calories, fat, sodium, and cholesterol; it also provides significant amounts of potassium, vitamin A, iron, thiamin, riboflavin, niacin, vitamins B6 and B12, phosphorus, magnesium, zinc, and copper.

In the developed world, tuna is available fresh, frozen, and canned (either in oil or in water). Canned tuna is easily made into tuna salads, with the addition of **mayonnaise** or **yogurt** and fruit juices and spices. Fresh or frozen tuna can be grilled, broiled, barbecued, baked, or even fried; added to salads; made into chowders or fish stews; or used in a fish dip.

Because tuna are predators and are high in the ocean's food chain, certain heavy metals (such as mercury) can accumulate in their flesh; consequently, women who are pregnant or nursing and children are often advised to avoid tuna.

Turkey

There are two species of turkeys, and both are natives of the Americas: the wild turkey (*Meleagris gallopavo*) is indigenous to North America and probably originated in Mexico; the ocellated turkey (*M. ocellata*) is native to Central America. The Mayan people of Central America probably domesticated the ocellated turkey by about 1000 B.C.E. The Aztecs, who came to prominence in Mexico in the 14th century C.E., may have domesticated the wild turkey, or these turkeys may have been domesticated by earlier civilizations. At any rate, the modern domesticated turkey is descended from the wild turkey, whose range now spreads from Mexico north and east to the Atlantic Coast of New England. Wild turkeys live in flocks in open forests; they may grow to 4 feet in height and 30 pounds in weight; the males have a very distinctive fan-shaped tail and a so-called beard. The English colonists in Massachusetts and Virginia probably never had to think about domesticating turkeys themselves, as the woods were full of wild birds easily trapped, snared, or shot. Spanish colonists probably brought turkeys to Europe from Mexico in the 16th century, and the birds were soon known in France, England, and Germany. Turkey would not have been known to the peoples of the Bible. Surprisingly, the English mistakenly believed that the birds actually came from the land known as Turkey; and nearly everyone else in Europe thought that turkeys came from India. Consequently, many European languages, as well as Arabic and Hebrew, came to refer to the turkey as the bird of India.

According to American folklore, the pilgrims feasted on turkey at the first Thanksgiving meal. Some historians dispute the inclusion of turkey on that menu. Nevertheless, turkey has become the traditional centerpiece of most U.S. Thanksgiving celebrations. The turkey became so quickly integrated into U.S. culture that Benjamin Franklin proposed it as the national symbol, proclaiming it to be a much nobler bird than the eagle. Turkey is also a traditional food of modern Purim celebrations.

Though there are still wild turkeys in North America, and though they have made a remarkable recovery in the last few decades, having been hunted or chased from their habitat to near extinction, most turkeys that now make their way to the dinner table come from turkey farms. Turkeys are raised for their meat, though even into the 1920s and 1930s most turkeys were raised for their feathers. Native Americans had prized turkey plumage as ornamentation, and European immigrants coveted the feathers for pillows, comforters, mattresses, and other bedding. Turkey feathers were also made into feather dusters.

Turkey flesh is extremely low in fat and calories; almost all the fat is located in the skin. Turkey meat is an excellent source of niacin, vitamins B6 and B12, phosphorus, iron, zinc, riboflavin, and magnesium. Nowadays, turkeys are classified according to how they can be prepared:

- Fryers/roasters are small (5 to 9 pounds) and are slaughtered when young and tender; they can be roasted, broiled, or grilled.
- Hens (females) are medium-sized (8 to 18 pounds) and can be roasted, broiled, or grilled.
- Toms (males) are slightly larger, up to 24 pounds, and can be roasted, broiled, or grilled.
- Mature hens or toms are older turkeys (older than about 8 months) and can be stewed or poached.
- Turkey parts are sections of the turkey, such as breasts, breast steaks, cutlets, tenderloins, thighs, drumsticks, and wings.
- Ground turkey can be used in place of ground beef, though it may require more seasoning.

Many turkeys are sold frozen, for extended storage. Once thawed, turkey should be cooked within twenty-four hours. Turkeys are often stuffed before cooking with **bread, rice**, nuts, fruit, meat, or other stuffings; these should be added just before cooking, and it is important that the stuffing (as well as the turkey itself) cooks thoroughly, to destroy any bacteria that may have migrated into the stuffing from the raw turkey. Cooked turkey will store in the refrigerator for up to four days, or it can be frozen for later consumption.

Veal

Veal is any cut of meat taken from very young calves of domestic **cattle** (*Bos taurus*). Although veal is extremely tender and tasty, the confined living conditions and slaughter of the young animals have caused a number of people to label the eating of veal as cruel and disrespectful of cattle.

Venison

Strictly speaking, venison is the meat of deer (*Cervidae* family), but in culinary terms, venison can actually mean the meat of any type of mammalian game (such as moose, elk, caribou, and antelope). Of course, the peoples of the Bible would not have come into contact with moose, elk, caribou, or whitetail deer, but antelope (such as ibex [*Capra* genus], oryx [*Oryx* genus], and gazelles [*Gazella* genus]) and certain deer (such as red deer [*Cervus elaphus*] and fallow deer [*Dama dama*]) were plentiful in the Middle East and were hunted and prepared for the table.

The tenderest venison comes from young male deer, with the loin and ribs the tastiest cuts. Marinating the meat can help mask some of the gamy taste. Roasting and broiling are the preferred methods of cooking, though venison stews and sauces are also delicious. Venison is generally low in calories, cholesterol, and fat and high in copper, iron, niacin, phosphorus, potassium, riboflavin, thiamin, and zinc.

VEGETABLES

Artichoke

The artichoke familiar to our dining tables is actually the unopened flower bud of the thistlelike plant *Cynara scolymus*. (Thistles are mentioned in Genesis 3:18, and are probably the plant referred to in Proverbs 24:30. Wild relatives of the cultivated artichoke are common in Jordan and are often referred to as thistles.) Also known as globe artichokes because of their shape, these buds consist of overlapping bright or olive-green leaves, which are extremely tough and inedible except at their base, where they are fleshy and tasty. Within this bud of leaves is the thistle, also known as the choke, which is light yellow or ivory in color and, toward the center, almost hairy. At the very base is a portion of tender, edible flesh, called the heart. Artichokes can vary greatly in size, from 2-ounce baby artichokes that can be trimmed, marinated, and eaten whole to 1-pound giants that are tastiest when stuffed with **cheese**-based or other fillings.

Originating in the Mediterranean region, perhaps in Sicily or Carthage, artichokes have been cultivated at least since the time of ancient Rome, and perhaps even by the ancient Greeks. The Saracens of Sicily and the Moors of Granada continued artichoke cultivation during the Middle Ages, when this vegetable fell out of favor, and in the 15th century artichokes spread north from Sicily to Naples and throughout the Italian peninsula. As a young bride of fourteen, Catherine de' Medici is reputed to have reintroduced the artichoke to French cuisine in the 16th century—causing a scandal, because she was very fond of eating them, and they were reputed to be an aphrodisiac. European immigrants brought artichokes to the Americas in the 19th century, and today they are most popular in Italy, France, and Spain, with some popularity in the United States. The cool, foggy climate of certain areas of California are so ideal for growing artichokes that California now produces 99 percent of the commercial artichoke crop worldwide.

Artichokes are high in vitamin C, folacin, and dietary fiber. They can be baked, steamed, boiled, sautéed, stir-fried, and marinated. Often eaten alone with a dipping sauce, they are delicious when stuffed or can be used as an ingredient in salads, stews, casseroles, omelets, and sauces.

Arugula

Also known as rocket, roquette, or rucola, arugula is the name for three species of leafy vegetable: *Eruca sativa, Diplotaxis tenuifolia,* and *D. muralis.* Somewhat like **lettuce**, arugula has had a place on the Mediterranean table since the time of ancient Rome, when it was used as an aphrodisiac. Arugula is thought by some scholars to have been one of the bitter herbs eaten by the Israelites at the first Passover. Up until very recent years it was usually collected from the wild; cultivation has spread in the past decade or so as people have developed a taste for different types of leafy greens.

Rich in beta-carotene, extremely high in calcium, and higher in vitamin C than most "lettuces," arugula has a peppery taste and aroma that tends toward the mustardlike. It adds flavor to soups, salads, vegetable dishes, sandwiches, and pastas.

Asparagus

Asparagus (*Asparagus officinalis*), a member of the Lily family, is a perennial plant whose geographic origins are difficult to determine. Currently, wild asparagus ranges from Iran to England, Russia to the Atlantic coast of Europe, and on all sides of the Mediterranean—not to mention across North America, though the plant is definitely not of American origin. The first to cultivate asparagus may have been the ancient Egyptians or perhaps the ancient Greeks, so perhaps the peoples of the Bible were familiar with it also. Certainly, by the time of ancient Rome, asparagus was a valuable garden vegetable, lauded by Cato (2nd century B.C.E.) in his *De Re Rustica*. Cultivated asparagus probably reverted to the wild after the fall of the Roman Empire, to be reintroduced into cultivation by monastic gardeners in the Middle Ages. Venetian farmers made fortunes in asparagus in the 16th century C.E., and Italian asparagus cultivars and methods became the standards against which all others were measured. At this time, European painters began including bunches of asparagus in their still lifes. French farmers also raised delicious asparagus, and the Huguenot refugees brought French cultivars with them when they fled to England in the 17th century, vastly improving the English asparagus, which had been extremely popular in England yet not very robust. English colonists brought asparagus to North America, but asparagus did not become a commercial crop in the United States until the 19th century.

The two main types of asparagus now grown are the white and the green. White asparagus is planted beneath piles of dirt, to block the sunlight that would help the plants produce green chlorophyll. The stalks of both the white and green varieties are usually cut when they are about a foot in length; the rhizome (root) will grow stalks again the following year. If allowed to continue growing, the plant will develop into a very tall (perhaps 10 feet in height), feathery stalk, which produces berries (seeds) devoured by birds.

Asparagus is very high in vitamins A, B6, C, and E and in copper, folacin, manganese, and potassium. Fresh asparagus must be refrigerated after it is harvested, as it decays rapidly and loses much of its vitamin content and flavor. And it should not be overcooked—quick boiling, steaming, blanching, or stir-frying works best, though it can be roasted and grilled and even served raw. Cooked asparagus can be served hot or cold, in vegetable salads, with pastas, or in soup.

Bean, Fava

Before the introduction of **green bean**s, the broad bean (*Vicia faba*) was a dietary staple in northern Africa and southwestern Asia. Commonly known as fava beans, the broad bean goes by a variety of names: faba, horse, field, and tic beans.

Fava beans have been cultivated since prehistoric times and have been found in Stone Age (circa 6000 B.C.E.) excavations and even in the ruins of the ancient city of Troy. Fava beans were certainly known to the peoples of the Bible, and if the Hebrew word *pôl* means "fava," as biblical scholars believe, then Daniel received fava beans as a gift and ground them into **flour** to make a **bread** for Ezekiel. An easy-to-grow annual, fava beans have no known wild equivalent; it is possible that the progenitor of the fava may be extinct. Easily shucked, the seeds of these beans are large, nutritious, and protein rich, eaten fresh or dried, mixed with grain and ground into flour to make bread, or used as fodder for livestock. Both black and white seeds have been known at least since ancient Greek and Roman times, when a white seed indicated "aye" and a black seed "nay" during elections. Ancient Egyptians stocked the tombs of the dead with dried fava beans, as provision for life in the hereafter, and beans played an important role in the funeral rites of the ancient Greeks. This association with death continues to the present: in Italy, fava beans are sown on November 2, All Souls' Day. During the Middle Ages in Europe, fava beans came to be associated with the supernatural (witches and fairies and ghosts), but they were often one of the few foods affordable by the poor. Fava beans crossed to the Americas in the 16th century C.E. but did not become widely cultivated until recent times.

Fava beans are rich in vicine, divicine, convicine, and isouramil, which can cause hemolytic anemia (the breakdown of red blood cells) in persons with Glucose-6-phosphate dehydrogenase (G6PD) deficiency, which may result in kidney failure and death. For this reason, G6PD has become known as favism. G6PD is the most common enzyme-deficiency disease worldwide; it is specific to certain ethnic groups and confers a certain level of immunity to malaria.

Fava beans are an important ingredient in modern Middle Eastern cooking. Whole fava beans are edible only when very tiny; shelled fava beans must also be skinned unless eaten when very young and tender. Fava beans go well in soups, risottos, and stews.

Bean, green

Green beans (*Phaseolus vulgaris*) are known by a variety of names, such as common bean, French bean, navy bean, string bean, flageolet or snap bean, American haricot bean, and wax bean, and may be bush beans or pole beans. Green beans are usually eaten whole—that is, both the seeds and the fleshy seed covering (pod) are consumed fresh—though the seeds are often removed from the pod, dried, and stored for later use. Such dried beans include pinto, **kidney**, **navy**, pea, great northern, and black turtle beans. High in protein and dietary fiber, beans are excellent sources of iron, potassium, selenium, molybdenum, and folate.

The green bean is native to the Americas and was certainly cultivated in prehistoric times, for it has been found in excavations dating to 7000 B.C.E. But it was not known outside the Americas until the so-called Age of Exploration (15th through 17th centuries C.E.) and the transfer of native species across the oceans. During this time, the green bean began to replace the broad bean in many European, Mediterranean, North African, and Middle Eastern dishes. Before the introduction of green beans, the broad or **fava bean** (*Vicia faba*) was a dietary staple in northern Africa and southwestern Asia.

Green beans are an important ingredient in modern Middle Eastern cooking. Generally, green beans are picked when still small and the seeds have not fully formed and are eaten whole. Whole green beans are delicious alone, cooked, pickled or marinated, or in salads and casseroles.

Bean, kidney

Kidney beans are varieties of the common or **green bean** (*Phaseolus vulgaris*). Usually dried for long storage, kidney beans have dark red, light red, or even white skin and have a shape that resembles that of a human kidney. Some types of kidney beans include Montcalm, Wells Red, Geneva, New York, and True Cranberry. These beans are used to make chili, soup, red beans and **rice**, and Creole dishes. As with other dried beans, kidney beans need to be soaked in water overnight to ready them for cooking.

Bean, lima

The lima bean (*Phaseolus lunatus*) is a native of the Americas, from modern-day Mexico to Argentina, and may have originated in what is present-day Peru. The large-seed variety of lima beans was domesticated in prehistoric times, probably about 6500 B.C.E. A small-seed variety was separately domesticated, probably about 800 C.E. Domestication spread to Europe during the 16th century. Lima beans would not have been known to the peoples of the Bible, but certain contemporary Middle Eastern dishes call for lima beans, which are high in fiber and iron. Also known as butter beans, lima beans are delicious alone or in company with roasted meat and poultry.

Bean, navy or white

Navy beans, also known as small white beans or pea beans or haricots, are a variety of the common or **green bean** (*Phaseolus vulgaris*). Usually dried for long storage, navy beans have a mild taste that complements the flavors of the foods with which they are served or combined. Some of the major varieties include Robust, Rainy River, Michelite, and Sanilac. To prepare the dried beans for cooking, they need to be soaked in water overnight. Then they can be boiled for serving as a bean dish, or they can be added to soups, stews, casseroles, and salads.

Bean Sprouts

Bean sprouts are the small sprouting plants of bean seeds. Most often allowed to germinate and harvested for their sprouts are the common or **green bean** (*Phaseolus vulgaris*), **chickpeas** (*Cicer arietinum*), **lentils** (*Lens esculenta*), and mung beans (*Vigna radiate*). (Alfalfa [*Medicago sativa*] and **mustard** [*Brassica* genus] sprouts are also commonly consumed.) Bean sprouts have less carbohydrates, iron, protein, and vitamins A and B than the beans (bean seeds) from which they grow, but they can have as much as five times the vitamin C. Bean sprouts are usually eaten fresh, added to salads or used as a garnish. They can be used in stir-fries, but cooking reduces the amount of vitamin C in the sprouts.

Beet

The beet (*Beta vulgaris*) is a root vegetable that is completely edible: both the roots and the green leaves are delicious, according to many palates. The species includes the common beet (also known as the red beet, beetroot, and table beet), the sugar beet (which is processed for sugar), mangle-wurzle (also known as mangel or mangold, and used as animal fodder), foliage beet (grown for its leaves), and Swiss chard (also grown for its greens).

Though the earliest written record of beet cultivation occurs in an 8th-century B.C.E. cuneiform tablet from Babylon, it is probable that beets were domesticated before 1000 B.C.E., along with the **carrot, cabbage, turnip,** and other like vegetables. Some botanists believe that the beet is native to the Mediterranean region. The ancient Greeks used beet greens for flavoring and as medicine, but beets grown specifically for their swollen roots may not have appeared until the time of ancient Rome. With the fall of the Roman Empire, beets, **radishes,** turnips, and carrots seem to have been lost to much of Europe until the Renaissance, when they again became essential garden vegetables. Beets have a relatively high tolerance for salt and grow very well in land reclaimed from the sea. They grow best in temperate to cool regions.

Beets are a biennial plant, producing their large, edible, red (or reddish, pinkish, or even white) root the first year and seeds the second (if they are allowed to remain in the ground).

Remarkably, the sugar beet has the highest **sugar** content of any vegetable. Andreas S. Marggraf, a German chemist, was the first to extract sugar from beets, describing in 1747 how he boiled beetroots in alcohol, allowed them to cool, and collected sugar crystals that were exactly similar to those of sugar cane. The first sugar extracting factory was established in Silesia in 1802, when the price of cane sugar from the West Indies was at an all-time high. Napoleon, at war with the English, encouraged the production of sugar beets, ordering the planting of 70,000 acres of them in order to undermine the English trade in sugar cane. In 1812 financier Benjamin Delessert opened a sugar-beet refinery in Paris. The Germans took the lead in the following years, when Moritz von Koppy developed the White Silesian beet, from which all of today's varieties of sugar beets have evolved. Today, nearly half the world's sugar comes from the sugar beet.

Beets are rich in folacin, vitamin C, and manganese. They have no cholesterol but are high in sodium. Beet greens are an excellent source of beta-carotene, calcium, and iron.

Fresh beets are always in good supply. They can be baked, boiled, or steamed alone to make a hot side dish. They can also be added to salads, pickled, spiced, made into a relish, and added to soups, including borscht, the traditional Russian soup so popular at modern Passover meals. Beet leaves can be steamed, sautéed, fried, and prepared just as other greens. So-called baby beets, which have been picked when immature, are a delicacy.

Broccoli

Like **cauliflower**, broccoli (*Brassica oleracea* form *cymosa*) is a **cabbage**. While cabbage has a long history of cultivation, it is not known when or where the broccoli form developed. Some scholars believe that it was known in ancient Rome and came from Asia Minor and the eastern Mediterranean. Others assert that the Etruscans developed it early in the common era. Certainly, it was well known in Italy by the 17th century and in the eastern Mediterranean before then. Some scholars state that broccoli came to the Americas with French or English settlers, as broccoli had made its way to England by the 18th century. Most believe that Italian immigrants brought broccoli to the Americas in the 20th century, though that may be simple folklore.

Broccoli is usually deep green, though purple-headed and white-headed types are known. One of the healthiest vegetables to eat, broccoli is extremely high in vitamins A and C and provides significant amounts of vitamin B6, folacin, manganese, and potassium.

Broccoli can be eaten either raw or cooked. If cooked, it should remain crispy and bright green—overcooking removes much of the vitamin content. Broiling, steaming, and stir-frying are the usual ways of cooking broccoli. Too often served with **cream** or **cheese** sauces (which add enormous amounts of calories and fats and mask the taste of the vegetable), broccoli is delicious if served plain with **lemon** juice or if mixed with pastas or added to soups.

Cabbage

The common garden cabbage (*Brassica oleracea capitata*), a member of the Cabbage family, exists as either red cabbage or white cabbage. It is very closely related to kale, kohlrabi, Brussels sprouts, collards, **broccoli**, and **cauliflower**. Indeed, cross-pollination is possible among these relatives and results in a relatively rapid reversion to the common wild ancestor: wild cabbage (sometimes called sea cabbage: *B. oleracea*). Generally, cabbage grows best in cool, moist climates, but wild cabbage is still found from England south to Spain, and relatives are native to Sardinia and Corsica (*B. robertiana*), northern Africa (*B. insularis*), and the eastern Mediterranean (*B. cretica*). The ancient Greeks knew of cabbage, and the ancient Romans considered it good for health: both Cato and Pliny the Elder mentioned cabbage in their writings—the latter as a source of medicine. It is certainly possible that the peoples of the Bible knew of and used cabbage in their cooking, though there is no conclusive evidence to that end and it is not mentioned in the Bible. Though probably native to northern Europe, red and white cabbage is not recorded there until the 14th century C.E., when the French court chef dared to serve cabbage at a banquet. Cabbage is recorded in the German lands in the 12th century, and in the Netherlands and perhaps England in the 16th.

Cabbage can be prepared in a number of ways: as a simple dish of boiled cabbage leaves; as the main ingredient in cabbage soup; and famously, as cole slaw and pickled as sauerkraut.

Cabbage, when raw, is a good source of vitamin C. It also contains moderate amounts of vitamin A. It is most nutritious when served fresh or lightly steamed. There is some evidence that eating cabbage might help lower the risk of gastrointestinal and respiratory cancers.

Carrot

The carrot (*Daucus carota*), an edible root, is probably a native of what is modern-day Afghanistan, Turkestan, and the Hindu Kush region of central Asia. There, carrots with red or purple roots still grow wild. Selective cultivation probably produced the reddish-purple, forked-root Asiatic carrot. The orange, yellow, or white single-root Western carrot was probably a later development. Carrot seeds have been found in Swiss and German archaeological sites dating from the 3rd millennium B.C.E., though archaeologists have concluded that early peoples ate only the seeds and left the roots in the ground. In the Fertile Crescent (from the Nile to the Indus Rivers), carrots were probably cultivated for their roots by 1000 B.C.E., so the Israelites may have encountered carrots during their captivity in Egypt. Linguistically, there is no reference to carrots until the 2nd century C.E., in the writings of Galen, a Levantine-Greek medical author. The people of modern-day Iran and northern Arabia were growing purple and yellow carrots by the 10th century; the range of yellow carrots expanded with the spread of Islam across northern Africa and into Spain. By the 13th century, carrots were known in Italy; by the 14th, Germany and the Netherlands; by the 15th, England. Carrots are reported in China from the 13th century; in Japan, from the 18th. Artists depicted carrots as purple or yellow; the orange variety first appeared in 16th-century art and probably developed in the Low Countries at that time. White carrots appeared in art at about the same time, indicating the domestication of wild, white-rooted varieties (though like orange carrots, white carrots may also have been selectively bred from yellow carrots). English colonists brought carrots to the Americas in the 17th century, and there they quickly escaped into the wild, and feral carrots have spread all over North America. In the 18th century the Dutch produced the Long Orange cultivar, the ancestor of all modern carotene (orange) carrots. Today, China and the United States are the top carrot producers, though carrots are grown around the world.

Carrots retain their high vitamin A content when cooked (vitamin A is essential in maintaining vision). Indeed, cooking carrots until they are just crisp-tender actually makes their nutrients more accessible to human digestion. Carrots are high in potassium and fiber (which helps to lower cholesterol) and may lower the risk of cancer of the lungs, larynx, and esophagus. Carrots also contain a lot of

sugar, though they are seldom prepared as a dish unto themselves. Usually, carrots are used in stews, soups, salads, **breads,** muffins, and even cakes.

Carrots are related to **parsley, dill, fennel, celery,** and the wildflower Queen Anne's Lace.

Cauliflower

Surprising as it may be, cauliflower (*Brassica oleracea* form *botrytis*) is actually a variety of **cabbage** and is the same thing as **broccoli:** both cauliflower and broccoli are types of cabbage whose flowers have been developed for eating. Essentially, humans have selectively grown cauliflower as an annual plant whose flowers do not mature but form into a head, a compact mass called the curd. Farmers developed broccoli as a biennial plant, picking it at the end of its first year of growth, when the flower buds had developed but before they could bloom during the second year. All of this selective cultivation occurred over many millennia: by the time of the ancient Romans, cauliflower was already part of the cuisine. Its exact origins are unknown, but the people of Asia Minor (which today is known as the eastern portions of Turkey) may have been the first to grow cauliflower. It's possible but unlikely that the people of the Bible ate cauliflower. Cauliflower did not cross north of the Alps until about the 14th century C.E., and it made its way to the Americas in the 17th. It became a favorite food for the Lenten season in northern Europe, as it was filling but unaffected by any rules for fasting. Enthusiasm for cauliflower has waned, except in Scandinavia (where long summer sunlight produces a tasty curd), Germany, England, and India (where curries add flavor to what some people say is an otherwise dull-tasting vegetable).

A large number of subvarieties of cauliflower are in cultivation, from white to green to purple. Cauliflower is very high in vitamin C and provides significant amounts of folacin, vitamin B6, manganese, and potassium; it has no cholesterol. Preparation includes boiling, sautéeing, and steaming, though the cooking time should be held to the absolute minimum, as overcooking will cause the nutrients to leach into the water. Also, cauliflower will turn yellow if cooked in aluminum and brown or blue-green if cooked in iron. Store cauliflower in a perforated plastic bag or wrap to allow carbon dioxide to escape and prevent the vegetable from developing an unpleasant taste and color.

Celery

Celery (*Apium graveolens*) is a biennial plant of the **Parsley** family. Grown from seeds, it produces a cluster of furrowed stalks with wedge-shaped leaves. In the wild, celery is coarse and somewhat rank; cultivation and blanching remove its acrid qualities and leave it with a mildly sweet, aromatic taste. Celery stalks are often chopped and used in salads and soups; the leaves are added to soups and stews for additional flavor; the seeds are used as a spice. Sometimes stringy, celery provides roughage that is beneficial to digestion. Celery was probably not known to peoples of the Bible, but it is a common vegetable in modern Middle Eastern dishes.

Chickpea

Also known as the garbanzo, garbanzo bean, and ceci, the chickpea (*Cicer arietinum*) grows in a pod, like **beans** and **peas**. Roughly spherical in shape, chickpeas are tan in color and have a slightly nutty taste with a firm texture.

Cultivation of the chickpea began so long ago that its original wild ancestor is now extinct. Presumed to be a native of the region between ancient Persia and the Caucasus, chickpeas have been found in prehistoric archaeological sites in Sicily and Switzerland. They were a staple in ancient Egypt and were grown in the hanging gardens of ancient Babylon. The Greeks of Homer's day relied on chickpeas in addition to beans, **lentils**, **onions**, and **garlic**, and the ancient Romans enjoyed chickpeas and bacon the way many people enjoy pork and beans. The chickpea would have been common across the Middle East during the biblical era. Chickpeas are now consumed worldwide: inexpensive with a high nutritional value, they are a staple in the diet of poor peoples and a contrasting favorite in the cuisine of the middle class and the well-to-do.

While high in calories, chickpeas are also high in protein, calcium, folacin, iron, phosphorus, and potassium and provide a good amount of dietary fiber. Chickpeas contain no cholesterol. Though to a lesser degree than other beans and legumes, chickpeas do contain some complex sugars that can cause indigestion, bloating, and flatulence. Not all people are affected, but those who are can minimize the effects by preparing the chickpeas in large quantities of fresh water, eating them in small amounts and in company with low-fat foods, having them earlier in the day rather than later, and avoiding other gas-producing foods like **cabbage**.

Around the world, people add chickpeas to salads, toss them with pasta, mash them to make hummus or falafel, and roast them for snacking. Like other beans, chickpeas tend to absorb the flavors of the foods they are cooked with and thus are extremely versatile. Dried chickpeas can also be ground into **flour** and used to make **breads** and other baked goods.

Cilantro

Cilantro is one of the common names for fresh **coriander**.

Cucumber

Cucumber (*Cucumis sativus*), belonging to the Gourd family, has been domesticated and cultivated for at least 4,000 years in India and Egypt, so it is probable that Abraham and his kin would have been familiar with it. Cucumber is mentioned in the book of Isaiah (1:8) and the book of Numbers (11:5). The cucumber is probably a native of the Himalayan regions. The plant grows as a vine, with large leaves that provide a canopy for the edible fruit (botanically, it is a fruit because the seeds are inside a fleshy shell; it is, however, a vegetable in the culinary, or cooking, sense), which can grow as long as 12 inches with a diameter of 2 or more inches. Cucumbers are eaten raw, cooked, or pickled. They are low in calories and provide few nutrients besides some minerals (unless pickled) but are filled with water and do constitute a refreshing dish on hot days.

Dandelion

The dandelion species (*Taraxacum* genus), members of the Sunflower family, are the common lawn weeds that annoy so many homeowners, but the leaves are quite nutritious. Picked before the plant develops its yellow flower (which turns into a puffball of seeds that scatter in the wind), the leaves taste slightly bitter, but they are high in calories, beta-carotene, vitamin C, calcium, and iron—in fact, dandelion greens have more calcium than whole milk. The leaves may be blanched, braised, sautéed, simmered, and steamed but are especially tasty if served fresh with a hot, garlicky vinaigrette. The leaves can also be steeped to make a **tea** and fermented to make **wine**. The flower buds are edible and are delicious fried, and the long taproot can be peeled and boiled and is less bitter if dug up in the spring or after autumn frosts. Ground and roasted, the roots make a passable **coffee**. **Honey** can be collected from dandelion flowers.

The ancient Mediterranean peoples ate wild dandelions, which were plentiful, and dandelions may have been among the bitter herbs that made up the Israelites' Passover meal. Dandelion greens were used as medicine up through the Renaissance period, though the presence of greens in the diet of European peoples had declined drastically during the Middle Ages. At the end of the 17th century, John Evelyn included dandelion greens in most of his salad recipes. Many African recipes, including the Algerian honey cake *yubba,* call for the addition of dandelion greens, and the African people sold into slavery brought their taste for dandelions with them to the Americas, where southern soul food developed to include dandelions in mixed-greens recipes. Bringing their recipes with them from northern Europe, the Pennsylvania Dutch prepared a dandelion salad dressed with hot **cider vinegar, sugar**, and bacon.

Eggplant

A member of the Nightshade family, eggplant, also known as aubergine, comes in two varieties: purple (*Solanum melongena*) and white (*S. esculentum*). Plants can grow 12 to 24 inches tall, producing large, pendulous fruits 6 to 12 inches long. When first harvested, the fruit is spongy and bitter to the taste, but upon cooking becomes tender, with a rich, complex flavor. First cultivated about 2000 B.C.E. in Southeast Asia, eggplant traveled to the Middle East and the Mediterranean and was quickly adopted into the regional cuisines. Abraham and his kin would probably have eaten eggplant, either as an ingredient in stews, as a paste to garnish **bread** or **endive**, or cooked in oil on its own. During the Middle Ages in northern Europe, eggplant fell out of favor because it was thought to cause fevers, epileptic seizures, and even insanity and came to have the nickname "Apple of Sodom." However, it remained popular in the Mediterranean, and its use in cooking has again spread across the world.

Endive

A member of the Aster family, endive (*Cichorium endivia*) is a leafy salad vegetable that is believed to have become known in ancient Egypt by 3000 B.C.E. Endive was probably one of the bitter herbs eaten by the Israelites at the first Passover. Both the ancient Greeks and Romans used endive as a vegetable and ingredient in salads. Often confused with chicory (*C. intybus*), endive is now known in three major varieties: Belgian endive, curly endive, and escarole. Endive is a very good source of potassium, fiber, selenium, and vitamin B. The best endive is either white with yellow tips or reddish; endive that is green has been exposed to too much light and has lost some of its taste and nutritional value. Crunchy yet tender, moist, and bitter, endive adds both texture and flavor to salads but can also be used as a scoop to complement **cheese-**, **yogurt-**, **honey-**, or **bean**-based dips or sauces.

Fennel

Fennel (*Foeniculum vulgare*), also known as sweet fennel, Florence fennel, and *finocchio,* is a member of the **Parsley** family. Although it may look like plump **celery**, fennel has quite a different flavor, tasting more like licorice or **anise**. Fennel has apparently had a long history of cultivation, though it has been seldom written about. Probably native to the Mediterranean, it has been a favorite of cooks on the Italian peninsula, and the ancient Romans sprinkled fennel seeds on **bread** and mixed fennel leaves in with other greens. They also preserved fennel stems in a mixture of **vinegar** and brine. Earlier, the ancient Greeks used the stalks and leaves, and their word for fennel, *marathon,* gave its name to that famous field of battle because it was overgrown with the plant. It was known among the ancient Gauls before the Roman conquest, and it is one of the traditional ingredients in Chinese **five-spice powder** (the others being anise seed, Szechuan **pepper**, **cloves**, and **cinnamon**). In India, fennel became an important ingredient in curries. In the Middle Ages, fennel was one of the four hot seeds (the others being anise, **caraway**, and **coriander**). Chaucer called it one of the nine holy herbs (though the identities of the other eight have been lost to history). In modern times, fennel has been considered one of the five roots that encourage appetite (the others being wild celery, **asparagus**, **parsley**, and knee holly [also known as butcher's broom]). Fennel is now part of modern Middle Eastern cuisines.

All parts of fennel are edible: the bulbs, leaves, stems, seeds, and flowers. Italian cuisine tends to concentrate on the bulbs and stalks, while French cooking uses the leaves as herbs. In general, the stalks can be used like celery and make a tasty addition to soups and stews, and the leaves make a flavorful herb. The bulbs can be baked, braised, sautéed, or steamed. Fennel adds a nice flavor to vegetable stir-fries, fish dishes, pasta sauces, and even fruit salads.

Fennel is very high in vitamins A and C and high in calcium, iron, magnesium, sodium, and potassium. It has no cholesterol and very little fat.

Garbanzo Bean
See **chickpea**.

Ginger Root
See **ginger**.

Grape Leaves
See **grape**.

Horseradish

A relative of the radish, the horseradish (*Armoracia rusticana*) is of indistinct origins: various botanists claim it is native to the Mediterranean, to southeastern Europe and western Asia, to western and southeastern Asia, to Siberia, to central or northern Europe, and so on. It is generally agreed that horseradish was known to the ancient Romans, as Cato mentions it in his agricultural treatises and a Pompeiian mural depicts the plant. The roots and leaves were used as both medicine and condiment, from southern Europe through Germany and Denmark.

The horseradish plant grows to about 5 feet in height, and the root is long and white. The greens are sometimes used as one of the bitter herbs of the Jewish Passover meal. Jewish cuisine also uses a sweetened horseradish-**vinegar** sauce called *chrain*. The root is often grated or crushed, used as a garnish for meats or fish, mixed with **salt** and distilled vinegar, or added to flavor sauces, though it can be eaten whole as crudité.

Horseradish is rich in vitamin C, potassium, calcium, magnesium, and phosphorous.

A wild horseradish (*A. lapathifolia*) is native to North America and was highly favored by no less a wild food expert than Euell Gibbons, proponent of natural diets and author of *Stalking the Wild Asparagus* and other classics of food lore.

Leek

The leek (*Allium ampeloprasum* var. *porrum*, otherwise known as *A. porrum*) belongs to the Lily family and is thought to be native to Central Asia, though it can withstand colder weather and flourishes in the British Isles and northern Europe; indeed, the leek is the national emblem of Wales. Leeks have been cultivated for millennia, and they are recorded as a staple of the builders of the Egyptian pyramids. They are also mentioned in the Bible (Numbers 11:5–6) when the Israelites were complaining about the blandness of their diet in the desert: "We remember the fish we used to eat in Egypt for nothing, the **cucumbers**, the melons, the leeks, the **onions**, and the **garlic**; but now our strength is dried up, and there is nothing at all but this manna to look at." Leeks have many health-promoting properties: they reduce disease-causing cholesterol, protect against prostate and colon cancer, and stabilize blood-sugar levels. Like onions, leeks are relatively easy to grow and are in season from the fall to the early spring. They are used in soups, salads, omelets, casseroles, stews, and many other dishes throughout the world.

Lentil

Like other legumes and beans, lentils (*Lens esculenta*) have been part of the human diet since time immemorial. Although their origin is unknown, they have been found in archaeological sites in northeastern Iraq dating from 6750 B.C.E., in Turkish sites from 5500 B.C.E., and in Egyptian tombs from before 1500 B.C.E. Documents from ancient Sumeria record their cultivation in Babylon by 800 B.C.E., but by then lentils had probably already spread well north into European lands and east into the Indian subcontinent. Lentils were certainly a staple in the cuisine of the peoples of the Bible: Jacob served them to his brother, Esau (Genesis 25:31), and Ezekiel made a **bread** with lentils (Ezekiel 4:9). The ancient Greeks and Romans considered lentils a food of the poor, though some wealthy Greeks and Romans did serve lentils at their meals, perhaps by choice, perhaps by necessity. In Europe, lentils were avoided during medieval times and did not come back into fashion until the 17th or 18th century C.E. Now they are consumed worldwide, though they are particularly important in the Middle East, India, and Africa.

Lentils come in a large number of varieties, from red to brown to green. They are relatively high in calories and calcium; high in protein, dietary fiber, iron, and phosphorus; very high in folacin. They contain no cholesterol and little fat. Though to a lesser degree than other beans and legumes, lentils do contain some indigestible complex sugars that can cause bloating and flatulence. Not all people are affected, but those who are can minimize the effects by preparing the lentils in large quantities of fresh water, eating them in small amounts and in company with low-fat foods, having them earlier in the day rather than later, and avoiding other gas-producing foods like **cabbage**.

Lentils cook quickly and, unlike other dried beans, do not require presoaking (though it does help to soften them). Their taste is relatively bland (some say it is mildly peppery), but they do pick up the flavors of accompanying foods. Use lentils in soups, salads, and stews; with other vegetables or with **rice**; or as a dish unto themselves.

Lettuce

Lettuce (*Lactuca sativa*) is perhaps the world's most important salad plant, but it probably entered cultivation by accident, its wild ancestors (*L. serriola*, *L. saligna*, *L. scariola*, and *L. virosa*) migrating out of the Caucasus region to grow as weeds in fields of **wheat** or **barley** that had been planted by denizens of the fertile Nile, Tigris, and Euphrates River valleys. Farmers would have begun cultivating these wild lettuces for the oil in their seeds, as the leaves would have been extremely bitter. It is believed that these wild lettuces would have been among the bitter herbs eaten by the Israelites at the Passover meal in Egypt (Exodus 12:8). Yet through ancient times lettuce was more of a medicinal and religious plant than a food plant. Many lettuces, particularly the *serriola,* exude a milky white latex when cut, and this bitter fluid contains a narcotic that induces sleep. By 2500 B.C.E. the ancient Egyptians were using this liquid in making poultices and in treating stomachaches and coughs, and they also made sacred offerings of lettuce to Min, their goddess of fertility, probably because lettuce's white fluid was a reminder of fertile semen. The ancient Greek physician Hippocrates (5th century B.C.E.) knew that lettuce juice would induce sleep, and the Romans were great fans of lettuce because of its soporific quality. But by the 1st century C.E., Roman farmers had begun to develop lettuces with tastier leaves.

Though Asia had indigenous lettuce (*L. indica*), the *sativa* lettuces made their way to China by the 8th century, and lettuce underwent further hybridization. In the Americas, as early as the 16th century colonists were growing European lettuces, which interbred with the bitter native lettuces (such as horseweed [*L. canadensis*]) to produce even more varieties. Today, seven types of lettuce, each with dozens of varieties, are recognized:

- Iceberg, the mildest tasting, resembling cabbage, pale green in color
- Crisphead, crunchy and mild
- Looseleaf, green or shading to deep red at the edges
- Romaine, also called Cos (in reference to its origin on the Greek/Turkish island of that name), with long, deep green leaves
- Butterhead, also called Boston or bibb, with a buttery texture, grass green in color
- Batavia, similar to butterhead
- Chinese, bitter and robust, with long leaves, good for stir-fries and stews

Of these types, romaine provides the most calcium, vitamins A and C, and folacin, though the butterheads provide more iron. In general, the darker lettuces provide more nutrients, though all lettuces provide a good amount of dietary fiber.

Lettuces are usually eaten raw, in salads, either alone or mixed with several varieties or with other vegetables, but lettuce can also be grilled, sautéed, steamed, and braised. Different lettuces can also be used as garnishes for sandwiches or Mexican dishes or as scoops for poultry or fish salads.

Lotus Root

The lotus (*Nelumbo nucifera*) is also known as the sacred lotus, Indian lotus, and sacred water lily. Native to India and Indonesia, the lotus is an aquatic perennial, growing to a height of about 5 feet. Each green leaf may be as wide as 2 feet in diameter, and the pink and white blossoms with yellow centers may be as wide as 8 inches in diameter. It was introduced into Egypt from Persia sometime between the 8th and the 4th centuries B.C.E., and traders probably brought it to the lands of the Israelites en route or soon thereafter.

Every part of the lotus is edible. The leaves are eaten as a vegetable, often as a wrap or container for other foods. The petals serve as garnish, while the dried stamens can be used to brew herbal **tea**. The seeds (nuts) can be eaten raw, dried and popped like popcorn, grilled, candied, or boiled into a paste; lotus seed paste is used in daifuku and **rice flour** pudding.

The rhizomes (roots) are generally about 8 inches long and 2 inches in diameter, with many large air pockets running lengthwise to make the plant buoyant (a cross-section of the rhizome will look like a wagon wheel). The rhizomes are delicious, used in soups and stir-fries and sometimes eaten raw. They can also be dried and ground into lotus flour, which can be used in baking a wide range of goods, from **bread**s and bagels to noodles and pancakes. In developed countries, fresh lotus root is difficult to find; it may be available in Asian markets, where one can encounter canned lotus root, which is almost as good for cooking. Asian markets may also have lotus flour.

In the Hindu religion, the lotus is associated with the divinities Vishnu, Brahma, and Lakshmi. Though it grows in mud, it yields a pure beauty, suggesting the spiritual potential of all souls, and the lotus' unfolding petals represent the soul's opening to the universe. In Buddhism, the lotus has come to symbolize purity—of body, speech, and mind—because it floats on top of muddy waters, detached from earthly desire. The lotus is closely associated with the Buddha.

Mallow

See *mulukhiya*.

Mulukhiya

Also known as Jews' (or Jew's) mallow (see Job 30:4), bush okra, nalta jute, and jute mallow, *mulukhiya* (*Corchorus olitorius*) is a type of jute, cultivated in the Middle East and Africa as an herb and in India, southeastern Asia, and the south Pacific for its fiber. It is believed to be native to India. Generally, when referring to the leaves consumed as a vegetable, the name *mulukhiya* (or *molokhiya*, *molohiya*, *mulukhiyah*, *mulukhia*, *molehiya*, or *molocheiya*) is used; when referring to the fiber obtained from the plant, the name *jute* is used.

As a summer vegetable, *mulukhiya* is available fresh or dried (powdered), and sometimes frozen (finely chopped leaves). Like **okra**, it can have a somewhat slimy (mucilaginous) texture when cooked.

Fresh *mulukhiya* is most often used to make soup (extremely popular in Egypt, Syria, and Jordan), and the leaves are sensitive to overcooking, which causes them to fall to the bottom of the soup pot instead of remaining suspended in the broth. It is also made into a stew with **chicken** and served over **rice** and sometimes **lentils**.

Mulukhiya is high in protein, vitamin C, beta-carotene, calcium, and iron.

Mushroom

"Mushroom" is the common name for a large number (perhaps as many as 38,000) of edible (and sometimes poisonous) fungi—plants that have no roots or leaves, do not flower or bear seeds, but reproduce by releasing spores, and do not require light to grow. Most mushrooms grow in the wild and have been collected as food since the time of the Egyptian pharaohs, who named them a royal food, and perhaps earlier. It is likely that mushrooms were known to the peoples of the Bible. The ancient Greek physician Hippocrates used mushrooms as both food and medicine. The Japanese may have been the first to cultivate mushrooms, having raised shiitakes for more than two thousand years. The French followed, though many years later, in the 17th century C.E., systematically cultivating mushrooms in caves. Commercial cultivation spread throughout Europe and the United States by the late 1800s, and Pennsylvania farmers developed methods of growing mushrooms indoors. Today, most mushrooms are grown in special buildings that closely regulate the light, temperature, humidity, and ventilation for maximum yield.

The most popular types of mushrooms include the button (*Agaricus bisporus*: sometimes called table, white, or common), cèpe (*Boletus edulis*: also known as bolete, cep, and porcino), chanterelle (the *Cantharellus* genus: also known as girolle or pfifferling), enoki (or enokitake or enoki-daki), Italian brown, morel (the *Morchella* genus), oyster (or pleurotus, tree oyster, phoenix, or sovereign), portobello (or portobella or Roma, a large brown strain of the button mushroom; immature portobellos are known as cremini), shiitake (*Lentinus edodes* or *Lentinula edodes*: also known as golden oak, forest, black forest, oriental black, or Chinese black), and wood ear (or tree ear or black tree fungus), not to mention the **truffle**.

In general, mushrooms provide more nutrition than they are usually credited for, containing a high amount of protein, B vitamins, copper, folacin, niacin, phosphorus, potassium, and riboflavin. They are low in calories and contain antibacterial and other medicinal substances; some have been reported to inhibit the growth of tumors.

Mushrooms can be prepared in a large variety of ways, from stir-frying and sautéeing to broiling and baking. They can be cleaned and eaten raw and whole, sliced for salads or sandwiches or pizza, stuffed with **cheese**, vegetables, or crabmeat, mixed in with **rice** or **barley** or other vegetable dishes, added to **tomato** sauces for pasta, and made into soups. They can also be dried, a process that tends to concentrate their flavor, and canned, to extend their shelf-life.

Given the prevalence of mushrooms in the field, mushroom lovers may be tempted to forego the store varieties and gather them wild. Only expert mushroom botanists should dare to do this, however, as many wild mushrooms are highly toxic, even deadly, and may be nearly identical in appearance to their edible relatives.

Okra

Okra (*Abelmoschus esculentus*) is an unusual vegetable in that it is picked and consumed when unripe because it is indigestible when ripe. It probably originated in the Ethiopian regions of Africa and spread from there to northern Africa and the

Middle East. There are some claims that okra was known in ancient Egypt; if true, okra would have been known to the peoples of the Bible. When native Africans were enslaved and taken to the Americas, they brought okra with them, and the name *okra* is said to come from its name in the Twi language, *nkruman* or *nkrumun*. However, okra is also known as *gumbo*, which is an abbreviation of its name in Umbundu, *ochinggombo* or *ngombo*. Although *gumbo* originally meant the actual vegetable, it now applies to any heavy catch-all American stew, even if that stew does not contain okra as a thickener. Okra is now consumed throughout the developing world, often used in soups and stews, sometimes eaten fresh, boiled, steamed, or pickled. It has been relatively unknown in Europe, though recent immigration patterns have been changing the variety of foods found in European markets.

Okra has a distinctive taste and a mucilaginous texture, which means that when it is sliced and cooked, it produces a sticky juice that thickens any liquid. Okra tastes particularly good when combined with **tomato**es, **peppers**, and **corn**. A good source of vitamin C, folacin and other B vitamins, magnesium, potassium, and calcium, okra is also high in dietary fiber, low in fat, and has no cholesterol.

Onion

The common onion (*Allium cepa*), like **garlic, leeks, chives, scallions**, and **shallots**, belongs to the Lily family. Usually known simply as the onion, common onions come in numerous varieties, from the Japanese onion to the tree or Egyptian onion, and from white to yellow to purple. The common onion is a biennial plant that is now grown worldwide.

No exact equivalent of the common onion occurs naturally in the wild, but five closely related species are found in central Asia, on the Tibetan plateau and on the Russian-Chinese border. Genetic comparisons indicate that onions have been cultivated and modified for a very long time, and the archaeological record provides additional proof. Traces of onion bulbs have been found at sites in Jericho, dating from about 5000 B.C.E. Carvings of onions appear on Egyptian tombs, and one of the pyramids built before 3000 B.C.E. records the amount of onions required to provision the laborers. The Bible also mentions onions (Numbers 11): when the Israelites grew tired of manna during their desert exile, they complained to Moses that they missed the onions that they had enjoyed while in Egypt.

Over the centuries, onion bulbs and seeds spread west to the Mediterranean basin and Europe. The ancient Greek physician Hippocrates, the ancient Greek philosopher/teacher Theophrastus, and the Roman writer Pliny the Elder all knew of onions, which by the time of the Roman Empire were available as either flat or round, yellow, red, or white, and mild or bitter varieties. Onions were ubiquitous in Europe during the Middle Ages, and seafarers took onions with them to Asia, Africa, and the Americas, where they quickly became a staple of agriculture.

Most onions have a sharp, strong smell and taste. Some onions, such as the white or silver Mediterranean onion, are mild, soft, and juicy; these tend to spoil quickly and cannot be stored for very long. Other onions, such as those cultivated in northern Europe, with reddish-brown skins, store nicely for longer periods, particularly when kept in cool vegetable cellars.

Because of their strong flavor and odor, and because they often induce tears when they are chopped or sliced, onions came to be known as the food of the poor. The Code of Hammurabi (about 1700 B.C.E.), from ancient Mesopotamia, stipulated a monthly ration of bread and onions for the poor. Cooking tends to mellow the strong flavor and odor of most onions, though some mild- or sweet-tasting onions are eaten raw. When cut, onions release sulfenic acid, which breaks apart quickly into a volatile gas; the gas combines with the fluid in the eyes to create a very mild sulfuric-acid solution, which causes the stinging sensation. The eyes produce tears to dilute and flush out this acid.

Onions are a good source of vitamin C and folacin. It is believed that onions may be at least somewhat effective against colds and may help to lower blood pressure and cholesterol levels.

Pea

The pea (*Pisum sativum* and *P. fulvum*) is technically a legume, like the bean, having a pod that surrounds fleshy seeds, but the pea does not require the long cooking times that other legumes often do. Humans have been eating peas since Neolithic times, and some say the oldest find of peas dates from 9750 B.C.E., located in the "Spirit Cave" on the border of Thailand and Myanmar (Burma). Other archaeologists claim the oldest peas to have been discovered in south-eastern Turkey, with a date of 7500 B.C.E. These all seem to have been peas gathered from the wild. The oldest of these would provide some indication of the geographic origin of the wild pea, which would necessarily have been a cooler area, and would indicate the direction in which peas migrated, either east to west or west to east. Or it is possible that there were different species of wild peas that had their own natural habitat and that may have hybridized to produce the species known today. The first evidence of cultivation comes from the town of Çatal Hüyük in Turkey, dating from circa 5750 B.C.E. From there, cultivation seems to have spread to Greece, Egypt, the Balkans, the Rhine Valley, the western Mediterranean lands, and, by circa 2000 B.C.E., to India. Peas were most likely known to the peoples of the Bible. Peas probably reached China by the 7th century C.E. To the end of the Renaissance, across Europe, peas were usually harvested when ripe, dried, and stored until they were ground into **flour**, mixed with **wheat** or **rye** flour, and made into **bread** or until they were soaked and used to make pease porridge or pudding, though sometimes they were eaten fresh in France. The Italians, who make an art of dining, seem to have adopted the custom of eating fresh peas in the 16th century, though consuming peas fresh did not really become common across Europe until the 17th century. Legend indicates that Christopher Columbus planted peas on Isabella Island in 1493 and that their cultivation spread rapidly among Native Americans, to Mexico by

1540, to Florida by 1602, and to New England by 1614. English colonists in both Massachusetts and Virginia planted their own garden peas too.

Besides their importance as a foodstuff, peas have played a major role in human scientific progress. Thomas Knight of England was the first to record his efforts to produce new cultivars of a standard crop under controlled conditions, and he experimented with pea cross-pollination in the late 18th century. More important were the experiments of Gregor Mendel, a Moravian monk who founded the science of genetics by hybridizing peas.

Generally, the best-tasting peas are the smallest. Peas are very high in nutrients, providing significant amounts of vitamins A, B6, and C, copper, folacin, iron, magnesium, manganese, niacin, phosphorus, and thiamin. They are often eaten raw, or they may be blanched, braised, steamed, boiled, or stir-fried. Added to **rice**, pastas, salads, soups, or eaten alone, peas are a colorful and delicious part of a meal.

Pepper

The pepper (*Capsicum annuum*) comes in a wide variety of shapes and colors and are either sweet or hot.

The most commonly known sweet pepper is the green bell variety, with three or four lobes, but bell peppers can also be yellow, red, orange, brown, or purple. Bell peppers generally have a sweet taste. Banana peppers, so named because in shape and color they resemble **bananas**, are also mild in taste. Cubanelle (light green or yellow, long and tapered) and pimento (red, heart-shaped) peppers are also among the sweet varieties.

The hot peppers, also known as chilies, include Anaheim (green or red, long and slender), poblano (also known as ancho; red to black), cascabel (green or red, tomato-shaped), cayenne (red, long and thin and pointed), cherry (red, cherry-shaped), Hungarian wax (yellow to orange-red, banana-shaped), jalapeño (green or red, short and thick), and serrano (green, torpedo-shaped). Some botanists classify these hot peppers as a different species, *C. frutescens*.

The *Capsicum* peppers originated in the tropical Americas and thus would not have been known to the people of the ancient Mediterranean regions. They were, however, an early domesticate of indigenous Americans, having been found in a Peruvian archaeological site dating from 2500 B.C.E. Transported across the Atlantic in the 16th century C.E., peppers gained immediate acceptance in Europe: plants flourished in the Mediterranean climate, and when the fruit was dried and ground, the result was an acceptable imitation of the much more expensive **black pepper**. Soon thereafter, peppers were also taken to India, China, and the Philippines. Today *Capsicum* peppers are cultivated worldwide and are an important ingredient in many cuisines, including Middle Eastern cooking.

All peppers are high in vitamins A and C, and the hot varieties provide capsaicin, which works as an anticoagulant and can help prevent heart attacks or strokes caused by blood clots.

Easily grown and readily available at any time of the year, peppers can be eaten raw, stir-fried, sautéed, baked, stuffed, blanched, or roasted. They can be made into relish, added to sauces or casseroles, sprinkled on **rice**, used in salsa—the possibilities are limitless, and peppers can add a colorful, flavorful, and healthful zest to almost any dish.

Pickle

The term "pickle" normally refers to cucumbers that have been pickled, but over the millennia humans have pickled many foodstuffs, from **cabbage, carrots, beans, onions, olives,** and **cauliflower** to **herring, eggs, plums, watermelon, lemons**— even snakes. Pickling has become so widespread because it extends the shelf-life of many perishable foods; it developed as a way of storing food for winter or during long voyages. The process involves soaking and storing the item in a brine (**salt**) and **vinegar** solution; herbs and spices (such as **dill, mustard,** and **cinnamon**) are often added to obtain different flavors.

Pimento

See **pepper**.

Potato

The potato (*Solanum tuberosum*) was assuredly not known to the peoples of the Bible, but modern cooks around the world, including those of the Middle East, now rely upon potatoes as a staple of their cuisine. A member of the Nightshade family, the potato is believed to be native to the Andes of South America and to have been widely cultivated by the pre-Columbian Incas. In the 16th century C.E. Spanish explorers brought potatoes to Europe, where they became extremely popular because they were easier to grow than **wheat** or **oats**, the prevalent staple crops. The edible part of the potato is not the green leafy stems (which are poisonous) nor the flowers that grow above ground, but the fleshy tubers that grow beneath the surface; these are simple to locate and unearth at the end of the growing season. Potatoes do not grow from seeds, as most vegetables do, but from buds (eyes) on the tubers; when planted, these buds grow into plants identical to the parent plant. Another reason why potatoes have spread world-wide is that they produce more food energy per acre than many other vegetables. Though they grow best in cool, moist climates, they are cultivated in most temperate regions. Additionally, they usually store well when kept cool and dry, and have carried many families over from one harvest to the next. High in carbohydrates, potatoes also provide potassium, calcium, and vitamin C. Potatoes come in many varieties. Their skin may be brown, yellow, pink, red, or purple (blue), and their flesh may be white or may match the color of their skin. Some are suitable for baking and/or roasting; others for boiling and/or mashing; still others for frying. They are eaten hot or cold, in stews, soups, casseroles, salads, and pancakes or alone as chips, fries, or gnocchi. Potatoes can even be fermented to produce **wine**!

Radicchio

A member of the Chicory family, radicchio (*Cichorium intybus*) is known as Italian red winter **lettuce** or Italian chicory. It resembles a small head of red **cabbage**, with leaves in shades or red, purple, white, and green. Still relatively expensive, it is used more as a color and flavor accent than as a base for salad, as it is slightly bitter in taste, and it is often used in the Passover meal to represent the bitter herbs of the Exodus. In addition, radicchio can be braised in broth for an unusual hot side dish. It can also be grilled (cut the head in half lengthwise) with oil, sautéed, and steamed. The raw curved leaves can be used to hold cooked vegetables, condiments, or other fillings. Radicchio is high in magnesium and potassium and relatively rich in vitamin A.

Radish

The radish (*Raphanus sativus*) is one of humankind's oldest root vegetables, believed to have been cultivated in Europe as early as the Neolithic era (3000–1500 B.C.E.). Its exact origins are not known: some botanists propose the Mediterranean wild radish (*R. raphanistrum*) as the ancestor; others, the Spanish radish (*R. maritimus*); still others, some long-lost Asian species, as the earliest record of radishes comes from China, in the document known as the *Rhya* of 1100 B.C.E. Herodotus (484?–425? B.C.E.) recorded that radishes were part of the diet of the workers who were building the Egyptian pyramids, and the ancient Egyptians were enthusiastic proponents of radish-seed oil. Radishes are traditionally used in the Passover meal to represent the bitter herbs of the Exodus. Both China and India grow special varieties of the radish particularly for their oils.

Whatever its origin, the radish is now cultivated worldwide, mostly for its root, but also for its pods, seeds, and leaves. *R. raphanistrum* and *R. landra* have leaves that can be eaten fresh in salads or boiled. The rat-tailed radish (*R. sativus* var. *caudatus*) grows pods of 8 to 12 inches that can be eaten raw.

As for the radishes cultivated for their roots, there are two types: summer and winter. The summer radishes are red or white, and spherical, oblong, oval, or conical in shape. Their taste is sharp and pungent, but they do not store well. The winter radishes grow more slowly but store much longer; these include the Japanese daikon (*R. sativus* var. *longipinnatus*), which can grow to 3 feet in length; a rose-colored Chinese radish; and several black radishes (*R. sativus* var. *nigra*). Winter radishes are frequently eaten raw, but they are also cooked and pickled and seem to have been more popular during ancient and medieval times than they are now.

Radishes are very low in calories and fat and have no cholesterol, and they are high in vitamin C and folacin.

In the United States, the most popular radishes today are the black, California mammoth white, daikon, red globe, and white icicles. To prepare them for consumption, radishes are scrubbed but not usually peeled. They can be eaten raw as a condiment or as part of a salad; they can also be boiled, steamed, or stir-fried and served alone or with fish or **chicken**.

Red Chili

See **pepper**.

Rhubarb

Rhubarb is descended primarily from wild rhubarb found in the colder region of the Tien Shan Mountains in Central Asia through Mongolia to western China. Humans first used rhubarb as a medicine because the roots are a source of anthaquinone: the first written record of rhubarb is found in the Chinese herbal book titled *Pen-King,* which dates from 2700 B.C.E. The roots of two species of rhubarb, *Rheum officinalis* and *R. palmatum,* when dried and crushed, are extremely effective in purging the digestive tract, and powdered rhubarb root is quite helpful in treating amoebic dysentery. By the 1st century B.C.E. rhubarb root was known in the Roman Empire, having been recorded as a pharmaceutical by Dioscorides, an army doctor from Cilicia in southeastern Turkey. With the fall of the Roman Empire, the use of rhubarb as a purgative seems to have been lost to Europe, though it continued to be used in Asia and was "rediscovered" by Marco Polo during his travels. Rhubarb powder commanded extravagant prices in France in the 16th century C.E. In the 17th, China began trading with Russia, which quickly took control of the rhubarb trade in Europe, but this monopoly fell apart when China was forced to trade with other European powers in the 19th century. The Chinese guarded the secret of growing and processing rhubarb, and efforts to produce the medicine outside of China were unsuccessful, as the only species of rhubarb that could be made to grow was *R. rhaponticum,* and its roots are not very rich in anthaquinone. However, the stems of *rhaponticum* (which is sometimes considered to be the same species as *R. rhabarbarum,* the contemporary garden rhubarb) are edible, and the English began to cook them as a vegetable in the 17th century. The stems do not have the medicinal effects that the roots possess. By the 18th century, when **sugar** became more readily available and less expensive, rhubarb pies, puddings, custards, and crumbles became popular. In North America, rhubarb became known as the Pie Plant. Although some people of northern European origin still cook rhubarb stems as a vegetable, rhubarb is used in Iranian stews and Middle Eastern dishes, and the Italians make an aperitif called *rabarbaro* from rhubarb stems, most of the time rhubarb is cooked as a fruit for dessert dishes.

Rhubarb is now grown either in hothouses (in which case the stalks are pink or light red) or in the field (in which case the stalks are dark red); hothouse rhubarb tends to be milder and less stringy. When buying or growing rhubarb, it is essential to remember to remove and discard all the leaves before cooking; rhubarb leaves, both raw and cooked, contain a deadly poison and must *never* be eaten! Rhubarb stems can be baked or stewed and sweetened with sugar or fruit juices. The stems are high in vitamin C, calcium, and manganese.

Rutabaga

The rutabaga (*Brassica napobrassica* or *B. napus* var. *napobrassica*) is a relative of the **cabbage** and the **turnip**. The first record of rutabagas dates from the 17th century C.E., and they were used mostly as animal feed in southern Europe, though they much prefer colder temperatures. They spread north, and their popularity in Sweden earned them their nickname the swede, swede turnip, yellow turnip, neep, or turnip. Rutabagas made their way to North America by the beginning of the 19th century. During World War I rutabagas saved many people from starvation; after the war, they became very unpopular in Europe, though they are still a food staple of European Jews.

Like turnips, rutabagas can be stored at low temperatures for long periods, and they overwinter well. They are at least 4 inches in diameter, with tan skin and a dark purple band at the top. Their flesh has a sweet, slightly peppery taste and can be eaten fresh or baked, roasted, boiled, braised, steamed, or stir-fried (they must be peeled first). They are often mashed with **potato**es or **carrot**s, added to soups, chowders, and stews, made into "coleslaw," or served with other crudités.

Low in fat, sodium, and cholesterol, rutabagas are high in vitamin C, folacin, and potassium.

Scallion

The scallion (*Allium fistulosum*) is often confused with the **shallot** (*A. ascolonicum* or *A. oschaninii*). Many authorities believe that they are actually the same species; others assert that neither one exists as a separate species but that both are simply varieties, or young specimens, of the **onion**. We will follow those botanists who state that the scallion and the shallot are both separate species.

The scallion is different in appearance from the onion: onions shade off to pale green or white at the bottom, while the scallion is dark green for the entire length of its leaves. Scallions and shallots have the same appearance, but scallions have a much stronger taste than shallots.

As a member of the Lily (or Onion) family, the scallion has a long history of cultivation, and it serves a variety of cuisines and dishes. Both the leaves and the roots can be eaten, in **tuna** or **potato** salads, **cheese** spreads, dips, **rice** dishes, **tomato** sauces, soups, omelets, and stir-fries.

Scallions are very good sources of vitamin C and folacin. In fact, scallion greens provide about five times more vitamin C than onions. Scallions also provide significant amounts of vitamin A and iron. With no cholesterol and very little fat, they are a nutritious addition to one's diet.

Shallot

The shallot (*Allium ascolonicum* or *A. oschaninii*) is often confused with the **scallion** (*A. fistulosum*). Many authorities believe that they are actually the same species; others assert that neither one exists as a separate species but that both are simply varieties, or young specimens, of the **onion**. We will follow those botanists who state that the shallot and the scallion are both separate species.

The preeminent shallot is the French grey or griselle (*A. oschaninii*). Small and mild tasting (milder than scallions and much milder than onions), the shallot bulb has a yellow or brown, onion-like skin. The interior is white with purple tinges but is divided into garlic-like cloves; but unlike those of **garlic**, the shallot cloves are not each enclosed in a separate sheath. When fresh, shallots and scallions have the same appearance—dark green along the entire length of their leaves.

As a member of the Lily (or Onion) family, the shallot has a long history of cultivation, having originated in central or southwestern Asia. Shallots serve a variety of cuisines and dishes, from Asian to Middle Eastern to French. Both the leaves and the roots can be eaten, in **tuna** or **potato** salads, **cheese** spreads, dips, **rice** dishes, **tomato** sauces, soups, omelets, and stir-fries. Shallot bulbs can also be pickled.

Shallots are very good sources of vitamin C and folacin and provide significant amounts of vitamin A and iron. With no cholesterol and very little fat, they are a nutritious addition to one's diet.

Spinach

Spinach (*Spinacia oleracea*) is a relative newcomer to the domestic garden. Its origins are as yet unknown: some botanists claim that it originated in Asia, where it continues to grow wild; others assert that it is native to the lands of Persia (in modern times, a wild spinach [*S. tetrandra*] has grown in that part of the world) and did not enter cultivation until the 7th century C.E., in China. It is almost certain that spinach was not known to the peoples of the Bible: there is no ancient Hebrew word for spinach, and there is no written or archaeological record of the consumption of spinach in the Middle East, the eastern Mediterranean, or northern Africa before the common era. However, spinach is used in many Middle Eastern dishes today. There are many conflicting accounts of spinach's entry into Europe: some say that the Moors brought it to Spain in the 9th century; others that it was new to England in the 16th century. Food historian Waverley Root has concluded that spinach came to Europe in the 11th century, brought either by the Moors or the Crusaders. It was fairly widespread throughout Europe by the 12th century and had made its way to the Americas by the 18th. Today it is grown worldwide.

Spinach is extremely rich in vitamin A and folacin. It is high in vitamin C, potassium, and magnesium, low in fat, but high in sodium and low in fiber. Although spinach is rich in iron and calcium, those minerals are bound into an insoluble salt that the body cannot easily absorb. It has no cholesterol. Three main types of spinach are available in the United States: savoy, with crinkly, curly leaves and a dark-green color; flat, or smooth-leaf, with unwrinkled, spade-shaped leaves; and semi-savoy, with slightly crinkled leaves. The growers of most U.S. spinach are in California and Texas.

Spinach does not store well, but it can be prepared in many ways: blanched, steamed, or sautéed for a dish of spinach leaves; used as a salad base instead of lettuce; added to vegetable soups or broths; mixed into soufflés or omelets; ground for appetizer dips; or baked into **bread**s.

Squash

Native to Mexico and Central America, the many species of squash (*Cucurbita* genus; not to be confused with gourds, which are in the same family) comprised one of the Three Sisters (maize [**corn**], **bean**s, and squash) cultivated by Native Americans. These three vegetables were usually planted together: the beans climbed the corn stalks, which shaded the squash, which kept the weeds down. Squashes are divided into two groups: winter and summer. The winter squashes include the acorn, gourd, pumpkin, and **butternut** squashes. The summer squashes (*C. pepo*) are the **zucchini** (green), patty pan (scallop), chayote (white), yellow straightneck, and yellow crookneck squash.

The summer squashes are harvested when the fruits are tender and relatively small. They contain large amounts of vitamin C and are low in calories, so they are often eaten raw (in salads or as finger food), though alone their taste is relatively bland. They are also boiled, sautéed, baked, and fried; added to sauces for pasta or seafood; and grated and used in **bread**s, cakes, muffins, pancakes, and omelets. Zucchini flowers are also a flavorful addition to pancakes. Termed a vegetable but botanically a fruit, summer squash would not have been known to the peoples of the Bible (though the word for "gourd" in the scriptures was often erroneously translated as squash) and did not enter Europe until introduced by Christopher Columbus in the 16th century C.E., at which time the cultivation of squash quickly spread to the Middle East, Africa, and Asia. (It is probable that the "squash" referred to by the Romans Pliny, Apicius, and Martial was really an edible gourd and not a true squash.) Now squash is a staple of many cuisines throughout the world, including the Middle East.

Squash, Butternut

Butternut squash (*Cucurbita moschata*) is a winter **squash** with a sweet, nutty taste. It has yellow skin and orange flesh, turning a deeper orange when ripe.

Butternut squash can be prepared in many different ways. It can be roasted or baked, puréed or mashed into soups, and added to casseroles, **bread**s, pies, and muffins.

This variety of squash is high in fiber, vitamin C, manganese, magnesium, and potassium.

Squash, Zucchini

Zucchini is a variety of summer **squash** (*Cucurbita pepo*), which also includes the patty pan (scallop), chayote (white), yellow straightneck, and yellow crookneck squash.

Termed a vegetable but botanically a fruit, zucchini would not have been known to the people of the Bible as it is a native of the Americas. Squash seeds have been discovered in Mexican burial caves dating from 8000 B.C.E., and their cultivation by Native Americans spread north into the Canadian lands. No squashes (or zucchini) were known in Europe before Christopher Columbus' voyages, but when he brought squash back with him in the 16th century C.E., it spread remarkably quickly throughout Europe and then to the Middle East, Africa, and Asia. Now squash is a staple of many cuisines throughout the world.

There are many varieties of zucchini: some are medium-green to gray-green, others are dark green; some have pale flecks or spots, others stripes; some are even golden yellow.

Zucchini grows best in warm, sunny weather. The plants fruit prolifically, and the squash can grow to several feet in length. However, these large fruits are generally seedy and starchy and very bland. The young, small fruit (about 6 inches in length) are the most tender and tasty. Zucchini contains large amounts of vitamin C and folacin. Low in calories, it is often eaten raw (in salads or as finger food), though with some kind of dressing or dip (which adds calories) because alone its taste is relatively unremarkable. Zucchini can also be boiled, sautéed, baked, and fried; added to sauces for pasta or seafood; and grated and used in **breads**, cakes, muffins, pancakes, and omelets. Zucchini flowers are also picked fresh for eating: they are very low in calories and are a good source of beta-carotene, vitamin C, and potassium. They can be fried or stuffed (which adds calories and fat), and they add a delicate flavor to omelets and other egg dishes, pancakes and waffles, and soups.

Tomato

The tomato (*Solanum lycopersicum* or *Lycopersicon esculentum*), although considered and used as a vegetable, is a fruit of the Nightshade family. Tomatoes originated in South and Central America and were probably first cultivated in what is now Peru. They would not have been known to the peoples of the Bible. Tomatoes were brought to what is now Mexico about 1000 B.C.E. The Europeans who settled in the Americas beginning in the 16th century C.E. believed the to-mato to be deadly poisonous; not until the 18th century did tomatoes become accepted as a food item in Europe and North America, and they did not become really popular until the end of the 19th century. Now they are grown worldwide and have become a staple of Italian, French, Middle Eastern, and other cuisines. Tomatoes are cooked in sauces, soups, stews, and casseroles; they are eaten raw in salads and as appetizers; they are squeezed for their juice; they are even pickled and fried. Tomatoes contain lycopene, an antioxidant that is believed to help prevent prostate cancer, and their consumption is believed to benefit the heart.

Truffle

Truffles are a type of fungi and are sometimes grouped along with the large number of **mushroom**s. The two main types of truffles are the black (*Tuber melanosporum*) and white (*T. magnatum*). The black grows mostly in France, Spain, and Italy; the white, which some gourmets consider superior in taste and scent, is found primarily in northern Italy. Chefs highly prize both black and white truffles for their flavor, but they are valuable because they are nearly impossible to cultivate and very difficult to harvest in the wild. Truffles grow beneath the ground, attached to the roots of oak or hazel trees; only specially trained pigs or dogs can sniff out the truffles, which truffle hunters, or *trufficulteurs,* must then carefully dig out of the earth. Truffle season is late fall and winter.

With a textured surface and a dense flesh, truffles have an earthy taste. Because of their strong flavor and expense, recipes normally call for only small amounts of truffles. They are sliced or grated raw over hot dishes. Black truffles are usually peeled before serving, the peelings used to flavor soups and stocks.

Ancient manuscripts mention the eating of "truffles" in Mesopotamia by 1800 B.C.E., and also in ancient Greece, Rome, and northern Africa, so it is possible that the peoples of the Bible would have known and used truffles in their cooking—but it is highly unlikely that the "truffles" mentioned were the true truffles now prized today, as truffles are a mushroom of the temperate zones. The first reliable mention of truffles occurs in the 15th century C.E., when the use of pigs to hunt truffles is described. At that time, truffles were mostly pickled, but in the 17th century the noted chef Pierre François de la Varenne began using truffles as other mushrooms were used. Because of their rarity and cost, truffles have been the food of aristocrats, and are even today.

Aside from black and white truffles, there are other brown, gray, and violet truffles found in France. Inferior tasting truffles grow wild in England and the United States. There are also three types of truffles from China (*T. sinensis* or *T. indicum; T. himalayensis;* and another without a scientific name), but these are not as tasty as the European varieties.

Black truffles are sometimes known as "the black diamond of the kitchen" or "the black pearl." Over the centuries, people have attributed an aphrodisiacal quality to truffles, but that is mere fiction. Truffles do provide some iron and other minerals. However, they have little nutritional value, and it is their taste alone that makes them so important in the kitchen.

Turnip

The turnip (*Brassica rapa*) is a member of the **Cabbage** family. A root vegetable with white or yellow flesh, turnips come in many shapes and sizes—some have weighed in at as much as 50 pounds.

Turnips were known in ancient India. Perhaps the first to cultivate turnips were the Babylonians, from whom the peoples of the Bible probably adopted this vegetable. From the lands of Asia Minor the turnip spread westward. The Romans also cultivated turnips, and turnips were a staple in the diet of medieval Europe. Both French and British settlers brought turnips to the Americas. Tolerating poor soils and ripening quickly, the turnip has often been considered a food of the poor.

Turnips are harvested in the fall and winter; they store very well at cool temperatures and can be part of a year-round diet. They can be baked and roasted, boiled, braised, steamed, stir-fried, mashed, puréed, and even eaten raw. Turnips are rich in vitamin C, relatively high in carbohydrates and sodium, and have no cholesterol.

Besides the root, turnip tops, or greens, are also widely consumed, particularly in the southern United States. The greens contain more calcium and iron than the roots.

Watercress

Watercress (*Nasturtium officinale*) is a cruciferous vegetable, a member of the **Cabbage** family, and is one of the oldest known leafy foods. Native to Asia and Europe, it grows quickly in streambeds and forms masses of pungent, dark-green sprigs that have a sharp flavor. It is used as a garnish and a salad and sandwich ingredient.

The ancient Persians, Greeks, and Romans all ate watercress, observing that soldiers who ate watercress were healthier than those who didn't. It is very likely that the various peoples of the Bible collected and ate watercress. Cultivation may have started very early, though one of the first mentions of cultivated watercress comes from Hippocrates in 400 B.C.E. European immigrants probably brought watercress to the Americas in the 18th century C.E.

Watercress is low in calories but high in iron, calcium, folic acid, and vitamins A and C. Some scientists now believe that watercress can help break tobacco addiction and can even prevent certain cancers.

FRUITS AND NUTS

Almond

The almond (*Prunus communis*) is a close relative of the peach. Originating in central Asia, the almond became indigenous to the Mediterranean basin and the Middle East. Wild almonds (*P. amygdalus*) continue to thrive in northern Africa and on the dry steppes of the Caucasus, Turkey, and Afghanistan. Almond trees grow to about 20 feet high in the wild and are larger when cultivated, primarily in California, South Africa, Australia, Spain, Italy, and Provence.

Although almonds are now the leading nut crop worldwide, they would not have been a likely candidate for cultivation. The nut seeds of wild almonds are extremely bitter; when placed in water, the seeds produce prussic acid, which is a fast-acting, deadly poison. A mouthful of raw wild almonds will kill a person. Fortunately, our early ancestors discovered that heating almond seeds makes them edible. Today, both bitter and sweet almonds are available in some countries, though it is advisable to stay away from the bitter ones, which if consumed in quantity can make one ill.

Almonds were domesticated before 2800 B.C.E. and have been identified at archaeological sites in the Dead Sea Basin, in Greece, and in Egypt. Before that, hunter-gatherer groups collected wild almonds for cooking and consumption. The Bible mentions almonds (Genesis 43:11; Exodus 25:33 and 37:19–20; Numbers 17:8; Ecclesiastes 12:5; Jeremiah 1:11), and peoples of the Bible would definitely have used almonds in their cooking.

Cooks in India and the Levant (that part of southwest Asia between the Mediterranean Sea, Mesopotamia, the Arabian Desert, and the Taurus mountains) still use almonds to flavor meat dishes. In Europe and the Americas, bakers use almonds or almond products (flakes, pastes, butter, extract) to flavor desserts, and both sugared and salted almonds are eaten as snack food. Almonds are extremely high in vitamin E, magnesium, calcium, iron, riboflavin, phosphorus, and dietary fiber. In some places, almond oil is a cosmetic and is so fine that it can be used to lubricate watches.

Apple

The apple (*Malus silvestris* spp. *domestica*) is, like the **apricot**—with which it has often been confused in Bible translations—a member of the Rose family. Native to the land between the Black and Caspian Seas south of the Caucasus Mountains according to many botanists (though others claim the apple is native to the Baltic region), the apple descended from the **crab-** (or wild) **apple** (M. *silvestris*). Spread by birds and animals, the crabapple mutated as it moved across Europe and Asia. Crabapples were part of the prehistoric human diet: archaeologists have discovered crabapple remains in Stone Age (before about 6000 B.C.E.) sites across Europe, from the Adriatic to the North Sea coasts. The first record of apple cultivation comes from a Babylonian tomb in the ancient city of Ur, dating from circa 2000 B.C.E. Apple remains have also been discovered at the Kadesh-Barne'a oasis, located between the Sinai and Negev deserts, dating from about 1000 B.C.E. And in the 13th century B.C.E. Ramses II planted apple trees in the Nile delta. By the 7th century B.C.E. the ancient Greeks were growing and using apples in their marriage ceremonies, and by the 6th century B.C.E. the ancient peoples of western Asia and the northern Mediterranean were growing apples, using grafting techniques learned from the peoples of Asia. One of the labors of Hercules was to capture the Golden Apples of the Hesperides, and the apple figures prominently in Greek mythology and lore, including the cause of the Trojan War (though those golden apples may actually have been lemons). Nevertheless, the apple was most likely not a common food of the ancient Hebrews; the Israelites may have known of apples from their time in Egypt, but they would not have been able to take apple trees with them on their wanderings through the desert, and they would certainly not have found wild apple trees there. It is possible that apples may have been growing in the Promised Land, but the climate there is not propitious for apple cultivation either.

The ancient Romans became sophisticated cultivators of apples: they were growing at least seven different types by the 2nd century B.C.E. and thirty-six varieties by the 1st century C.E. The Romans worshipped a goddess of fruit, Pomona, who, along with Venus, was often shown holding apples. Apple remains have been discovered from Roman Britain. Indeed, apple cultivation has a long history in England; many famous apple varieties (Old English Pearmains, Costards, Cox's Orange Pippins, Cox's Pomonas, and Bramley's Seedlings, among many others) developed there, and the apple even inspired Isaac Newton to propose his theory of gravity. The French were also great apple growers and originated the Pippin varieties. Domestic apple varieties probably did not make their way to China until the Middle Ages.

English colonists brought apples (seeds and cuttings) to the Americas in the early 17th century, finding there a perfect environment for apple cultivation, which needs cold winters and hot summers (the apple requires at least two months of winter to regain its strength after harvest). By the mid-18th century, New England was exporting apples. In the early 19th century the legendary Johnny Appleseed (born John Chapman) took a load of apple seedlings and a bible and set off down the Ohio River, preaching and planting wherever he roamed, from western Pennsylvania to Indiana. Because the apples grown from seed did not often produce fruit the equal of that grown on grafted trees, they were sometimes made into cider or fed to livestock. Some of the finest eating apples were accidental hybrids or chance trees grown from seed: the Northern Spy, the Spitzbergen, the Jonathan, and the Rhode Island Greening all were discovered by chance and further cultivated by grafting. Henderson Llewelling (or Luelling), a farmer from Iowa, took several wagonloads of apple trees and other plants to Oregon in 1845; though his family of pioneers was afflicted with cholera, attacked by Native Americans, and abandoned by the rest of their wagon train, he persevered, made it to the Willamette Valley, planted his trees, and became wealthy by selling the fruit on the West Coast. Apple orchards are now most prevalent and productive in Washington, Michigan, and New York, with many orchards found throughout New England and down the Atlantic Coast as far south as Virginia.

The Victorian English were great lovers of apples, developing famous varieties such as Bramleys, Russets, Swaars, Gravensteins, Golden Reinettes, and Red Astrakhans. During the same years, American farmers developed the Delicious, the Golden Delicious, and Grimes Golden. Golden Delicious is now famous around the world, though many say that its taste is much inferior to that of the older and more delicate cultivars.

Today, about 7,500 varieties of apples are grown worldwide, but there are eight apples that make up 80 percent of domestic U.S. production. These are:

- Red Delicious, a bright red apple that accounts for almost half the U.S. domestic crop. It is sweet, crisp, and juicy and is best eaten raw.
- Golden Delicious, a golden-yellow or yellow-green all-purpose apple that can be eaten fresh or baked, used in pies, or made into applesauce. When cut up, its

flesh does not turn dark as quickly as that of other apples. It is unrelated to the Red Delicious.

- Granny Smith, a green, all-purpose apple with a tart flavor and crisp flesh.
- Jonathan, a deep-red apple used for eating, baking pies, and making applesauce.
- McIntosh, a green-and-red all-purpose apple that is slightly tart and very juicy. It is the parent apple of such varieties as Cortland and Empire.
- Rome Beauty, a red or red-striped apple that is best when cooked or used in baking.
- Stayman, a purplish-red all-purpose apple with slightly tart and juicy flesh.
- York, also known as York Imperial, a pinkish-red baking apple with yellow and somewhat juicy flesh.

Of course, many apples are delicious eaten fresh from the tree, but there are many ways of preparing apples: baking them whole or stuffed, using them in pies and cakes, cooking them into applesauce, adding them raw to salads, squeezing them into cider, fermenting them into hard cider, even turning them into so-called apple butter, which is really a jamlike product. One of the appealing features of the apple is its long shelf life: when kept in cold storage, apples go into a sort of suspended animation that prevents them from further ripening and protects them from spoilage.

In general, the entirety of the apple fruit is edible, but one should avoid eating too many apple seeds, as they contain tiny amounts of the poison cyanide. Apples are generally high in vitamin C, moderate in dietary fiber, beta-carotene, potassium, and boron, low in calories and fat, and have no cholesterol.

Apricot

The apricot (*Prunus armeniaca*) is a member of the Rose family, along with the **almond, cherry,** peach, **apple,** and **plum.** Native to what is now eastern Tibet and northern China, it has small, unpalatable fruit in the wild. It is not known when the Chinese first began cultivating apricots—perhaps as early as 2000 B.C.E.—but the fruit made its way rather quickly to ancient Mesopotamia and was reported in the Hanging Gardens of Babylon. By the 1st century B.C.E. apricots had spread west to the Levant (that part of southwest Asia between the Mediterranean Sea, Mesopotamia, the Arabian Desert, and the Taurus mountains) and were well known in ancient Rome, though not in ancient Greece. It is generally accepted that the peoples of the Bible were familiar with and fond of apricots. Many biblical scholars believe that the fruit referred to in the Garden of Eden story was really an apricot, not an apple, as the early English translations stated. With the fall of the Roman Empire, apricots seem to have disappeared from Europe, to appear again with the Moorish colonization of Spain, and then again with the return of the Crusaders from the Holy Land.

The orange-yellow flesh of apricots is drier than that of peaches and peels away easily from the stone, or pit. Apricots are rich in vitamins A and C, iron, and potassium. They are low in fat and calories and have no cholesterol. Apricots are most nutritious when eaten fresh, but they can be broiled, grilled, poached, and dried, and they can also be squeezed for nectar. Untreated apricot pits contain amygdalin, a chemical that breaks down into, among other components, hydrogen cyanide, which can be poisonous. Another extract of the pits, known as Laetrile, is thought to help eradicate cancer, though no tests have definitively proved this theory.

Apricot trees are relatively delicate; they require a temperate climate with cool winters, when they go dormant, but early, warm springs, as they are extremely susceptible to frost. The United States (California) is the world's leading producer of apricots, but they are also grown widely in Europe, particularly in Hungary, Spain, France, Italy, Greece, and Turkey. Some of the more popular varieties of apricots include the Blenheim, Tilton, Patterson, and Castlebrite.

Banana

The banana (*Musa* cultivars of the Banana family) may have been one of the first fruits cultivated by humankind. Originating in the wet tropics of southeastern Asia, perhaps in the Malaysian peninsula, the banana is really a treelike perennial herb—the world's largest herb, in fact. Botanists have identified about forty species of bananas growing wild in the region, and it is likely that more have yet to be discovered. Most of these have seedy, generally inedible fruit, technically a false berry, which develops from the unfertilized female flowers of the plant. Prehistoric mutations produced a sterile plant that yielded seedless, edible fruit, and early peoples liked the fruit and began to cultivate them, taking the plants along when they migrated northwest toward India. These mutations hybridized with a hardier species of wild banana to produce the ancestors of the bananas so widely enjoyed today.

Recent archaeological evidence from Papua New Guinea indicates that banana cultivation was common by 5000 B.C.E., perhaps even by 8000 B.C.E. The first written mention of bananas dates from the 6th century B.C.E., in the Indian Buddhist literature. Bananas became known to the Mediterranean world only when Alexander the Great entered India about 330 B.C.E., but neither he nor his followers brought banana plants back with them. Not until Islam claimed Palestine and the eastern Mediterranean in the 7th and 8th centuries C.E. did the banana become at all known in Europe. In fact, the banana may be the Tree of Paradise mentioned in the Koran, and bananas have become an important ingredient in Middle Eastern cuisine. But climate prevented bananas from becoming established north of the Sahara Desert; instead, they spread southward into the African heartland. From there they made their way to the Canary Islands, and Spanish settlers took them to the Caribbean and then to Central and South America in the 16th century. Simultaneous with their westward spread, bananas may have been taken eastward from Malaysia through Polynesia and the Pacific.

But the perishable banana did not become an important trade product until the 19th century, when shipbuilders learned how to construct vessels that could cross the oceans quickly enough so that the bananas would not spoil before reaching their destination. These schooners, often called banana boats, raced one another from Brazil to New York and from the Caribbean to Liverpool to capture the market. Refrigerated steamships made the trade even more competitive and so lucrative that the United Fruit Company of Boston could use the profits generated from selling bananas to build railways and finance governments in Central and South America. Virtually servants of the company, the governments of Costa Rica, Panama, and Honduras became known as "banana republics." Today, Ecuador, Costa Rica, Colombia, and the Philippines are the world's major banana producers.

Bananas are extremely high in carbohydrates and so are an excellent source of energy. They are also rich in potassium and are recommended to people suffering from high blood pressure. Bananas may help ease both constipation and diarrhea.

Bananas occur in a large variety of sizes and colors, from small, inch-length to larger, foot-length fruits, and from green to yellow. The most commonly available varieties are the sweet M. *acuminata* and M. *x paradisiaca*, both of which are available fresh year-round. Most of the bananas exported outside of the tropics are of the Cavendish cultivar.

Bananas and plantains, which are a harder and starchier variety, are the staple food of many tropical and subtropical regions. Of course, bananas are eaten fresh, peeled and removed from the skin, either alone or in fruit salads, with ice cream, or even with peanut butter. Unripe bananas are often fried. Ripe bananas are sometimes mashed to produce a starchy paste that can also be fried or mixed with **bread** or cake batter. Bananas make a fine jam. They can be dried, either sliced or whole, and eaten as a snack. The flowers and the tender core of the trunk are also served either raw with dips or cooked in curries and soups. The long, large leaves can serve as building, clothing, and cooking materials.

Cantaloupe

The cantaloupe (*Cucumis melo cantalupensis*) is actually a type of **muskmelon** (*C. melo*). The cantaloupe got its name from Cantalupo, Italy, where in the 18th century C.E. the pope's gardener imported the melon's seeds from Armenia and began to grow them for the papal table. The French developed a variety of cantaloupe called Charentais, which has pale green skin. The popular Netted Gem cantaloupe with a beige rind and sweet orange flesh is actually a W. Atlee Burpee Company hybrid, introduced in the late 19th century.

Cantaloupe is delicious when eaten fresh from the rind, either chilled or at room temperature. It makes a fine addition to fruit salads. Wrapped in prosciutto, it adds color and flavor to antipasti. Seeded cantaloupe halves make a colorful and tasty serving bowl for cereals, **cheeses**, and even soups. Cantaloupe juice can also be distilled into liqueurs.

Of the melons, cantaloupe is highest in vitamin C and potassium. It is also extremely high in vitamin A and has no cholesterol.

Carob

Carob is the flesh of the pods of the carob tree (*Ceratonia siliqua*), an evergreen shrub native to the Mediterranean and Middle East. Growing to a height of more than 30 feet, the trees produce small red flowers and seed pods that are several inches in length. The flesh of the pods has a taste similar to that of **cocoa**, but carob has no caffeine and can be substituted for cocoa in a wide variety of ways. For millennia, carob was one of the few sweeteners known to humankind and so was an important ingredient in Middle Eastern cooking. Members of the Legume family, carob trees are quite resistant to drought and thrive in semiarid climates, such as the desert areas where John the Baptist conducted his ministry, and it is believed that the "**locusts**" often referred to as part of his diet (Matthew 3:4; Mark 1:6) were really carob pods (the translators of the Bible knew them as locust beans). Carob pods are also called St. John's bread.

Cherry

The cherry is related to the **apricot**, peach, **plum**, and, surprisingly, **almond**. Like them, the cherry belongs to the *Prunus* genus of the Rose family, and the cherry's ancestors also originated in the mountain valleys and upland forests of central Asia.

The cherry comes in two main varieties: sweet and sour. The sweet cherry, represented primarily by the Gean (*Prunus avium*), is a large tree that can reach 80 feet or more in height. Its flowers are white and its fruit is reddish-black. Its scientific name means "bird's cherry," an indication that birds find the fruit particularly tasty. It is now native to Europe, northern Africa, Turkey, and the greater Caucasus region, having migrated millennia ago from its land of origin. The sweet cherry was certainly part of the diet of early human hunter-gatherers: cherry stones from Gean fruits have been discovered in Neolithic and Bronze Age sites (5000–1500 B.C.E.) from Turkey to Portugal to Central Europe. By about 500 B.C.E. the cherry had been put into cultivation in Greece and Asia Minor. It is a rather difficult plant to cultivate, requiring cross-pollination from other trees for fruit to set. Also, it propagates best by grafting, a technique unknown in Europe until the time of ancient Greece, having made its way west from China, where it was invented. Plato's pupil Theophrastus wrote about the cultivation of cherries in *History of Plants,* and there is a Roman fresco that depicts a bird eating cherries. It is possible that cherries were known to the peoples of the Bible. The best-known sweet varieties today are the Bing, Lambert, Van, Chapman, Larian, and Black Republican, not to mention the lighter-skinned Rainier and Royal Ann.

The sour cherry, primarily represented by the Morello (*P. cerasus*), is likely a cross between the sweet cherry and the ground cherry (*P. fruticosa*), a shrub native to central and eastern Europe whose fruit is small and bitter. The Morello is a short tree, reaching about 25 feet in height, and it is capable of self-pollination. Because of the sour taste, its fruit is used mostly for jams and liqueurs. Today, the Montmorency variety is the best-known sour cherry.

Cherry cultivation in Europe declined with the fall of the Roman Empire, coming back into vogue during the 16th century C.E. European colonists brought cherries with them to the Americas: the sour varieties liked the climate of the Atlantic coast, while the sweet varieties found the Midwestern climate more suitable.

But North America already had indigenous cherries, which millennia ago had made their way east from central Asia through China (which now boasts the beautiful Chinese cherry *P. tomentosa*) and Siberia, across the Bering Land Bridge, and down the Pacific coast before crossing the continent. The American cherry populations became intermixed as European colonists began cultivating the American wild sand cherries (*P. besseyi* and *P. pumila*), and the Gean and Morello cherries escaped into the American wild. American natives also include the chokecherry (*P. virginiana*), the pin cherry (*P. pennsylvanica*), the sweet black cherry (*P. serotina*), and the southwestern chokecherry (*P. melanocarpa*), among others. Today, the United States is one of the leading producers of cherries.

Sweet cherries are high in calories, vitamin C, and potassium. Prized for their taste, they can be added to fruit salads, **yogurt**s, pies, cakes and muffins, cookies, pancakes and waffles, and meat and poultry dishes; they can even be used to make a delicious chilled cherry soup. Sour cherries, which are also high in vitamin A, are used most often for pie fillings and for jams, though **sugar** is usually added to temper the sour taste.

Clementine

See **orange**.

Coconut

The coconut palm (*Cocos nucifera*) is a tall palm tree that produces large numbers of coconuts, which are not true nuts at all but rather fibrous drupes, with a hard outer shell, a fibrous inner shell, and a juicy liquid center. The coconut palm has spread across much of the tropics, but its origins are somewhat obscure, as coconuts float and take root wherever they happen to wash ashore. Some botanists claim the tree is native to southeastern Asia; others, northwestern South America. Dating from more than 15 million years ago, fossils of a small, coconut palm–like plant have been found in New Zealand and India. Coconuts were known in Egypt in the 6th century C.E., brought in from the shores of the Indian Ocean, and they are often used today in Middle Eastern cooking. They did not become known again in Europe until Marco Polo journeyed to Asia in the 13th century. They were "discovered" again by Ferdinand Magellan during his voyages to the East Indies and the South Pacific in the 16th century. It is unlikely that coconuts would have been known to the peoples of the Bible, as the coconut palm requires sufficient rainfall and circulating ground water in order to thrive.

Coconut palms produce coconuts at five to seven years of age. The individual coconuts can take an entire year to ripen, but the trees bloom year-round, and each flower spike can develop into a cluster of six to twelve coconuts; thus a tree can yield as many as seventy-five coconuts each year. Immature coconuts, known as spoon coconuts, are a delicacy: the interior is still soft and gelatinous, with a lively flavor, and is eaten from the shell with a spoon. Coconut milk, which is widely used as a cooking liquid in the tropics, is not actually the liquid found in the center of the coconut; that liquid is called coconut water. Coconut milk is the juice that comes from squeezing grated coconut meat that has been soaked in water. Coconut oil is extracted from copra, the dried coconut meat.

Coconuts are high in B vitamins, vitamin C, iron, potassium, and phosphorous. They have no cholesterol but are high in saturated fatty acids.

Coconuts are delicious when eaten raw, fresh from the shell. Their meat can also be dried, to extend its shelf-life and concentrate its nutrients.

Hearts of palm, also known as "millionaire's salad," are the interior of the growing tip of the coconut tree; unfortunately, harvesting the tip will result in the death of the tree.

In addition to the fruit and its uses, coconut palms have also provided fiber for ropes and mats, lumber for construction, fronds for weaving and roof thatch, fuel for cooking, and even trunks that have been hollowed out into drums and canoes. Known in Sanskrit as "the tree which provides all the necessities of life" and in Malay as "the tree of a thousand uses," the coconut palm truly lives up to its reputation.

Cranberry

The cranberry is a low, creeping shrub that grows in acidic bogs throughout the cooler Northern Hemisphere. Cranberries are part of the *Oxycoccus* subgenus of the *Vaccinium* genus, though some botanists name the genus *Oxycoccus*. The four species of cranberry are

- the common or northern cranberry (*V. oxycoccus* or *O. palustris*), which is native to northern Europe, northern Asia, and northern North America, and which produces a small pale pink berry
- the small cranberry (*V. microcarpum* or *O. microcarpus*), which is native to northern Europe and northern Asia
- the American cranberry (*V. macrocarpon* or *O. macrocarpus*), which is native to the northeastern part of North America and is the largest species
- the southern mountain cranberry (*V. erythrocarpum* or *O. erythrocarpus*), which is native to the high altitudes of the southeastern region of North America

Cranberries would not have appeared on the menus of the peoples of the Bible. Since prehistoric times, cranberries have been part of the diet of Arctic and northern peoples, who ate them both raw and cooked. Because raw cranberries are extremely acidic, native peoples often cooked them with **honey** or maple syrup used as a sweetener. They also pounded cranberries in with dried meat and melted animal fat to produce an edible mixture that could be stored for very long periods. Dried cranberries alone will keep almost indefinitely and are easily transportable. According to tradition, Native Americans introduced the starving Plymouth settlers to cranberry sauce in the early 17th century C.E., and the cranberry has been part of the U.S. Thanksgiving feast ever since.

The cultivation of cranberries probably began in the early 19th century in Cape Cod, Massachusetts. They are planted in diked fields, and when the berries are ripe, the fields are flooded and the bushes jostled about. The berries float and are easily skimmed off the surface of the water.

Cranberries provide potassium and vitamin C. They are made into jams, jellies, and juices. Fresh or dried, they are added to cakes, muffins, **breads**, and cookies. There is some evidence to suggest that cranberry juice reduces the rate of urinary tract infections. They are common today in Middle Eastern cooking.

Currant

Growing in clusters on vines like grapes, the currant is a member of the Gooseberry family. Currants come in three main varieties—red and white (*Ribes rubrum*) and black (actually, very dark purple or blue: *R. nigrum*)—though there are more than one hundred species of *Ribes*. The white is the sweetest, though the rarest; the red is the most common; the black is cultivated mainly for use in jams, jellies, liqueurs and cordials (crème de cassis and kir), and even ice cream, as it is very bitter when eaten fresh.

Native to temperate climates in the Northern Hemisphere (Europe, North America, and northern Asia), the currant would not have been known to the peoples of the Bible. Currant seeds have been found in a Danish archaeological site dating from before 4000 B.C.E., and Native Americans almost certainly enjoyed the plentiful red currants they could gather. Historic records indicate that the cultivation of currants began in the 16th century C.E. in Denmark, the Netherlands, and along the Baltic, though it is possible that currants were under cultivation before then. The currant quickly spread to England and France. By the 17th century, colonists had brought black currants to the Americas, where they flourished alongside the native red currants.

Though they are still common in Europe, currants are difficult to find today in North America because currant farming was banned in the United States in the early 1900s. Currant plants are host to a fungus that leaves them unaffected but moves on to cause blister rust, a disease that kills white pine trees. Because this pine was so valuable to the lumber industry, drastic steps were taken to eliminate the fungus. A resurgence of interest in native food products has brought the currant back into favor.

Currants are very high in vitamin C, potassium, and fiber. Of the varieties, the black currants have the most nutritional value when fresh but lose much of their vitamin C when cooked.

What are often referred to as "currants" in the Bible were really dried **grapes** (**raisin**s). The word *currant* was a corruption of *Corinth,* where by circa 500 B.C.E. Dionysius had become the patron deity of vines and **wine**. This corruption carried over into Greek translations of the scriptures.

Date

Among the sweetest of fruits, the date is the ripe fruit of the towering date palm (*Phoenix dactylifera*), which thrives in the dry, desertlike regions of northern Africa and the Middle East but is also now cultivated in California and Arizona. It is believed that dates originated in the area of what is present-day Iraq. Dates were domesticated before 3000 B.C.E.—indeed, they were one of the first fruits to be cultivated deliberately—and have become a staple of Middle Eastern cuisine. The peoples of the Bible would certainly have enjoyed dates, both fresh and dried; the Bible describes Jericho as the city of palm trees (Deuteronomy 34:3; Judges 1:16; II Chronicles 28:15), and Jericho was noted in the ancient world for the quality of its dates. Dates became available in Europe during the Middle Ages and were well known in England during Elizabethan times, though they were very expensive. Not until the European colonization of Africa and the Middle East did dates become easily affordable, and cultivation in California did not begin until the early 20th century C.E.

Dates come in three varieties: soft, semisoft, and dry. The semisoft Deglet Noor is the most often found in the market, though the semisoft Zahidi and Medjool are also available. The soft Barhi and the dry varieties are less popular, though dry dates are more likely to be stocked in health-food stores. Dried dates store extremely well, but semisoft dates need to be refrigerated.

Dates are high in dietary fiber and rich in **sugar**. They are often eaten alone, as a snack, or stuffed (with **almonds**, **cheese**, or fruit fillings). Dates can also add a sweet touch to stews, casseroles, and meat dishes, and they are a fine addition to many desserts.

Fig

The fig (*Ficus carica*), a member of the Mulberry family, has an ancient history. Probably native to Asia Minor, the fig was likely brought into cultivation circa 3500 B.C.E., as indicated by evidence found at archaeological sites in the Jordan Valley and Dead Sea region, and Sumerian clay writing tablets reveal that figs were being grown in Mesopotamia by 2500 B.C.E. Egyptians also recorded figs as early as 2750 B.C.E. Of course, Neolithic populations gathered and consumed wild figs, and remains have been found at archaeological sites dating from as early as about 7500 B.C.E. Ancient Athens was famous for its figs, and both Greek and Spartan athletes trained on a diet of them. Homer mentioned figs in both his *Iliad* and *Odyssey,* and archaeobotanists believe that the Greeks were accomplished cultivators of figs by the 7th century B.C.E. As the Greeks and Phoenicians colonized the Mediterranean basin, figs spread to Italy, Spain, and northern Africa, and by the 1st century C.E., about two dozen different varieties of figs were known throughout the Roman Empire. The Romans held the fig in high esteem: Romulus and Remus, the supposed founders of Rome, were said to have been suckled by the wolf beneath a fig tree, consequently held sacred by Romans; and on the first day of their year, many Romans gave one another presents of figs. There is also a sacred fig tree in Anuradhapura, Sri Lanka, which is believed to be a cutting of the bo tree that shaded the Buddha when he achieved nirvana. The Jewish tradition is not so kind to figs. The Bible mentions figs very early in the story of humankind, stating that Adam and Eve made clothing from fig leaves to hide their nakedness from God (Genesis 3:6–7); some scholars believe that the Tree of Knowledge mentioned in the Garden of Eden story may have been a fig tree. The Christian tradition is no kinder, for in the Gospels of Mark (11:13–14) and Matthew (21:19), Jesus curses the fig tree that has no fruit. At any rate, it is certain that the peoples of the Bible knew and enjoyed figs: for example, Isaiah instructed that a poultice made of figs be applied to cure King Hezekiah of his boils (II Kings 20:7). Figs spread as far north as England, and Shakespeare mentions them in both *Othello* and *Antony and Cleopatra.* Spanish colonists brought the fig to the Americas; California is now a major producer of figs.

By nature, the fig has an odd and unique botany. The "fruit" that humans consume is not actually a fruit but is, in fact, a hollow, fleshy receptacle containing tiny flowers. These flowers are pollinated and ripen their seeds without ever being exposed to the light. Wild figs are either male or female, and the "fruit" on the female trees will drop off unless pollinated by the male trees. The only way pollination can occur is by means of the tiny fig wasp (*Blastophaga psenes*), which lays its eggs in the male trees and then, as an adult, picks up pollen, flies to the female trees, and enters the "fruit" through a tiny hole to pollinate the flowers. This process is called "caprification" and was understood as early as the classical Greek era. The Smyrna variety of figs still requires caprification. As the product of centuries of cultivation and selection, the Common (or Adriatic) fig and the Mission fig produce mature, edible fruit without need of pollination. Figs come in a wide variety, large and small, winter and spring and summer, round and ovoid, and black, brown, red, purple, violet, green, yellow-green, yellow, and white. Some botanists list as many as seven hundred and fifty species of fig.

Beneath a pliable skin, figs have a sweet, soft, fleshy texture; the seeds are edible. Unfortunately, fresh figs have the shortest lifespan of any marketable fruit: about a week. As a result, the vast majority of the world's fig harvest is dried. Dried figs are a powerful nutritional package: high in energy (calories), fiber, potassium, calcium, magnesium, and iron.

Both fresh and dried figs can be eaten as they are; they can also serve as a supplemental or primary ingredient in baking, garnish salads or vegetable dishes, flavor poultry or pork recipes, and, because of their sweetness, serve as a wonderful base for jams and syrups.

Grape

The grape is one of the oldest cultivated fruits. Neolithic and Bronze Age archaeological sites in present-day Switzerland, Germany, France, and the Balkans have turned up grape seeds, and archaeobotanists believe that the cultivation of grapes began about 8000 B.C.E. in the Fertile Crescent, the area between the Tigris and Euphrates Rivers, along with the growing of olives, pomegranates, dates, and perhaps figs. Egyptian tombs from about 4000 B.C.E. are painted with scenes of grape cultivation. The ancient Sumerian epic *Gilgamesh* (dating from about 3000 B.C.E.) mentions grapes as part of the diet of the times, though these perhaps were the wild variety. The first reliable archaeological evidence of grape cultivation comes from a 3500 B.C.E. site in the Jordan Valley and a 3200 B.C.E. site at Jericho. Other archaeological evidence indicates that the ancient Greeks cultivated grapes by 1700 B.C.E., and the tomb of Tutankhamun (dated c. 1350 B.C.E.) contained a jar labeled as unfermented grape juice. Grapes were grown in the Hanging Gardens of Babylon, and the Bible often mentions grapes, as early as Genesis (the first book of the Bible), which relates the story of Noah and what happened to him after he left the ark (9:20). By the time of the ancient Greek civilization, special varieties of grapes were being developed, some for eating as a dessert, some for fermenting into wine. The Romans further developed viticulture (the cultivation of grapes), probably spreading the grape into France, Spain, the Germanic lands, and other parts of Europe. Grape seeds have also been discovered in Native American sites dating from about 1800 B.C.E.; likely, Native Americans gathered grapes from the wild, though limited cultivation may have occurred. While the exact origins of the grape are unknown, it is believed that its birthplace is somewhere between the Caspian and Black Seas, where it still grows wild. The grape is now cultivated around the world in all but the coldest climates.

The wild grape (*Vitis vinifera silvestris*) is naturally a dioecious plant: individuals are either male or female and must grow in close proximity to produce pollination and fruit. Over the centuries, however, many varieties (some botanists count about eight thousand) have been developed, for both table eating and fermenting into wine, and most modern cultivars are hermaphroditic (both male and female) and can self-pollinate. Colonists brought European vines to the Americas, and French wine producers began to import American vines in the 1860s when an aphid (*Phylloxera vastatrix*) was decimating the French vineyards; grafting and crossing the aphid-resistant American species with the flavorful French species saved the French wine industry, but the search for a perfect combination continues.

Grapes can be eaten fresh or dried, dried grapes being known as raisins. Whether fresh or dried, grapes can be added to salads, pastas, chicken or fish or other meat dishes, breads, and baked desserts like cakes, cookies, and muffins. Frozen grapes make a fun and particularly refreshing treat. The ancient Romans used grape sugar as a sweetener, and the ancient Greeks stuffed grape leaves with various fillings, then cooked them for a succulent treat. Even grape seeds are edible, as garnishes, and some recipes call for grape-seed oil. Grapes can also be squeezed for their juice, and grape juice is one of the sweetest fruit juices available. The juice of grapes can be mixed with the juice of other fruits, such as **lemons** or grapefruits, to create particularly thirst-quenching drinks. The fermentation of grapes will be treated under **wine**.

The American and the European are the two basic types of grapes grown today, with the European being more popular and versatile. Seedless varieties have been developed over the centuries, though many gourmets insist that seeded grapes are more flavorful. The European grapes (V. *vinifera*) include the Black Beauty (Beauty Seedless), Calmeria, Cardinal, Champagne (Black Corinth), Emperor, Exotic, Flame Seedless, Italia (Italia Muscat), Perlette Seedless, Queen, Red Globe, Red Malaga, Ribier, Ruby Seedless, Thompson Seedless, and Tokay (Flame Tokay). The American grapes (V. *labrusca* and V. *rotundita*) include the Concord, Delaware, Niagara, and Steuben. In general, American grapes tend to have skin that separates easily from the flesh but seeds that are tightly embedded in the pulp.

Grapes are high in vitamin C; they are also high in calories but have no cholesterol.

Hazelnut

There is much confusion between references to the hazelnut and the filbert, and the terms are often used interchangeably. One might say that the nuts are called hazelnuts in the Americas and filberts in Europe, although some experts say that they are altogether different. At any rate, the two are so closely related as to be almost indistinguishable, both in appearance and taste. They are the seeds of the deciduous shrubs (really, small trees) of the *Corylus* genus. Some of the varieties include the C. *americana*, C. *avellana*, C. *maxima*, and C. *cornuta*.

Hazelnuts (to use the American term) are generally thought to be native to southeastern Europe and southwestern Asia, though they are found throughout the northern temperate zone. Hazelnut remains have been found in Mesolithic dwellings in Europe and in Eocene sites in central Asia. Both the ancient Greeks and Romans cultivated hazelnuts, and they were known to the peoples of the Bible: Jacob flavored his cattle's drinking water with hazel twigs to help them conceive (Genesis 30:38). During the Middle Ages, hazelnut cultivation declined, as wild nuts were plentiful and easy to gather. Though many people consider the hazelnuts of North America to be inferior in taste to those of Europe and Asia, Native Americans flavored their cornmeal cakes with hazelnut powder. Today, hazelnuts/filberts are largely cultivated in Europe, Asia, Turkey, Australia, Washington, and Oregon.

Hazelnuts/filberts are rich in protein and folacin and provide significant amounts of calcium, thiamin, niacin, phosphorus, potassium, iron, and magnesium. They are also high in both calories and fat. Often eaten whole or chopped, hazelnuts make a nutritious snack. Hazelnut **flour** is used in many baking applications, as are hazelnut paste and butter, which also make delicious candy. Hazelnuts are one of the main ingredients of Nutella spread, and they are also used to flavor **coffee**s and lattes.

Juniper Berry

Also known as juniper bush and juniper bark, juniper "berries" are the blue-black seed cones of the common juniper (*Juniperus communis*), a small evergreen tree that ranges throughout the temperate northern hemisphere. As the berries can take more than a year to ripen, a single plant will have both green and blue berries, and only the riper blue ones are ready for harvesting.

Ancient Greek and Arabian physicians used juniper berries to treat various diseases, and juniper trees are mentioned in I Kings, the book of Job, and Psalm 120 of the Bible. During the Black Death, desperate people sucked on the berries to protect themselves from infection, but juniper berries provide no protection against bubonic plague. During the early years of surgery, **tea** made from juniper berries was used to disinfect medical implements. Various peoples around the world have used juniper berries to treat warts and skin growths, cancers, upset stomach, kidney diseases, even hangovers. Today, juniper berries and their extracts help to treat urinary tract, bladder, kidney, and prostate infections. They also work as a diuretic, helping the body eliminate waste and toxins. They may also serve to improve digestion and ease stomach and intestinal cramps. Some herbalists claim that juniper berries can relieve rheumatic and arthritic pain, relieve congestion, and treat asthma.

Because they are very bitter, juniper berries are seldom consumed fresh. They are usually dried and crushed and serve to flavor luncheon meats, sauces, stuffings, and strong game meats. They are particularly important in making sauerbraten and sour **beef** stew. They are also one of the main flavoring agents in the production of **gin**.

Lemon

The lemon (*Citrus limon*) probably originated in the eastern foothills of the Himalayan Mountains, as wild lemon trees still exist in that region, although historians occasionally suggest that lemons originated in the Indus Valley, in present-day India. On the other hand, some botanists assert that the lemon is not a distinct species at all but a hybrid, as it will not grow from seed. The history of the lemon, or citron as it is also known, is uncertain. The domestication and grafting of lemon trees is documented by the 4th or 3rd century B.C.E., but citron seeds are present in an archaeological site in Cyprus dating from 1200 B.C.E. It is possible that lemons were known to the peoples of the Bible, but lemons are not mentioned in the scriptures. However, they are today a key ingredient in Passover and Purim meals, and lemon juice is widely used in Middle Eastern cooking. By the time of the Roman Empire, lemons were common all around the

Mediterranean region, where they thrived in the warm dry summers and cool wet winters. The Romans used the lemon tree more for timber, decoration, and medicine than for food. By the 8th century C.E., Muslims began uprooting **grape** vineyards and planting citrus groves, and their cuisine did feature the use of lemons and other citrus fruits for flavoring. The lemon symbolized fidelity in Renaissance art but did not gain wide acceptance in European cooking until the 17th century, when French cooks began using citrus juices in sauces for flavoring meat dishes, although the Italians may have begun using lemons in cooking as early as the 15th century. Christopher Columbus probably brought lemons to the Americas, and lemons were grown in Florida by the 16th century. Today, Sicily and California are major lemon-producing regions.

There are three types of lemons: common (or acid), which are the most readily available in the supermarkets of the world; rough, which are used primarily as rootstock for other citrus fruits; and sweet, which are not actually sweeter than other lemons but simply less acidic. Of the common lemons, the two main varieties are Eurekas and Lisbons.

Lemons are high in vitamin C and potassium and are used principally for the flavor they add to sauces, stews, dressings, and garnishes, as well as for lemonade (which must be sweetened somehow to be made palatable).

Lime

The lime (*Citrus limetta*) is a very close relative of the **lemon**, though some botanists believe that the lime is actually biologically identical to the lemon and is really a hybrid or mutation thereof (*Citrus x aurantifolia*). The history of limes, therefore, is probably similar to that of lemons, although some botanists believe that limes may have originated in Tahiti. It is not likely that the peoples of the Bible knew of limes, though they are currently an important ingredient in Middle Eastern cooking.

The main varieties of limes currently cultivated are Persian and Bearss, both of which are greenish-yellow when mature. Like lemons, limes grow more abundantly in California than Florida. Another type of lime is the Key lime of southern Florida, used primarily for pie flavoring. Like lemons, limes are used as flavoring in sauces, stews, and dressing, but they are also used in some cocktails. Limes are high in vitamin C and potassium and low in sugar.

An interesting historical note: Sailors of the Royal Navy became known as "limeys" because the British discovered that the consumption of citrus fruits prevented scurvy and thus provisioned their ships with limes and **lemons**.

Mango

There are hundreds of varieties of mango (*Mangifera indica*), which has been under cultivation since prehistoric times. It is thought to be native to the region of the eastern Indian subcontinent through to the land now known as Myanmar (or Burma), but there is no real way of knowing its origins. Given their preferred climate (wet and hot, without any possibility of frost), it is doubtful that mangoes were known to the peoples of the Bible, though mangoes are now not uncommon in Middle Eastern cuisine. The first reliable mention of the mango occurs in the account of Hwen T'sang, a Chinese traveler, in the 7th century C.E. News of the mango probably did not reach Europe until the 14th century, though Persian travelers probably brought mangoes to Africa by 1000. Mangoes were planted in Brazil in 1700 and in the West Indies shortly thereafter. By 1825 mangoes were being grown in Florida, the only state where they can reliably flourish. India remains an important mango producer, though Mexico, Central America, and Haiti are also major producers.

Mango trees grow to a height of 60 feet and begin to yield fruit when they are about seven years old. An individual fruit may weigh from 6 ounces to 5 pounds, depending on the variety. Usually round, oval, or kidney-shaped, they may also be shaped like hearts, pears, or peaches. Most mangoes are green when unripe and become golden, yellow, or red as they ripen, with orange flesh. The most common variety of mango is the Tommy Atkins, which is oval-shaped and somewhat fibrous with a bland taste. Other varieties include Haden, Kent, and Keitt, all of which have a rich flavor and smooth flesh, and Francine, which is completely green.

Mangoes are relatively high in calories and carbohydrates, but they are extremely rich in vitamins A and C and provide significant amounts of vitamin E and potassium. Usually eaten raw, mangoes are somewhat difficult and messy to extract from the peel and to separate from the interior pit. Raw mangoes are often combined with other fruits in a tropical fruit salad, used to garnish waffles or pancakes, mixed with **yogurt**, blended with other fruits and **milk** for a breakfast shake, used as a topping for cakes and puddings, or eaten as a fresh peach would be. Slightly underripe mangoes can be cooked in the same way as **apples** or peaches, and they add a nice flavor to meat and fish dishes. Mangoes are also a required ingredient for Indian chutneys.

Mulberry

Berries are not often mentioned in the Bible, but mulberry trees are mentioned in II Samuel 5, I Chronicles 14, and Luke 17:6; and Isaiah's mention (17:6) of berries probably referred to mulberries, for the mulberry is one of the few berries that would have been available in biblical times in the Middle and Near East. Actually, there are twelve species of mulberry; all but one are Asian in origin. The three main species are the black (*Morus nigra*) and the white (*M. alba*) from Asia, and the red (*M. rubra*) from North America.

The cultivation of black mulberries dates from at least 2000 B.C.E.; they were grown in ancient Mesopotamia and Egypt and so would have been known to the peoples of the Bible. Both the Greeks and Romans ate mulberries, which very slowly spread north and west throughout Europe until their cultivation reached England in the 16th century C.E.

The white mulberry, generally held to be excessively sweet, is a traditional staple in Afghanistan, and some people in other parts of southwest Asia grind them to use as **flour**. White mulberry leaves are also used to feed silkworms.

The red mulberry is indigenous to the Atlantic and Gulf coasts of North America, and it was so important that the Natchez named a month after it.

In general, mulberries contain high amounts of sugar and are rich in vitamin B and potassium. They can be eaten alone, combined in fruit salads, made into jams or jellies, added to desserts, or used to flavor other dishes.

Muskmelon

As with all melons, **cucumbers**, and **squashes**, muskmelons (*Cucumis melo*) grow on low vines and like sandy, well-watered soil. Unlike squashes, which are native to the Americas, however, muskmelons and other melons originated in Africa and Asia. It is possible that early human ancestors may have domesticated melons as early as 2 million years ago, though hard archaeological evidence is limited to melon seeds found in Iran dating from perhaps 2000 B.C.E. and other seeds found in Greece dating from about 1000 B.C.E. The peoples of the Bible would have been familiar with muskmelons, either from Mesopotamia or from Egypt. Chinese writings from about the same time mention both sweet muskmelons and bitter pickling melons, and Chinese farmers have been growing melons since then. The ancient Romans grew melons that were probably far inferior to the sweet muskmelons we know today. It is believed that muskmelons did not truly become part of Mediterranean agriculture until introduced by Muslim farmers in the 8th century C.E. Marco Polo told of other melons he encountered during his travels in the 13th century, and melons became extremely popular in England during the 16th and 17th centuries. European colonists introduced melons to the Americas, and that's when confusion over nomenclature began, for what is called a cantaloupe in America is called a muskmelon in Europe, the European cantaloupe being an entirely different type of melon (see **cantaloupe**).

Often eaten fresh, muskmelons make a wonderful addition to fruit salads, **yogurt**, and cereals and a fine complement to **chicken** and **tuna** salads, ice creams, and sherbets. Muskmelon can be puréed and made into a cold soup or fruit drink, and melon slices can even be grilled.

Muskmelons are generally high in vitamins A and C and potassium.

Olive

The olive (*Olea europea*) has been a staple of the human diet for many millennia. Olive pits (or stones) have been found in archaeological deposits at Mount Carmel dating from 9000 B.C.E., though it is impossible to say whether these particular olives were gathered from the wild or cultivated. The first conclusive archaeological evidence of olive cultivation comes from Tuleilat Ghassul, north of the Dead Sea in modern-day Jordan, at a site that dates from the 4th century B.C.E. It is believed that the olive was cultivated in Crete by 3500 B.C.E. Sites in Palestine and

Syria indicate that the ancients were pressing olives into oil by about 3500 B.C.E. Olive berries, trees, wood, and oil were very important to the peoples of the Bible and are mentioned scores of times in the Judeo-Christian scriptures.

The cultivated olive is probably a descendant of the wild olive (*O. europea* ssp. *oleaster*), which is native to the Mediterranean region and grows particularly well in Greece and the islands of the Aegean Sea. In the wild, the olive is a straggly evergreen. Olives are basically inedible when picked and need to be soaked in a salt solution to temper their bitterness, though fruits that have fallen from the trees and "aged" for a time on the ground are more palatable, and such are probably the first olives that ancient humans consumed.

The ancient Greeks began cultivating olives by 1000 B.C.E., and Greek and Phoenician colonists planted olives all along the North African, Italian, Sicilian, and Spanish coasts and perhaps even in the Canary Islands. The trees are very easily rooted and grown from cuttings. Spanish settlers brought the olive to the Pacific coast of South America, where it flourished in Chile and Peru. By the 17th century C.E., Jesuit missionaries had brought the tree to Mexico and California, where it thrived. The olive also took root in parts of Australia and in South Africa. Olive trees need full sunlight; they do not tolerate hard frosts or freezing temperatures; they thrive on 8 to 10 inches of annual rainfall but will not produce fruit if the climate is wet or humid; they rarely grow on land that is above 2,000 feet in altitude; and they may live for three hundred to six hundred years.

Olive oil was a real luxury among the ancient Greeks, who used it, for example, as an after-bath moisturizer and as an oil for anointing the dead. As time passed, it became more available and took its place in the common home, providing oil for cooking, oil for lamps, and soap for baths. Whole, green olives were soaked in a solution made from ashes and then pickled in brine, to make them edible. In ancient Rome, the well-to-do ate olives as appetizers and as end-of-the-meal fresheners; main courses also relied heavily on olives. Olives and **bread** were said to have been the staple foods of the Roman working classes. The Romans also cooked the fragrant parts of the olive tree (such as the flowers, leaves, or roots), which they then mixed with olive oil to make a scented oil, or perfume. The ancient Greeks, Hebrews, and Romans also believed olive oil capable of restoring health and adding longevity; and we now know that the olive tree does contain salicylic acid, the active ingredient of aspirin. (We also know that olives are high in unsaturated fats and thus can help prevent the buildup of cholesterol in the body.) In ancient Egypt, olive oil was thought to have been used as a lubricant for moving large stones. Throughout the Mediterranean, olive oil helped preserve fish. The Israelites used olive wood, hard and strong and beautifully grained, to construct the tabernacle of Solomon's temple.

The ancient Greeks also used olives as a symbol of peace, victory, wealth, and prosperity. Both victors in athletic contests and successful warriors were decorated with olive sprays. Suppliants bestowed gifts of olive branches or trees to indicate peaceful intentions or submission.

Olives today come in a variety of flavors resulting from different curing and pickling processes. Essentially, however, there are two types of olives: green, picked and cured before they ripen, and black, picked when they are ripe.

Orange

The most widely grown fruit in the world, the orange is thought to have descended from trees native to what is now southern China. Chinese records indicate that cultivation of oranges (probably the bitter orange, *Citrus aurantium*) began as early as 2400 B.C.E., but oranges made their way east very slowly. There is no reliable record of oranges west of the Indian subcontinent until the 1st century C.E., when coast-hugging Arab boats brought oranges to the Roman port of Ostia, via the Red Sea, the Nile, and the Mediterranean. Always sensitive to cold, oranges did not receive sufficient care after the collapse of the empire and so disappeared from Europe. The Moors reintroduced oranges to Europe when they conquered Spain and by the 12th century had planted vast citrus orchards in the lands surrounding Granada, Seville, and Valencia. In Sicily, the Saracens cultivated oranges by the 11th century, and oranges made their way back to Rome by the 13th century. They were imported to England from Spain as early as the 13th century and were grown in Mediterranean France by the 14th century. Christopher Columbus brought oranges to the Americas, where they thrived in the Caribbean climate and from there spread to Mexico, Brazil, Florida, and eventually California. They also made their way to Australia. Brazil is today the world's largest producer of oranges.

There are several important oranges grown today: the bitter, which is probably the ancestor of the others and which is best for cooking and is used for **marmalade**; the sweet (*C. sinensis*), which the Portuguese brought to Europe in the 16th century, and of which the Valencia is the most widely grown; and the mandarin (*C. deliciosa* and *C. reticulata*), which is believed to be a mutation of the sweet orange and is sometimes known as the tangerine (although the tangerine may be a subgroup of the mandarin). The navel orange, prevalent today, is probably a mutation of the sweet orange and first appeared in Brazil in the 17th century. The **clementine**, first discovered in Algeria in 1902 by Clement Rodier, is thought to be either a mutation of the sweet orange or a hybrid of a sweet orange and a mandarin. Other important types include the Jaffa orange, which originated as a mutation on a tree near Jaffa, in present-day Israel, in the 19th century, and the blood orange, which is extremely sweet.

Oranges are consumed whole (once peeled), squeezed for their juice, or used in cooking. They are extremely high in vitamin C, which is concentrated in the white pulpy layer just beneath the peel, and there is some conflicting evidence about whether vitamin C helps to heal cuts, prevents cancer, lowers cholesterol, or shortens or prevents colds and the flu. Oranges are also high in potassium and have significant amounts of folacin and calcium. But they are also high in sugar and low in fiber. Oranges are a source of expensive perfume oils, extracted from either the rind or the flowers.

Orange trees are still susceptible to freezing temperatures, but genetic manipulation has produced trees with inferior fruit that can survive cold winters. Further manipulation and hybridization may eventually produce a hardy tree that bears high-quality fruit.

Oranges would probably not have been known to the peoples of the Bible, but the fruit is now an important ingredient in Middle Eastern cooking.

Pecan

The pecan (*Carya illinoensis*, also known as *C. olivaeformis*) is a peculiarly North American nut, produced by the tree known as the Illinois hickory. This hickory naturally ranges from Illinois to the Gulf of Mexico and from Alabama to the Rocky Mountains and received its scientific name because French missionary-scientists probably first encountered it in the Illinois area. Thomas Jefferson brought the trees to the Atlantic coast. Today, Georgia is the leading producer of pecans in the world, and 95 percent of the world's pecan harvest is produced in the United States.

The pecan was a versatile food staple for Native Americans, who pressed oil from the nuts to use in cooking, ground the nuts to thicken stews, mixed the whole nuts with vegetables, and even roasted the nuts to preserve them for consumption during long hunting or other journeys.

Pecans are very high in energy (calories); of all the nuts, they are among the highest in fat and the lowest in protein.

The pecan is a difficult tree to grow. It requires high summer temperatures both day and night and is often particular about the soil in which it grows. The trees require a large amount of space and take a long time, sometimes twenty years, to reach full productivity, at which point a tree can give from 100 to 600 pounds of nuts each year. Because of these difficulties, and because the taste of the pecan has been considered too close to that of the **walnut**, which thrives in Europe and other parts of the world, the pecan tree has not been widely planted outside of North America, though it has been cultivated in Israel, with significant success.

Pecans would not have been known to the peoples of the Bible, but modern Middle Eastern cooks rely upon a variety of nuts, including pecans, to flavor their foods.

Persimmon

There are perhaps as many as two hundred species of persimmon, but only five produce fruit that is readily eaten: the American persimmon (*Diospyros virginiana*), which is native to North America; the Japanese (*D. kaki*), which is actually native to China; the black; the date plum (*D. lotus*), from the Himalayan region; and the monkey guava, swamp ebony, African ebony, bush kaki, or *soun-soun* (*D. mespiliformia*), which is grown in tropical Africa. Native Americans gathered persimmons for centuries before the European colonization of the Americas. The Japanese imported and adopted their persimmons so long ago that it has become one of their traditional New Year foods. Persimmons would not have been known to the peoples of the Bible but are often found in modern Middle Eastern recipes.

The persimmon is the latest ripener of all tree fruits, reaching ripeness well into autumn, after cool, even cold, weather has set in. Persimmons are either astringent or nonastringent, and the astringent fruits, though sweet and spicy when ripe, are extremely bitter and unpalatable when not. Because of its ripening schedule, the persimmon has not become widely popular, and most of the persimmons eaten in the United States are imported Japanese varieties: the Hachiya and the Fuyu.

Persimmons are high in vitamins A and C and potassium. Persimmons can be eaten like an **apple**, whole, peeled, or pared, or added to salads. They can be pressed to make a dessert sauce or a sauce for **chicken** or other meat dishes. Sliced or chopped, they can be used like apples in cakes and muffins. Mashed, they can substitute for applesauce in some baked goods.

Pineapple

The pineapple (*Ananas comosus*) is a member of the Bromelia family. Native to the Caribbean islands and to Central and South America, the pineapple would not have been known to the peoples of the Bible, though it has entered some Middle Eastern kitchens in modern times. It was first "discovered" by members of Christopher Columbus' expeditions, though Native Americans had been cultivating the pineapple for so long (many millennia) that it had already lost its ability to produce seeds. European explorers fell in love with the pineapple, so-called because of its resemblance to a pine cone (*piña* means "pine" in Spanish), and within a very short time the pineapple was imported to tropical areas around the world. The pineapple is relatively easy to propagate: the crown of the fruit can be planted and will readily grow if the climate is right. By the 16th century pineapples were abundant in India, Java, and even China. They made their way to Africa by the 17th century and to the Pacific islands by the 18th. By the 17th century they were even cultivated in hothouses in England, France, and the Netherlands. Today most pineapple comes from Hawaii, the Philippines, Thailand, Mexico, and Central American countries. Pineapples are ripened on the plant and spoil quickly on the shelf, so it is important to get them to market quickly, and shoppers should choose those that are as fresh as possible.

The three major varieties of pineapple are Smooth Cayenne, which is the most popular as many people consider it to taste the best; Red Spanish, which has a tough shell that protects it during shipping; and Sugar Load, which is the largest, weighing from 5 to 10 pounds.

Pineapples are high in vitamin C, potassium, and manganese and have no cholesterol. Fresh pineapple contains the enzyme bromelain, which aids in the digestion of protein; if pineapple is used as a base for a marinade, this enzyme will break down the connective tissue of the marinating meat, and lengthy exposure will turn the meat to mush. Cooking the pineapple destroys the enzyme, and any meat dishes that rely upon pineapple will usually call for cooked pieces (or for the pineapple to be cooked simultaneously with the meat). Pineapple is most often eaten raw, sliced or cubed, fresh from the shell. It can be combined with other tropical fruits into a salad, added to **lettuce** salads, or mixed with **yogurt** or **sorbet**. Pineapple pieces and pineapple juice can sweeten vegetable dishes and can be baked with **chicken** or pork, stir-fried with chicken or shrimp and vegetables, or added to curry. Thick pineapple slices can even be grilled with seafood, chicken, and other fruits and vegetables.

Pine Nut

The pine nut—also known as the pignoli, piñon nut, and Indian nut—is a collect-all name for the various seeds that come from the pine cones of nut pine trees, of the Pine family. These nuts range from the slender ivory-colored pignolis of the Mediterranean, gathered from the Stone pine (*Pinus pinea*) and the Swiss pine (*P. cembra*), to the much larger nuts of the Americas, mostly from the Colorado pinyon (*P. edulis*), the single-leaf pinyon (*P. monophylla*), and the Mexican pinyon (*P. cembroides*). Eight other types of American pinyons produce pine nuts, as well as the gray pine (*P. sabineana*), Torrey pine (*P. torreyana*), and sugar pine (*P. lambertiana*). There are also several Asian pines that produce edible pine nuts: the Korean pine (*P. koraiensis*), the Chilgoza pine (*P. gerardiana*), and, to a lesser degree, the Siberian pine (*P. sibirica*), the Siberian dwarf pine (*P. pumila*), the Chinese white pine (*P. armandii*), and the lacebark pine (*P. bungeana*). In South America, the nuts of the monkey-puzzle tree (*Araucaria araucana*) are often called pine nuts, as are the nuts of the bunya-bunya (*A. bidwillii*) of Australia.

High in protein but also high in fat, rich in thiamin, iron, and magnesium, pine nuts have been a staple of the human diet since ancient times. Nowadays, they are relatively expensive, as the harvesting process is lengthy: the pine cones must be dried to release the nuts, then the nuts must be shelled to free the kernels.

Archaeologists believe that nut pine trees have been cultivated since about 4000 B.C.E. Of course, for many millennia before, humans collected pine nuts from the wild, to provide supplementary protein and energy-rich fat for their diet. It is likely that the peoples of the Bible gathered and consumed some type of pine nuts.

Pine nuts, particularly pignolis, are an essential ingredient of pesto but add flavor and texture to meat, fish, and vegetable dishes, as well as **chocolate** desserts and baklava. The shelf-life of unshelled pine nuts is long if they are dry and refrigerated, but once shelled, pine nuts do not last more than a few weeks.

Pistachio

The pistachio (*Pistacia vera*) is probably a native of Persia, in southwestern Asia, and has been part of the human diet since prehistoric times. The earliest pistachio nuts have been found at an archaeological site in what is now northeastern Iraq, dating from 6750 B.C.E. But the pistachio did not become an important part of the diet until about 2000 B.C.E., when the population of the area increased significantly, and it has not left the table since then. Pistachios were grown in the Hanging Gardens of Babylon (about 700 B.C.E.) and are mentioned in the Old Testament (Genesis 43:11), so many peoples of the Bible favored pistachios in their meals. According to tradition, Emperor Vitellius brought pistachios to the Roman Empire sometime before 69 C.E. Cooks of the Middle Ages preferred almonds to pistachios because of the latter's expense, but it is believed that the Moors planted many pistachio trees in Spain and Sicily and northern Africa, and from there pistachio cultivation spread throughout the Mediterranean. Nowadays, California and Florida grow a good number of pistachios, but Turkey is a major producer. A relative, *P. mexicana*, is native to Mexico; its nuts are slightly less flavorful than pistachios. There is also a Chinese relative, *P. chinensis*, but it is almost exclusively ornamental.

High in protein, pistachios are also high in energy, or calories (mostly from fat). They also supply significant amounts of iron, thiamin, and phosphorus.

In cooking, appearance and presentation are as significant as taste, texture, and aroma, and as one of the few green ingredients suitable for desserts, pistachio nuts have become a popular addition to cakes, pastries, and even ice cream.

The shells of pistachios are tan or light brown, and they naturally split open as the pistachios mature to reveal the light-green nut inside. During the 20th century, many importers and growers dyed (and some still dye) their pistachio shells red in order to make them distinctive in the marketplace. But the dye colors the nuts as well as the shells. As there are some health threats associated with the red dye, it is safest to use natural, undyed pistachios.

Plum

The plum is one of the most succulent fruits provided by nature. Related to the nectarine, peach, and **apricot**, plums have developed into a wide variety of colors, shapes, sizes, and flavors. Two species dominate plum cultivation: the common (also known as European) plum (*Prunus domestica*) and the Japanese (also known as salicina) plum (*P. salicina*).

The common plum has blue or purple skin and golden-yellow flesh, and is usually freestone (the flesh separates easily from the pit). These are the plums invariably dried for **prunes**, as they tend to be small and dense. They are also used for baking, stewing, and making preserves. Some of the better-known varieties include Italian, President, Empress, Stanley, and Tragedy.

The Japanese plum has red to black-red skin and yellow or red flesh and is usually clingstone (the flesh clings to the pit). They are usually eaten fresh, though some serve for cooking. Among the better-known varieties are El Dorado, Freedom, French, Santa Rosa, Red Beaut, Friar, Nubiana, Queen Rosa, Casselman, Laroda, Simka, and Elephant Heart. Wickson and Kelsey are unusual green-skinned varieties.

The original wild plum is not known, and the common plum is probably a hybrid or fusion of several species:

- the sloe plum (*P. spinosa*), whose pits have been discovered in Swiss Neolithic or Bronze Age sites
- the bullace plum, which may also be *P. spinosa* but which many botanists classify as *P. institia*
- the damson plum (*P. damascena*), which the ancient Romans imported from Damascus by the 1st century C.E.; these plums had been cultivated in ancient Mesopotamia and had been among the plants in the Hanging Gardens of Babylon (and would have been known to the peoples of the Bible)
- the cherry plum (*P. cerasifera*), which originated in Asia Minor as well

The ancient Romans may have been the ones to bring these species together to produce the common plum.

The Japanese plum is probably native to China but was adopted by Japan so long ago and improved so much since then that it now is truly Japanese. The many varieties of Japanese plums adapt well to different soils and climates and are resistant to insects and diseases.

A third plum that has some agricultural importance is the American plum (*P. americana*). Native to either North or South America, the American plum entered cultivation under the Incas in the 1st or 2nd century B.C.E. It has continued to be a wild tree in North America; English colonists in the 17th century C.E. planted common plums, much superior to the American plums, and did not see the need to try to bring the native species into the garden.

Among a number of other North American species, there is also the beach plum (*P. maritima*), which grows along the Atlantic coast. Small with tough skin, it is somewhat acidic but makes marvelous preserves, jams, and jellies.

Fresh plums are high in vitamin C, carbohydrates, and calories; they have no cholesterol. Japanese plums are the ones most often consumed raw, while the common plum is better suited for cooking purposes. Fresh plums are delicious in fruit salads, with **yogurt**, or over cereal. Puréed plums can be made into a dessert sauce or fruit soup. Plum pieces can be added to muffins, **breads**, and **lettuce** salads. Plums can be baked or poached and served whole, sliced, or chopped. Plum preserves and jellies are quite popular, and Chinese duck sauce is a sweet-and-sour mix of **vinegar**, hot **peppers**, **sugar**, **soy sauce**, **garlic**, **ginger**, apricots, and plums. Plums are also fermented into **wine** and distilled into **brandy**.

Prune

Quite simply, the prune is a dried **plum**, commonly of the California French or d'Agen plum variety, allowed to mature on the tree so that they are fully ripe and sweet, then harvested, dried, sorted, and moisturized before storing. Prunes are extremely high in soluble fiber, which may help to lower blood cholesterol. Also high in calories and carbohydrates, prunes provide significant amounts of vitamins

A and B6 and E, copper, iron, magnesium, manganese, niacin, phosphorus, potassium, and riboflavin.

Portable and convenient, prunes can be eaten as a snack or diced and added to cakes, cookies, breads, and other baked goods. They can be puréed into fruit shakes, served with **yogurt**, and added to pancakes or cereal. **Chicken, beef, lamb**, and pork roasts and stews can be sweetened with prunes, as can stuffings, mashed **potatoes**, and **squash** dishes. Prunes can even be cooked in **brandy** and served as a side dish; and prune juice is sweet enough to serve as a **sugar** substitute. Like plums, prunes are often called for in Middle Eastern recipes.

Raisin

Raisins are dried **grapes**. As a dried fruit, they are a concentrated source of calories and nutrients, including vitamin B6, copper, iron, magnesium, manganese, phosphorous, potassium, and thiamin. They are also high in dietary fiber and have no cholesterol.

Raisins were probably first "discovered" when a prehistoric hunter-gatherer picked naturally dried grapes from a wild vine, but by 1000 B.C.E. farmers were deliberately picking grapes and laying them out to dry in the sun. The process is almost unchanged to this day. Middle Eastern merchants profited from a thriving raisin trade in ancient times, and raisins would have been precious to the peoples of the Bible. Both the ancient Greeks and Romans would have enjoyed raisins, which have an extended shelf-life and thus can provision travelers who embark on long journeys. Spanish missionaries brought raisins to the Americas, and today approximately half of the world's raisins come from California.

Four kinds of grapes are used to produce most raisins: Thompson Seedless (which are the popular green grapes found in the fresh-produce sections of grocery stores), Muscat, Sultana, and Black Corinth. The raisins themselves are classified as follows:

- Natural seedless raisins, which are sun-dried Thompson Seedless grapes; dark brown, they constitute a vast majority of the raisins on the market
- Currants, which are made from Black Corinth grapes; they are seedless, very dark, and tiny, about one-quarter the size of natural seedless raisins
- Golden seedless raisins, which are oven-dried Thompson Seedless grapes; they are chemically treated to keep them light
- Monukka raisins, which are dried Monukka seedless grapes; they are large and dark
- Muscat raisins, which are dried Muscat grapes; large and brown, they have seeds unless they have been mechanically de-seeded
- Sultanas, which are dried Sultana grapes; they are large and soft and tend to be yellow-green in color

Raisins can be eaten as a snack, either alone or mixed with nuts and other dried fruits. They are stirred into **yogurt**, added to cereal and oatmeal, used in **breads**, cakes, and cookies, and mixed into applesauces and puddings. They provide a sweet flavor to stuffings for meat or poultry, vegetable dishes, curries, pilafs, and salads.

Raspberry

Human hunter-gatherers have been gathering and eating raspberries throughout northern Europe, Asia, and North America since prehistoric times. Raspberry seeds have been discovered in Denmark at an archaeological site dating from the 3rd millennium B.C.E. and in Bronze Age and ancient Roman sites in northern Europe. Native Americans also gathered berries from the indigenous raspberry canes, taking advantage of the plant's wide range and abundant productivity. The three main native raspberry species are the red raspberry of Europe (*Rubus idaeus*), the red raspberry of America (*R. strigosus*), and the black raspberry of America (*R. occidentalis*), though there are hundreds of others, particularly in Asia. Botanists believe that all raspberries originated in eastern Asia and spread west and east from there. It is doubtful that the peoples of the Bible were familiar with raspberries, which do not thrive in dry regions, but modern irrigation has made them available to today's Middle Eastern cooks.

In ancient Greece and Rome, the wild raspberry was known for its medicinal effects: its blossoms were thought to make a salve for sore eyes and a potion for stomach ailments, according to Pliny the Elder. By the 4th century C.E., raspberries had supposedly been domesticated in Italy, according to the poet Palladius, though even through the 16th century the raspberry was still considered a medicinal plant in Europe, and wild raspberries were so plentiful that there was little need to domesticate them. Raspberry leaf **tea** was a popular (and effective) remedy for diarrhea, sore throats, and burns and other wounds. As the Renaissance progressed and fresh fruits and vegetables became more acceptable for eating, gardeners began improving raspberries to produce larger and more abundant fruit. Colonists brought these new raspberry canes with them to the Americas, where they crossbred with the native American raspberries to create high-yielding cultivars that were resistant to heat, cold, and drought. In the 20th century new viruses and diseases threatened raspberry farming, and farmers and botanists are using cutting-edge genetic manipulation techniques to create stronger raspberry cultivars. Today, red raspberries are farmed mainly in Scotland, England, eastern Europe, western North America, Chile, New Zealand, and southern Australia. Black raspberries are grown in western North America. Other varieties include those with yellow, apricot, amber, and purple fruit.

Raspberries are the most fragile of all the berries, and they have a very short shelf-life of only a day or two. Fortunately, raspberries are easily and safely frozen: wash and drain them thoroughly, spread them out in a single layer on a nonstick surface, and place them in the freezer. When they are frozen solid, they may be gathered together into a plastic container and will store for almost a year.

But they are delicious when freshly picked, and they make a refreshing addition to fruit salads or fruit and **yogurt** shakes, a sweet topping for waffles or cereal, and a flavorful ingredient for **breads** and muffins. Cooked with other berries and berry juices and combined with **cornstarch**, raspberries will make an intriguing dessert sauce. They can even be added to sparkling **wines** for an elegant effect.

Raspberries, though high in calories, are also high in vitamin C and potassium.

Sultana

The Sultana is a type of **raisin**.

Walnut

The walnut (*Juglans regia*) is otherwise known as the Persian nut or Persian walnut because the ancient Romans obtained walnuts from Persia. The original range of wild walnuts, however, extends much beyond Persia to include southeastern Europe all the way to the Himalayas. By prehistoric times, the walnut had spread well beyond this range, and Neolithic remains in Switzerland include stores of walnuts. The Babylonians grew walnuts; the Greeks pressed out walnut oil; and the Romans considered walnuts a luxury to be eaten as dessert. While not specifically mentioned in the scriptures, walnuts would almost certainly have been part of the diet of the peoples of the Bible. Walnuts also spread east and were recorded in China by 100 B.C.E. Intensive cultivation of walnuts began in the Grenoble region of present-day France as early as the 4th century C.E., and walnuts were used to flavor other foods. By the 11th century, walnut oil was used as a flavoring in Paris. Menus of the 14th century listed walnuts as dessert offerings, and walnut paste began to flavor sauces and to thicken stews and soups. Walnuts arrived in the British Isles in the 16th century. The English brought walnuts to the Americas, but this species of walnut did not survive the climate and did not take root in the Americas until they were introduced in Oregon and California.

The Americas, however, had their own native walnut: the Eastern black walnut (*J. nigra*). Archaeological findings indicate that Native Americans had been eating black walnuts since at least 2000 B.C.E., though it is probable that black walnuts were a part of their diet well before then.

Both species of walnut are readily available in the marketplace today. The Persian walnut is generally thought to be finer in flavor and is much more common; while sweet and oily, the black walnut has a stronger taste that some people find unpalatable, and it has a thicker, tougher shell than the Persian. Yet black walnuts combine extremely well with **chocolate** and are superior for flavoring ice cream.

Of late, walnuts, particularly the Persian variety, have made somewhat of a comeback as a main-course food because the proteins in walnuts are perhaps the closest among those of all vegetables, except soybeans, to animal proteins.

Walnuts are now used in salads, combined with vegetables, and used in many dessert treats, in addition to being eaten alone. While rich in fats, they are also valuable sources of potassium, magnesium, calcium, phosphorus, and sulphur acids.

Watermelon

The watermelon (*Citrullus lanatus* or *C. vulgaris*) is a type of melon that originated in southern Africa, probably evolving from the tsamma melon (*C. lanatus* var. *citroides*), which still grows wild. It is a vinelike flowering plant, usually low growing, that bears a false berry (an accessory fruit that develops when the sepals, petals, and stamens all ripen along with the ovary; other examples of false berries include **bananas**, **cucumbers**, **squashes**, pumpkins, **cranberries**, and blueberries). It is possible that our human ancestors domesticated melons as early as 2 million years ago, though hard archaeological evidence is limited to Egyptian hieroglyphs from about 3000 B.C.E., and archaeologists believe that pharaohs had watermelons placed in their tombs to feed them in the afterlife. In Egyptian myth, watermelons came from the semen of the god Set. The ancient Israelites would have become familiar with watermelons during their time in Egypt. The Chinese were growing watermelons by the 10th century C.E., and the Moors brought watermelons to Europe by the 13th century. The melon had made its way to England by the 17th century. Some botanists believe that watermelons may also be indigenous to North America, though most assert that European colonists and African slaves brought watermelon seeds to the Americas, beginning in the 16th century, and that the climate of North America was so favorable that watermelons spread quickly, either through cultivation or by escaping from domestic gardens into the wild.

About fifty different varieties of watermelon are now grown worldwide, the larger types being called "picnic" melons and the smaller, "ice-box" melons. The skin or rind of watermelons varies from gray to deep green, either dappled, streaked, or solid in color, with the underside yellowish. Almost all watermelons have sweet red flesh, but a few have orange or yellow flesh, and the flesh is about 92 percent water and 8 percent sugar. Watermelon flesh provides vitamin C, potassium, and beta-carotene and is usually eaten fresh from the melon, though it is delicious when used in a fruit salad or blended with other fruits and fruit juices in a refreshing drink called a smoothie. Watermelon seeds are also edible; they tend to be high in fat calories, but they are tasty when roasted and salted. Some seedless varieties of watermelon have been developed. Watermelon rinds are sometimes eaten as a vegetable, and the Chinese stir-fry, stew, and pickle the rinds; pickled watermelon rind is popular elsewhere as well.

The watermelon can also be used to make an alcoholic treat called a hard watermelon. A hole is cut into the rind, then the liquor or liqueur is poured inside; after some time, when the alcohol has permeated the watermelon's flesh, the melon is cut and served in intoxicating slices.

GRAINS

Barley

Barley (*Hordeum vulgare*), cultivated for food and livestock feed, is a member of the Grass family. Probably originating in the highlands of what is now Ethiopia, modern barley is thought to have descended from wild barley (*H. spontaneum*), which is still found in the Middle East, and to be one of the first plants cultivated for food. There is some archaeological evidence of domesticated barley in Syria by about 8000 B.C.E., but the first recorded mention of barley is in Egyptian hieroglyphics dating from 5000 B.C.E. and Sumerian cuneiform tablets from about 3500 B.C.E. It was being grown in northwestern Europe and in the Indus River valley by 3000 B.C.E. The two "immortal sons of heaven" of the early Vedic literature are barley and **rice**, and a 2800 B.C.E. Chinese writing lists barley among the five sacred crops of China (the others being soybeans, rice, **wheat**, and **millet**).

The ancient Hebrews used barley extensively in **bread**-making. One of the plagues visited upon Pharaoh to convince him to let the Israelites leave Egypt was a rain of hailstones that ruined the barley (Exodus 9:31). Barley was one of the riches of the Promised Land that God held in store for the Israelites (Deuteronomy 8:8). Ruth arrived in Bethlehem with her mother-in-law, Naomi, at the beginning of the barley harvest and gleaned barley from the harvested fields (Ruth 1:22 and 2:17). Absalom destroyed Joab's barley fields to weaken his enemy (II Samuel 14:30). God instructed Ezekiel to make a bread with barley (Ezekiel 4:9). And Jesus took five barley loaves and fed 5,000 people, with such abundance that afterward his followers were able to collect twelve large baskets of leftover bread (John 6:1–13).

Barley was the chief grain of the Greek Homeric epics, and it may have been the venerated grain spike of the fertility rituals of the Demeter ("Mother-Goddess" or "Bringer of Seasons," sometimes known as "Barley-mother") cult of the ancient Greeks, who also fermented barley grain into a mildly alcoholic beverage. The ancient Romans preferred barley bread over all others and at one point even demanded a barley tribute from Carthage. Barley remained the major bread grain in Europe until the 16th century C.E. Spanish colonists planted barley in South America, and English colonists brought it to North America, where it thrived in Pennsylvania (and was later fermented with limestone water to make whiskey).

Barley is low in gluten and does not respond to yeast, so it lost its popularity when leavened bread became the standard for bread-making. Nowadays barley is primarily used for feeding livestock and making **beer**, though where wheat is difficult to grow, barley remains an essential grain for the human table—in fact, it is the fourth most important cereal crop in the world. It is tolerant of both cold and salty conditions. Today, the major producers of barley are Russia, Canada, the Ukraine, Turkey, Spain, Australia, Morocco, the United States, Iraq, and Iran, in order of decreasing barley cultivation.

Three species of barley are widely farmed, differing by the number of rows of kernels in the barley head: two-row barley (*H. distichum*), four-row barley (*H. tetrastichum*), and the most common, six-row barley (*H. vulgare*). The species differ in both protein and enzyme content, with two-row barley having less protein but more enzymes.

Barley commonly is available in several forms:

- Flakes (or flaked barley) are flattened grains.
- Grits are barley grains that have been toasted and cracked into small pieces.
- Hulled barley is barley that has had only the outer, inedible hull removed; the bran remains, so it is rich in dietary fiber and iron and other minerals.
- Pearl (pearled) barley is barley that has been scoured during milling to completely remove the double husk and the bran layer. This process shortens the grain's cooking time but removes many nutrients. This is the form most commonly found in the supermarket.
- Pot (Scotch) barley is barley that has been scoured, but not quite so thoroughly as pearl barley, and the bran layer remains intact.

Barley can be eaten alone or as a side dish, but it is often used in soups, casseroles, stuffings, stews, and salads. Chilled cooked barley can even be made into a pudding. In general, barley is high in calories and dietary fiber but low in fat and cholesterol. It provides vitamin B6, copper, folacin, iron, magnesium, manganese, niacin, phosphorus, thiamin, and zinc.

Barley Flour

The grains of **barley** (*Hordeum vulgare*) can also be ground into **flour**, which can be made into **bread**s and porridge. Indeed, barley bread is a staple of many regions where wheat is difficult to cultivate, as barley is hardy and can be grown in land that is unfriendly to **wheat**.

Basmati

Basmati is a small, long-grained variety of **rice**. Its name comes from Hindi and means "queen of fragrance," and it is justly famous for its aroma and flavor. Basmati has been grown on the Indian subcontinent for centuries and is one of the rices popular in the Middle East today.

Bulgur Wheat

See **wheat**.

Chickpea Flour

Dried **chickpeas** (*Cicer arietinum*) can be ground into a versatile **flour** that can be used to make flatbreads and to thicken soups and stews. This flour can also be mixed with flours from other grains to create baked goods with different textures and flavors. Chickpeas are the main ingredient in hummus, a popular Middle Eastern dish.

Corn

Corn (*Zea mays*) is one of the most versatile and important grain crops in the world, as corn production (600 million metric tons in 2003) has recently surpassed that of wheat. Also known as maize, sweetcorn, and Indian corn, corn is native to the Americas, growing wild in what is now southern Mexico as long as 70,000 years ago. Some botanists believe that Native Americans may have begun to bring corn under cultivation as early as 10,000 B.C.E. The earliest archaeological evidence of corn cultivation comes from the Guila Naquitz Cave in the Oaxaca Valley, Mexico, where tiny maize cobs dating from about 4250 B.C.E. have been discovered. As the wild varieties of corn yield very small edible portions, many centuries of selective cultivation and hybridization and perhaps many chance mutations must have been required to produce plants with ears large enough to be worth cultivating. By the time of Christopher Columbus' voyages, Native Americans from present-day Massachusetts to present-day Argentina were farming corn in silty river valleys, cutting and burning trees to clear the forests. In North America they tended to grow corn, **squash**, and **beans** in tandem; these plants worked together and were known as the Three Sisters: the corn provided support for the bean plants, and the squashes covered the ground and helped prevent weeds from taking over. Native Americans would use a particular plot for about a decade before allowing it to go back to the wild and moving on to another piece of land. In Central and South America, corn agriculture was the economic power base for the empires of the Toltecs, Aztecs, Mayans, and Incas. In the early 17th century corn helped save the starving survivors of both the Plymouth, Massachusetts, and the Jamestown, Virginia, colonies.

Native Americans developed five different types of corn:

- Sweet corn for eating
- Flint (hard-grained) corn for feeding animals
- Dent (dimpled-grained) corn for feeding animals
- Popcorn, with kernels that explode when heated
- Flour corn, with soft kernels used for baking

To mature properly, corn needs long hot summers and drying autumns. These types of corn (called maize in Europe) quickly made their way across the Atlantic, taking root in the Mediterranean region. North American settlers also took corn with them as they spread westward, planting it in the Ohio River valley and eventually converting much of the Great Plains of North America into cornfields. Now, about four centuries and many hybrids later, corn is farmed in places as diverse and widespread as France, China, India, Indonesia, South Africa, and Australia.

Corn grows to a height of 7–10 feet. At the top of the plant is the flower, called the tassle, which drops pollen onto the tufts of silk that grow out from the joints where the leaves meet the stem. Pollinated silk develops the corn cobs, or ears, each pollinated strand leading to a developed kernel of corn. Each kernel is about the size of a mature pea and is usually yellow or yellowish in color, though different varieties of corn may produce red, white, orange, and even blackish and brownish kernels. A single corn stem can produce half a dozen ears of corn, though modern hybrids can yield much more.

Native Americans in Mexico used **corn meal** or corn **flour** to create tortillas and cornbread and used corn husks to make tamales. Farther north, local tribes baked corn paste into flat cakes called corn pones. North American pioneers called these cakes "journey-cakes," or "johnny-cakes," because they ate them on their way over the Appalachian Mountains. Farmers in Bourbon County, Kentucky, developed corn alcohol and used it to make **bourbon** whiskey. Nowadays, corn has many additional uses. Bleaching corn kernels with lye yields hominy. Coarsely grinding the kernels produces grits. Popcorn and cornflakes have become popular snacking and breakfast foods, respectively. Corn syrup is used in sweetening other prepared foods. Some corn is processed into ethanol, which is added to gasoline. Corn cobs and even corn kernels are used as heating and cooking fuel. Dried corn cobs are hollowed out into pipes, and some multicolored corns are grown for decorative purposes. Primarily, though, corn is grown to feed livestock. For example, in recent years U.S. livestock consumed 5.6 billion bushels of corn—57 percent of all the corn grown in the United States. In fact, 80 percent of all U.S. corn was fed to livestock around the world.

But for the human table, corn has an incredible number of uses. Corn can be eaten fresh off the cob, or it can be made into soups, added to salads and salsas and vegetable dishes, pickled, creamed, used in casseroles and meat loaves, turned into relish, mixed in with muffin and **bread** batter, and prepared into puddings and custards. It can be barbecued, grilled, roasted, baked, boiled, fried, stir-fried, and steamed. It can also be ground into flour or pounded into paste and used in baking breads.

Corn is relatively high in vitamin C, folacin, magnesium, phosphorus, and thiamin. It has no cholesterol, is low in fat, and provides a good amount of dietary fiber.

In many parts of the world, the word "corn" is used to name the most common cereal grain, and the word "maize" is used to name what people in the Americas think of as corn.

It is interesting to note that the King James Version of the Bible often refers to corn; however, corn is a uniquely American plant and would not have been known to the peoples of the Bible. Where it does appear, it should be properly translated as grain (**barley**, **wheat**, or some other type).

Cornmeal

Also known as *masa harina*, mealie meal, and *farina di granturco*, cornmeal is made from **corn** (*Zea mays*) that is dried, then ground, either by hand with a stone or in a steel gristmill. Cornmeal that has been stone-ground includes the hull and germ and thus has a bit more flavor and nutrition than steel-ground cornmeal, for which the hull and germ have been removed. Stone-ground cornmeal is, however, more perishable. Blue cornmeal is made from grinding blue corn or by adding coloring to the cornmeal.

Usually mixed with boiling water to form a thick mush, cornmeal becomes grits in the southern United States, polenta in Italy, and *ugali, nsima, sadza,* and *mealie pap* in different parts of Africa. Cornmeal is also the basis for cornbread, muffins, pancakes, johnny-cakes, hoecakes, cornpones, hush puppies, dumplings, waffles, biscuits, and even cookies, cakes, and puddings.

Couscous

Couscous has been popular in North Africa since biblical times. It is a fine meal made from semolina, which is a coarsely ground durum **wheat** product. The name *couscous* comes from the Maghreb Arabic (north of the Sahara and west of the Nile River) *kuskusu,* which in turn comes from the Berber (of Algeria and Morocco) *seksu.* In northern Africa, parts of the Middle East, and France, couscous is usually served as a bedding beneath a spicy meat (**chicken, lamb,** or mutton), fish (or squid), or vegetable (such as **carrot** and **turnip**) stew. Couscous grains are usually about 1/16 inch (1 millimeter) in diameter when cooked. Traditionally made by rolling the semolina grain by hand and then sieving the pellets to produce a batch of the proper size, couscous needs to be steamed rather than boiled to prevent it from sticking together in a large mass (though packaged couscous available in the United States has been pre-steamed and dehydrated so that only the addition of boiling water is required to make it ready to eat).

Cream of Wheat

Also known as farina, cream of wheat is the finely milled endosperm of the **wheat** grain. While milling removes the bran and much of the germ of the wheat, cream of wheat is usually enriched with vitamins and minerals. It is consumed as a breakfast cereal or cooked like polenta.

Filo

Also known as phyllo (from the Greek word *phyllon,* which means "leaf"), filo is a dough that is made in extremely thin layers, often leaf-thin or paper-thin. In traditional Mediterranean and Middle Eastern cuisines, this dough is used to make pastries, such as *börek* in Turkey, *byrek* in Albania, sometimes *pita* in Greece, and *strudel* in Austria, Germany, and Hungary. Layers of filo can be stuffed with apples (*apfelstrudel*), cheese (*peynir börek* and *tiropita*), **chicken** (*tavuklu börek* and *kotopita*), meats (*kiymah börek* and *kreatopita*), nuts and syrup (*baklava*), **potatoes, cherries,** or **spinach** and **feta** (*ispanak börek* and *spanakopita*). It can also be served sprinkled with powdered **sugar** (*sekerli börek*).

Flour

"Flour" is a term used to describe any soft, dry powder that comes from the grinding of grain, vegetables, fruits, legumes, nuts, even fish—though "flour" usually signifies a grain product. Finely ground grain has been used since prehistoric times, and for most of that time grain kernels were ground between stones. Nowadays, mechanical rollers are used to mill flour.

Because of the importance of **wheat** in agriculture and cooking, and because of its gluten content, which gives wheat dough strength, elasticity, and the ability to rise, wheat flour is processed into a wide variety of products. There are two main types: refined wheat and whole wheat.

Refined wheat flour, sometimes called white flour, represents the vast majority of flour available today. To make this flour, only the endosperm of the wheat kernels is milled. The result is a very light flour with an unequaled ability to rise. However, loss of the bran and germ from the kernels before milling means a significant decrease in the amount of dietary fiber, vitamins, and minerals present in the flour, so white flour is often enriched with iron, thiamin, niacin, calcium, vitamin D, and riboflavin. Some of the kinds of white flour available are:

- All-purpose flour (also called family, plain, white, or general-purpose flour), which is made from blending soft and hard wheats. This flour usually comes presifted, which means that it has been milled to a very fine level and aerated to make it lighter.

- Bleached flour, which is treated with chemicals to turn the naturally yellow flour a white color. This process also accelerates the flour's gluten-making capability (natural aging of flour does the same at a slower rate).

- Bread flour, which is made from hard wheat with a high gluten content that promotes the quick rising of **bread** dough.

- Bromated flour, which contains a maturing agent that develops the gluten in the flour. Maturing agents include bromate, phosphate, ascorbic acid, and malted **barley**.

- Cake flour, which is made from soft wheat. It is an extremely fine flour with a low gluten content.

- Durum flour, which has the highest protein content of all flour and, thus, produces the most gluten. Durum flour is often used to make pastas.

- Farina, which is used in pastas and cereals.

- Gluten flour, which has about twice the gluten potential of other flours. It often strengthens other low-gluten flours.

- Instant flour (also called instant-blending, quick-mixing, or granulated flour), which has a very powdery texture and high starch content. It mixes quickly with liquids and serves to thicken sauces and gravies.

- Pastry flour (also called cookie or cracker flour), which is suitable for light pastries because its gluten content lies between that of cake flour and that of all-purpose flour.

- Self-rising flour, which contains **salt**, leavening (such as **baking soda** or **baking powder**), and a substance to start the process. It is made from soft wheat.

- Semolina, which is milled from durum wheat. It is high in protein and is used in pastas and breads.

Whole wheat flour is made by recombining the ground bran and germ with the milled endosperm of the wheat kernels. Sometimes called graham flour, whole wheat flour has more fiber, vitamin E, B vitamins, minerals, and proteins than even enriched white flour. However, the bran decreases the flour's ability to develop gluten, so whole wheat flour produces baked goods that are denser than those made with white flour.

There are many types of non-wheat flours, which generally have little or no gluten and so will not rise. Some of these flours include:

- Amaranth flour, which is ground from amaranth (*Amaranthus* genus) seeds. It has more fiber than wheat and rice flours and more protein than most others. Amaranth flour is good for making cookies, cereals, and crackers.
- Arrowroot flour, which is milled from the roots of the maranta plant (*Maranta arundinacea*). This tropical plant's roots are extremely high in starch, and the flour is very easy to digest.
- Buckwheat flour, which is ground from buckwheat. It is used for pancakes and Japanese *soba* noodles.
- **Cornmeal** flour, which is made from **corn**.
- Oat flour, which is milled from **oats**.
- Potato flour, which is also called potato starch. Made from steamed, dried, and ground **potato**es, it is used to make breads, cakes, and pancakes and to thicken sauces.
- Rye flour, which is ground from **rye** grains (*Secale cereale*).
- Soy flour, which is used to increase the protein content of baked items. It is made from ground, defatted soybeans (*Glycine max*).
- Tapioca flour, which comes from ground cassava (*Manihot esculenta*) root. It is used to thicken puddings, pies, and soups.
- Triticale flour, which is made from triticale (*X Triticosecale*), a wheat-rye hybrid.

In general, flour does not store very well. It absorbs moisture from the air and can develop strange flavors and yield unpredictable results. If flour is to be stored for longer than a month or two, it can be frozen to keep it fresh.

Grain flours are basic to many biblical meals, though "flour" is specifically mentioned only a handful of times in the scriptures.

Matzoh

Matzoh, also known as matzo, matzah, and matza, is an unleavened **bread** (bread that does not rise; made without **yeast** or any leavening) made from **flour** and water. It is one of the main foods of the Jewish Passover meal. According to the account in Exodus (chapters 11 and 12), God sent several plagues to Egypt to convince Pharaoh to allow Moses to lead the Israelites out of bondage. The final plague, the death of the firstborn males of Egypt, was a frightful curse that caused Pharaoh to let the Israelites leave his land. God spared the Israelites from this plague by instructing them, through Moses, to mark the doors of their homes with the blood of a newly slaughtered **lamb**, to prepare a quick meal of roasted lamb, bitter herbs, and unleavened bread, and to eat the meal with their sandals on and their belts around their waists, in preparation for a hasty departure. The unleavened bread used at Passover (for the plague "passed over" the houses of the Israelites) has come to be known as matzoh.

According to some Jewish traditions and laws, Passover meals may not include any **wheat, barley**, spelt, **rye**, or **oats** unless they are dry-roasted or made into matzoh. Any dough made from these five grains during Passover must be baked or otherwise used within eighteen minutes (eighteen being a sacred number) of the time the dough is moistened or it cannot be considered unleavened.

Matzoh can be ground into meal, which can be substituted for flour during Passover cooking.

Millet

"Millet" is a name used to denote a number of small-seeded species of cereal crops grown worldwide for food and fodder (both for livestock and for pet birds). This group includes pearl millet (*Pennisetum glaucum*), foxtail millet (*Setaria italica*), proso millet (*Panicum miliaceum*), finger millet (*Eleusine coracana*), barnyard millet (*Echinochloa* spp.), kodo millet (*Paspalum scrobiculatum*), little millet (*Panicum sumatrense*), guinea millet (*Brachiaria deflexa*), browntop millet (*Urochloa ramosa*), teff (*Eragrostis tef*), and fonio (*Digitaria exilis*). Sorghum (*Sorghum* spp.) and Job's tears (*Coix lacrima-jobi*) are sometimes included among the millets.

Some botanists believe that the various millets probably originated in northern Africa; others believe millets are native to Asia. Wherever they first sprang up, millets have been a staple in Asia, India, parts of the Middle East, and parts of Africa for millennia. In fact, some archaeologists speculate that millet in some form may have been the very first cultivated cereal (though others give that distinction to **wheat**). The first written record of millet dates from a 2800 B.C.E. Chinese writing that lists millet among the five sacred crops of China (the others being soybeans, **rice**, wheat, and **barley**). Millet was grown in India during prehistoric times, and millet remains have been found in Swiss lake settlements of the 3rd millennium B.C.E., though millet did not become common in Europe until the 1st millennium B.C.E. It seems that millet migrated to Europe via the Eurasian steppes and not by the Mediterranean sea routes. Millet was among the plants in the Hanging Gardens of Babylon (about 2300 B.C.E.) and is mentioned in the Old Testament (Ezekiel 4:9), so it was known to the peoples of the Bible. The ancient Gauls and Etruscans were growing millet before the arrival of the Romans. Charlemagne (8th century C.E.) had millet stocked as a food for Lent, and Marco Polo (13th century) reported vast quantities of millet in China. Europeans grew more millet than wheat during the Middle Ages.

Millets are extremely hardy cereals, thriving in the wild but also responding well to cultivation. In general, they go dormant during times of drought but grow quite fervently when water returns. Millets thus manage very well in monsoon climates, from the Arabian Sea to China. All of the millets have tiny seeds, which are spread and sown easily by small birds or the wind. Millet seeds store well (some can keep for up to five years if unthreshed), making any of the millets the perfect grain to keep in reserve against times of famine. However, the tiny seeds are somewhat difficult to handle and contain no gluten, so millet **flour** will not rise and is suitable for **flatbread** only. Many people also consider millet grain to taste inferior to other grains.

Millet grain can be cooked or prepared in the same way as other grains. It can be simmered like **rice**, prepared as a pilaf, or steamed like **couscous**. If prepared as a hot cereal, it blends well with **milk**, fruit, and **yogurt**. It can be added to hamburger and meatloaves, casseroles, and soups. Mixed with **cucumbers** and **tomato**es, millet grain makes a light side dish. It can even be added to cookies or mixed with **honey** and fruit as desserts.

Millet grain is high in phosphorus, magnesium, thiamin, folacin, iron, manganese, and copper. It has no cholesterol and is low in protein but rich in carbohydrates.

Oat Bran

Oat bran is the outer layer of oat groats (see **oats**). Available in bulk or as a cereal, oat bran has fewer calories than whole oats but more dietary fiber and higher concentrations of magnesium, manganese, phosphorus, and thiamin.

Oatmeal

Oatmeal is made from processed **oats**. In most of the English-speaking world, *oatmeal* refers to any coarsely ground grain such as **cornmeal**, wheatmeal, and peasemeal. In North America, however, *oatmeal* means crushed, rolled, or cut oats, as well as the porridge made from these oats.

Oatmeal has many uses in the kitchen: as an ingredient in cookies and cakes, as a poultry stuffing, even as a **cheese** coating. Oatmeal has also been used in alcoholic beverages, in cosmetics, in soaps, and in topical medicines. Oatmeal as a porridge, combined with **brown sugar, honey, cinnamon,** or maple syrup; **butter** or **margarine; milk, cream,** or **yogurt; raisins, apples,** or other fruits, makes a filling and tasty breakfast.

Certain medical studies have indicated that eating a bowl of oatmeal daily can help lower cholesterol. Other studies have shown that oatmeal may help reduce the risk of heart disease. In both cases, a low-fat diet is recommended as well.

Oats

Oats (*Avena sativa*) are a plant of cool climates and probably originated in the greater region of northern Germany. They do not require much summer heat (in fact, they go dormant if it gets too hot) and are tolerant of rain, cold, and even late frosts or snow. An annual, oats are planted either in the fall for late summer harvest (or plowed under in the spring to serve as green fertilizer) or in the spring for early autumn harvest. Some archaeologists claim that oats did not enter cultivation until the 1st century C.E.; others assert that oats were being grown in Germany, Denmark, and Switzerland by 1000 B.C.E., and perhaps even earlier. Although both the ancient Greeks and Romans knew of oats, they used this grain sparingly, and oats never established firm roots in the Mediterranean region. Oats would not have been known to the peoples of the Bible (though modern Middle Eastern cooks sometimes use oats in their recipes).

Though many peoples have readily used oats as livestock feed, just as many have disdained oats for human consumption. Oats were particularly favored in Scotland and other Celtic lands and in Germany, and cooks of the Middle Ages placed bags of oatmeal in kettles while cooking salted foods, as the oats would absorb enough of the salt to make the rest of the meal palatable.

Oats are generally available in only a few forms: as oat groats, which are whole kernels that can be cooked like **rice**; steel-cut oats, which are groats that have been sliced lengthwise and so require longer cooking times (about twenty minutes); and rolled oats, which are flattened kernels that cook relatively quickly (about five minutes). **Oat bran**, the outer layer of oat groats, is also available in bulk or as a cereal. While oat bran has fewer calories than whole oats, it has more dietary fiber and higher concentrations of magnesium, manganese, phosphorus, and thiamin.

Oats are one of the main ingredients in granola and muesli. Groats can be prepared like a pilaf and resemble the taste of wheatberries; they can be added to steamed or grilled vegetables, soups, stews, stuffings, poultry or fish breadings, **wheat breads** and muffins, cookies, cakes, and even pancakes.

Oats do not contain gluten and so constitute a safe grain for people who are wheat- or gluten-intolerant.

Potato Flour

Potato flour is made by steaming, then drying, then grinding **potatoes** (*Solanum tuberosum*). **Bread**s, biscuits, pancakes, and cakes can be made using potato flour, which is also used as a thickener for sauces.

Rice

Rice (*Oryza sativa*) has been the staple food of more than half the world's population since prehistoric times. Rice is native to Asia (probably northern Thailand, where rice grains have been found at an archaeological site dating to 3500 B.C.E.). Rice was named one of the two "immortal sons of heaven" in the early Vedic literature (along with **barley**) by about 3000 B.C.E., though the documents themselves, along with carbonized rice grains found in Uttar Pradesh, date from about 1000 B.C.E. A 2800 B.C.E. Chinese writing lists rice among the five sacred crops of China (the others being soybeans, barley, **wheat**, and **millet**), and rice husks mixed with potsherds (pottery fragments) dating from 2000 B.C.E. have been found in China. Rice was also the basis for an ancient Chinese dish called the Eight Marvels, made from rice, oil, **onions**, **mushrooms**, pork, ham, **eggs**, and **soybean sauce**. Rice made its way to Japan by the 1st century B.C.E., though it had reached all of southeastern Asia, the Philippine islands, and Indonesia much earlier. Moving westward, rice became one of the most important foods of the Middle East. Brought to Spain by the Moors in the 8th or 9th century C.E., it became the basis for paella. From there it made its way to Italy, certainly by the 15th century, and became the famous Italian risotto. It arrived in North America in the late 17th century and is now a major export of the United States. It is also an important crop in the West Indies, parts of Central America, and Brazil.

Needing warm, wet climates to thrive, rice can be divided into two types: paddy rice and upland rice. Paddy rice is grown in fields that are flooded for most of the growing season; the water prevents the growth of weeds, and the fields are drained when it is time to harvest. Upland rice does not require flooding but does need wet soil, and this rice is often grown in terraced fields.

Rice is either long-grain, medium-grain, or short-grain and is available in four forms: brown, white, aromatic, and glutinous:

- Brown rice is the most nutritious because only the husk is removed during milling; the bran is left intact, so brown rice has more fiber, folacin, iron, riboflavin, potassium, phosphorus, zinc, copper, and manganese than white rice. It also has vitamin E, which is absent in all the other rices.
- White rice, also called milled rice, is the more popular type of rice. White rice has had the husk, bran, and most of the germ removed during milling. It is worth noting that much white rice is enriched after milling to replace the nutrients lost in the milling process.
- Aromatic rices are long-grained and have a nutty or toasty flavor. These include **basmati**, jasmine, texmati, wehani, and wild **pecan** rices.
- Glutinous (sweet) rice is short-grained, starchy, and sticky; it turns translucent when cooked.

Rice, in general, is high in calories; it also has significant amounts of vitamin B6.

Rice dishes can be plain or elaborate. Cooking rice in broth or adding spices and herbs to the water will add a great deal of flavor. Any number of vegetables, nuts, fruits, spices, sauces, and dressings can be added to rice after it is cooked. Rice has become a necessary part of curries, gumbos, goulashes, stews, and stir-fries and can replace pasta in many dishes. It can also be added to soups, stuffings, and salads. Rice pilaf and risotto are specialty dishes that are relatively easy to prepare. Rice can even be made into a dessert pudding.

Rye

Closely related to **wheat**, rye (*Secale cereale*) is thought by some to be native to Asia and to have spread westward as a weed, and by others to be native to northern Europe and to have spread southward and eastward. Wherever it originated, it was being cultivated in Britain, Germany, and central Europe by 1000 B.C.E. It was known in ancient Greece, but not in ancient Rome, Egypt, or India. In the Middle Ages, rye was the principal cereal crop in north-central Europe and Russia. Although some versions of the Bible incorrectly identify a certain rough-grained wheat as "rye," it is unlikely that what we know as rye was known to the peoples of the Bible. Rye, however, is commonly used by Jews of the Diaspora, particularly those who settled in Eastern Europe and Russia. Rye proliferates under conditions that are too wet or too cold for other grains, so it became a staple of Scandinavia, Russia, and northeastern Europe. Another reason for its prevalence is that rye **breads** have a much longer shelf-life than wheat breads; like wheat, rye contains gluten (which makes bread rise) and other grains do not. French colonists were probably the first to plant rye in the Americas—in Nova Scotia in 1606. Dutch and English colonists also brought rye to New England, where it grew much better than wheat and became a staple of bread-baking (such as Boston brown bread) and a cereal grain.

Whole rye is available as

- Whole rye berries, also called whole kernels or groats, which resemble **wheatberries**;
- Cracked rye, which are whole groats cracked open; and
- Rye flakes, which are made by heating and then pressing the berries.

Whole rye can be prepared as a casserole or added to soups. Rye flakes can serve as a hot breakfast cereal, like **oatmeal**. Cracked rye can be added to soups or prepared as a pilaf or hot cereal.

Rye is very high in dietary fiber, calories, and carbohydrates, high in protein, and very low in cholesterol. It provides significant amounts of vitamins B6 and E, copper, folacin, iron, magnesium, manganese, niacin, phosphorus, riboflavin, thiamin, and zinc.

Unfortunately, rye sometimes gets sick with ergot (contamination by the parasitic fungus *Claviceps purpurea*), which causes uncontrollable and violent muscular fits and hallucinations, and sometimes death, in humans who consume it. Over history, instances of ergot poisoning have often been attributed to spells cast by witches or to demon possession, and many historians believe that the citizens of Salem, Massachusetts, who were hanged as witches in 1692 were convicted because the town's rye had been contaminated and caused the townspeople to exhibit odd behaviors.

Rye Flour

Rye flour is made by grinding **rye** seeds (*Secale cereale*). There are three types of rye flour:

- Light, sometimes called "bolted," which has been sifted to remove the germ and bran

- Medium
- Dark, which is unsifted and has more fiber

Rye flour is most often used to make **bread** and crackers.

Tahini

Also known as *tehina* in Hebrew, tahini is a paste made from ground **sesame seeds**. In Middle Eastern markets, tahini is available fresh, in cans, in jars, or dehydrated. The sesame seeds are also available, either hulled or unhulled. Tahini made from unhulled seeds is bitter but it has more vitamins, calcium, and protein than tahini made from hulled seeds.

Tahini is a major ingredient in hummus and other vegetable and meat dishes. It is also used as a spread on **bread**, as the base for a sauce with **lemon** juice and **garlic**, or as a side dish by itself.

Wheat

It might easily be said that wheat is the most important cereal crop in the world, for wheat nourishes more people than any other grain. One of the oldest cultivated grains—and perhaps the first crop deliberately planted and raised for harvest—wheat is believed to be descended from a wild grass, probably einkorn, native to Asia Minor, somewhere between modern-day Afghanistan and Ethiopia. Stone Age people began growing wheat before 6000 B.C.E., and it has been found in archaeological sites dating from that era as far from its origins as the French Pyrenees. Wheat kernels have also been found at a site in Turkey dating from 5500 B.C.E. Sumerian writings of 3100 B.C.E. (Sumerian being the oldest known written language) describe how wheat was used for making **bread** and **beer**. Thereafter, the cultivation of wheat was recorded in ancient Babylonia, Mesopotamia, and Egypt. Egyptian pictorial representations of wheat date from earlier than 2600 B.C.E. Wheat was cultivated in India by 2500 B.C.E. and in China perhaps by 2800 B.C.E. Wheat is frequently mentioned in the Bible, and the Israelites would probably have learned how to leaven bread dough from the Egyptians, though the escape from Egypt may have happened so quickly that there would have been no time to take the leavening mixture with them. This would explain the commemorative meal of unleavened bread. When they finally reached the Promised Land, the Israelites may have begun to cultivate "yeast," by which was meant the froth of any fermenting liquid. This froth would have been used in making raised bread, though the entire process by which real **yeast** causes dough to rise was not understood until the 19th century when Louis Pasteur discovered that yeast is a living organism. The ancient Greeks imported most of their wheat from Egypt and Sicily and the Black Sea lands. Carthage, Malta, and Gaul were very important regions of wheat agriculture during the Roman Empire.

Wheat agriculture continued to spread north, to Britain by the 7th century C.E. and to the Baltic by the 13th century. The Moorish colonization of Spain and southern Europe was nearly disastrous for European wheat production; the

Moors brought barberry, which is an intermediate host for the parasite that causes black stem rust in wheat. In France, **rye** overran the wheat fields during Renaissance times, and the French could not separate the wheat from the rye until the 19th century. As a result, England became the primary supplier of wheat to Europe, with occasional help from Russia, which had become a great wheat-growing country. Christopher Columbus was the first to plant wheat in the Americas, at Isabela, Puerto Rico. Wheat did not grow well in the Caribbean, but Spanish conquistadors brought it to modern-day Mexico, Ecuador, Peru, and California. Native Americans of the southwestern United States began to cultivate wheat, and wheat came to New England and Virginia early in the 17th century with the Dutch explorers and the English settlers. But wheat did not truly flourish in these areas. Not until the early 18th century, when wheat was planted in the Mississippi Valley, did wheat agriculture really establish itself in the Americas. Wheat is tolerant and adaptable and is now grown virtually world-wide, though Australia, the United States, Canada, Argentina, and Russia grow the vast majority of the world's wheat today.

Although there are more than thirty thousand varieties of wheat grown world-wide, agronomists and botanists now divide wheat into six classes based upon their planting season, the hardness of their grain, and the color of their kernels. These classes are Hard Red Winter, Hard Red Spring, Soft Red Winter, Hard White, Soft White, and Durum. The winter wheats, planted in the fall, lie dormant until the spring and may be harvested in early summer. The spring wheats are sown in the early spring and harvested in late summer. The harder wheats have a greater protein-to-starch ratio than the others, and Durum is the hardest of all.

Bread and all-purpose **flours** are ground from the kernels of Hard Red Winter, Hard Red Spring, and Hard White. Baking flour comes from Soft Red Winter and Soft White. Pastas are made from Durum.

Aside from grinding and milling wheat into flour, there are numerous ways to process and use whole-wheat products. **Bulgur**, produced when whole-wheat kernels are steamed, dried, and cracked, is used for pilaf, cereal, and tabbouleh. **Wheatberries** (also known as groats) are whole, untreated wheat kernels; with a nutlike flavor, they often work as a side dish or an accompaniment to main dishes. Cracked wheat, made from ground wheatberries, is often served as a breakfast cereal; it can also be mixed into baking recipes and substituted for bulgur or **rice** or other grains in most dishes. Farina, milled from the endosperm of the wheat grains, is almost exclusively used as a breakfast cereal. Rolled wheat (also known as wheat flakes) is made by flattening whole wheatberries and can be used in baking or cooked as hot cereal. Wheatena, a finely cracked wheat product, is used as a hot cereal.

Simmering is the usual way of cooking wheatberries, cracked wheat, and bulgur. Whole wheatberries can be sprouted, and the sprouts can be used like **bean sprouts,** or allowed to grow longer and used as wheat grass. Bulgur, rolled wheat, farina, and wheatena can be cooked by steeping.

Whole-wheat products are high in dietary fiber and can be beneficial to those with a family history of colorectal cancer. Whole wheat is also a good source of protein, B vitamins, iron, magnesium, and manganese.

Wheatberry

See **wheat**.

Wild Rice

Contrary to common belief, wild rice is not a type of **rice** but a type of grass that grows in shallow water, in lakes, ponds, and streams. There are four main species of wild rice:

- Northern wild rice (*Zizania palustris*), native to the Great Lakes region of North America; it is an annual plant.
- Wild rice (*Z. aquatica*), native to the Saint Lawrence River and the North American Atlantic and Gulf coasts; it is also an annual plant.
- Texas wild rice (*Z. texana*), limited to the San Marcos River in Texas; it is a perennial plant.
- Manchurian wild rice (*Z. latifolia*), native to China; it is a perennial.

Now cultivated primarily in Minnesota, wild rice is relatively expensive, but it was once a staple of the diet of the Chippewa and the Dakota. It is high in calories and higher in protein and iron, zinc, thiamin, niacin, and vitamin B6 than true rices.

Wild rice is cooked in much the same way as true rices, though it may have a somewhat chewy texture. It also has a nutty flavor that makes it enjoyable to eat. It is a nutritious substitute for traditional rice, though it would not have been known by the peoples of the Bible.

HERBS AND SPICES

Allspice

Allspice (*Pimenta dioica*), a member of the Myrtle family, is native to the tropical Americas, particularly Jamaica and the West Indies; it was first brought to Europe around 1600 C.E. and would not have been known to the peoples of the Middle East until much later. Allspice is so named because it has a taste and aroma somewhere between pungent and mild, resembling a combination of **cloves**, **pepper**, **cinnamon**, and **nutmeg**. It is readily available as both ground powder and whole dried berries, and it will have the best flavor and will keep the longest if ground fresh. Allspice is generally used to flavor stews and sauces, pork or **chicken** dishes, **sausages**, meat pastries, and pickled vegetables.

Anise

The anise flavor, which is quite like licorice, comes from two unrelated plants. The major source is the European anise (also called green anise and African anise: *Pimpinella anisum*), a flowering annual that is a native of the eastern Mediterranean—Egypt, Greece, Crete, and Asia Minor. It has been known since the time of the ancient Egyptians and would have been known to the peoples of the Bible, and it was used by both Greeks and Romans to flavor **breads** and cakes to aid digestion. Roman weddings also featured anise cake, perhaps a precursor of spicy wedding cakes and today's sugar-coated, anise-flavored **almond** candies. The Romans also believed that aniseed would prevent bad breath and remove wrinkles and that an anise plant hung over the bed would take away bad dreams.

The other plant is Chinese star anise (*Illicium verum*), a tree belonging to the Magnolia family. Coming to Europe through medieval Russia, Chinese anise became for a time the basis for French anisette until political relationships made it too expensive.

Oil of anise, which comes from the gray-green aniseeds, is also the basis for French **anisette**, Turkish raki, and South American aguardiente, all liqueurs. It is also commonly used to mask the taste of bitter medicines.

Basil

Basil (*Ocimum basilicum*) is a member of the large **Mint** family. It is believed to have originated in India or Asia, though the location of its first cultivation is lost to history. It is not specifically mentioned in the Bible, but basil is thought to have been brought to the Mediterranean world via the ancient spice routes and to have been known to the ancient Israelites. Archaeologists have found basil in mummies removed from the pyramids and believe that the ancient Egyptians used it as an embalming herb. Both the Greeks and the Romans used basil. The Greeks called it *basilikon phuton,* which means "magnificent, royal, or kingly herb," and it is possible that only Greek rulers were allowed to use it. The generic name *Ocimum* comes, perhaps, from the Greek word *okimon,* which means "fragrant," as basil is a strongly fragrant herb. The Romans called it *basiliscus,* which refers to a basilisk, a fire-breathing dragon, believing perhaps that basil was a charm against this beast. The Roman belief may have given rise to a wider use of basil as a medicinal cure for venomous bites. People of the Middle Ages thought that basil could actually produce scorpions, and basil is associated with the symbolism for the astrological sign of Scorpio. In contrast, basil came to be associated with love in the Italian and Romanian regions: Italian maidens wore basil in their hair if they wished to be courted, and Romanian girls gave basil to the boy they wished to marry. The people of India consecrated basil to the Hindu god Vishnu, whose wife, Tulasi (or Tulsi), became basil when she visited earth. When someone dies, Hindus will still bathe the head in basil water and place a basil leaf over the heart.

There are more than sixty known varieties of basil, and these range from green to red to purple, each with a distinctive flavor. Basil leaves are used in sauces, pestos, salads, soups, and more, and for best results should be picked before the plant flowers. Either fresh or dried, basil is now an essential ingredient in many recipes.

Bay Leaf

Bay leaves of several species have a long association with humans. The ancient Greeks used the leaves of the Mediterranean bay leaf shrub (*Laurus nobilis*) to adorn their victorious athletes at the Olympic games, and Greek poets and scholars were granted wreaths of bay leaves upon completion of their studies; the modern word *baccalaureate*, which is the degree granted upon completion of undergraduate work, derives from the word for laurel berries and is a carryover from the Greek custom. The ancient Romans adopted this custom of bestowing laurel wreaths, but transferred it to their victorious warriors. The Romans also believed that lightning never struck the bay leaf tree and so wore crowns of its leaves as protection during thunderstorms. It is possible that the peoples of the Bible were familiar with the bay leaf, though it is not mentioned therein.

Bay leaves have a distinctive flavor, which is so strong that a single leaf can alter the taste of an entire stew or soup, so they are employed with restraint and in combination with other spices like **parsley**, **thyme**, and **rosemary**.

There are two other bay leaves used in cooking besides the Mediterranean bay leaf: the California bay leaf (*Umbellularia californica*), also known as California laurel, Oregon myrtle, and pepperwood; and the Indian bay leaf (*Cinnamomum tejpata*). The California variety is similar to the Mediterranean but has a stronger flavor. The Indian tree, though similar in appearance, has an entirely different flavor, more like that of **cinnamon** bark, and so is used in much different ways in the kitchen.

When using whole dried bay leaves, place them in the pot at the start of the cooking process so that they have time to release their flavor, but remove them before serving the meal. Powdered bay leaves are also available but are less common.

Benzoin

Also known as benzoinum, benzoin resin, benzoin gum, gum Benjamin, or balsamic resin, benzoin is the dried sap that seeps out from injured benzoin trees (*Styrax benzoin*), which are native to Sumatra, Java, and Thailand. Because benzoin is very fragrant, it is used to make perfumes and incense. It also contains benzoic acid, which makes it an effective antiseptic, stimulant, and inhalant. Among the varieties of benzoin, those from Siam and Sumatra benzoin trees are considered the finest. For centuries, benzoin has been mixed with **frankincense** or **myrrh**, particularly in the Middle East, to scent private homes and places of worship.

Borage

Borage (*Borago officinalis*) is a traditional medicinal and culinary herb native to the Mediterranean region and probably first cultivated in the lands now comprising Turkey and Syria; it would probably have been known to the peoples of the Bible. The Moors brought it to Spain, and from there it spread all over Europe. The name is from the Arabic *abu rach*, which means "father of sweat," possibly because tea made from borage can help reduce fevers and ease chest colds.

Both the leaves and the small blue or pink flowers have culinary uses. The leaves are said to taste like **cucumbers**; both the leaves and flowers are used in salads, dips, and soups. The Frankfurter Grüne Sauce, also known as Green Sauce, relies on borage leaves as one of its seven ingredients. Chopped borage leaves can be added to stews during the final minutes of cooking, and they can also be cooked with **cabbage**. Both the leaves and the flowers often garnish **gin**-based cocktails, and the flowers are frozen in ice cubes to decorate other drinks. The candied flowers make splendid cake decorations.

Since ancient times, borage has been used to dispel melancholy and induce euphoria; it is also used to treat catarrh, rheumatism, and skin diseases. The oil from the seeds helps regulate the hormonal system and aids in lowering blood pressure. Borage is rich in potassium.

Also known as Starflower, borage is a lovely, easily grown garden plant. It blooms from June through September, growing to a height of about 8 inches. It is an annual, but it resows itself.

Caper

The caper is the unopened flower bud of the Sahara caper tree (*Capparis spinosa*), which is really a trailing shrub. It is believed that the caper originated in the Sahara Desert (thus its common name) then spread around the Mediterranean. Requiring strong sunlight but capable of absorbing moisture from the air through its leaves, the caper is first recorded around 600 B.C.E., when ancient Greeks brought some to the region of southern France. Likely, the Greeks (or at least those living in the lands now known as Turkey) used capers long before then. The Romans were great fans of capers. Given the desert origin of this piquant spice, it is highly likely that the peoples of the Bible called upon capers to flavor their stews and meat dishes.

The caper buds are usually pickled, though sometimes they are allowed to mature and the berries are collected for use. Even today, the collection of capers is labor-intensive, so they tend to be relatively expensive. Yet a small amount will give a significant lift to an otherwise bland dish.

Caraway Seed

Caraway (*Carum carvi*) is a member of the **Parsley** family. Its origins are not known, though caraway seeds have been found in Swiss Neolithic lake settlements. It prefers cool weather, and the Romans may have imported it from Gaul (present-day France) or Spain. Some authorities claim that caraway originated in Egypt, as the medical papyrus of Thebes, which dates from 1552 B.C.E., mentions it, though other authorities claim that the reference is to **cumin**. Many translations of the Bible still use the word "caraway" instead of "cumin," though the latter is what the peoples of the Bible would have known and used.

Although the roots of the plant are sometimes eaten, the caraway seed is what is most often called for. The flavor is pungent, and caraway is a common flavoring for **bread**s and cakes, casseroles, **cheeses**, **pickles**, **carrot** and **potato** dishes, sauerkraut, salads, pastas, and even liqueurs. The oil from caraway seeds also flavors soaps, lotions, and perfumes. The ancient Romans may even have chewed caraway seeds to alleviate bad breath.

Cardamom

Cardamom (*Elettaria cardamomum*), a pungent, aromatic spice, is native to the moist mountain forests of what is now southwestern India, and it is first mentioned in the ancient Vedic medical texts of 1000 B.C.E. By the 4th century B.C.E., it had been imported to Greece; thus it is doubtful that Abraham and his kin would have known about cardamom. But in the intervening years it has become an important ingredient of Middle Eastern cooking, and it is most often used to add spice to **coffee**, either by adding freshly ground cardamom seeds to the coffee powder or by steeping a few cardamom pods in the hot coffee. Middle Eastern cooks also use cardamom to flavor meat and **rice** dishes. A member of the **Ginger** family, cardamom is often considered the third most expensive spice in the world, after **saffron** and **vanilla**. It quickly loses its flavor when ground and should be purchased only as whole pods and crushed immediately before use.

Cayenne Pepper

Sometimes known as simply cayenne or hot red pepper, cayenne pepper is made by grinding up hot red cayenne peppers or chilies (*Capsicum frutescens*; see **Pepper**). Used in many Mexican, Indian, Italian, Caribbean, Chinese, and Cajun recipes, cayenne also adds a kick to marinades and barbecue sauces for meats and poultry. Cayenne pepper has spread worldwide and is often found in Middle Eastern kitchens.

Celery Seed

Celery seed comes from the **celery** plant (*Apium graveolens*). The seeds have a mild celery flavor and often add a nice taste to split-**pea** soup, fish chowders, **tomato** sauces and soups, vegetable and **potato** dishes, **bread**s, and stuffings. They are also an important ingredient in pickling and curry recipes. Celery seed figures importantly in the cuisines of Germany, Italy, Russia, and Asia and has been adopted by Jews of the modern Diaspora.

Chamomile

There are at least three herb species that go by the name "chamomile":

- German chamomile (*Matricaria recutita* or *M. suaveolens*; also *Chamomilla recutita* or *C. chamomilla*)
- Wild chamomile (or pineapple weed: *M. matricarioides*; also known as *M. discoides*, *M. suaveolens,* and *C. suaveolens*)
- Roman chamomile (*Chamaemelum nobile*; also known as *Anthemis nobilis*)

German chamomile, also known as wild chamomile and scented mayweed, is an annual of the Sunflower family and is native to Europe and temperate Asia; it is an invasive species in temperate North America and Australia. Its flowers have white petals surrounding the bright yellow center, which has a strong, aromatic fragrance. Usually consumed in the form of an herbal **tea** (tisane), the dried flowers help relieve upset stomach, work as a sleep-inducing relaxant, and help guard against mouth infections.

Wild chamomile, an annual, is native to both North America and northeastern Asia. Its flowers are yellowish-green, without petals, and have a **pineapple**/chamomile aroma. They can be steeped to make an herbal tea (tisane) or added to fresh salads, and they help to calm the stomach and relax the body; if crushed and applied externally, they can soothe itching and skin irritation.

Roman chamomile is also known as garden chamomile, ground apple, low chamomile, and whig plant. A perennial that is native to Europe, it produces single flowers with yellow centers and silver-white petals. Infusions of the flowers can help ease flatulence and digestive cramps and can sometimes help abate fevers. The oil from the flowers can help soothe calluses, bruises, and painful joints.

Jews of the modern Diaspora, particularly those who settled in Europe, used chamomile, and it is now a common tea in the Middle East.

Chervil

The "herb of joy," according to the ancient Greeks, chervil or garden chervil (*Anthriscus cerefolium*) is an annual herb that is a member of the **Parsley** or **Carrot** family. Native to southwestern Russia and western Asia, chervil was widely known around the Mediterranean during the classical period. In the ancient Middle East the roots were boiled and added to soups and salads, as well as used fresh. The ancient Greeks used it to flavor foods, while the Romans ate it as a vegetable. It is likely that chervil was known to the peoples of the Bible. The Gauls cultivated chervil, and it is still widely in use in French cuisine and has an established place in Italian recipes; it is much less common in English and American kitchens.

Chervil leaves are consumed fresh in salads or dried as herbs. It is one of the ingredients in *bouquet garnis* and *fines herbes* and is used to flavor poultry, some seafoods, and vegetables. The seeds are also aromatic.

Chili Powder

Chili powder, also known as chili mix, is a combination of spices such as **cumin, garlic, oregano, paprika, salt,** and ground chili **peppers.** Used to add spice to chili, chili powder can also flavor other dishes, such as guacamole, **tomato** sauce, **cornbread,** tamales, enchiladas, **chicken** stew, hamburgers, nachos, and **bean** dip. The first chili powders were sold commercially in Texas in the 1890s, and chili powder has become part of spice cabinets worldwide.

Chives

Chives (*Allium schoenoprasum*) are a member of the **Onion** family. They originated in Asia and are recorded in China as long ago as 3000 B.C.E. Some scholars believe that chives spread over the Siberian-Alaskan land bridge to the Americas long before Marco Polo brought them to Europe. Other authorities assert that the ancient Romans used chives in their cooking, for chives now grow wild around the Mediterranean. It is unlikely that chives were part of the diet of the peoples of the Bible, though they are used in the recipes of Jews of the modern Diaspora.

Chives have an arresting flavor that is both delicate and incisive. They are used to flavor cold soups, stir-fries, **cheese** and **cream** sauces, dips, and **potato** dishes. The blossoms are also delicious in salads and can be used to flavor **vinegar.**

Chives are relatively challenging to grow from seed, but they are easily grown from bulbs. In fact, the clump of bulbs needs to be separated every couple of years for best results. The edible portion is the greenery, and the bulbs will regularly send up new growth to replace the cut leaves. If not cut back, chives will produce a lovely purple flower.

Cicely

Often confused with **myrrh** (and therefore appearing in some biblical translations as such), cicely (*Myrrhis odorata*), sometimes known as sweet cicely, is a perennial probably native to central and southern Europe. The leaves, seeds, and roots are all edible, the leaves tasting slightly like those of **chervil** or **anise.** Cicely was very popular in France and England in the 16th and 17th centuries, but its use has much declined since then in favor of milder-tasting herbs. Cicely is now used mostly to flavor fish dishes.

Cinnamon

Cinnamon (*Cinnamomum zeylanicum* or *C. aromaticum*) is a light-brown spice with a fragrant aroma and a warm, sweet flavor. A member of the Laurel family, it is a native of what is now Sri Lanka, India, and Myanmar (Burma), though it was probably known in China by 2800 B.C.E. Cinnamon was also recorded in Egypt by 1500 B.C.E. and was certainly familiar to the Hebrew tribes by 1000 B.C.E. (it is mentioned in Exodus, for example, as an ingredient for an oil of anointing). In ancient times, because of its flavor and its scarcity, cinnamon was worth as much as fifteen times the value of silver. In Middle Eastern cooking, cinnamon is used to flavor both fiery curries and subtle, fragrant **rice** dishes. In Western cooking, cinnamon was very popular in the 16th to 18th centuries C.E. but is now used primarily to flavor desserts such as stewed fruits or spice cakes and rarely used in spicy dishes.

Clove

The clove (*Syzygium aromaticum*) is a native of Indonesia. Cloves were known in China during the Han Dynasty (c. 200 B.C.E.–c. 200 C.E.), and from China made their way to India. Cloves reached the Roman Empire by 335 C.E., brought by Arab traders. But cloves disappeared from Europe with the collapse of the Roman Empire, to reappear when the Saracens conquered Sicily, when the Crusaders brought spices back from the Holy Land, and when the Portuguese made their way by sea to India. By the 13th century, cloves were becoming an important and expensive import to Europe—and thus an object of numerous "trade wars" among competing merchants. Cloves are sometimes mentioned as one of the rare spices that the Queen of Sheba gave to King Solomon in II Chronicles 9:9 and are a very common spice in Near and Middle Eastern cuisine.

Clove trees are evergreens, growing to a height of 60 feet. They thrive in Indonesia, Madagascar, and Zanzibar. The cooking spice comes from the buds of the tree, picked just before they open, then dried, separated from their husks, and dried further, whereupon they resemble brown, black, or rusty nails. Indeed, the name "clove" derives from the French word *clou,* which means nail. Harvesting is very labor-intensive. Often used whole, cloves are also ground into a powder.

Modern-day cooks use cloves to flavor meats, salad dressings, and desserts. Cloves are an essential ingredient in **ketchup** and **Worchestershire sauce**s. They are also used to flavor certain **coffee**s and can even be made into cigarettes. As it is a strong spice, only a small amount is necessary to create an impression.

Cocoa

Cocoa is a product of the seeds of the cacao tree (*Theobroma cacao*), which is native to the low Andean foothills and the Amazon and Orinoco River basins. Introduced into Central America by the Mayans, and later cultivated by the Toltecs and the Aztecs, the tree grows to a height of 25 feet and requires humid conditions, regular rainfall, and good soil in order to thrive. The trees produce ovoid pods about 12 inches long, and each pod contains twenty to sixty seeds; but a single mature tree may yield only about twenty pods in a year, and from three hundred to six hundred seeds are required to make 2 pounds of cocoa paste, so many trees are needed. One of the most important active ingredients in the seeds is theobromine, a chemical that is similar to caffeine. It is interesting to note that *theobroma* means "food of the gods," and many people would say that cocoa is just that. The Aztecs were great lovers of cocoa drinks, which they flavored with **vanilla** and other spices.

The three main cultivars used for making cocoa are the Criollo Group, which produces beans that are less bitter and more aromatic than the others; the Forestero Group, which are hardier than the other cacao trees; and the Trinitario Group, which is a hybrid of the other two. Beans from Criollo trees are extremely expensive and are used in only about 10 percent of chocolate, though it is considered to be the best tasting of all.

The Spanish conquerors of Mexico brought cocoa back to Europe and also planted cacao trees in the West Indies and the Philippines. Cacao trees were also planted in Africa. Today, most of the world's cocoa comes from trees in Africa and Brazil, and the Netherlands and the United States are the leading processors of cocoa. Cocoa would not have been known to the peoples of the Bible, though it is now consumed worldwide.

Because of its wonderful taste, cocoa is a favorite ingredient in many drinks, cakes, **creams**, cookies, toppings, and other recipes. It is also a health food, with about twice the anticancer antioxidants of red **wine** and three times those of green **tea**.

Coriander

Coriander (*Coriandrum sativum*), a member of the **Parsley** or **Carrot** family, was one of the first spices used in cooking. Archaeologists have discovered coriander seeds in both Bronze Age ruins on the Greek Aegean islands and in Egyptian tombs. The Ebers Papyrus mentions coriander, and the ancient Assyrians, Babylonians, and Mycenaeans grew it. The Hindus used coriander in religious ceremonies, and the Hebrews, adopting it perhaps from the Egyptians, perhaps from the Babylonians, used it in cooking (Exodus 16:31 and Numbers 11:7, where the taste of manna is compared to that of coriander). The Romans spread the cultivation and use of coriander throughout Europe, and it has been grown as far north as the southern part of England. Spanish settlers brought coriander to the Americas, where it quickly became a favorite of Native American peoples in Mexico and the southwestern regions of the United States.

Cooks can most easily find coriander powder, but the taste is much better if one buys the seeds and grinds them as needed. The flavor is both pungent and sugary, and it can serve as a complement to almost any dish, from wild game to **chicken**, curry to omelets, soup to **bread**, and pudding to cake. While many people use coriander as a spice, coriander leaves are also used as a salad. The fresh leaves are known by the common name "**cilantro**."

Cream of Tartar

Cream of tartar (the potassium **salt** of tartaric acid) is a byproduct of **wine**-making and might well have been known in biblical times. During the fermentation of **grape** juice, tartar crystallizes in the wine casks. The crystals are collected, purified, and ground, producing a white, odorless, acidic powder. Cream of tartar has many uses in cooking: for example, it can stabilize egg whites, increasing their heat tolerance and volume; prevent **sugar** syrups from crystallizing; and decrease discoloration in boiled vegetables. When combined with **baking soda** it produces an effective laxative.

Cumin

Cumin (*Cuminum cyminum*), a member of the **Parsley** family, is native to the Mediterranean and the Middle East. It was an important spice during biblical times, noted by Egyptian medical writers (in the medical papyrus of Thebes) by 1552 B.C.E. and by Greek palace scribes earlier than 1000 B.C.E., and it was also mentioned by the author of Isaiah (28:25, 27). Cumin has often been confused with **caraway**, but scholars now assert that their origins and uses are quite distinct. The Roman scientist Pliny considered cumin an appetite stimulant. The cumin seeds, which are really fruits, have a warm, bitter flavor. In modern times, European cooks use cumin only for **cheese** flavoring; it is much more important to cooks throughout the rest of the world. In Indian cooking, for example, cumin is used to flavor **lentil** or other vegetable dishes or curries and as an essential ingredient in *tandoori* recipes. According to folklore, cumin also has a medicinal application, as a stimulant and antimicrobial.

Dill

Dill (*Anethum graveolens*) is another early spice, thought to have been well known to the ancient Romans, who called it *aneth* and used its oil as a tonic. Frequently mistranslated in the Bible as "**anise**," true dill was mentioned in Hebrew law texts as a plant whose stems, leaves, and seeds were subject to tithe; hence the admonition in Matthew 23:23: "Woe unto you scribes and Pharisees, hypocrites! for ye tithe **mint** and dill and **cumin**, and have left undone the weightier matters of the law." Cooks of northern Europe, North America, and the Indian subcontinent use it regularly; elsewhere, it is relatively unknown.

Dill is most familiar because of its use in flavoring **cucumbers** and making **pickles**. Dill often adds spice to **potato** salads and sauerkraut, **vinegar, cabbage** and other vegetable dishes, stews and soups, sauces, pork and fish—even **bread, apple** pie, and chutney. The entire aromatic plant is edible.

Five-Spice Powder

Five-spice powder is a spice mixture that originated in China. Balancing the yin and yang in the taste of food, this powder incorporates the sweet, sour, bitter, pungent, and salty. Most recipes for this powder call for mixing Tung Hing **cinnamon**, powdered cassia buds, powdered star **anise** and aniseed, **ginger** root, and ground **cloves**. Sometimes the recipe will consist of cinnamon, **black pepper** (or Szechuan pepper), **cloves, fennel** seed, and star anise. The powder is most often used in cooking **duck** and **beef** stew. Its use has spread to more than a few Middle Eastern kitchens.

Frankincense

Frankincense is the resin or gum produced by injured forest trees (*Boswellia thurifera*) native to Somalia and parts of Arabia. Frankincense is a stimulant, and in ancient times it was widely used as such. The Babylonians, Assyrians, Persians, Greeks, Israelites, and Romans used frankincense for religious purposes. Mentioned frequently in the Bible (for example, Exodus 30:34; I Chronicles 9:29; Matthew 2:11), it was presented with the shew-**bread** every Sabbath and was stored in the Temple at Jerusalem. In ancient Egypt, it was used to scent perfumes and makeup.

Today, besides its use in the making of incense, frankincense has little value, aside from possibly aiding in the treatment of bronchitis and laryngitis.

Galangal

Also known as galingale and galanga, galangal is the common name for four species of the **Ginger** family: greater galangal or Chewing John (*Alpinia galanga*), lesser galangal (*A. officinarum*), sand ginger (*Kaempferia galangal*), and Chinese ginger or fingerroot (*Boesenbergia pandurata*). Galangal is best known in Thai and Laotian cuisine, but it was common in medieval European cooking and is well known to Jews of the Diaspora. It is frequently used in the Near and Middle Eastern and North African kitchen. Although it is not true ginger, galangal is like ginger in both appearance and taste, though with a bit more citrus flavor and perhaps a touch of soapiness. It is readily available from merchants of Asian spices, either as a powder or whole.

Garlic

Garlic (*Allium sativum*), a member of the **Onion** or Lily family, is native to Central Asia and grows wild in Sicily and southern France. It was known in Egypt as long ago as 3000 B.C.E. From tomb paintings, we know that the ancient Egyptians made offerings of garlic to their gods, and bunches of garlic were placed in the pyramids to provision the deceased in the afterlife. The book of Numbers (11:5) offers evidence of the esteem in which the ancients held garlic: when Moses had led the Israelites into the desert, they complained, "We remember the fish we used to eat in Egypt for nothing, the **cucumbers**, the melons, the **leeks**, the **onions**, and the garlic; but now our strength is dried up, and there is nothing at all but this manna to look at" (NRSV). The Chinese cultivated garlic as early as 3000 B.C.E., the oldest Vedic writings of India mention garlic, and the Babylonians made extensive use of garlic in the 8th century B.C.E. Greek and Roman military leaders urged their soldiers to eat garlic in order to get fired up for battle. During the centuries of Roman rule, however, garlic fell into disrepute: it has an acrid taste, and its strong, sometimes offensive odor was considered unsuitable for the aristocracy, so it became a staple of the lower classes. (The well-bred citizens of Rome did not know that fresh **parsley** can alleviate "garlic breath.") Furthermore, it was believed to have certain magical properties, such as the ability to ward off vampires, protect children or farm animals from sorcery, or keep seafarers safe on their voyages. It was believed to have aphrodisiacal powers too. It may have actual medicinal uses, such as the easing of hypertension, the lowering of cholesterol, or the prevention of cancer. Garlic is now an important ingredient in such diverse cuisines as Italian, Korean, and Californian and in sauces, stews, and salad dressings. Garlic bulbs can be dried and stored, and individual segments (cloves) peeled off and chopped or crushed, then added to flavor recipes; the dried cloves can also be ground into powder for longer storage.

Ginger

Ginger is the dried root of the perennial ginger plant (*Zingiber officinale*). Native to tropical Asia, ginger has been under cultivation for so many millennia that its wild forebears have disappeared; botanists might guess that they came from India and Malaysia. Confucius is the first to mention ginger in his writings circa 500 B.C.E. The name *ginger* comes from the Sanskrit *sringa-vera*, which means "horn-root" or "horn-body," and that is an apt description of the root, which is strangely knobby. Some speak of the roots as hands; others, as races, which makes sense because the Portuguese-Spanish word for "roots" is *raíces*. The plant itself grows to a height of 3 feet, and the 6-inch roots are unearthed once the upper plant dies.

The ancient Romans imported vast quantities of ginger and taxed it heavily because it was in such high demand, so it was likely known to the peoples of the New Testament. After the fall of the Roman Empire, ginger became rare in Europe, and Marco Polo remarked how inexpensive ginger was in Asia compared with its cost in Europe. Use of ginger declined in many parts of Europe except England, which enjoyed its pungent flavor and found a ready supply in India (at one time a part of the British Empire). English colonists brought ginger to the Americas, where it became and still is a favorite ingredient in cookies, **breads**, candy, carbonated beverages (ginger ale and ginger **beer**), and even ice cream.

Over the years many effects have been attributed to ginger: the Portuguese thought it an aphrodisiac; New Englanders believed it prevented belching and flatulence; a French doctor said that it gave the person who eats it power over tigers; it was even used as a suppository for horses to make them act lively for potential buyers. Truthfully, ginger adds a special flavor to curries and to spice blends. Often it is purchased fresh and sliced thinly for consumption; the French were the first to dry and pulverize the roots into usable powder. Ginger oil is also used in the cosmetics industry, mostly for men's *eau de cologne* and shaving lotions.

The farming of ginger has spread throughout the tropics, and today it is part of the agriculture of Australia, South America, Indonesia, western Africa, Jamaica, and Puerto Rico, in addition to India and China.

Lemon Balm

Also known as bee balm or sometimes simply as balm, lemon balm (*Melissa officinalis*) is so called because it has a slightly lemony scent. It is a perennial native to southern Europe. "Balm" is mentioned many times in the Bible but probably refers to the gum of the balsam tree. It is possible that cooks of the Middle East would have learned of lemon balm from the Romans. Throughout history, it has been used medicinally, as it was believed to have mild sedative properties and to be able to relieve gas, reduce fever, and increase perspiration. In the Middle Ages lemon balm was steeped in **wine** and consumed to lift the spirits, heal wounds, and treat venomous bites. It was also used as a disease preventative, its oils and extracts possessing antibacterial and antiviral qualities.

Sprigs of lemon balm make a refreshing garnish for cocktails, salads, and main dishes. Either fresh or dried, the leaves make a delicious **tea**. The dried leaves are added to potpourris, and the oil is an ingredient in perfumes.

Lotus Oil

Lotus oil is an extract of the flower of the sacred lotus (*Nelumbo nucifera*). Although the flowers are relatively large (about 8 inches in diameter), each one yields only a tiny amount of oil, so lotus oil is very expensive. But it is also very concentrated, so it is usually diluted or blended with other lighter oils. Commonly, lotus oil is added to bath or massage oils or diffused in the air to create a pleasing scented atmosphere. For more information on the lotus, see **Lotus Root**. The royal courts of Persia would likely have been familiar with lotus oil.

Mace

Mace is a spice made from the bright scarlet netting, called the aril, that surrounds the seed of the nutmeg tree (*Myristica fragrans*); the seed itself is **nutmeg**. Although the nutmeg tree is native to the Spice Islands of Indonesia, the Roman naturalist Pliny wrote about a tree that produced two different spices, and it is thought that he might have been describing the nutmeg tree. However, the earliest reliable record of the spice's entry into the Mediterranean world dates from the 6th century C.E., and it is probable that neither mace nor nutmeg was known to the peoples of the Bible.

The flavor of mace is similar to but stronger than that of nutmeg, and mace can be used much the way nutmeg is. Mace is, however, the classic spice for poundcake. It is available primarily as a powder and most flavorful when whole, but it is difficult nowadays to find "a blade of mace," as called for in old cookbooks. When it is used in Middle Eastern cooking, it is often for sweet dishes.

Marjoram

Botanists seem to be somewhat confused about marjoram. Many believe it to be the herbal plant *Origanum majorana*; others say it is the herbal plant *Majorana hortensis*; some mix things up entirely and say it is *O. hortensis*. The confusion stems from the popular belief that marjoram is a close relation to **oregano**, a belief fostered by Carl Linnaeus in the 18th century when he incorrectly classified marjoram as *O. majorana*, but the two plants are not at all related: marjoram is a plant of the *Majorana* genus; oregano, of the *Origanum*. Marjoram is thus correctly classified as *Majorana hortensis*, a perennial herb, and it is commonly known as garden marjoram, sweet marjoram, annual marjoram, or knotted marjoram, all of which are descriptive of its characteristics.

Marjoram originated in the Mediterranean region, but exactly where is lost to antiquity, as it has been under cultivation since prehistoric times. The ancient Greeks and Romans used marjoram in bridal wreaths as it symbolized love and honor, and the former believed that the growth of marjoram on a gravesite indicated that the deceased was enjoying eternal peace. Marjoram is mentioned in the Bible (Leviticus 14:4), but it is often mistranslated as "hyssop," a plant that looks very similar. A member of the **Mint** family, it reaches a height of 2 feet and, unlike other members of its family, does not release its fragrance until crushed. It is an herb that is much more pungent dried than fresh.

Marjoram adds a pleasant, sweet flavor to **pickles**, **sausages**, **lamb**, **beef**, pork, **chicken**, and fish. It also works well in **tomato** dishes, stuffings, **breads**, salad dressings, and chowders. Italian, French, northern African, Middle Eastern, and North American cuisines and spice blends such as *bouquet garni* and *fines herbes* often call upon marjoram. As well, it is an ingredient in potpourris and scent bags and sachets, and marjoram oil is used in perfumed soaps.

Mastic

Mastic is a hard, aromatic, transparent resin that is harvested from injured mastic shrubs (*Pistacia lentiscus*). Native to the Mediterranean, from Turkey west to Spain, Morocco, and the Canary Islands, mastic shrubs grow to 12 feet in height. It is mentioned in the apochryphal book of Susannah (verse 54). Some scholars speculate that it may have been the substance called "manna" in the book of Numbers. Mediterranean peoples have been treating gastrointestinal distress with mastic for many centuries, as attested by Dioscorides, the 1st century C.E. Greek physician. Recent medical studies have reinforced mastic's healing properties, showing that mastic oil is a strong antibacterial and antifungal agent and that mastic can help heal peptic ulcers and reduce tooth plaque caused by bacteria.

In the kitchen, mastic is a key ingredient in Turkish ice cream. It is also used to make chewing gum, which can help freshen the breath, and a liqueur called mastica.

Mint

There are about twenty true varieties of mint, from peppermint (*Mentha piperita*) and spearmint (*M. spicata*) to apple mint (*M. suaveolens*), water mint (*M. aquatica*), and even chocolate mint (*M. x piperita "Chocolate mint"*). All are vigorous perennials originating in the Mediterranean region, but they now grow in a wide range of conditions. Menthol, a local anesthetic and counterirritant that has long been used as an ingredient in soothing balms, is the compound that gives mint its scent. The mint called pennyroyal (*M. pulegium*) was well known in Greece by 1200 B.C.E. as a flea repellant and an abortifacient (a substance that can induce abortions), and according to the Roman naturalist Pliny, both the Greeks and the Romans used peppermint (or a wild ancestor) as adornment and table decoration. There is evidence that the Egyptians cultivated a variety of mint, and the Israelites would have adapted it to their cooking during their years in Egypt, using it to add zest to fruit or grain salads, beverages, vegetable dishes, and soups. Some biblical scholars believe that mint was among the bitter herbs mentioned in

Exodus 12:8 and Numbers 9:11. The mint mentioned in the gospel of Luke (11:42) would probably have been some type of peppermint.

Mustard

Mustard is a member of the Cruciferae family, so called because the four petals of their flowers are arranged in the form of a cross. The most common mustards are the black mustard (*Brassica nigra*), white mustard (*B. alba*), field mustard (*B. campestris*), and Indian mustard (*B. juncea*). The consumption of mustard dates from prehistoric times, in Asia to Europe to northern Africa: early humans ate both the seeds and the leaves. It was known to the Egyptians, Romans, and Hindus, and mustard is so productive, even in the wild, that cultivation was hardly necessary; indeed, it became among the Hindus a symbol of fertility. Mustard has a prominent place in the Bible, in Jesus' parable of the mustard seed (Matthew 13:31–32; Mark 4:30–32; Luke 13:18–19); most scholars believe that black mustard must have been the plant referred to, even though the plant grows to a height of only three feet. Today, mustard is second only to **pepper** in the world spice trade.

Mustard seeds can have either a pleasantly nutty taste or a pungent, hot flavor. Compounds made from their oils have helped the body absorb scar tissue, relieved strained muscles, and disinfected surgeons' hands. Powdered mustard has helped relieve pulmonary congestion and has aided sinus and throat congestion.

Today, mustard is grown mostly for use in condiments or cooking oils, though mustard greens are a necessary ingredient in what is now called soul food and are a very good source of vitamins A and C.

Myrrh

Often confused with **cicely**, myrrh is the dried reddish-brown, highly aromatic resin of the myrrh tree (*Commiphora myrrha*), although other trees (such as *C. erythraea, C. opobalsamum,* and *Balsamodendron kua*) also produce sap that is called myrrh. The myrrh tree is native to Somalia, but the name "myrrh" comes from the Hebrew *murr* or *maror,* which mean "bitter." Because it has a very pleasant aroma, solid myrrh has been used in perfumes and embalming oils and as an aromatic additive to **wine** for many centuries. However, when burned, myrrh gives off a repulsive odor, and it has been used extensively in penitential incenses. Myrrh is mentioned in the Old Testament (e.g., Genesis 37:25; Exodus 30:23; Esther 2:12); and in the New Testament (Matthew 2:11) as one of the gifts that the Magi brought to the baby Jesus, perhaps as a foreshadowing of the bitterness that the infant and his parents would experience in years to come. Today, myrrh is sometimes added to toothpowders and mouthwashes.

Nutmeg

Nutmeg is a spice made from the seed of the nutmeg tree (*Myristica fragrans*); another spice, **mace**, also comes from this tree, which is native to the Spice Islands of Indonesia. The Roman naturalist Pliny wrote about a tree that produced two different spices, and it is thought that he might have been describing the nutmeg tree. While ancient Indian and Arabian literature mention the medicinal uses of the spice from the two-spice tree, the earliest reliable record of nutmeg's importation to the Mediterranean region dates from the 6th century C.E. A mild, slightly sweet spice, nutmeg is used to flavor stews, **sausages**, meats, soups, preserves, beverages (especially alcoholic beverages), and vegetable and fruit dishes; it is also an important ingredient in baking. Nutmeg can also be used as a sedative and as a treatment for diarrhea, vomiting, and nausea. When used in Middle Eastern and North African cooking, it is often in sweet dishes.

Old Bay

Old Bay is a trademarked seasoning produced by McCormick & Company. Named for the Chesapeake Bay region of the United States, it was first blended by Gustav Brunn in the 1940s. Old Bay contains **celery seed**, **mustard** seed, red pepper, **black pepper**, **bay (laurel) leaf**, **cloves**, **allspice**, **pimento**, **ginger**, **mace**, **cardamom**, **cinnamon**, and **paprika** (many of the spices of the Bible). A "hot" seasoning, it has come to be associated with steamed crabs and shrimp.

Oregano

Often confused with **marjoram**, oregano (*Origanum vulgare*) is believed to be a native of the Mediterranean region, though like marjoram it has been under cultivation for so long that its exact origin is lost to prehistory. Like marjoram, oregano was highly favored in ancient Egypt, Greece, and Rome and would have been known to the peoples of the Bible. Like marjoram, oregano is a perennial. Unlike marjoram, however, oregano can tolerate cool weather, thriving as far north as the British Isles, and more arid soil.

The name *origanum* comes from the Greek words meaning "mountain" and "joy," and indeed, the Greeks still appreciate the flavor that the "joy of the mountain" adds to their meals. Oregano has a stronger taste than marjoram and is much preferred for Mediterranean cooking. It has certainly become necessary for Italian **tomato** sauces and pizzas, Middle Eastern tomato and **eggplant** dishes, and, of course, Greek mutton kebabs. But the English use it in Exeter stew, the French add it to many sauces, and the Swedes sprinkle it on **pea** soup.

Orris Root

Orris root is the underground stems, or rhizomes, of three species of iris plants: *Iris germanica*, *I. florentina*, and *I. pattida*. These irises are native to southern Europe. Both the ancient Greeks and Romans used orris root to make perfumes and scented balms, as it has a lovely violet-like scent when dried. It would probably have been known to the wealthy people of the Middle East during New Testament times. Orris root was also used to flavor candies, toothpastes, and mouthwashes, and orris root **tea** was (and still is) taken for cases of bronchitis, colds, coughs, diarrhea, and dropsy. It is also used in cosmetics and potpourri.

Paprika

Paprika is the name for the dried, ground pods of the sweet red **pepper** (*Capsicum annuum*). Fragrantly sweet, paprika is bright red, and chefs prize it because even its color adds zest to their cuisine. A member of the Nightshade family, the paprika pepper is believed to have originated in South America; it was probably first domesticated in Mexico. Spanish colonists first brought this pepper to Europe. It would not have been known to the peoples of the Bible. The paprika pepper now grows worldwide, though Spain, Central Europe, and the United States are the major producers. Many Spanish and Hungarian (and some Middle Eastern) dishes call for paprika, and it adds color and flavor to poultry and fish, chowders, salad dressings, soups, and vegetable dishes.

In addition to its culinary popularity, paprika is famous because it was the fruit from which vitamin C was first identified, by Hungarian scientist Albert Szent-Györgyi, who won the Nobel Prize for his work. Paprika peppers are also high in beta-carotene (a source of vitamin A), as well as vitamins B1 and B2.

Parsley

Parsley (*Petroselinum crispum* and *P. neapolitanum*) is a native of the Mediterranean region, and both the ancient Greeks and Romans used it as a seasoning and a garnish. The Greeks also wreathed the heads of their young war or athletic heroes with crowns of parsley and used it to treat rheumatism and kidney pains; and the Romans believed parsley could prevent intoxication. It is possible that the Israelites used parsley as one of the bitter herbs that were part of their Passover meal. A bright-green, biennial herb, parsley adds a fresh, crisp flavor and decorative color and texture to almost any dish. In the Middle East today, it is an essential ingredient of *hummus* and *tabbouleh*.

Pepper, black

It is not an exaggeration to say that black pepper (*Piper nigrum*) ranks as one of the most important spices in world history. Originating on the Indian sub-continent and in Indonesia, black pepper is first mentioned in the Sanskrit literature about 1000 B.C.E. It probably made its way to the Mediterranean world by the 4th century B.C.E., carried by caravans from market to market. Thus it would most probably not have been known to the peoples of early biblical times but would have entered their cooking perhaps during the times of exile. In the Mediterranean region, black pepper was initially considered a medicine. Its merits as a seasoning soon recognized, black pepper became a common ingredient, called for in almost every type of dish except desserts. In fact, the ancient Romans were so enamored of pepper and other spices that the Emperor Domitian built a special spice market, the *horrea piperataria*, which, as can be seen, derives its name from pepper. When the Roman Empire collapsed, pepper became scarce in Europe— and thus all the more valuable. During the Crusades, Venetian ships transported soldiers to the Holy Land and pepper and other spices back to Europe, and it might almost be said that the spice trade became as important a cause for a crusade as any theological or political reason. Trade in pepper brought wealth to merchants from cities as far-flung as Venice, Genoa, Augsburg, Lisbon, Amsterdam, Brugges, and Alexandria. During the Middle Ages pepper also served as currency: tenants paid their rent in peppercorns, landholders paid their taxes in pepper, and pepper was used to bribe city officials. Consumption of pepper was enormous, due to the prevalence of foodstuffs such as salted pork, dried and salted fish, the rare bit of "aged" **beef**, and the need in all cases to mask their unpalatable taste. By the 17th century, however, overspicing with pepper began to fall from fashion, as raw and fresh foodstuffs seasoned with milder spices and herbs made their way to the table. At one time the most valuable of all spices, pepper is still the most widely used and the most easily recognized by taste.

Black pepper actually comes in three colors—green, white, and black—which are merely peppercorns picked at three different stages of ripeness; all come from the tropical climbing bush *P. nigrum*. Once treated and dried, the berries can be stored whole or ground into powder. Because pepper has a volatile, fast-fading aroma and taste, ground pepper loses its flavor rapidly, and many connoisseurs insist on buying the peppercorns to grind their own.

Poppy Seed

The poppy seed comes from the poppy flower (*Papaver somniferum*), an annual, which has been cultivated at least since 2000 B.C.E. The exact origins of the poppy are not known, though some botanists believe that they are native to the northern Indian subcontinent or perhaps to southwestern Asia; thus, it may have been known to the peoples of the Bible. Although the poppy is the source of the narcotic opium, dried poppy seeds do not have a narcotic effect. Instead, they contain an oil that adds a nutty flavor to **bread**s, vegetables, and salad dressings. Crushed poppy seeds, which are extremely small and slate blue in color, are mixed in with other spices to create unique blends for use in Indian and Turkish dishes.

In Greek mythology, the goddess Demeter (known as Ceres to the Romans) was believed to favor the poppy. Demeter's daughter Persephone, kidnapped by the god of the underworld Hades, was thought to bring the rebirth of the world with her when she ascended from the shadowy realm every spring, and her fertility became associated with the poppy, each flower of which produces millions of tiny seeds.

In the United States, the poppy has lost its connection to fertility; instead, it is used to commemorate Veterans' Day.

Rosemary

Native to the Mediterranean region, rosemary (*Rosmarinus officinalis*) received its name from the Roman author Pliny, who described it as a flowering plant that grows so close to the shore that foam (*ros*) from the sea (*mare*) sprays upon it. Both the ancient Greeks and Romans placed a high value on rosemary, the Greeks believing that their gods would prize a wreath of rosemary above one of gold, and the Romans offering the plant to their house gods and dedicating it especially to Venus. Ancient Greek students wore rosemary to strengthen their memory during examinations, and it became a widespread symbol of remembrance, featured in both weddings and funerals. Early Christians believed that during the flight to Egypt, when the Virgin Mary made a bed for the Christ Child upon a clump of rosemary, the plant's flowers turned blue, a color that represented eternity, truth, and wisdom. It is believed that rosemary was not used for cooking until the Middle Ages, when it became popular as a means of masking the taste of **salt**-preserved meats, but surely the many ancient peoples of the Middle East who preserved their meats with salt would have known and taken advantage of rosemary's fresh, slightly bittersweet taste. A member of the **Mint** family, rosemary is a perennial herb that is very tolerant of dry climates and is easily cultivated. Rosemary leaves do not lose their flavor through long cooking, as other leaves do, and are more aromatic when dried than when fresh. They are most frequently used to flavor fish, meat (particularly **chicken**), **potato**, and vegetable dishes. The taste of rosemary is very strong, and cooks must take care not to overdose their recipes with it.

Rose Oil

Rose oil is the extracted oil of rose petals, usually the petals of the damask rose (*Rosa damascena*). Roses are native to the lands from eastern Asia to western Europe, though the exact origins are now unclear. One of the ancestors is believed to be *R. gallica*, which continues to grow wild in the Caucasus Mountains. The damask rose is a hybrid of *R. gallica* with *R. phoenicia* or *R. moschata*, and damask roses were first known in western Asia in the Bronze Age and were cultivated by the ancient Greeks and Romans. Rose oil has also been distilled from the blooms of *R. centifolia*, *R. gallica*, and *R. rugosa*. The rose appears numerous times in the Bible: e.g., Ecclesiastes 24:14, 39:13, 50:8; Wisdom of Solomon 2:8; II Esdras 2:19.

Rose oil is very precious because many flowers are needed to create even an ounce of oil. Furthermore, the content of oil is highest on the first morning when the blooms open, so the flowers must be picked by hand, a process that makes rose oil even more expensive. Today, the main producers of rose oil are France, Bulgaria, Turkey, and Iran.

Rose oil is used mostly in perfumes, cosmetics, massage and bath oils, and incenses. It can also be used to flavor jams, jellies, **honey**, **butter**, **tea**, and **vinegar**, as well as desserts, especially baklava, a Middle Eastern favorite.

Rue

Rue is the name of a genus (*Ruta*) of highly fragrant evergreen shrubs native to the Mediterranean and southwestern Asia. There are a number of species of rue, the most common being

- Common rue (*R. graveolens*)
- Egyptian rue (*R. angustifolia*)

- Fringed rue (*R. chalepensis*)
- Corsican rue (*R. corsica*)
- Mountain rue (*R. montana*)

Many people consider rue to have a strongly disagreeable odor, and the best-known literary references to rue (in William Shakespeare's *Hamlet* and *Richard III*) refer to rue as a reflection of inner heartache. It is also mentioned in the Bible when Jesus dines with the Pharisee (Luke 11:42).

The ancient Greeks considered rue an antidote to poison, and people of the Middle Ages used dried rue as an antimagical herb and a protection against witches. In the Renaissance, rue was used to prevent epileptic fits, earache, and vertigo, and it was believed to bestow second sight. Some Italians still add fresh rue to salads, as it is supposed to help keep the eyesight clear. In modern times it is employed as an asperges for distributing holy water during Roman Catholic masses of repentance.

Saffron

Saffron (*Crocus sativus*) is the spice made from the dried stigmas of the saffron crocus, a member of the Iris family. No longer a wild species, saffron crocus probably originated in the Near East or Asia Minor and was one of the earliest domesticated food species. The word *saffron* is believed to be derived from Sumerian, the language spoken by the peoples of the southern Tigris and Euphrates River Valleys more than 5,000 years ago. A Chinese book of medicine dating from 2600 B.C.E. provides the earliest written reference to saffron, and an Egyptian text of about 1500 B.C.E. describes the crocuses in the palace gardens at Luxor. People of the Phoenician cities (which thrived about 1500–1000 B.C.E.) used saffron-dyed sheets on their wedding nights, and Buddhist monks wore (and still wear) saffron-colored robes as a sign of holiness; it also became a color reserved for the higher classes. The Israelites certainly knew about saffron, and the ancient Hebrew text known as the Song of Solomon (or the Song of Songs [4:14], probably written in the 10th century B.C.E., or perhaps later) mentions a garden filled with saffron crocuses. Saffron had made its way to ancient Greece via Crete and the Minoan civilization by this time, and Greek mythology included at least two different stories to explain the origins of the saffron crocus. The Greek physician Hippocrates and the Roman physician Celsus both used saffron in their remedies, particularly to treat abdominal ailments, and saffron also came to be known as an anti-intoxicant among Roman revelers. Roman emperors such as Hadrian and Heliogabalus also used saffron to mask unpleasant smells and improve the odor in public places.

The saffron crocus blooms in the late summer, and the flowers must be picked early in the morning, before the scent is lost to the heat of the day, and then the appropriate parts of the flower must be separated by hand. About 150,000 flowers are required to make 2 pounds of saffron. Consequently, saffron is perhaps the most expensive spice ever cultivated.

Saffron has a pleasant spicy scent, a slightly bitter taste, and colors food yellow to orange. It is used in many **rice** dishes and in the preparation of soups, meat and seafood stews, **breads**, **egg** dishes, and vegetables.

Sage

Silvery-gray in color, sage (*Salvia officinalis*) is available either as whole leaves (known as cut sage) or as a fluffy, cottony powder (known as rubbed sage). It is most common as rubbed sage.

The ancient Greeks used sage for its medicinal properties as early as the 4th century B.C.E., believing in its curative powers, particularly against fevers. Judean sage is the plant after which the flower design on the Temple menorah was patterned (Exodus 37:17) and was well known to the peoples of the Bible. Native to southern Europe, sage was planted and cultivated throughout Europe by the time of Charlemagne in the 9th century C.E. People of this era believed that sage strengthened the memory, and to this day wise people are known as sages.

The use of sage has declined somewhat since the Middle Ages, though it is still employed to flavor stuffing, poultry, **cheese**, **sausages**, **breads**, vegetable dishes, and even some desserts. Some people favor eating the young shoots in salads; others enjoy pickled sage leaves—although both dishes would be very pungent.

Sesame Seed

Sesame seed is the dried seed of *Sesamum indicum*. High in protein, the seeds are oval shaped and have a nutlike flavor when toasted. Sesame was native to Indonesia and eastern Africa but spread to Mesopotamia by the 2nd millennium B.C.E. The ancient Babylonians used sesame seeds to make cakes, to flavor **wine** and **brandy**, and to provide oil for both cooking and perfuming purposes. By 1500 B.C.E. the Egyptians were using sesame oil as a medicine. The peoples of the Bible would have used sesame seeds in their cooking.

The indigenous peoples of Africa and Asia treat sesame seeds as a grain, but in Europe, Japan, and the Americas, sesame has entered the diet as cooking oil. In recent years sesame seeds have been used to flavor **breads**, crackers, and salad dressings.

In folklore, the magical password "Open Sesame" that unlocked the cave for Ali Baba in *The Thousand and One Nights* probably was a play on the fact that ripe sesame seed pods pop open loudly with a slight touch. Also, sesame seed was so common that "sesame" would not have been considered important enough to be used as a secret password.

Sumac

Sumac (*Rhus coriaria L.*) or sumach is native to the Mediterranean region and is a member of the Cashew family. It produces clusters of bright or dark-red fruit, berries, or drupes. Drupes are the type of fruit in which the outer fleshy part (exocarp [skin] and mesocarp [flesh]) surrounds a shell (endocarp) with a seed inside. In the Middle East, the hairy covering of the drupes is harvested, ground, and used as a spice. This purple-reddish powder has a tart and sour taste and is used to flavor **rice** dishes and stews. In some parts of the Middle East, sumac berries are cooked in water until they reduce to a thick, sour essence that is then added to meat and vegetable dishes. Other Middle Eastern cooks mix the berries with **onions** and serve the mélange as an appetizer. Sumac was also used as a dyeing and tanning agent, as in the ram's skins mentioned in the book of Exodus.

Tahina

See **Tahini.**

Tarragon

Tarragon (*Artemisia dracunculus*) is a perennial plant that can reach 4 to 5 feet in height but can easily be grown in a corner garden or window box. Its land of origin is thought to be the steppes of Asia. Invading Mongols introduced it to the Near East in the 12th century C.E., and the Crusaders brought it to Europe soon thereafter. Tarragon was probably one of the bitter herbs of the Bible, often mistranslated as "wormwood" (Revelation 8:11). Tarragon has been served as a vegetable in the Near East, though its use as an herb for flavoring is much more widespread. Tarragon is usually available dried; unfortunately, the dried leaves are much less flavorful than the fresh. Its species name, *dracunculus,* means "little dragon," from the Roman superstition that a twig of tarragon would protect the bearer against snakes and dragons. Its names in French (*estragon*), Spanish (*estragón*), Italian (*targone*), Swedish (*dragon*), and German (*Estragon, Dragon*) convey the same meaning.

Tarragon complements the flavor of poached, baked, or broiled fish or poultry. It also works well with shellfish and **eggs**, and it adds a nice touch to vinaigrettes and other salad dressings, cooked **potato**es, and vegetable dishes.

Thyme

Thyme (*Thymus vulgaris*) is a small perennial member of the **Mint** family. Native to the Mediterranean basin, it entered the herb garden early, being used by the ancient Sumerians by 3500 B.C.E. The Egyptians used thyme for embalming, and it would have been familiar to the peoples of the Bible (Revelation 18:12, according to the Wycliffe New Testament). It was said to be one of the few fruits and spices that could be easily gathered in the fields of Israel during the First Temple Period. The Greek physician Hippocrates considered it a healing herb, and to the Greeks, thyme also symbolized courage. Roman soldiers sometimes bathed in thyme water because it was thought to give strength in addition to courage. The ancients also believed that **tea** made from thyme would lift depression and dispel nightmares. In the Middle Ages, knights wore scarves embroidered with sprigs of thyme to fortify their bravery, and some folk to this day call upon thyme to help them see elves and fairies.

Garden thyme now exists in many varieties, including orange, lemon (*T. citriodorus*), caraway, camphor, and even turpentine. Wild thyme (*T. serpyllum*) still thrives from Greece to the British Isles.

Thyme is considered an essential ingredient in stuffings and is used to flavor meats, stews, soups, fish, and wild game dishes, or even salads. It is part of **zaatar**, *herbes de Provence*, and *bouquet garni*, and it is required in the making of jerk pork and curries. It also adds a nice touch to desserts that include **lemon**, such as custards, **creams**, and sherbets.

Turmeric

Turmeric (*Curcuma longa*) most probably originated in South Asia (the Indian subcontinent) or Southeast Asia and spread to the Middle East and eastern Mediterranean lands as a result of Alexander the Great's conquest of Central Asia (achieved from 334 to 326 B.C.E.). Thus turmeric would not have been known to the peoples of the Bible until New Testament times.

Turmeric is a perennial member of the **Ginger** family, and its thick rhizome is harvested, cleaned, cooked, sun-dried, polished, and ground into a powder. This deep yellow-orange powder is a key ingredient in curry powder and is also used to color sauces and syrups and **rices** and to flavor meat and vegetable dishes. Turmeric is sometimes used as an inexpensive, though much less flavorful and aromatic substitute for saffron. It also has wide use as a cloth dye. Today, it is very common in Middle Eastern dishes.

Vanilla

Native to the West Indies, Central America, and northern South America, vanilla (*Vanilla planifolia*, formerly known as *V. fragrans*) made its way to Europe on the ships of Hernán Cortés and would not have been known to Middle Eastern cooks of biblical times. Vanilla is a member of the Orchid family and is a lush trailing plant that can climb up to 100 feet in its native tropical rainforest environment. It produces 2–3 inch yellow-white flowers in clusters, and when pollinated, these flowers yield 10-inch pods (incorrectly called beans) containing vanilla seeds. Most of the fragrance resides in the seeds and the surrounding oily liquid. Vanilla is a very expensive spice, second in value only to **saffron**, because the production of vanilla is very labor-intensive. To capture the vanilla spice, the pods must be either blanched or steamed, then cured and dried, a time-consuming process that might take up to a full year, before they are ready for use. Additionally, although vanilla plants are self-pollinating (that is, pollen from one flower can be used to fertilize other flowers on the same plant), they are adapted to pollination by insects (butterflies or bees) or hummingbirds; unfortunately, the original pollinator of vanilla disappeared centuries ago, and long before Christopher Columbus first tasted vanilla in 1502, the flowers were all pollinated by hand. Called *tlilxochitl* by the Aztecs of Central America, vanilla was harvested and used to improve the taste of **chocolate** drinks, which were very spicy (containing, for example, chilis, **paprika, peppers**), sweetened with **honey**, colored deep red (like blood) by the addition of annatto, and drunk cold. The Mayans consumed their chocolate drinks hot or cold and did not necessarily sweeten them. Columbus brought vanilla to Europe, where it soon became an essential ingredient in chocolate drinks; Europeans almost always sweetened their chocolate, added spices such as **cinnamon** or **anise**, and used a **milk** base instead of a water base, which gave the drink a much thicker consistency. In Western cuisine, vanilla is now used almost exclusively in sweet recipes, such as cookies, cakes, puddings, pastries, and ice creams, though it remains a staple of spicy recipes in certain cultures. Scientists were first able to create artificial vanilla in the 19th century, but it still does not have nearly the prized aroma or taste of natural vanilla. Today, vanilla is used extensively in Middle Eastern cooking.

Vanilla, Madagascar Bourbon

Many connoisseurs consider Madagascar Bourbon vanilla to be the best **vanilla** ever produced. It comes from vanilla beans grown and processed on the islands of Madagascar and Réunion (formerly Bourbon) in the Indian Ocean since the 19th century, but it did not come into great demand worldwide until the 1960s. It is used to flavor baked goods, ice cream, and French toast.

Zaatar

Zaatar is a mixture of powdered **thyme**, whole **sesame seeds**, and powdered **sumac**. Some recipes for zaatar also include **oregano, marjoram**, savory, and **salt**. It is a staple of modern Middle Eastern kitchens.

MILK, MILK BEVERAGES, CHEESES, AND OTHER MILK PRODUCTS

Butter

The making of butter is almost as old as the milking of **goats**, cows, and other milk-producing animals. Butter is easily made by letting a pan of **milk** set quietly until the **cream** floats to the top. The cream is skimmed off and allowed to sour and thicken into a form called clabber cream. Churning or other techniques are then used to shake up the cream and separate it into a liquid (**buttermilk**) and a solid fat (butter). Butter consists of 80 percent fat.

Butter is solid but soft at room temperatures. It stores well when refrigerated and can even be frozen to extend its shelf-life. It also melts easily but resolidifies quickly. Butter is usually pale yellow, though the actual shade of yellow depends on the milk animal's diet.

Butter is usually salted, though unsalted butters are now available. Sweet butter (or sweet cream butter) is made from unfermented milk in the same ways as other butters.

Butter appears often in the Old Testament (e.g., Genesis 18:8; Deuteronomy 32:14; Judges 5:25; II Samuel 17:29; Job 20:17). Over the millennia, butter has been used as a medicine and a cosmetic. During the Middle Ages, butter was also used as a packing medium to protect fragile articles during transport: the item was submersed in melted butter, moved when the butter had solidified, then melted out of the butter at its destination.

Buttermilk

Buttermilk is the liquid left after **butter** is made from full-cream **milk**. Buttermilk has a slightly sour taste and is a popular refreshing drink, particularly in India. Nowadays, buttermilk is cultured by adding souring agents (such as lactic acid) to whole milk. Buttermilk is an important ingredient in many Middle Eastern **breads**, creamy soups, and **cream** sauces.

Cheese

Made in nearly every country where **milk** is produced, cheese is a solid food made from curdled milk, primarily the milk of cows, **goats**, **sheep**, reindeer, camels, and water buffalo. To make cheese, milk is first cultured with bacteria, as in the making of **buttermilk**. The milk is then curdled (broken into solid [curds] and liquid [whey]) by adding a curdling agent such as rennet (sometimes known as rennin, which is the pure enzyme), **vinegar**, or **lemon** juice. The whey is drained away, and the curds may be pressed to remove additional moisture before they are aged (sometimes called ripened) to allow them to dry further and develop flavor. Sometimes the curds are exposed to molds or bacteria, washed with **beer** or **brandy**, smoked over fragrant woods, coated with herbs and spices, or even encased in wax to give them particular flavors or consistencies.

Cheeses are either natural or processed. The natural cheeses include

- Soft, unripened (fresh) cheeses, such as Cottage Cheese, Cream Cheese, Farmer Cheese, Mascarpone, Mozzarella, **Ricotta**, and String Cheese. These are generally low in fat and sodium and relatively neutral in taste so that they combine readily with many other foods.

- Semisoft cheeses, such as Bel Paese, Brick, **Edam**, Fontina, Gouda, Jarlsberg, Liederkranz, Limburger, Muenster, Port Salut, Provolone, and Tilsit. These comprise the largest category of cheeses; they are relatively moist and delicate-tasting, and they slice and melt well for use in sandwiches or in cooking.

- Soft-ripened cheeses, such as Brie and Camembert. These cheeses are aged after their surfaces are sprayed with penicillin, developing soft, edible rinds. They are generally lower in calories than firm cheeses.

- Firm (hard) cheeses, such as **Cheddar**, Colby, Gruyère, Monterey Jack, and Swiss. These cheeses are quite popular for cooking, and they have a robust flavor that makes them ideal for snacking. Losing moisture as they age, they provide a more concentrated source of calcium than softer cheeses.

- Very hard (grating) cheeses, such as Asiago, Dry Jack, Parmesan, Romano, and Sapsago. These cheeses have dense textures and highly concentrated flavors. They grate finely, and can even be grated when frozen.

- Blue-veined cheeses, such as Gorgonzola and Stilton. These cheeses are inoculated with molds and allowed to ripen until they develop blue-green veins and intense flavors.
- **Goat's-** and **sheep's-milk cheeses,** such as Chèvre, **Feta,** and Roquefort. These cheeses tend to be higher in fat but lower in cholesterol than cow's milk cheeses.

Processed cheeses are made by melting one or more ground natural cheeses to form a smooth mass, pasteurizing, adding sweeteners, pouring out, and then slicing when the cheese recongeals.

Most cheeses are high in protein, vitamins A and B12, calcium, phosphorus, riboflavin, and zinc. They are also high in calories, fat, cholesterol, and sodium. The actual nutritional content varies depending on the type of cheese and the process by which it is made. In general, the harder cheeses provide more calcium than the softer. Cheese appears at least three times in the biblical texts (I Samuel 17:18; II Samuel 17:29; Job 10:10), where it denotes curdled milk. Cheeses of all types are very common in Middle Eastern cooking.

Cheese, camel's-milk

Camel's-milk cheese is made, of course, from **camel's milk,** though the processing of camel's milk into cheese is said to be more difficult than the processing of other milk into cheese because camel's milk is more difficult to curdle, or thicken. Furthermore, the cheeses made from camel's milk tend to be soft and perishable. On the other hand, camel's-milk cheese is high in vitamins, low in cholesterol, and low in lactose. One cheese, kadchgall, is sometimes made from camel's milk clotted with **yogurt,** though it is usually made from sheep's milk. Camel's-milk cheese is most likely the curds indicated in Genesis 32:15 (KJV).

Cheese, cheddar

Cheddar cheese is a firm cheese that is the favorite of U.S. consumers, representing about 33 percent of the total U.S. cheese consumption. Ranging from white to deep orange, cheddar is mild and slices easily. It is used in sandwiches and salads, as a snack or appetizer, and in cooking. It is usually made from cow's or **goat's milk.**

Cheese, Edam

Edam is the famous Dutch cheese that comes covered in red wax or red cellophane. A semisoft cheese, mild and buttery-tasting, it is made from part-skim **milk.**

Cheese, feta

First developed in Greece, feta cheese can be made from either **goat's** or **sheep's milk.** It is chalky-white in color and very porous. Feta cheese, made in brine, has a high sodium content; the sodium can be reduced by draining the cheese and rinsing it in fresh cold water.

Cheese, ricotta curds

Ricotta is a soft, unripened cheese made from whey and whole or skim **milk**. Finely textured, it can be eaten alone, though it is most often used as an ingredient in Italian pasta dishes (such as lasagna and cannelloni) and pastries.

Cheese, sheep's-milk

A variety of sheep's-milk cheeses are available, from salty **feta** to pungent Roquefort. Sheep's-milk cheeses tend to be higher in fat than those made from cow's **milk**.

Cream

Cream is the fatty layer that rises to the top of unhomogenized **milk**. (Homogenization is the process whereby the milkfat is distributed evenly throughout the milk, usually by forcing the milk through small openings to break the fat into tiny particles that remain suspended instead of rising to the surface.) There are two types of cream: sweet and sour. Sweet creams include half-and-half, light cream (also called **coffee** cream or table cream), light whipping cream, and heavy cream. Heavy cream will contain 36 percent milkfat, while half-and-half will contain between 10.5 and 18 percent milkfat. Sour creams include dairy sour cream, sour half-and-half, lowfat sour cream, light sour cream, and fat-free sour cream. Sour creams contain at least 18 percent milkfat, and they are made by culturing cream with lactic acid bacteria.

Cream, sour

See **Cream**.

Cream, whipping

See **Cream**.

Kashkaval

Also known as *caciocavallo*, kashkaval is a type of cottage **cheese**, usually made from cow's or **sheep's milk**. It originated in Sicily, probably in the 14th century C.E., where it was most likely made from the milk of mares (hence the name *caciocavallo*, which means "cheese on horseback"—or the name may relate to the practice of hanging the cheese molds astride horizontal rods; in old Italian street talk, to "end up like *caciocavallo*" meant "to be hanged"). Now it is popular throughout southeastern Europe, from Hungary to Turkey. It has a mild, slightly salty flavor that becomes more pungent as it ages; soft when young, it is granular and ideal for grating when mature.

Kefir

Kefir is a liquid drink that is somewhat like **yogurt**. Originally from eastern Europe, it was made from mare's milk and fermented with a cultured starter until it became slightly alcoholic. Modern versions of kefir are made from cow's or camel's **milk**, are nonalcoholic, are less tart than plain yogurt, and are available plain or flavored with fruit.

Milk

Milk is perhaps the one food that every human being has consumed in his or her life, as every human baby is dependent on milk—either its own mother's breast milk, the breast milk of a wet nurse, or milk from another animal—for sustenance and survival. Humans have taken milk from many mammals over the millennia: **goats**, **sheep**, mares, llamas, donkeys, buffalo, camels, reindeer, and yaks, in addition to cows, which provide the vast majority of milk for human consumption. For most of history and much of human prehistory, people (primarily young children) drank milk fresh, soon after the animals (whichever they were) had been milked; but milk is also the raw material for **butter, cheese, cream,** and **yogurt** and has been processed in many ways to suit the human palate.

Perhaps the first peoples to consume the milk of another species were the nomads of the Eurasian steppes, who preferred mare's milk to all other types, even though they had sheep and goats. In historic times, the first record of milking comes from a 2900 B.C.E. frieze found at Ur, in ancient Mesopotamia. For both the ancient Israelites and Egyptians, milk, mostly **goat's milk** but perhaps also from sheep and cows, was a rare treat, synonymous with wealth: thus the Promised Land was called the "land flowing with milk and **honey**." The milking of buffalo in China began about 2000 B.C.E., though again, milk seems to have been accessible only to the wealthy. When the Aryans entered India about 1750 B.C.E., they brought their herds of cows along; these nomads depended so heavily on milk products that the cow became sacred on the subcontinent. The ancient Greeks had milk from goats and sheep, preferring the former, but used it primarily to make cheese. The ancient Romans seem to have preferred sheep's milk; they also used it to make cheese but did mix milk with **wine** for drinking.

Of all the milks, donkey's (or ass's) milk is the closest to human milk. Human milk has more fat, but otherwise they are similarly digestible. Next would be mare's milk, which was probably the first that humans consumed on a regular basis, and goat's milk, which is sweeter than cow's milk, followed by sheep's, **camel's**, and reindeer's. At the bottom of the scale of digestibility by humans are the milks of cows, buffalo, and yaks. Why, then, does about 90 percent of the milk consumed by humans come from cows? The reason lies both in the animals' docility and in their responsiveness to selective breeding, which has rendered certain breeds of cows mere milk-producing machines.

While some people praise the practice of breastfeeding because it provides exactly the correct nutrients for a human baby and also transfers certain antibodies from the mother to the infant, others claim that mother's milk has such high levels of antibiotics, pesticides, and other pollutants that it is unsafe for human consumption. It is true that chemicals tend to become concentrated in humans, who are high on the food chain; cows and goats and other milk-producing animals also ingest high levels of antibiotics and pesticides, so their milk is also adversely affected. Additionally, the required pasteurization of milk, a process by which it is purified for human use, destroys all the vitamin C and beneficial bacteria that were present in the milk when it was produced by the milk animal. Milk does contain significant amounts of calcium, phosphorous, and riboflavin, and calcium- and vitamin-fortified milk is often available for purchase.

At the same time, the human habit of drinking the milk of other animals is actually contrary to nature. Milk contains a rich **sugar** called lactose; cow's milk has a lot of it, and goat's milk has very little of it. Human babies produce an enzyme called lactase in their intestines, and only this enzyme can serve to digest lactose. As human babies mature into childhood and then into adulthood, their systems produce less and less lactase, until they are unable to digest milk (or most milk products) at all. Fully 80 percent of the world's people of color and many Mediterranean peoples are lactose intolerant, meaning that their digestive systems are unable to handle most milks, the result being painful gas, flatulence, cramps, and diarrhea. In recent years, lactase supplements have become available for those who enjoy milk, cheese, ice cream, and butter. A more natural solution would be to avoid milk and its derivatives: the body seems to know what is healthful for it to consume.

Milk, camel's

Camel's milk is heavy and sweet (some might say unpleasantly so and might compare it to evaporated milk), but it is a highly prized luxury of desert peoples. Unfortunately, a milk camel can give only 6 to 10 quarts of **milk** per day, even under completely favorable conditions. For this reason, camel's milk is not a major staple of the human diet.

Milk, goat's

Goat's milk is generally sweeter than cow's milk. The fat in goat's milk is present in smaller globules than that in cow's milk, making raw goat's milk more digestible by humans; however, homogenization of milk breaks the fat globules apart anyway, so in the long run homogenized cow's milk is no less digestible than goat's milk. Additionally, goat's milk has slightly less lactose than cow's **milk**.

Yogurt

Although yogurt has been a staple food in Asia, the Middle East, and eastern Europe for millennia, it did not become popular in the United States until the 1970s. To yogurt has been attributed the ability to cure everything from insomnia to cancer, but scientific research has not substantiated any of these claims. It is true, however, that yogurt provides calcium, protein, riboflavin, phosphorus, and vitamin B12. It is versatile, delicious alone or with fruit, and can be substituted for **mayonnaise**, heavy **cream**, whipped cream, or sour cream in many recipes.

To make yogurt, pasteurized and often homogenized **milk** is curdled with purified cultures of *Lactobacillus bulgaricus* and *Streptococcus thermophilus*, special bacteria that turn the milk sugar (lactose) into lactic acid. Warmed in an incubator, the yogurt thickens and develops its distinct flavor. Sometimes nonfat-milk solids are added to make the yogurt even thicker. Usually, the bacteria survive the process; sometimes, the yogurt is pasteurized again, which kills the bacteria.

Because the lactose has been reduced by the bacteria, yogurt is generally more digestible for people who are lactose intolerant; yogurt with live cultures (that is, yogurt that has not been heat treated after culturing) is most easily digested by such persons. The live cultures also help digest casein and may even help restore the beneficial bacteria to a digestive system that has been cleaned out by the use of antibiotics.

Yogurt is available plain or flavored, in nonfat, low-fat, and whole-milk forms. It is also available in frozen form, often as dessert products. Yogurt makes a fine topping for cereals. Blended with fresh or frozen fruits and/or fruit juices, it makes a low-fat shake. It can be mixed with **scallions**, **chives**, curry powders, herbs, or **mustard**s to make a tangy dip for vegetables or chips. Yogurt can add texture to soups and guacamole and is a nutritious dressing for **cucumber, chicken,** and **tuna** salads. It is a low-fat substitute for sour **cream** atop baked **potato**es and can serve as a tangy marinade for chicken and fish.

If the whey is drained from yogurt, the result is yogurt **cheese**, which is a soft milk product that can be used in place of cream cheese, sour cream, or crème fraîche. Yogurt cheese is delicious in low-fat dips and spreads, in tuna or chicken salads, and in desserts. Yogurt is a popular ingredient in many Middle Eastern recipes.

BEVERAGES

Angostura Bitters

Angostura bitters is a compound made primarily from gentian (genus *Gentiana*), a flowering plant with bitter-tasting leaves. Gentians are native to temperate regions from Asia to Europe to North America, with some of its many species found in northwestern Africa, eastern Australia, and the Andes. Gentians can be annuals, biennials, or perennials.

J.G.B. Siegert, a German physician living in Angostura, Venezuela, first developed Angostura bitters in 1824 as a remedy for stomach maladies. Although the compound did not perform as expected, it was exported to England and Trinidad, where it was adopted as an ingredient in cocktails, as the bitters do help in mild cases of nausea or upset stomach. Angostura bitters is generally about 45 percent alcohol by volume.

Besides its use in cocktails such as Bermuda Rum Swizzle, **Bloody Mary**, Manhattan, Old Fashioned, and Rob Roy, Angostura bitters can also be added to soups, glazes for poultry or pork, **turkey** stuffings, fish dishes, even **tomato** sauces, custards, and fruit medleys.

Bitters are mentioned in the Bible (Exodus 12:8, Young's Literal Translation) but the reference is probably to bitter herbs.

Anisette

Anisette is a liqueur made from the seeds of the **anise** plant (*Pimpinella anisum*). Aniseeds have a distinctive licorice taste and are used in making not only anisette but sambuca, anis, ouzo, raki, arak, and pastis. Usually, anisette is served after a meal, to aid digestion or relaxation, either at room temperature, mixed with water, on the rocks, or added to **tea** or **coffee**. Sometimes it is mixed with **brandy** and is used to flavor baked goods, fruit dishes—even seafood.

Anisette is also used to make a number of cocktails, such as Jelly Bean, Oyster Bay, Lady in Green, Dance with a Dream, Green Opal, Malayan Gold, and Brandy Champarelle.

Apple Cider

Apple cider (often known simply as cider) is made from the juice of **apples**. In North America, cider is traditionally an unfermented beverage; in other parts of the world, cider means fermented apple juice, which is known in the United States as hard cider.

Cider is not the same as apple juice. Cider is usually made from early apples, which tend to be less sweet and more acidic, so cider has more tang than apple juice. Often, ciders are made from a number of different apple varieties (and these are not usually the varieties used for eating), to produce a balanced taste, and the exact proportions have become highly guarded secrets at cider mills. Cider also tends to be unfiltered, with suspended solid particles that make it opaque.

To make cider, the apples are ground to a very fine pulp. This pulp is compressed into a cake (called a cheese) that is then placed under pressure until all the juice (called must) has been squeezed out. The juice is placed in vats or casks for slight aging before being sold as cider. Many connoisseurs consider fresh cider superior in taste, but because of the possibility of salmonella and *E. coli* contamination, health regulations now generally require apple ciders to be pasteurized before they can be sold. The pulp is used as livestock feed or as the base for apple liqueurs such as apple **brandy**.

Hard cider is produced from fermenting the must (juice) that is used to make cider. Hard cider is usually above 6 percent alcohol by volume.

Another alcoholic beverage made from cider is applejack, which results from freeze distillation or evaporative distillation. Applejack can have as much as 30–40 percent alcohol by volume, but home-produced applejack may also contain deadly toxins and is thus illegal in many places.

During colder weather, cider is often served hot or mulled (that is, flavored with **cinnamon, orange** peel, **nutmeg, cloves,** and other spices). Sparkling cider is also available; it is a carbonated, nonalcoholic cider or apple-juice beverage.

Beer

Beer is one of the oldest manufactured beverages, probably dating from about 5000 B.C.E. The oldest recorded evidence is believed to be the ancient Sumerian tablet of 4000 B.C.E., which shows a group of people drinking from a communal bowl through reed straws. The *Epic of Gilgamesh,* which dates from about 1900 B.C.E., provides the oldest beer recipe and relates how beer was made from **barley bread.** Beer was a popular beverage in all the ancient civilizations: Mesopotamian, Egyptian, Greek, and Roman, although **wine** came to replace beer, which began to be seen as fit only for "barbarians." Beer was undoubtedly known to the ancient Israelites from their time in Egypt. Nevertheless, beer maintained its importance through the Middle Ages and the Renaissance, gradually moving from home-based to commercial breweries, with pubs and even monasteries becoming major manufacturers of beer. Up until the 15th century C.E., many beers were made without hops, though hops had been introduced to beer brewing by the 11th century, and perhaps as early as the 9th. Unhopped beers were known as ales; hopped beers were called beer. However, by the 16th century, all ales and beers were made with hops, and any strong beer was called an ale. Beer-making is now an enormous industry, with major breweries producing large quantities of brand-name beers for worldwide consumption and microbreweries making small amounts of specialty beers for local use.

Today, most beers are either ales or lagers. Ales are brewed using top-fermenting **yeasts,** at higher temperatures than lagers. The result is a significant amount of esters and other flavor and aroma products, which makes ales very flavorful. Lagers, on the other hand, are brewed by using bottom-fermenting yeasts, with two phases, the fermentation and the lagering, both of which take place at temperatures lower than those used for ales. The lagering process was discovered only in the 16th century, by accident.

Beer is made from a combination of water, malted barley or other grains, hops, and yeast. Sometimes adjuncts such as **corn** or **rice** are added, as a source of **sugar,** to increase the alcohol content of the final product. Clarifying agents are also involved, to rid the beer of any particulate residue.

Because **water** is the principal ingredient of beer, it has a large effect on the character of the beer. In general, harder water is best for darker beers such as stouts and porters; softer water, for light-colored beers like pilsners.

As a source of malt, barley is the most commonly used, but **wheat,** rice, **oats, rye,** maize, and even sorghum can be substituted. Malt forms when the grain is allowed to soak in water and germinate, then dried in a kiln. This process yields the enzymes that convert the grain starch into fermentable sugar.

Hops are grown specifically for use in brewing beer. Hops add a certain bitterness to the end product, to balance the sweetness provided by the malt.

Contributing aroma, hops also provide an antibiotic effect that facilitates the activity of the yeast and determine the endurance of the beer's foamy head.

The fungus yeast causes the fermentation of the sugars in the grains, producing alcohol and carbon dioxide. The major strains of yeast are ale yeast (*Saccharomyces cerevisiae*) and lager yeast (*S. uvarum*). Beers average 4 to 6 percent alcohol by volume, though some beers have alcohol content as low as 2 percent and others as high as 14 percent. Specialty beers may even have as much as 20 percent alcohol.

Brewing beer requires the following steps:

- Mashing: The malted grains are ground, then soaked in warm water to yield a malt extract. During this step, the starch is converted into fermentable sugar.
- Sparging: Water is sent through the mash, dissolving and absorbing the sugars. The result is a dark, sugar-laden liquid called wort.
- Boiling: The wort is boiled, removing excess water and killing bacteria. Hops are then added.
- Fermenting: The yeast is added to the mixture and begins to ferment the sugars. Sometimes the mixture goes through two fermentations, the second of which allows the yeast and other particles to settle.
- Packaging: The mixture is carbonated, sometimes by adding carbon dioxide directly to the beer, sometimes by adding extra sugar or fermenting wort for a short refermentation called cask- or bottle-conditioning.
- Kegging, casking, bottling, or canning: The beer is prepared for consumption. Some beers are unpasteurized and may contain live yeasts that continue to ferment and cause the development of secondary flavors; these strong beers may require significant aging or conditioning periods, perhaps as long as a year or more.

Finally, the taste of a beer depends significantly on the temperature at which it is served, the container from which it is consumed, and the manner in which it is poured. Many beers are not meant to be served ice-cold, and most beers are meant to be drunk from specially shaped glasses. Some beers also need a bit of time to settle after they are poured, so that their full flavor can be appreciated.

Today's beer connoisseur can choose from an almost endless variety of beer, from those of Albania to those of Zimbabwe. Some of the major brands include Coopers, Fosters, Amstel, Tuborg, Stella Artois, Guinness, Labatt, Molson, Moosehead, Tsingtao, Pilsner Urquell, Budweiser, Carlsberg, Beck's, Dinkelacker, Karlsberg, Rheingold, St. Pauli Girl, San Miguel, Harp, Murphy's, Sapporo, Corona, Dos Equis, Heineken, Colt 45, Löwenbräu, Bass, Courage, Whitbread, Michelob, Samuel Adams, Coors, Miller, Pabst, and Rolling Rock. There are even hybrid beers, such as fruit or vegetable beers, in which a fermentable fruit or vegetable adjunct has been introduced (very popular in the Benelux countries); herb and spiced beers, in which roots, seeds, or flowers have been used instead of or in addition to hops; wood-aged beers, which have been aged in contact with wood (in barrels or mixed with chips or cubes) in order to assimilate a woody flavor; and smoked beers, whose malts have been processed to produce a robust flavor.

Besides being a satisfying beverage, beer is also a wonderful seasoning. It tenderizes meat, fish, or seafood when used as a marinade. When simmering meats and vegetables, beer can be used instead of water; it brings out the richness of the food and, as the alcohol evaporates during cooking, leaves only a delicate beer flavor behind. Beer imparts a rich color to roasted or broiled foods when it is used in the basting sauce. It provides a surprising lift to **cheese** and other dips, soups, and salad dressings. Most surprising, beer can be used in baking, adding a lightness to biscuits, pancakes, breads, and cakes.

Bloody Mary Mix

Bloody Mary mix is used, not surprisingly, to make a cocktail called a Bloody Mary. There are many variations, but the mix generally consists of **horseradish**, **lemon** juice, **pepper**, **garlic**, **onion**, and **Worcestershire** or Tabasco sauce, plus ingredients guarded as trade secrets by the various manufacturers. The mix is added to vodka and **tomato** juice and often served with a stalk of **celery** and a **lime** wedge to make a Bloody Mary.

Bourbon

Bourbon is North American whiskey, made from **corn**, **wheat**, or **rye**. The whiskey is distilled to no more than 160 (U.S.) proof (about 80 percent alcohol by volume), then aged in oak barrels for at least two years before being bottled and sold.

The name "bourbon" comes from Bourbon County, Kentucky, which is where this alcoholic beverage was first developed. An act of Congress in 1964 declared bourbon to be "America's Native Spirit" and restricted the name "bourbon" to this particular type of whiskey made in the United States. Some aficionados claim that bourbon is not really bourbon unless it is made in Bourbon County.

Today, most bourbon is made by the sour-mash process: each new fermentation is conditioned by spent beer (previously fermented mash separated from its alcohol), much the way that starter is used to make sourdough **bread**. The acid in the sour mash controls bacteria that could harm the whiskey.

Usually, bourbon is reduced to 80–100 proof before it is bottled. Occasionally, bourbon is bottled at cask strength, which would be of significantly higher proof. Recently, 80 proof and lower has been the norm, as many U.S. jurisdictions prohibit the sale of alcoholic beverages with greater than 40 percent alcohol content.

Some common bourbons include Early Times, Jim Beam, Old Crow, Old Forester, Wild Turkey, and Kentucky Gentleman.

Besides its obvious attraction as a beverage, bourbon can add a tasty flavor to many recipes. It can be used in marinades for meats, **chicken**, and seafood;

barbecue sauces; candied yams; custards, cheesecakes, **pecan** pies, and mud cakes; and julep and punch drinks. Bourbon is often used today in Middle Eastern dishes in combination with **pomegranate** juice and other fruit juices.

Brandy

Brandy is short for brandywine, a term for **wine** that has been distilled. As early as the ancient Babylonian civilization (c. 2000 B.C.E.), wine and alcoholic beverages were concentrated by evaporation, for preservation and transportation purposes. All of the ancient civilizations, including the Greek and Roman, generally added water to their wines, both to make them more palatable and to dilute their alcoholic effects. The peoples of the Bible were probably familiar with concentrated wines. In the 8th century C.E. Muslim scientists invented modern distillation, a process of removing the water from wine or other liquids but leaving all the other ingredients, and this process made its way to Europe and began to be applied to wines by the 12th century. By the 14th century, connoisseurs had realized that distilled wine stored in wooden casks was remarkably tasty and strongly alcoholic, and modern brandy was born.

Three main types of brandy are now made:

- Grape Brandy is produced by distilling fermented **grape** juice. Grape brandies include the **Cognacs**, Armagnacs, and U.S. brandies. These brandies are served at room temperature or slightly warmed in a brandy snifter.
- Pomace Brandy is made from fermented **grape** pulp, seeds, and stems—everything that remains after the grapes are pressed. Pomace brandies include Grappa and Marc.
- Fruit Brandy is distilled from other fruits such as **apples, plums**, peaches, **cherries, raspberries**, blackberries, and **apricots**. Usually clear, fruit brandies are served chilled over ice. Examples include Calvados and Kirsch.

Brandies need to be aged, and the aging is done in one of the following ways:

- Single-barrel aging, in oak casks, yielding brandies that are golden or brown.
- Solera process, using a series of barrels or other containers; a portion of the brandy from the last barrel is removed and bottled, then the last barrel is filled from the next-to-last, and so forth, until the first barrel is filled with new wine. Sherries, Madeiras, Marsalas, Mavrodaphnes, and even **Balsamic vinegar**s are aged by the solera process.
- No aging: many pomace and fruit brandies are not aged after distillation.

Brandies are classified according to how long they have been aged. The following system is usually followed:

- A.C.—at least two years old
- V.S. (Very Special)—at least three years old

- Napoleon—at least four years old
- V.S.O.P. (Very Superior Old Pale)—at least five years old
- X.O. (Extra Old)—at least six years old
- Hors d'Age—too old to determine the age

Generally speaking, the older the brandy, the more expensive it will be.

Brandy can add a wonderful flavor to many recipes, including those for **chicken** and **turkey**, **beef** and pork, prime rib, meatballs, seafood, wild-game dishes, goulashes, salad dressings, stuffings, **yams**, **cabbage** dishes, **cheese** balls, tofu, pancakes, puddings, cakes and pies, **coffees**, eggnog, parfaits and sundaes, and fruit cakes. Brandies are now popular in Middle Eastern desserts such as *Ataif, haroset,* and baked **figs**.

Coffee

The world's most popular beverage, coffee is made from the roasted beans (seeds) of the coffee plant, either *Coffea arabica* or *C. canephora (robusta)*. The former is native to the Arabian Peninsula; it is more susceptible to disease but is considered to yield superior tasting coffee than the latter. The latter is more disease-resistant because it contains much more caffeine, which is a natural insecticide.

The first people to drink coffee may have been the inhabitants of Ethiopia, where the coffee plant is believed to have originated. According to legend, a goatherder observed his goats becoming energized after eating certain berries; he tasted the berries and became energized himself, thus beginning the human consumption of coffee beans. Coffee was first cultivated in Yemen, perhaps as early as the 12th century C.E., but was not known outside of Arabia, Egypt, and Turkey until the 16th century, when the British and Dutch East India companies brought it to Europe. By the 17th century, London, Boston, Paris, and Vienna boasted a number of coffeehouses. Coffee was first planted in the Americas—in Brazil—in the 18th century. Today, coffee is the world's second most valuable commodity, behind only oil. Brazil produces the most coffee, followed by Vietnam, Indonesia, and the Philippines, though Kenya, Ethiopia, Hawaii, Jamaica, Sumatra, Yemen, and Tanzania all produce significant amounts of coffee. It is possible that the peoples of the Bible were familiar with coffee beans; certainly, coffee is now practically a "staple" of Middle Eastern cuisine.

Many coffee brands blend beans from the two different coffee species or from the different regions, as growing conditions, environment, and processing can affect the flavor of the beans. Mocha-Java is a very old blend, combining beans from Yemen and Indonesia. Other beans are so flavorful that they have become very expensive: examples include Jamaican Blue Mountain and Hawaiian Kona; these are often blended to improve the flavor of less expensive beans.

The production of coffee is a complicated process of aging, roasting, grinding, and brewing.

Many types of coffee improve as they age, becoming less acidic and more balanced in flavor. Often, beans are aged for three years, though some are aged for as long as eight years.

After aging, the coffee beans are roasted, becoming enlarged and changing color. Light roasting allows the beans to retain some of the flavor that reveals their place of origin; this flavor depends on the soil and weather where the coffee was grown. Dark roasting removes much of the "origin" flavor and imparts the flavor of roasting. Sometimes beans are roasted in **butter** or **sugar**, and very dark roasting can even result in a burnt flavor that completely masks the origin flavor. Because roasted coffee beans quickly turn bitter and deteriorate in flavor, they are usually stored in pressurized cans or bags.

When the consumer is ready to make coffee, the beans need to be ground. In general, the degree of grinding needs to match the brewing method to be employed in order to get the most flavor from the beans and to avoid bitterness or weakness. Coarse grinding works best when the coffee grounds are to be brewed for a lengthy time, and fine grinding works best when the brewing method is very quick. Grinding the beans does make them deteriorate more quickly, so it is best to grind them just before brewing; otherwise, refrigeration, even freezing, can retard the deterioration of ground coffee.

There are four primary methods of brewing coffee: boiling, pressure brewing, gravity brewing, and steeping. In each case, hot water passes through or comes in contact with the coffee grounds, absorbing soluble components that impart flavor to the water. The recommended brewing temperature is 204°F: cooler temperatures will not release all the flavors, and hotter temperatures will pull unpalatable tastes from the grounds. Boiling is used to make Turkish and so-called cowboy coffees. Espressos are made by pressure brewing, which can employ a pressure percolator or a vacuum brewer. Gravity brewing makes use of gravity to cause the hot water to drip down onto the coffee grounds, which are placed in a coffee filter; this is sometimes called drip brewing, and older electric percolators use this method. Steeping coffee requires the coffee grinds to be placed in a coffee bag or special cafetière, allowing the hot water to seep into the grinds, which are then easily removed en masse, leaving the coffee.

Once the coffee is brewed, there are many ways of serving it:

- Black coffee, to which **sugar** may be added
- White coffee, with **milk** or **cream** added, and sometimes sugar
- Cappuccino, which is a mixture of equal parts of espresso, steamed milk, and frothed milk, sometimes flavored with **cinnamon, cocoa,** or other spices
- Caffè e latte (also called café latte or simply latte), which is a mixture of equal parts of espresso and steamed milk, often topped with frothed milk
- Café au lait, which is a mixture of equal parts of drip-brewed coffee and milk, sometimes sweetened with sugar
- Americano coffee, which is espresso diluted with hot water

- Iced coffee, which is sweetened coffee with milk, on ice
- Flavored coffee, which is coffee flavored with spices such as cinnamon and **nutmeg,** light fruit syrups, or **chocolate**
- Irish coffee, which is coffee flavored with whiskey and topped with a layer of cream
- Indian filter coffee, which is drip-brewed for several hours, then served with milk and sugar
- Vietnamese coffee, which is drip-brewed coffee mixed with sweetened condensed milk
- Turkish (or Greek or Armenian) coffee, which is boiled coffee served with sugar, **cardamom, anise,** and other spices
- Frappé coffee, which is made from instant coffee and served cold, with or without sugar and milk

There are innumerable other ways of preparing coffee, and each culture has created its own favorites. It is important to note that if brewed coffee is kept heated, it will quickly become unpalatable; sealed off from oxygen, it will retain its flavor longer.

To make coffee preparation easier, both instant and soluble coffees have become available. In these types, coffee grounds have been dried into powders or granules, which dissolve in hot water. Many coffee gourmets believe that instant, even freeze-dried, coffees are markedly inferior to freshly brewed coffees.

Coffee naturally contains caffeine, a stimulant. For people who are sensitive to or even addicted to caffeine, decaffeinated coffee (or decaf) has been developed, the caffeine being removed from the raw beans either by soaking them or subjecting them to a chemical solvent. However, caffeinated coffee is sometimes believed to improve the effectiveness of migraine medication and some other pain killers, to prevent gallstones and gallbladder disease in men, to reduce the risk of suicide in women, and to decrease the incidence of diabetes, liver cirrhosis, colon and bladder cancers, and heart disease in both men and women. In some people, however, caffeinated coffee can produce caffeine jitters (caffeinism).

Cognac

Cognac is a type of **brandy.** Double distilled in large pots, cognacs include brands such as Martell, Rémy Martin, Hennessy, and Courvoisier (which was favored by Napoleon Bonaparte).

Cointreau

An **orange**-flavored liqueur that is both sweet and bitter, Cointreau was first distilled by Edouard-Jean and Adolphe Cointreau of Angers, France, in 1849. This liqueur generally is 80 proof (40 percent alcohol content) and is most often consumed as an after-dinner drink, or *digestif.* It is also used to make cocktails or mixed drinks, such as B-52 shooters, Cosmopolitan, Singapore Sling, Long Island Iced Tea, Sidecar, and Pink Flamingo. Cointreau is considered to be a very high quality triple sec, which means that it has been distilled three times. Cointreau is often used in Middle Eastern dessert recipes.

Cranberry Juice
See **cranberry**.

Gin

Gin is an alcoholic drink made from the distillation of white grain spirit and **juniper berries**. Juniper berries are the seeds of trees of the *Juniperus* genus, of which there are several dozen species found around the world. Gin was first made in the Netherlands in the 17th century, created by Francis de la Boe, but spread to the British Isles when William and Mary became the regents of England in 1689. In the 18th century gin became very popular in England when the government allowed its manufacture to proceed unlicensed while heavily taxing imported spirits. Gin became much less expensive than **beer** and became a favorite drink among the poor, but it was blamed for many social problems, and terms like "gin joint," "gin mills," and "gin-soaked," which date from this era, indicate the negative feelings that became associated with its consumption. Gin production was licensed by the mid-1700s, and drinking gin became more respectable in the 19th century with the introduction of a dry style and the use of gin in quinine-based tonic drinks (gin and tonic) in areas of the British Empire that were subject to malaria. The creation of the martini in the United States at the end of the 19th century did much to establish gin's reputation as a sophisticated spirit. Gin-based cocktails became quite popular during Prohibition in the United States (because it is clear and looks like water), and gin has remained a common base for mixed drinks ever since.

The original name for gin was *jenievre*, or *jenever* (sometimes *genever* or *geneva*), which was shortened to *gin* when the beverage made its way to England.

Today, gin comes in at least four main types:

- London dry gin, which is usually made in a column still. This high-proof spirit is redistilled after botanicals like **orange** or **lemon, anise, cinnamon**, cassia bark, **cardamom**, licorice, **orris root**, and bitter **almonds**, in addition to **juniper**, are added to the base.
- Dutch gin, often called jenever, which is the original gin.
- Plymouth gin.
- Old Tom gin, which is supposed to be reminiscent of the pot-distilled spirits of the 18th century.

Some of the popular brands of gin include Beefeater, Bombay, Gilbey's, Gordon's, Seagram's, and Tanqueray.

Gin is not often used in cooking but can serve as a splendid flavoring for roasted wild boar, caribou, elk, pheasant, salmon, and seafood. It also serves as a special ingredient in marinades, fruit salads, sorbets, cookies, and cobblers. In modern Middle Eastern cooking, gin is added to fish dishes and light desserts.

Grand Marnier

First created in 1880 by Alexandre Marnier-Lampostolle, Grand Marnier is an alcoholic beverage made from a combination of various **cognacs**, distilled essence of **orange**, and other flavorings and ingredients. About 40 percent alcohol by content (about 80 proof), Grand Marnier is often consumed "neat" or "straight" (by itself); it is also mixed with other spirits and beverages for a variety of mixed drinks.

The main types of Grand Marnier include

- Red Label, also known as Cordon Rouge: This is usually called simply Grand Marnier and is consumed either neat or in mixed drinks.
- Yellow Label, also known as Cordon Jaune: This is a scarce type, made with grain alcohol instead of cognac, and is considered to be of inferior quality; it is used for mixed drinks and in cooking recipes.
- Black Label: Another scarce type, this is considered to be of a higher quality and is generally very expensive; it is consumed neat.
- 100: Officially called Cuvée du Centennaire (Centennial Edition), this is made with twenty-five-year-old fine cognacs; it is very expensive and is consumed neat.
- 150: Officially called Cuvée Spéciale Cent Cinquantennaire (Special Sesquicentennial Edition), this is the finest and most expensive Grand Marnier available; it is made with fifty-year-old fine cognacs and is consumed neat.

In just a short time, Grand Marnier has found an extremely important place in the kitchen. It adds a touch of flair and a special flavor to ice cream, cake, crêpes, soufflés, flambés, tortes, **chocolate** dips, fruit salads, and **coffees** and iced **teas**. It is an especially delicious addition to **chicken** and pork marinades, stuffings, shrimp salads, and scallop dishes, and it adds a wonderful flavor to marmalades and jams.

Some mixed drinks that use Grand Marnier include Red Lion, Cosmopolitan, B-52, French Connection, Grand Royale, and even Sangria. Grand Marnier is often an ingredient in Middle Eastern sauces, puddings, **creams**, and pastries.

Grape Juice

See **grape**.

Grenadine

Grenadine is, strictly speaking, the juice or syrup extracted from **pomegranates**. Deep red in color and intense in taste, grenadine is often used to sweeten and color cocktails such as 77 Sunset Strip, Arizona Sunrise, Bahama Mama Sunrise,

Boxcar, California Lemonade, Cherry Blossom, Cotton Candy, Flamingo Cocktail, Hawaiian Punch, Jamaican Rum Punch, Zombie, Watermelon Shooter, Tequila Sunrise, Shirley Temple, Ruby Slipper, Pink Lady, and many more. Grenadine is a popular addition to Middle Eastern marinades, desserts, and sauces, as well as savory vinaigrettes.

Lemon Juice

See **lemon**.

Lime Juice

See **lime**.

Orange Blossom Water

Orange blossom water is simply **water** that has been flavored with **orange** blossoms, either by adding an extract from the blossoms to the water or by boiling the water and blossoms together, then filtering and cooling the water before consumption. It is often an ingredient listed in recipes for baklava and other Middle Eastern pastries.

Orange Juice

See **orange**.

Pear Juice (Pear Nectar)

Pear nectar is the juice extracted from the fruit of the pear tree (*Pyrus* genus), which is, surprisingly, a member of the Rose family. Native to central Asia, pears spread across temperate Asia and Europe, mutating and speciating until today there are about thirty types of wild pears that inhabit various ecological niches from Spain to China. Pears were an important part of the diet of prehistoric humans, and pear remains have been discovered in archaeological sites dating from before 4000 B.C.E. in Germany, Switzerland, Italy, and Greece and in a Chinese tomb dating from 2100 B.C.E. The earliest written record of pears is found on an ancient Sumerian tablet dating from about 2750 B.C.E., and it is possible that this is also the first record of cultivated pears; an Egyptian wall painting dating from about 1400 B.C.E. shows a pear that may have been cultivated. It is possible that the ancient Israelites knew of pears, though the fruit would not have been readily available to nomadic peoples. Pears are mentioned in some translations of the Bible (e.g., Douay-Rheims Version of II Kings 5:23 and I Chronicles 14:15); but the reference is most likely erroneous. Reliable records of pear cultivation date from about 1000 B.C.E., when the people of the Aegean region began to understand grafting techniques. By the time of Aristotle (c. 300 B.C.E.), pears were an important fruit of the Greek garden, and the ancient Romans continued to develop pear cultivars and spread cultivated pears as far north as the British Isles. Pear cultivation continued throughout the Middle Ages, kept alive by monastics. Pears did not cross the Atlantic until the 16th century C.E., carried by Spanish missionaries and spreading rapidly along the Pacific Coast. They made their way to New England with English colonists and then spread westward, and French missionaries also introduced pears to the Iroquois.

The pears first cultivated in Europe are probably descendants of *P. pyraster* and *P. caucasica,* which grow wild in Europe, Asia Minor, and the Caucasus. The pears first cultivated in Asia probably descended from *P. pyrifolia* and *P. ussuriensis,* which grow wild in the Far East. There are now more than three dozen species of pears under cultivation, the most notable being the European pear (*P. communis*). Some well-known varieties include Anjou, Bartlett, Bosc, and Comice; lesser-known but just as tasty varieties include Seckel, Winter Nellis, Clapp, and Forell. Asian pears (*P. pyrifolia*) are relatively difficult to find in the United States.

Pear trees can live to be a hundred years old and can grow to heights of sixty feet. They need sunny exposure and little winter chilling to produce profuse white blossoms and fruit. Cultivated pears are almost always picked before they are ripe and are allowed to ripen in the market or at home.

Pears are a delicious fruit to eat fresh or as part of a fruit salad. The skin contains most of the vitamin C to be found in pears, so they should not be peeled. Pears can be baked, poached, sautéed, and made into "pearsauce," flavored with **cinnamon, nutmeg, cloves, allspice, brown sugar, rum,** or **orange** juice. They go well with **raisins, figs, dates, yogurt, cheeses,** poultry, and pork.

Pear nectar is relatively high in **sugar** and so has more calories than most fruit juices.

Pomegranate Syrup

Pomegranate syrup is extracted from the fruit of the **pomegranate** tree (*Punica granatum*), which is actually a large, drought-resistant bush growing to a height of about 16 feet. The pomegranate is probably a native of central Asia, perhaps the mountains of Afghanistan, though its origins are lost to prehistory, as it entered cultivation about 8000 B.C.E. Cuneiform writing tablets from ancient Mesopotamia (about 2500 B.C.E.) refer to pomegranates, and their remains have been discovered in archaeological sites at Jericho from about the same time, in Egypt from about 1800 B.C.E., and in Greece and Cyprus from about 1500 B.C.E. By this time pomegranates had spread throughout the eastern Mediterranean and into India. To the Israelites, pomegranates were one of the fruits of Egypt that they longed for during their desert wanderings (Exodus 28 and 39 and Numbers 20) and one of the fruits to be expected in the Promised Land (Deuteronomy 8:8); the temple of Solomon also incorporated a pomegranate design into its decorations (I Kings 7:17). Homer mentioned pomegranates in the *Odyssey,* and the ancient Romans also grew pomegranates, though they imported many more than they raised. Pomegranates made their way to China by about 100 B.C.E. but seem to have been lost to Europe after the collapse of the Roman Empire, to be reintroduced by the Moors in the 9th and 10th centuries C.E. The fruit had made its way to England by the 16th century, and to the Americas with the Spanish by the

17th. Today, pomegranates are raised in many tropical and subtropical regions, but they are not as important as they once were, for citrus fruits and melons have replaced them as a thirst-quenching fruit in many areas.

Pomegranates have a thick, reddish skin, red pulp, and an extraordinary number of seeds and are about four inches in diameter. Because of the great number of seeds, in ancient times the pomegranate was a common symbol of fertility. Its red juice, reminiscent of blood, also made it a symbol of death. It was associated with Cybele, the Great Mother Goddess of Asia Minor, and with Persephone, whose annual journeys to and from the underworld marked the turning of the seasons. Early Christians baptized the pomegranate and made it a symbol of fidelity, and in Christian art the Holy Family, the Blessed Mother, and the Christ Child are all depicted with pomegranates. Pomegranates are still a traditional part of the Jewish Rosh Hashanah and Sukkot meals. Muslims also honor pomegranates as one of the fruits to be found in the Garden of Paradise.

Usually peeled and eaten fresh, pomegranates are extremely high in vitamin C and are a good source of folic acid and antioxidants. Their taste ranges between sweet and sour.

Pomegranate juice is still a popular drink in the Middle East. Pomegranate (grenadine) syrup—simply thickened and sweetened pomegranate juice—is used to dress various Middle Eastern dishes such as *baba ganoush* and *shawarma*. It is also used to make cocktails (see **grenadine**) and can be fermented and distilled to make a liqueur.

Rose Water

Rose water is simply **water** that has been flavored with roses, either their petals, buds, or hips. Extracts from these parts of the rose can be added to water, or water can be boiled together with the petals, buds, or hips, then filtered and cooled before consumption. It is often used as a flavoring in Middle Eastern pastries such as baklava.

Rum

Rum is an alcoholic beverage, fermented and distilled from sugarcane byproducts (**molasses** and sugarcane juice), then aged in wooden casks. Modern rum was not developed until the 17th century, but peoples of ancient India and China produced fermented beverages from sugarcane juice, and the practice spread to Malaysia and beyond. Systematic rum production did not occur until sugarcane had been planted in the Caribbean. There, perhaps in Barbados, plantation slaves took molasses, which is a residue of **sugar** refining, and fermented it into an alcoholic drink. Distillation removed impurities, creating the first true rums.

Rum became quite a popular drink and helped create the so-called triangular trade in the 17th and 18th centuries: Europe was in great need of sugar and so purchased cane sugar and molasses from the Caribbean, distilling the molasses into rum; European ships then took the rum to the western coast of Africa, where slavers traded the rum for Africans, who were sold or traded to them as slaves and transported to the Caribbean; there, the slaves were sold to the sugarcane plantations, where they worked the fields to grow, harvest, and process the cane. The American colonies became involved in two ways: as owners of rum distilleries (in the Northeast), and as owners of cotton plantations (in the South) in need of slave labor, the cotton being sold to textile mills in England. This triangular trade created enormous profits for the merchants and owners and enormous pain and suffering for those who had been sold into slavery.

The triangular trade in sugar-rum-slaves was one of the causes of the American Revolution. In 1733 Parliament passed the Sugar Act (also known as the Molasses Act), levying a tax upon all molasses purchased from the French West Indies; the intention was to force the American colonies to purchase sugar from the British West Indies. However, British sugar was more expensive than the French, and there was not enough of it to supply the demand; consequently, the act was widely ignored. To bolster enforcement, the British passed the Revenue Act in 1764, and this crackdown on sugar smugglers caused hardships for the New England rum distillers and fostered further resentment of British rule of the colonies.

Rum was a popular drink in the new United States until supplanted by the development of U.S. whiskey in the 19th century. Rum continued to be one of the most popular beverages in England until very recent years. When the British captured Jamaica in 1655, the Royal Navy stopped granting its seamen a daily ration of French **brandy** and substituted a daily ration of rum. The ration was served neat, or mixed with a small amount of **lemon juice** (which helped prevent scurvy), but in 1740 the Royal Navy began watering down the rum ration to minimize its alcoholic effects. This mixture of water and rum became known as grog, after the grogram cloak worn by Admiral Edward Vernon, who first directed the mixing of the rum ration with water. The Royal Navy continued this practice until 1970, when **beer** replaced the rum ration.

In New South Wales, Australia, rum became a medium of exchange (a substitute for money). Governor William Bligh (who had lost his ship HMS *Bounty* to a mutiny in 1787), thinking to curb a problem with drunkenness, outlawed the use of rum as a substitute for money, but this provoked a mutiny of the New South Wales Corps, who arrested Bligh and took control of the colony until a new governor arrived.

Nowadays, rum is made mostly from molasses, though some producers use sugarcane juice. **Yeast** is added to start the fermentation process, and different yeasts will cause the rum to have varied tastes and aromas. Afterward, the mixture is distilled, using either pot stills or column stills. Then the rum is aged, often in wooden barrels but sometimes in stainless steel tanks, for extended periods. Filtering and blending to adjust the final color and taste complete the process.

Rum is usually classified according to the following types:

- Light Rums, also known as silver or white rums: These are clear and generally sweet but have little other flavor and so are best used in making mixed drinks and cocktails.
- Gold Rums, also known as amber rums: These are medium-bodied, usually yellowish in color, having darkened from aging in wooden barrels, and are flavored by the addition of spices and caramel.
- Dark Rums: These are much darker in color, having been aged for longer periods in charred casks; they have a strong flavor, with hints of spices and molasses, and are used in many rum drinks and in cooking.
- Flavored Rums: These have had **mango**, orange, citrus, or **coconut** flavors added and are generally used in tropical fruit drinks.
- Overproof Rums: These rums have more than 40 percent alcohol and are commonly 150 to 160 proof.
- Premium Rums: These are well aged and specially prepared, having more character and flavor than other rums; premium rums are usually consumed neat.

However, there is no worldwide standard for defining or grading rum, so the varying rules and laws of the producing countries apply. For example, some countries require rum to have at least 50 percent alcohol by volume; others, only 40 percent. Some countries require at least eight months of aging; others, a year or two. But there are some general guidelines:

- Spanish-speaking countries traditionally produce light rums.
- English-speaking countries usually make darker, richer rums.
- French-speaking countries produce mostly agricultural rums, those made from sugarcane juice that retain the sugarcane flavor.

Most of the world's rum is produced in the Caribbean islands and in parts of South America. Some of the major brands are Bacardi, Captain Morgan, Cruzan, Mount Gay, Myers, and Pusser's. Among the favorite drinks made using rum are Planter's Punch, Daiquiri, Piña Colada, Mai Tai, Zombie, Mojito, Rum Toddy, and Hot Buttered Rum. Certain liqueurs, such as spiced rum, are also manufactured from rum.

Rum has achieved a special place in the kitchen too. Rum adds a distinctive touch to **coffees**, **teas**, and ciders. It flavors special desserts, such as rum balls and rum cakes, **bananas** Foster, fruit cakes, fritters, ice cream, and some hard sauces for pastries. As a marinade ingredient, rum works wonders on **chicken**, pork, shrimp, and fish. It is also an important component of many Caribbean dishes, and not a few Middle Eastern rich desserts.

Seltzer (Seltzer Water)

Quite simply, seltzer is **water** containing carbon dioxide. Also known as carbonated water, soda water, sparkling water, and club soda, seltzer was inspired by spring-fed mineral waters that naturally contained carbon dioxide and became quite popular in the 19th century as a curative. In the 18th century English chemist Joseph Priestley invented a method of carbonating water (that is, dissolving carbon dioxide in water) by locating a bowl of water over a vat of fermenting **beer**. What he called a method of "impregnating" water was also discovered independently by Swedish chemist Torbern Bergman, who applied sulphuric acid to chalk to produce carbon dioxide. Both men believed the carbonated water would help improve the health of anyone who consumed it.

Nowadays, water is carbonated by passing carbon dioxide through it under pressure, and the pressurization allows more carbon dioxide to dissolve than would be possible under standard atmospheric pressures. This is the reason why carbonated beverages bubble when opened: the release of the pressure allows the gas to emerge from the solution. On old-fashioned seltzer bottles, the release of pressure was controlled by a handle on the side, and the liquid would shoot out in a stream.

Many seltzers are now flavored or tinged with fruit juices, and others are sweetened, flavored, colored, and sold as soft drinks (soda, pop). Seltzer water is also used to make cocktails and fruit spritzers and is a common ingredient in matzoh-ball soup recipes and Middle Eastern lemonades.

Sherry

Sherry is a very specific type of fortified **wine**, made exclusively in Spain from three types of **grapes**: Palomino, Pedro Ximénez, and Muscat (Moscatel). The name derives from the place where it was originally produced, Jérez (in Andalusia, southern Spain), which was known during Moorish times as Xerex (pronounced "shareesh"). At times, sherry has been known as sack. Other countries besides Spain produce sherries, but they must be named according to their place of origin.

Sherry became extremely popular during the 16th and 17th centuries aboard oceangoing ships of the Spanish, British, and French navies. Wines would spoil easily and quickly during ocean voyages because they were subject to huge temperature changes and extreme jostling. Fortifying wines with **brandy** served to stabilize them, as well as making them more alcoholic, so sherries (along with ports and marsalas) became a regular part of the captain's "wine" store.

Sherry begins its life like other wines, but after fermentation it is fortified with brandy. If it is to be a Fino-style sherry, **yeast** is allowed to grow. If it is to be an Oloroso-style sherry, the fortification is so strong that yeast cannot grow. Then the sherry is aged according to the solera system: using a series of casks or other containers, a portion of the sherry from the last barrel is removed and bottled, then the last barrel is filled from the next-to-last, and so forth, until the first barrel is filled with new sherry. Bottling occurs about twice a year.

Several varieties of sherry are commonly identified:

• Amontillado, medium-dry sherries that are medium in color and sweetness between the Finos and Olorosos

- Fino (which means "fine" in Spanish), the driest and palest sherries, consumed young before they become too sweet
- Manzanilla, very pale, dry, and somewhat salty sherries
- Oloroso (which means "scented" in Spanish), sweet, dark sherries that are aged for considerable periods

Other sherries include the cream sherries, the pale cream sherries, and the brown sherries, most of which are made from Olorosos.

For some cooks, sherry has become an essential ingredient. Sherry is used in making vinaigrettes, **mustard**s, and salad dressings, marinades for **chicken** and pork and **lamb**, gravies, jams and jellies, soups, fruit salads, fish and seafood, vegetable dishes, **rice, bread**s, bread pudding, and even chili. It also adds flavor to cakes, fruit bars, cookies, custards, **chocolate** desserts, trifle, and ice cream. Sherry eggnog is also a favorite holiday beverage.

A number of cocktails also rely on sherries; some examples include Apricot Collins, Cream Sherry Flip, In the Sack, Jerez Cocktail, Nelson's Nightcap, Radio City, Spanish Guitar, Winter Garden, and Xerex Cocktail.

Sherry is a very popular ingredient in Middle Eastern recipes, especially in chicken dishes, with **lentil**s and rices, and in desserts.

Tea

Tea comes from the tea shrub (*Camellia sinensis*), which is believed to be native to southeastern Asia, possibly China. Tea has exerted such an influence on human culture that it has become fixed in ancient mythologies. According to Chinese legend, about 3000 B.C.E. the emperor Shen Nung (Shennong) ordered the boiling of all drinking **water** to prevent sickness. One day, while his servants were boiling his water, dried leaves fell into the pot, and the water turned dark. Curious, the emperor tasted the liquid and was refreshed by it; he also found that it eliminated "poisons" from the body. Tea thus became both a medicine and a beverage in China. According to Buddhist legend, it was the Buddha who had this experience of a leaf accidentally flavoring his drinking water. Another legend relates that tea bushes miraculously sprouted from the place where master and monk Bodhidharma, the founder of Zen Buddhism and the Shaolin school of Chinese martial arts, had thrown his eyelids, which he had removed in order to keep himself awake while he was meditating.

Most archaeologists believe that tea was grown and brewed in China by about 1000 B.C.E., though specific written references to tea date from the Tang Dynasty (7th–10th centuries C.E.). During this era, the performer-turned-scholar Lu Yu wrote the *Ch'a Ching (Cha Jing)*, a book that recorded in detail the Chinese methods of tea cultivation and preparation. A Buddhist priest named Yeisei, who had studied in China, brought tea seeds and the culture of tea to Japan, where tea preparation became a form of art, as embodied in the Japanese Tea Ceremony known as *Cha-no-yu*. Tea houses were built to accommodate the ceremonies, and the geishi (geishas), Japan's cultural and artistic hostesses, specialized in performing the tea ceremony. The practice often lost its meditative aspects, but by the 16th century Zen Buddhist priests succeeded in integrating the art of tea so completely into Japanese life that even soldiers meditated over tea before battle.

If Marco Polo ever encountered tea, he never mentioned it; the first European to make reference to tea was Jasper de Cruz, a Portuguese Jesuit priest-missionary, in 1560, soon after Portugal had won trading rights with Japan. The Portuguese shipped tea to Lisbon, where the Dutch purchased it for shipment farther north; by the early 17th century the Dutch had entered the Pacific trade in tea themselves. Tea was initially very expensive, but by the beginning of the 18th century it had become common in food stores in the Netherlands and France. Tea made its way to England by 1600 but did not become the national beverage until Charles II (who grew up in Holland) and his Portuguese bride brought their love of tea with them when he ascended the throne and helped England establish trade routes to Asia. By 1700 tea became so popular in England that a new meal, "afternoon tea," was established as part of the daily routine. So-called low tea was served in aristocratic society and consisted of tea, light refreshments, and conversation. So-called high or "meat" tea was considered the province of the working classes and consisted of a full dinner served with tea. By the end of the 18th century the Royal Navy controlled most of the world's sea-lanes, and the British East India Company had a virtual monopoly on the tea trade. Tea became the primary beverage served in English coffeehouses, and the English also planted tea gardens, where low tea could be enjoyed outdoors.

Earlier, in the 17th century, the Chinese had introduced tea to Russia, and Russians became great tea drinkers, adapting the Tibetan "hot pot" to create the Russian samovar.

Also in the 17th century Dutch settlers brought tea to New Amsterdam (New York). By the early 18th century tea drinking had spread to Boston and Philadelphia, and tea had become an important trading commodity between the American colonies and England. Seeking to cash in on a lucrative business, smugglers found ways to bring contraband tea into the colonies. To protect its monopoly on tea, the John Company (predecessor of the East India Company) pressured the English Parliament to take action, and in 1767 it passed the tea tax, which was promoted as a way to make the colonists pay for the cost of the French and Indian War. To avoid paying the tax, the American colonists reacted by purchasing Dutch tea. When the John Company was merged with the East India Company and allowed to bypass colonial merchants and sell directly to consumers, the American colonists refused to buy any English tea and, in 1773, raided English ships in Boston harbor and tossed hundreds of pounds of tea into the water, an action now known as the Boston Tea Party. Events moved quickly: the British closed the harbor and occupied Boston, and colonial leaders soon declared independence.

Despite the war in the Americas, the British continued their extensive trade in tea with the Chinese. To cure the trade deficit that developed on the British side of the exchange, the John Company (and then the British East India Company) began to grow poppies in India, which the British had recently colonized, and to sell opium to China. Though the caffeine in tea is addictive, opium is much more so, and the British created a limitless market—and also sparked another war. In the Opium War (or wars), which lasted until the early 20th century, British (and other European) military forces prevented the Chinese from forcing the British out of China. At the same time, the British attempted to create tea plantations in India, but their early efforts failed, and Indian tea did not become a profitable enterprise until the end of the 19th century.

Meanwhile, the newly independent United States, looking to develop its own commercial interests, entered the tea trade with China at the start of the 19th century. By constructing fast sailing vessels called clipper ships, and paying with gold instead of opium, the United States was able eventually to end the British monopoly in tea. John Jacob Astor was one of the U.S. merchants who made his fortune in the tea trade.

Iced tea was an invention of necessity at the 1904 World's Fair, as the steamy weather in St. Louis made fair-goers uninterested in sampling hot tea. In 1908 the tea bag was invented, to enable New York restaurants to avoid the mess of loose tea leaves when brewing tea. Tea dances became popular at this time as places for single young men and women to meet and socialize; during Prohibition, the tea dance became a secret opportunity to enjoy bootleg alcoholic beverages, and gay men also gathered for tea as a way of meeting other like-minded men.

Today, tea is grown worldwide, in China, India, Bangladesh, Pakistan, Iran, Korea, Sri Lanka, Taiwan, Japan, Indonesia, Nepal, Australia, Argentina, and Kenya. But tea is not usually classified by its place of origin. Rather, it is classified by its processing. After the tea leaves are picked, they are heated and dried; although this process is called "fermentation," it does not involve true fermentation, but it does stop the leaves from oxidizing (breaking down). The amount of oxidation determines the type of tea:

- White tea consists of young leaves and new buds that have not been oxidized; this tea is relatively expensive.

- Green tea consists of leaves that have undergone only a slight amount of oxidation; this tea is processed within a couple of days after the leaves are picked.

- Oolong tea consists of leaves that have been oxidized for two to three days.

- Black tea (also known as red tea) consists of leaves that are completely oxidized, a process that takes from two weeks to a month.

- Pu-erh tea consists of leaves that have gone through a second stage of oxidation, then aged for some time (perhaps years).

- Yellow tea consists of tea leaves processed in the same manner as green tea leaves, but with a longer drying phase.

Like **coffees**, teas are often blended, to achieve consistent taste and affordability. Some of the more popular blends include

- Breakfast teas, which are blends of black teas
- Jasmine tea, which is flavored with jasmine flowers while it is drying
- Earl Grey tea, which is a mix of black teas with extract of bergamot added
- Indian chai, which is flavored with spices such as **ginger, cardamom, cinnamon, cloves,** and **nutmeg**
- Touareg tea, which is a very strong green tea flavored with **mint**
- Jagertee, which is flavored with **rum**
- Gen Mai Cha, which is a Japanese tea flavored with roasted **rice**
- Lapsang souchong, which is a black tea dried/smoked over burning pine wood

Because tea is so popular, its effects on the body have been extensively studied. Certain teas are high in antioxidants, and there is evidence that drinking tea can help prevent cancer, heart disease, and arthritis, and promote weight loss.

The term "tea" properly denotes an infusion made from tea leaves; other infusions, such as those of other herbs or fruits, may be commonly known as "herbal teas," but they are properly known as "tisanes."

Though probably unknown to peoples of the Bible, all types and colors of tea figure prominently in Middle Eastern recipes.

Vermouth

Vermouth is classified as a fortified **wine**—a wine to which alcohol has been added. Originally, fortifying wine was a method of preservation; nowadays, it is a matter of taste. After being fortified, the wine is aromatized—flavored with aromatic spices and herbs. The Germans used wormwood (*Wermut* in German) to impart the aroma, and the French turned the word into vermouth.

Three styles of vermouth are recognized:

- Dry, about 36 proof (18 percent alcohol), which is white and is used in martinis
- Sweet, about 32 proof (16 percent alcohol), which is either white (bianco) or red (rosso) and is served as an aperitif, usually straight, but also in cocktails
- Half-sweet

The most popular vermouths are now French and Italian made; among these are Martini & Rossi, Cinzano, Campari, and Dubonnet. Cocktails that include vermouth are Dry Manhattan, James Bond Martini, Perfect Rob Roy, and American Beauty.

Water

It may seem odd to "define" or "explain" water in a book about cooking and the history of food, but water is absolutely vital to human life. The human body is more than half water by weight, and all the body's processes depend on water. But the body loses water daily, through perspiration, evaporation, and urination. Although most of the food consumed by humans can consist of as much as 85–95 percent water, this does not yield enough water for the human body to survive. People have to drink water—at least six to eight large glasses a day, and more if one is active or lives in a very dry or cold climate. Other beverages can add water to the body, but usually not enough to supply the body's needs; and alcoholic and caffeinated drinks can even result in the loss of more water. Drinking lots of plain water is the best way to keep the body hydrated. Water does not contain any nutrients except those that might have been mixed in with it, either deliberately or from contact with the earth.

Wine

Wine is, strictly speaking, an alcoholic beverage made by fermenting **grapes** and **grape juice**. Wild grapes were native to the mountainous areas south of the Caspian Sea, and archaeologists believe that the cultivation of grapes began by 8000 B.C.E. in the Fertile Crescent. Fermentation probably followed not long afterward, though the oldest archaeological artifacts of wine production and consumption date from 5400–5000 B.C.E., having been discovered in Hajji Firuz Tepe in Iran. Some scholars maintain that earlier wine has been discovered in Jiahu, China, dating from 7000–6000 B.C.E., but it is not certain whether this fermented beverage had been made from wild grapes or hawthorn fruit. In ancient Mesopotamia, archaeological evidence of wine consumption dates from 3500–3100 B.C.E. By 2700 B.C.E. the ancient Egyptians were importing grapes and possibly wine from Canaan (Palestine); Egyptian tombs depict scenes of wine-making, and wine was included among the provisions buried with the dead to nourish their journey through the afterworld. Egypt had planted its own vineyards for growing wine-making grapes by 2100 B.C.E. The peoples of the Bible certainly drank wine, as it is mentioned in Genesis, the first book of the Bible, in the story of Noah (9:21). The ancient Israelites included wine in all their important rituals, from Passover to Purim, and modern Jews still follow these ancient wine customs. The Greeks introduced wine-making to Europe, planting vineyards in their colonies throughout the Mediterranean, and became large wine exporters themselves. Wine performed an important role in Greek religious ceremonies: libations of wine were offered to the gods for success in battle, bountiful harvests, and plentiful hunting; and certain cults employed wine to inebriate both sacrificial victims and the priests/priestesses who performed the sacrifices. The ancient Romans spread wine culture even farther, planting vineyards in Gaul and Central Europe, classifying grapes, recording vintages, introducing the use of bottles to store wine, and perhaps taking the consumption of wine to excesses hitherto unknown. When early Christians began to develop their rituals and theologies, wine came to stand for the sacrificial blood of Christ. After the fall of the Roman Empire, the Roman Catholic Church and its monasteries preserved and advanced the knowledge of grape growing and the practice of wine-making in Europe. At the same time, the Arab peoples continued to be producers and connoisseurs of fine wine until the rise of Islam in the 7th century C.E., which prohibited (and still does) the consumption of alcoholic beverages. When Europe exploded into creativity during the Renaissance, numerous new wine grape cultivars were developed and wine varieties were produced. During the Reformation, the Roman Catholic Church began to lose its absolute control over the land, and some wine vineyards came under royal or private ownership. In the 16th century Spanish missionaries planted vineyards in Argentina and Chile and, in the 18th century, in California, establishing the beginnings of a thriving wine industry that continues to this day. In the 16th and 17th centuries French and British colonists planted vineyards along the Atlantic Coast of North America, but European grapes did not thrive until crossed with the native wild grapes to produce hardy hybrids. The Dutch transplanted wine grapes to South Africa in the 17th century, and British colonists established vineyards and wine-making in Australia and New Zealand in the 19th century. Today, France, Italy, Spain, the United States, Australia, Argentina, Germany, South Africa, Portugal, Chile, Greece, Georgia (former Soviet republic), Romania, and Hungary are the world's largest producers of wine.

Almost all wine today is made from grapes that are descended from the wild Eurasian grape (*Vitis vinifera sylvestris*), native to the lands between Spain and Central Asia. Some wine is made from native North American grapes (*V. labrusca, V. aestivalis, V. rupestris, V. rotundifolia,* and *V. riparia*); more often, these grapes have been hybridized with *V. vinifera* to produce hardy, disease-resistant varieties. The quality of the wine depends, of course, on the quality of the grape, and many variables affect the taste, juiciness, and aroma of the grapes: the soil of the vineyards, the amount of rainfall and sunshine, the temperatures during the growing season, not to mention the quality of the local **yeast** cultures used in fermentation, the material used to make the wine barrels and casks, the length of fermentation and aging, the blend of grapes used, the additives included, and so on. One year's wine cannot be duplicated the following year.

Making wine is a relatively simple process. Basically, the ripe grapes are harvested and crushed. The result is called must. When yeast is introduced into the must, it causes fermentation, converting the **sugar** in the must to carbon dioxide and alcohol. The carbon dioxide is allowed to evaporate, and the result is an alcoholic beverage called wine.

Generally, wines are named by the grape variety used (such as Sauvignon Blanc and Pinot Noir) or by the place where the wine is made (such as Bordeaux and Burgundy). But there are many ways to classify wines. The most common is by their vinification method:

- Still wines, which are the most common, are either red or white wines. A wine's color is independent of the color of the grape used to make it; rather, red wine is made by allowing the grape skin to remain with the juice mixture during fermentation. Rosé wine is made by leaving the red grape skins in the fermenting mixture for a short time.

- Sparkling wines, such as champagnes, which contain carbon dioxide, retained during the fermentation process or added later
- Fortified wines, such as marsala, madeira, port, and **sherry**, which are sweeter and more alcoholic than still wines, having been fortified with alcoholic spirits
- Distilled wines, such as **brandy**, which are made from fermented grape juice or pomace

Wines can also be classified by harvest year:

- Vintage wines, which are made from the grapes of a single year's harvest, often develop improved flavors as they age.
- Nonvintage wines, which are made from the grapes of multiple harvests, do not improve with age and are intended for immediate consumption.

Vintage wines tend to be more expensive than others, and wines that are deemed to be of superior or super-premium vintage can command tremendous prices as they age; of course, there is also the risk that they will spoil and turn to **vinegar**.

Wines can be classified by taste:

- Dry wines, which contain little residual sugar after fermentation
- Fruity wines
- Sweet wines, which contain significant amounts of residual sugar

And wines can be classified by use:

- Aperitifs (or appetizer wines), which are intended for consumption before eating, to awaken the appetite. Examples include sherry, **vermouth**, and madeira.
- Table wines, which contain no more than 14 percent alcohol by volume. Table wines include:
  - Red dinner wines, which are usually dry, are intended to be served with a meal's main course, usually red meat dishes, stews, or pastas with **tomato** sauce. They are most flavorful when served at room temperature. Examples include claret, Burgundy, Chianti, and Cabernet Sauvignon.
  - White dinner wines, which are either very dry or sweet, are also intended to accompany the main course, usually seafood, white meat, and poultry. Examples include Chablis, wines from the Rhine, Pinot Grigiot, and Chardonnay.
- Sparkling wines, which are usually served at celebratory occasions. Examples include champagne and sparkling Burgundy.
- Dessert wines, which are sweet, are served with desserts. Examples include port, sweet sherry, muscatel, and often rosé.
- Cooking wines, which are the lowest grade of wine and are usually salty.

Wines can also be used to make cocktails, punches, spritzers, and coolers.

Recent medical studies have indicated that drinking one or two glasses of wine daily can lower the risk of coronary heart disease and reduce mortality rates. Overconsumption of wine can, however, increase the risks of liver cirrhosis, mouth cancer, and upper respiratory tract infections. Some people can also have allergic reactions to the sulfites that are added to wines as preservatives; also, the histamines in wine can induce headaches and hangovers.

OILS

Canola Oil

Canola is a cultivar of rapeseed (*Brassica napus*), a plant that is widely grown for animal feed, vegetable oil, and diesel lubricant. Canola was selectively developed (in Canada) to have a low erucic acid content (an acid that can cause health problems), so successfully that canola oil is probably the healthiest vegetable oil available, with a ratio of 15.7:1 of unsaturated to saturated fats. The name canola stands for "Canadian oil, low acid."

Corn Oil

Corn oil is extracted from the kernels of **corn** (technically called maize: *Zea mays*). Corn oil is a healthful alternative to oils made from animal fats, with a ratio of unsaturated to saturated fats of 6.4 to 1. Corn oil is used to make **margarine**, cooking oils, and even salad dressings. In general, corn oil is high in vitamins A (if made from yellow corn) and C and the B vitamins, as well as potassium.

Margarine

Margarine is a catch-all name for a range of **butter** substitutes, made from a wide variety of both animal and vegetable fats and often mixed with **milk** and/or butter. Generally, margarine comes in three main forms:

- Hard, usually colorless, margarine is used for cooking and baking and contains a high percentage of animal fats.
- So-called traditional margarines, which are used as spreads, are made from either animal or vegetable fats and contain a relatively high percentage of saturated fats.
- Mono- or polyunsaturated fat margarine, made from safflower, **sunflower**, soybean, cottonseed, or **olive oils**, are generally considered more healthful than butter or other margarines.

Some of today's table spreads are blends of margarine and butter, providing the taste of butter without the cost or fats.

The history of margarine begins in 1813 when Michel Chevreul discovered what he called margaric acid in animal fats, but in 1853 Wilhelm Heintz realized that margaric acid is really a combination of stearic and palmitic acids found in animal fats. But it was French chemist Hippolyte Mège-Mouriés who first used the name "margarine" when he created oleomargarine in response to Emperor Louis Napoleon III's contest (in the 1860s) to create a butter substitute for soldiers and poor citizens. Mège-Mouriés made his oleomargarine (sometimes referred to as oleo, but commercially sold as margarine) by extracting the liquid from clarified **beef** fat and allowing it to solidify, then combining it with water and butyrin (a liquid fat naturally present in butter). By 1873 margarine was being exported from France, and by 1880 margarine was being made in the United States and other countries.

In the United States, the dairy industry quickly lobbied to restrict the sales of margarine. Laws were passed concerning how margarine could be labeled (it had to be made clear that it was not real butter), and by 1885 the federal government levied a sales tax on margarine and required makers or sellers of it to purchase an expensive license. The most effective means of protecting butter, however, was color bans on margarine. Margarine is naturally white or almost white, and by 1900 many states had passed laws banning the use of yellow food coloring in margarine production. Some manufacturers supplied food coloring capsules along with the tubs or blocks of margarine so that it could be colored before serving. These bans, regulations, and taxes were copied in other countries around the world. Both world wars brought an upswing in the consumption of margarine, as butter was difficult to obtain and very expensive, but the restrictions against margarine were not fully lifted until the 1960s. In the United States, margarine still cannot be sold in packages larger than one pound. Yet by the year 2000, U.S. consumption of margarine was about twice that of butter.

Because of the chemical process of hydrogenation (converting unsaturated fatty acids to saturated ones, to make margarines solid at room temperatures), margarines are made of saturated fats. A process called partial hydrogenation yields the formation of trans-fats as well. Although trans-fats are unsaturated, they have been implicated in causing coronary heart disease and atherosclerosis. Some maintain that this makes margarine less healthy than butter; others argue the opposite. Manufacturers have responded by creating new varieties of margarine that have fewer trans-fats, though often these are not able to be made solid enough for baking. In general, the more solid the margarine (or shortening, or oil), the higher the content of saturated fats and the more adverse the effects on health. Liquid, unsolidified margarines and vegetable oils are best for the health.

Usually, however, margarine can be used in all the ways and for all the same purposes as butter.

Olive Oil

Olive oil is one of the few vegetable oils with a recognizable taste and aroma. Composed primarily of monounsaturated fatty acids, olive oil is extremely beneficial in preventing cholesterol buildup, helping to maintain high levels of the high-density lipoproteins that carry cholesterol out of the blood and to lower the levels of low-density lipoproteins that deposit cholesterol in the arteries.

Made by pressing ripe **olives**, olive oil is available as either virgin (from the first pressing) or pure (from the first and second pressings). Additionally, olive oil is graded according to the presence of free oleic acid, which indicates that the molecules of the oil have begun to break apart: virgin (4 percent free oleic acid); fine virgin (3 percent); superfine virgin (1.5 percent); and extra virgin (1 percent).

Sites in Palestine and Syria indicate that the ancients were pressing olives into oil by about 3500 B.C.E., and it was certainly of widespread use among the peoples of the Bible (Exodus 25:6; Numbers 11:8; II Kings 18:32; Zechariah 4:12; etc.). Olive oil was a real luxury among the Greeks, who used it, for example, as an after-bath moisturizer and as an oil for anointing the dead. As time passed, it became more available and took its place in the common home, providing oil for cooking, oil for lamps, and soap for baths. The Romans cooked the fragrant parts of the olive tree (such as the flowers, leaves, or roots), which they then mixed with olive oil to make a scented oil, or perfume. The Greeks, Hebrews, and Romans also believed olive oil capable of restoring health and adding longevity; and we now know that the olive tree does contain salicylic acid, the active ingredient of aspirin. In ancient Egypt, olive oil was thought to have been used as a lubricant for moving large stones. Throughout the Mediterranean, olive oil helped preserve fish. Today, olive oil is a major staple of Middle Eastern cooking.

Store olive oil in a cool, dark place to prevent it from turning rancid.

Peanut Oil

Peanut oil is extracted from peanuts (*Arachis hypogaea*), which are technically a legume but are consumed as nuts. Unlike other nuts, the peanut pods grow below the ground and must be pulled up and dried before consumption. Also known as goobers, ground peas, ground nuts, earth nuts, and monkey nuts, peanuts are an annual plant native to South America, perhaps Brazil or Peru. Depictions of peanuts have been found on Chimu pottery dating from the 14th century C.E., and either the Chimu or the Incas (who conquered the Chimu in the 15th century) first cultivated peanuts. Christopher Columbus found peanuts in Haiti, and Hernán Cortés found them in Mexico. The peanut's entry into the United States is not documented, but Thomas Jefferson records having grown them, and they quickly became a popular crop. George Washington Carver discovered more than three hundred uses for the peanut, creating peanut soup, peanut-flour **bread**, peanut oil dressing, peanut ice cream, peanut cookies and candy, and even peanut "**coffee**." But peanut butter became the most common of its uses in the United States, followed by roasted, dried, or salted peanuts eaten as a snack food and dried peanuts used to make candy. Peanut agriculture has spread throughout the rest of the world: in the 16th century the Spanish brought peanuts to Malaysia, from where they spread to China and other parts of Asia, and the Portuguese brought them to Africa from Brazil in the 17th century. The peoples outside the

United States have many other uses for peanuts: they are eaten like other dried legumes and beans; they are pressed to make peanut oil; they are ground into flour. Roasted under pressure in safflower or **sunflower oil**, peanuts can also be defatted.

In the United States, commercial peanuts fall into three main types:

- Runners, grown in the U.S. South and Southwest, are usually used to make peanut butter.
- Virginia peanuts are usually sold roasted in the shell.
- Spanish peanuts, which are round with reddish skin, are generally used in candy and are salted as a snack.

Probably because they are legumes, peanuts have more protein than any other nut. They are moderately fatty but are high in dietary fiber. They also provide large amounts of folacin, magnesium, niacin, phosphorus, and thiamin and significant amounts of vitamins B6 and E, copper, iron, manganese, potassium, and zinc.

Peanut oil is generally neutral in flavor, which makes it ideal for cooking dishes that need no flavor competition. It is popularly used to make salad dressings, to fry meats and vegetables, and even to lubricate pasta and **rice** dishes. It is worth noting that many people who suffer allergic reactions to peanuts do not exhibit the same symptoms after having consumed peanut oil, possibly because peanut oil contains very little peanut protein. Peanut oil is found in many Mediterranean and Middle Eastern pastries.

Sesame Oil (Sesame Seed Oil)

Sesame seed oil is extracted from the seeds of the sesame plant (*Sesamum indicum*). This oil is rich in polyunsaturated fatty acids and has a ratio of unsaturated to saturated fats of 4.4 to 1. Sesame oil is used to make margarine, cooking oils, and salad dressings and is a healthful alternative to oils made from animal fats. Remarkably, in both India and China, sesame oil is used as fuel in oil-burning lamps. Sesame oil is the key ingredient in *halvah*, the Middle Eastern confection, and is the base for **tahini**.

Sunflower Oil

Sunflower oil is derived from black-shelled seeds of the sunflower (*Helianthus annuus*). The gray-and-white shelled seeds are those generally used for snacking and cooking purposes. Sunflower oil is high in vitamins B6 and E, copper, magnesium, manganese, niacin, phosphorus, potassium, riboflavin, and zinc. It is also rich in calories, but in terms of its ratio of unsaturated to saturated fats, it is the third best oil to use, behind **canola** and safflower oils.

The sunflower is an annual plant that can reach heights of 10 feet, with flowers reaching a foot in diameter. The name "sunflower" originates in its ability to turn and face the sun, a behavior known as heliotropism. This ability is also recorded in the French and Italian names, *tournesol* and *girasole*, respectively.

Native to the Americas, sunflowers were domesticated sometime about 1000 B.C.E. They did not make their way to Europe, where they are now grown in great abundance, until the 16th century C.E.

What gardeners generally call the flower is actually a composite flower, also known as a head—that is, numerous flowers crowded together. On the outside of the head are yellow, maroon, or orange ray florets, which are sterile. Inside the ray florets are the disc florets, which produce the seeds. Remarkably, the disc florets are arranged in such a way that a pattern of spirals is formed, with one system of spirals going clockwise and an interlacing system going counterclockwise.

Sunflower oil is now a standard ingredient in Middle Eastern recipes.

Vegetable Oil

Many types of vegetable oils are available. The most common are **canola**, safflower, **sunflower**, **corn**, **soybean**, **olive**, **peanut**, **sesame seed**, cottonseed, **palm** kernel, and **coconut**, in order of their ratio of unsaturated to saturated fats (canola having the best ratio). In general, vegetable oils contain less saturated fatty acids than animal oils and are a healthful substitute for them; but it is important to be aware of how a particular vegetable oil compares. For example, coconut oil has a higher percentage of saturated fat than animal oils, while corn oil has a lower percentage. Vegetable oils have a wide variety of uses and have become essential ingredients in salad dressings, in stir-fries, and in cakes and brownies.

Vegetable Shortening

Vegetable shortening is hydrogenated vegetable oil that is solid at room temperature. Hydrogenation is the process whereby unsaturated fatty acids are changed to saturated fatty acids, resulting in the solidification of the oil. Many vegetable shortenings are only partially hydrogenated, but all are 100 percent fat. Shortening gets its name from its ability to inhibit the formation of long **wheat** strands in wheat-based doughs, thus giving them a short texture. Vegetable shortening has become important in the kitchen, used in making pie crusts and shortbread cookies, in particular. The most popular shortening, Crisco, was first produced in 1911. As one might imagine, vegetable shortening is greatly used in Middle Eastern cooking, particularly in **breads** and cakes and in meat dishes.

Walnut Oil

See **walnut**.

OTHER INGREDIENTS

Baking Powder

Baking powder is a leavening agent that is used to make dough rise. First used in the early 19th century C.E., baking powder comes in two forms: single-acting and double-acting. Single-acting baking powder contains acid salts such as **cream of tartar**, calcium phosphate, and citrate that react with alkalis (such as **baking soda**) at room temperature to produce carbon dioxide, a higher temperature, and an increase in the volume of the dough. Double-acting baking powder contains these **salts** and also contains acid salts such as calcium aluminum phosphate that react with alkalis at higher temperatures to create even more carbon dioxide and dough volume.

Many cake, muffin, and **bread** recipes that use all-purpose **flour** call for the addition of baking powder.

Though baking powder (as we know it) did not exist in biblical times, it performs many of the same functions as leaven, a term of frequent biblical usage.

Baking Soda

Baking soda is also known as bicarbonate of soda, sodium bicarbonate, and sodium hydrogen carbonate. It is a crystalline alkali that combines with an acid (such as those in **baking powder**) to release carbon dioxide and **water**. When this reaction occurs in the mixing of doughs and batters, the carbon dioxide serves to increase the volume and raise the temperature of the mixture. Today, baking soda is essential to the success of Middle Eastern **breads**, desserts, gravies, and sauces.

Berry Vinaigrette

Berry vinaigrette is a mixture of **vinegar** that has been flavored and aged with the addition of berries (for example, blueberries, **raspberries**), **vegetable oils** (such as **olive oil** or **sunflower oil**), herbs, and spices. Berry vinaigrette is delicious when used on **lettuce** salads, pastas, and **chicken** dishes.

Bread

Generally speaking, there are two types of bread: unleavened (flat) and leavened (raised).

The making of unleavened breads dates from prehistory, when early humans combined ground grain with **water** and cooked the mixture on hot stones. Flat breads like matzoh, tortillas, and chapatis are still quite popular today.

The ancient Egyptians invented leavened bread, perhaps by accident when wild **yeasts** somehow contaminated **wheat** dough and caused it to rise. Egyptian cooks learned to add a portion of dough from a risen batch to an unleavened dough to cause it to rise too. The Hebrews adopted the Egyptian techniques, and the Romans carried the making of leavened bread to all parts of their world. Though raised bread became commonplace, the process of leavening was not fully understood until quite recently. Louis Pasteur (1822–1895) discovered that yeast is alive and that it causes fermentation, and that this fermentation yields carbon dioxide that in turn makes dough rise.

Bread consists of three necessary ingredients and three optional ones. The necessary ingredients are:

- **Flour**, which is the main ingredient. For flat breads, any type of flour will work, from wheat to **potato** to **corn** to soybean. For raised breads, **wheat flour** is the best, then **rye**. Wheat flour contains proteins that combine with liquid to form gluten. The gluten, in combination with the yeast, creates a strong yet elastic cell network; the cells are able to expand during leavening but remain strong enough to trap the carbon dioxide produced by the action of the yeast. Gluten also traps starch, which solidifies during baking. Both the gluten and the starch provide the bread's texture.

- Liquid, which distributes the flour evenly. In raised breads, the liquid also dissolves and spreads the yeast throughout the dough; the formation of gluten and the solidification of starch also require a liquid. Different liquids produce different types of bread: for example, **water** yields a bread with a crispy, thick crust; **milk**, a bread with a thinner, tender crust. Fruit juice, potato juice, and even **beer** can be used as the liquid in bread-making.
- Yeast, which is necessary only for raised bread. Yeast ferments the carbohydrates present in wheat flour, yielding alcohol and carbon dioxide. The gluten present in the flour traps the carbon dioxide in the dough, and the dough increases in volume. The alcohol evaporates during cooking. Yeast also makes the dough more elastic and sticky and provides certain flavors and aromas.

The nonessential bread ingredients are:

- **Salt**, which strengthens the gluten and controls the multiplication of the yeast. It also adds flavor to the final product.
- **Sugar**, which serves as energy for the yeast at the beginning of the leavening process (though too much sugar will slow the action of the yeast).
- Fat, which increases the dough's elasticity and facilitates the leavening process. It also adds flavor (and calories).

Over the centuries, many different forms of leavened bread have been developed. Some of the more popular are English muffins, French baguettes, Italian bread, focaccia, pita, pumpernickel, **rye**, sandwich bread (white or whole wheat), multigrain breads, challah bread, **cheese** breads, **raisin** breads, potato breads, bagels, croissants, rolls, and sourdough.

Because there are so many different ways to make bread, the nutritional content of bread products will vary widely. In general, wheat breads are very high in phosphorus, thiamin, magnesium, niacin, iron, and folacin and very low in cholesterol, though they also tend to be very high in calories and sodium.

Bread is probably the most important part of the Middle Eastern meal and is usually broken to signify the start of the feast.

Chocolate

Chocolate is a substance made from the beans of the cacao (also known as **cocoa**) tree (*Theobroma cacao*), which is native to the tropical Americas. Christopher Columbus "discovered" cacao beans in 1502 and sent them back to Spain, but they were so bitter that no one was interested in eating them. In 1519, however, Hernán Cortés tasted chocolate prepared by the Aztecs and sent cacao beans and instructions to Spain. Mixed with cane **sugar**, newly introduced into Europe at about the same time, the cacao paste was a chocolate novelty that became popular throughout Europe. Spain kept the recipe a secret and maintained a monopoly on the production of chocolate for almost a hundred years, until expelling its Jewish citizens, who brought the recipes for chocolate-making to France. Chocolate made its way to England in the 17th century, and by about 1700 the English had added **milk** to chocolate. James Baker opened the first chocolate factory in North America, in Massachusetts, in 1765. The Swiss did not begin making chocolate until the mid-19th century; in 1876 they introduced milk chocolate on a commercial scale. Worldwide, more than 600,000 tons of cacao beans are now consumed annually.

The word *chocolate* comes from the Nahuatl language of the Aztecs. They made a drink called *xocoatl* from cacao beans and often flavored it with **vanilla, chili pepper,** annatto, **pimento,** and other spices. The drink was supposed to help prevent fatigue; it was also associated with Xochiquetzal, the Aztec goddess of fertility.

To make chocolate, the cacao beans are fermented, roasted, and ground. Most of the fat of the cacao bean (cocoa butter) is extracted, leaving cocoa liquor, paste, or powder, depending on the amount of dessication. In the process, a lot of the nutrients naturally found in the beans are eliminated. Sugar is usually added, as is vanilla; sometimes **honey, coffee, almond** extract, **mint, cinnamon,** and fruit extracts are also used to add interesting flavors.

There are several types of chocolate available:

- Bitter or unsweetened or baking chocolate, which is used in cooking, has no sugar added. With the addition of sugar, it becomes the basis for cakes, brownies, and cookies.
- Dark (also called plain or sweet) chocolate has sugar but no milk.
- Couverture chocolate, used by professional chefs and sold in specialty food stores, contains a high amount of chocolate liqueur and cocoa butter. Fluid when melted, these chocolates have exquisite flavors. Some common brands include Lindt, Guittard, and Valrhona.
- Milk chocolate is chocolate with milk powder or condensed milk added in.
- Semisweet chocolate, a dark chocolate, has a high sugar content and a low cocoa content; it is used for cooking.
- Bittersweet chocolate is made by adding sugar, cocoa butter, and vanilla to chocolate liqueur; it is not quite as sweet as semisweet chocolate.
- White chocolate is made from cocoa butter without any cocoa solids.
- Cocoa powder is made by grinding partially defatted chocolate liqueur to remove nearly all the cocoa butter; it is used in baking to react with **baking soda** and make the batter rise.

According to recent studies, dark chocolate contains antioxidants that promote cardiac health, help prevent cancer, and counteract mild hypertension. However, eating milk chocolate or white chocolate, or even drinking milk with dark chocolate, can negate any health benefits. Also, chocolate tends to be rich in calories, so too much chocolate can be the cause of other health problems, such as obesity and diabetes. The theobromine and caffeine found in chocolate can act as weak stimulants. There is no conclusive evidence that eating chocolate causes acne.

Chocolate, semisweet

See **chocolate**.

Cider Vinegar

See **vinegar**.

Cornstarch

Cornstarch, sometimes called cornflour, is the starch of the **corn** grain. Used as a thickening or binding agent in puddings, sauces, and gravies, it also serves as an anticaking agent in powdered or **confectioners' sugar**. Cornstarch is an important additive in Middle Eastern candies, casseroles, and vegetable dishes.

Corn Syrup

Corn syrup is extracted from sweet **corn** for use in sweetening other prepared foods. It is a key ingredient found in Middle Eastern pastries, particularly baklava.

Crabapple Jelly

Crabapple jelly is made from the fruit of crabapple trees (*Malus* genus), which are native to the temperate regions of North America, Europe, and Asia (see **apple**). The fruit of crabapples is generally small and sour, often unpalatable. The addition of lots of **sugar** can counteract the bitterness of the crabapples. Although crabapple jelly is a relatively common homemade product, crabapple trees are generally cultivated for their lovely red, white, pink, or purplish spring blossoms, attractive shapes and foliage, and decorative fruit. Crabapple jelly is often found on modern Middle Eastern tables as a side dish to accompany **turkey** breast, *tagines*, and **lamb** casseroles.

Eggs

Human beings have consumed eggs since time immemorial, though for most of prehistoric times the eggs were gathered from the nests of wild birds. Over the millennia, people have eaten the eggs of **ducks**, geese, peacocks, ostriches, plovers, partridges, **quail**, gulls, and **chickens**. (People have also enjoyed eating the eggs of various fishes like sturgeon, **salmon**, **mullet**, shad, and **herring**, as well as the eggs of certain turtles and crocodiles.) Today the three most important eggs commercially are those of the chicken, the duck, and the ostrich, in that order, but chicken eggs were very late in entering the kitchen. The people of India probably first ate chicken eggs when they domesticated wild jungle fowl about 2000 B.C.E. By 1400 B.C.E. the Chinese were artificially incubating eggs; these may have been duck eggs, but chicken eggs were certainly a part of Chinese cuisine by that time. Chickens did not appear in the Mediterranean region until sometime between 1100 and 700 B.C.E. It is possible that the peoples of the Bible had chickens and ate eggs, but the only certain mention of chicken eggs is in the New Testament (Luke 11:12), and it is difficult to know if the few references to eggs in the Old Testament and Hebrew scriptures apply to chicken eggs or to the eggs of other creatures (partridge in Jeremiah 17:11 [KJV]; swallows and sparrows in Psalm 84:3 [The Message]; owl in Isaiah 34:15 [NIV]). The ancient Greeks and Romans ate lots of chicken eggs (but initially little chicken, as the birds were probably too tough and thin for good eating; toward the end of the Roman Empire the people had learned how to raise plumper fowl). During the Middle Ages and the Renaissance, eggs served as a staple and available source of protein, and chickens were kept for their egg-laying qualities and not for eating. While Christopher Columbus probably introduced chickens to the Caribbean, they did not appear in North America until imported by the settlers of Jamestown and Plymouth in the 17th century.

The consumption of chicken eggs today is enormous, and eggs are sometimes used as the standard against which other foods are measured to determine their nutritive value. Chicken eggs are an inexpensive source of high-quality protein; they are also rich in vitamins B12 and E, riboflavin, folacin, iron, and phosphorus. Indeed, eggs would be a near-perfect food were it not for the high cholesterol found in egg yolks. Yet based on recent studies, the American Heart Association has recommended that people with healthy cholesterol levels can eat as many as four whole eggs per week. Egg whites, which are almost pure protein, can be consumed without concern.

Because of the risk that even fresh eggs can carry salmonella bacteria, eggs should be cooked thoroughly before eating. There are numerous ways to cook eggs: boiling, frying, scrambling, poaching; making omelets and French toast; adding them to recipes for pancakes, waffles, cookies, cakes, pies, and other desserts; and using cooked eggs to garnish salads, vegetable dishes, and so on.

Food Coloring

Many foods are artificially colored to make them more attractive to the consumer. Certain foods lose their natural coloring during transport and storage, under varying moisture, light, and temperature conditions. Some foods have natural color variations that make them unappealing. Sometimes food coloring can even protect the flavor and vitamin content of certain foods.

Much food coloring has natural origins. Light-brown coloring comes from caramelized **sugar**. A reddish-orange dye called annatto can be made from a tropical seed. Algae are the source of the green coloring known as chlorella. The red dye cochineal comes from cochineal insects. Other natural colorings come from **beet** juice, **turmeric**, **saffron**, and **paprika** and are common in Middle Eastern dishes, especially those with **rice**.

There are also artificial food colorings. These are known as either dyes or lakes. Dyes dissolve in water and can be used to color beverages, baked goods, dairy products, powdered mixes, and even pet foods. Lakes are made by combining dyes with an insoluble material. Ideal for adding color to foods containing fats and oils, such as chewing gums and hard candies, lakes are oil dispersible.

Some people have adverse reactions, such as hyperactivity, depression, and asthmatic symptoms, to certain artificial food colorings. FD&C Yellow No. 5 and FD&C Red No. 3 in particular, when consumed in large quantities, have been found to be potentially harmful to one's health.

Honey

The Bible mentions honey numerous times, and honey is associated with the stories of biblical heroes such as Moses, Samson, and Jonathan. The peoples of the Bible considered it a necessity, for it was the best or sometimes the only sweetener they had. **Grape** sugar, **carob** pods, **date** or **fig** syrup, even **sugar**cane were not always available and then not often equal to honey. Although keeping bees may date from as early as 2600 B.C.E. in Egypt, the Israelites were too nomadic to tend beehives. For a long time most of the Mediterranean peoples preferred wild honey to domesticated varieties anyway, but the ancient Romans were great practitioners of beekeeping and passed on their art to the peoples they conquered. During the Middle Ages, all feudal manors maintained beehives, and honey continued to be the principal source of sweetening right through the Renaissance, until cane sugar became plentiful enough, cheap enough, and palatable enough to replace honey. In the Americas, both the Aztecs and the Mayans raised bees for their honey. European settlers brought their own bees with them to the Americas, and swarming domesticated bees escaped into the wild and crossed the continent.

Honey bears the distinctive flavor of the flowers from which it is made. Some of the favorites over the centuries are honeys from **thyme**, acacia, **apple** blossom, **orange** blossom, heather, **rosemary**, clover, chaparral, and **sage** blossom. The flower nectar also determines the color of the honey: for example, rosemary honey may be almost pure white, while thyme honey is clear and golden.

Although consumed "raw," honey is a processed food—processed, that is, by the bees themselves. When a bee eats nectar from a blossom, its digestive juices begin to transform the nectar into sugars. At the hive, the gatherer feeds these sugars to the youngest bees, who manipulate it in their mouths to evaporate the **water** content; their glandular secretions cause additional changes too. The young bees then transfer the fluid to the honeycomb, where it undergoes further concentration in the high temperatures maintained inside the hive. After a time, the honey is ready. When the honeycomb is removed from the high temperatures of the hive and the honey removed from the comb, it may crystallize; placing it in warm water will return the crystals to liquid form.

Honey has little nutritive value aside from providing sugar to the diet. Many cooks prefer to substitute honey in dessert recipes calling for processed sugar, but other adjustments to the recipes often need to be made. Honey can also be used in fish dishes and sauces, in salad dressings, as a garnish on nuts, and even to sweeten **wine**. Honey is everpresent in the Middle Eastern kitchen.

Ketchup

Also known as tomato sauce in the United Kingdom and catsup elsewhere, ketchup is a condiment made from **tomatoes**, **vinegar**, **sugar**, **salt**, **allspice**, **cloves**, **cinnamon**, and sometimes **onions**, **celery**, and other vegetables.

The term "catchup" was first used as early as 1690 to denote an East Indian sauce. Up until the end of the 19th century, ketchup was any sauce made with vinegar. In the early days, ketchup was made from **mushrooms** and fish brine with herbs and spices. Other popular ketchup recipes included anchovies, oysters, lobster, **walnuts**, **beans**, **cucumbers**, **cranberries**, **lemons**, and **grapes**. In fact, tomatoes were a late addition to ketchup, as many people of the early 19th century believed that tomatoes were poisonous. Yet a few tomato ketchup recipes from the early 1800s have been found, including one by Thomas Jefferson's cousin Mary Randolph.

The H. J. Heinz Company introduced the first commercial ketchup, and it was a radical departure from previous ketchups. To avoid the use of benzoate as a preservative, the safety of which the U.S. Food and Drug Administration had called into question, Heinz used pickled ripe tomatoes, which had a long shelf-life; previously, unpickled unripe tomatoes had been used, and the ketchups were less vinegary and more bitter and salty. Heinz's recipe made ketchup simultaneously more sour and pungent and sweeter. His innovations influenced the recipes of all modern ketchups, and ketchup has become the premier condiment in use in the United States.

Ketchup is generally high in vitamin C and lycopene, but it is also loaded with sodium and calories. In the Middle East, ketchup is used particularly as a sidedish with falafel, **rice**, beans, roasted meats, and **bread** salads.

Lemon Sorbet

Lemon sorbet (also known as sorbetto or sorbeto) is a frozen dessert made from iced **lemon** purée. Sorbets contain no **milk** and are generally served between the appetizer course and the main course of a meal, in order to cleanse the palate. According to legend, the Roman emperor Nero had snow mixed with **honey** and **wine**, creating the first sorbet. However, the Chinese had been mixing snow, fruit juice, and fruit pulp as a refreshment for hundreds of years before. Food historians believe that Catherine de' Medici brought frozen desserts to France in the 16th century C.E.; by the end of the 17th century, the people of Paris could buy sorbets from street vendors, and sorbets had become popular in England and throughout Europe. Sorbets, made from any number of fruit juices, are a delicious nonfat (or low-fat) dessert. Sorbets are often on the dessert menu of Middle Eastern restaurants and eateries.

Mayonnaise

Mayonnaise is a sauce made from **vegetable oils**, **egg** yolk, **vinegar** or **lemon** juice, **salt**, and spices, often **mustard**s. Usually white or light yellow, it is used as a sandwich spread, a condiment for French fries, and a base for chilled sauces and salad dressings such as

- Aioli, which is **olive oil**, mayonnaise, and **garlic**
- Tartar sauce, which is made by adding **capers** and **pickles** to mayonnaise
- Russian dressing, which is a combination of mayonnaise and **tomato** sauce (or **ketchup**)
- Thousand Island dressing, which is Russian dressing with pickles and herbs added

The first use of the word *mayonnaise* occurred in an English cookbook in 1841. Today, mayonnaise is used in Middle Eastern recipes that feature fish, **rice** or **potatoes**, salads, dips, spreads, and vegetarian fare.

Mint Jelly

Mint jelly is made from the leaves of any number of **mint** species in the *Mentha* genus. To make the jelly, the leaves (and sometimes the stems) are boiled; then the **water** is strained and combined with **lemon juice** and **sugar**. The mixture is boiled again, and fruit pectin is added. After further boiling, the mixture (now a hot jelly) is poured into jars for canning. Variations on this basic recipe would add **apples** or gooseberries, or **lime** juice instead of lemon juice, or other herbs like **basil** and **parsley**. Mint jelly is often served as a sauce or complement to **lamb** or mutton dishes or with steak or **eggplant**s.

Molasses

Molasses, sometimes called treacle, is a thick sugary liquid extract of either the **sugar**cane plant (*Saccharum* genus) or the sugar **beet**.

In the 17th and 18th centuries, molasses was very popular because it was much less expensive than refined sugar. England's American colonies imported great quantities of molasses from the Caribbean, and in 1733 Parliament passed the Molasses Act, which levied a tariff on molasses produced in lands not under British control. This act was one of the first causes of colonial unrest that eventually led to the American Revolution.

Sugarcane molasses is available in three types:

- Unsulphured, the finest quality, is made from the juice of cane that has ripened in the sun; the juice is then clarified and concentrated.
- Sulphured is made from unripe sugarcane and treated with sulphur fumes as the sugar is extracted.
- **Blackstrap** is the result of multiple rounds of processing and boiling of the cane juice. The result of the primary round is called first molasses, which has the

most sugar. Second molasses is the result of a secondary round of boiling and processing, and it is slightly bitter. Additional rounds yield blackstrap molasses, which is considered to be the most nutritious of all.

Sugar beet molasses is the result of the final crystallization stage of the sugar beet juice; intermediate stages yield high-green and low-green juice. Sugar beet molasses is very sweet, about 50 percent sugar, but it is not very palatable and is generally used as livestock feed.

Molasses of either type can be fermented to make **rum**.

Today's largest producers of molasses are the United States, the Philippines, Thailand, Taiwan, Brazil, and India.

Molasses, Blackstrap

Blackstrap molasses comes from **sugarcane** (*Saccharum* genus) and is the result of multiple rounds of processing and boiling of the cane juice. Most of the sugar has been removed, but blackstrap molasses is still an energizing mineral-rich sweetener, very high in iron, manganese, copper, potassium, calcium, magnesium, vitamin B6, and selenium. It is sold in most health-food stores. It is also used to flavor baked beans, gingerbread, cookies, cakes, and **turkey** and **chicken** dishes. Blackstrap molasses is considered the premier type of **molasses**.

Orange Marmalade

Orange marmalade is a sweet jam-like spread made from **orange**s, usually large sour oranges from Seville, with orange peel, **sugar**, and a gelling agent. It is most often spread on toast, muffins, bagels, and other **bread** products.

Marmalades were probably first made by the ancient Greeks, who slow-cooked quince with **honey** to make a thick, sweet-and-tart spread. The ancient Romans learned from the Greeks and added new **wine** to produce a particular Roman marmalade. The English learned about marmalades from the French by the 15th century C.E., and in the 17th century, when England began to import a plentiful supply of citrus fruit, marmalade began to be made with oranges and **lemons**. As a result of Britain's worldwide empire, marmalade is now popular around the globe, and is quite popular in the foods of Middle Eastern kitchens.

Salt

Salt, also known as table salt and edible salt, is basically sodium chloride, with other trace minerals. Essential for regulating the body's fluid balance, salt is available in crystalline form in rock deposits or dissolved in sea **water**. Salt is also a superb food preservative.

The use of salt predates the historic record, and the earliest humans ingested salt when consuming foods (especially meats) and beverages (like **milk**) that are naturally salty. With the advent of herding and then of agriculture came the need to provide seasonings for food—both to improve the flavor of vegetables and to obtain the necessary amounts of salt. The invention of cooking pots made the need for added salt even more imperative, as the natural salt content of meats, which is conserved during roasting, leaches during boiling. Neolithic humans obtained some salt from the ash left by burning salty plants, but it was not enough, and other sources were needed. Discovering that certain earths, such as former seabeds, were rich sources of salt, people began to mine rock salt. Some of the oldest salt mines are in Austria, though Asia, Africa, and the Americas have many salt plains where rock salt is plentiful. At the same time, some coastal peoples began to obtain salt by evaporating sea water. But quantities of salt were extremely difficult to obtain in some regions, and salt became one of the earliest and most highly valued trading commodities, carried over the deserts by camel caravans, over the oceans by convoys of sailing vessels, and over roads built especially for the transportation of salt by ox- and donkey- and horse-drawn wagons. At times, salt was so precious that it was traded for an equivalent weight of gold: hence the saying "worth its weight in gold." Conflicts arising over the salt trade caused wars and brought about the rise and fall of governments.

All of the ancient peoples knew the importance of salt, and salt figures importantly in the Bible stories: the ancient Israelites even included salt in their sacrificial offerings to God. Salt also played a role in the religious rituals of the ancient Aryans, Egyptians, Greeks, and Romans. Among the Semitic peoples, an offer of salt was an offer of hospitality, with its accompanying obligations of protection, but casting salt across the threshold of a house or tent was a warning that strangers were not welcome. This custom was perhaps the beginning of the superstition that spilling salt brings bad luck—though because salt was so expensive, wasting it would certainly not have been looked upon favorably. One of the most prominent representations of this superstition is Leonardo da Vinci's painting *The Last Supper,* which depicts Judas overturning his salt container. The Christian Church embraced the belief in salt's sanctity and spread the idea that salt was a protection against the devil and other lesser demons.

Perhaps the first to do so, Chinese governments taxed salt as long ago as 2200 B.C.E. Ancient Roman soldiers received their pay in quantities of salt, and the Romans established salt roads through much of Europe for the safe transportation (and taxation) of this precious commodity. Cities, states, dukedoms, and nations have imposed salt duties and taxes right up till the present, the best known being the salt tax that sent Mahatma Gandhi on a march to the sea in 1930 (see **sea salt**). Salt even influenced the location of cities: Timbuktu was an enormous salt market, and Liverpool became a large port to accommodate exports of salt mined nearby. At the end of the 19th century, mechanization made the mining of salt much easier, and the price of salt became more reasonable. The addition of iodine to salt also made it better for one's health.

The main types of salt include:

- Unrefined salt (also called sea salt).
- Refined salt, mainly sodium chloride, is today prepared primarily from rock salt (mineral deposits that contain large quantities of edible salt), formed

centuries or millennia ago by the evaporation of salt lakes. Rock salt is often mined, but water may also be injected into the ground to dissolve the salt, and the brine solution can then be pumped to the surface for the removal of the salt. The salt is then purified through a process of recrystallization, multiple evaporations, and kiln drying. Anticaking agents (such as potassium iodide, tricalcium phosphate, and magnesium oxide) are added, to absorb humidity and prevent the salt crystals from sticking together. Refined salt is sold primarily for commercial purposes.

- Table salt is about 95 percent sodium chloride and is usually iodized by the addition of potassium iodide. Iodized table salt has helped prevent hypothyroidism, goiter, cretinism, and myxedema by enabling the thyroid to produce the hormones necessary to keep the body functioning properly. Table salt is used in cooking and as a seasoning.

Over the centuries, salt has been used to preserve fish and meats for long storage because bacteria, fungi, and other organisms that might cause decomposition or disease cannot live in a highly salty environment. During times of religious fasting, fish was the only permitted "meat," and salting it was the only way to transport and preserve it. Pickling is another form of salting, using brine (salt water) instead of dry salt. Today, certain meats (ham, bacon, **sausage**), **cheeses**, and fish are still salted for taste.

Just as the lack of salt can cause health problems by disrupting the body's electrolyte balance, the excessive consumption of salt can cause high blood pressure. Persons with high blood pressure are often required to follow a low- or no-salt diet, and salt substitutes (such as products containing potassium chloride) are readily available at the grocery store.

Salt, Kosher

Unlike common table **salt**, kosher salt contains no additives. Salt is called kosher not because of the way it is produced (which is exactly the same as table salt is produced) but because it is used to make meats kosher: when meats are coated in large-grained kosher salt, the salt does not dissolve, and the blood is allowed to leach out of the meat, rendering it kosher.

Salt, Sea

When sea water evaporates, the residue that is left is called sea salt. Often used in cooking and sometimes used in making cosmetics, sea salt is not pure sodium chloride like table **salt** but contains other minerals that impart a slightly different taste. France (*fleur de sel*), Ireland, Hawaii, and Cape Cod are four places that continue to specialize in producing sea salt, though in the past sea salt was the only source of salt for many peoples. Sea salt has also played an important role in political history: for example, in 1930 Mahatma Gandhi led thousands of people on a march to the sea to collect salt rather than pay the British government's salt tax, a protest that came to be known as the Salt Satyagraha.

Though some gourmets believe that sea salt is superior to table salt, particularly in taste, most sea salt is only about 20 percent sodium chloride by weight. Additionally, sea salt contains much less iodine than iodized table salt, and the thyroid gland needs iodine to function properly.

Many Middle Eastern recipes call for sea salt to enhance delicate flavors.

Soy Sauce

Soy sauce (also known as soya sauce) is a sauce made by fermenting a mixture of soybean (*Glycine max*) juice, roasted grain, **water**, and **salt** (or **sea salt**). Alcohol is usually added during bottling as a preservative. This salty brown sauce originated in China, but its use has spread throughout Asia. However, Chinese soy sauces are not the same as Japanese: Chinese soy sauces are made primarily from soybeans and have only small amounts of other grains, while Japanese soy sauces are made primarily from **wheat** and are slightly sweet. One type should not be substituted for another.

Because soy sauces are salty (even low-salt brands), persons on low- or no-salt diets should avoid them. Additionally, soy sauce contains naturally occurring MSG (monosodium glutamate), so lactose-intolerant persons may not be able to digest it.

Soy sauce is used to flavor **beef**, pork, fish, and **chicken** dishes, vegetables, noodles, **rice**, sushi, soups, and numerous other foods.

Soy sauce is now appearing often in Middle Eastern restaurants and at takeout stands.

Sugar

Sugar (sucrose) is an extract of certain plants, such as sugarcane (*Saccharum* genus), sugar **beets** (*Beta vulgaris*), the **date** palm (*Phoenix dactylifera*), sorghum (*Sorghum vulgare*), and the sugar maple (*Acer saccharum*). The vast majority of the world's sugar comes from sugarcane or sugar beets.

Sugarcane no longer exists in its wild state, so its exact origins are unclear. Many botanists believe that it is native to New Guinea; others, to the Indian subcontinent. It seems to have spread rapidly into Malaysia, Indonesia, Indochina, and southern China. The first record of sugarcane cultivation dates from the 8th century B.C.E. in China, but it is likely that cultivation and even processing had begun at a much earlier date. It probably reached Persia by the 5th century B.C.E., and Alexander the Great's army brought news of sugarcane back to the Mediterranean region with them—but did not bring any plants, sugar, or cane juice. Neither the ancient Greeks nor the Romans sweetened their food or sought the source of the stories of sugarcane. Sugar finally made its way to Europe, but the time and source are, again, obscure; either the Crusaders carried it back with them from the Holy Land, or the Arabs began a trade in sugar products. What is certain is that by the 13th century C.E. Venice had established a sugar monopoly, at first importing processed sugar from Alexandria in Egypt, and by the 15th century purchasing sugarcane and refining it within its own boundaries. The Italian aristocracy went crazy over sugar, adding it to almost every dish, as did the French nobles in the 14th century. But sugar remained a medicinal, used to treat various ailments from melancholy to fever, and did not become common in the kitchen until the 15th century, when Italian cooks began to follow the Arab example of making desserts that relied heavily on sugar. The Portuguese explorer Vasco da Gama ended the Venetian monopoly in sugar trading when he reached India in 1498, and Lisbon became Europe's sugar capital; the Portuguese planted sugarcane in the Cape Verde Islands and even the Canaries.

The colonization of the Americas, and the early establishment of sugarcane plantations in the Caribbean, changed history. Christopher Columbus first planted sugarcane in the West Indies in 1494; within a few years, the Spanish had planted sugarcane in Hispañola, Cuba, and Mexico, the Portuguese in Brazil, the Dutch in their island and mainland holdings, the English in Barbados, and the French in Martinique. The demand for sugar became insatiable, driving planters to establish huge cane farms. By the 17th century, sugar was worth its weight in gold. Sugarcane cultivation is extremely labor-intensive, and abundant, cheap labor was needed—and at that time in history, cheap labor meant slavery. At first, the native peoples were enslaved to work the plantations, but the working conditions, along with exposure to diseases like smallpox against which they had no immunities, decimated their numbers. The Spanish, Portuguese, French, and English began to import African slaves, who were resistant to malaria and yellow fever. From the Caribbean, slavery spread north and south; and slavery became an established institution in North America, transferring its work force to cotton and tobacco plantations. The New England colonies exported salt cod to the West Indies to feed the slaves; in return, the plantations sent **molasses** to New England and sugar to England. New Englanders soon had a surplus of molasses, so it was fermented into **rum** and loaded aboard ships bound for Africa, where the rum was traded for slaves.

Originally, sugar was extracted from sugarcane by means of chewing. Early refining processes involved grinding or pounding the cane to extract the juice, then boiling the juice (or drying it in the sun) to produce gravelly sugar crystals. The improvement of the sugar press in the 1390s permitted the expansion of sugarcane refining. By the mid-16th century the Portuguese had built hundreds of sugar mills in Brazil, and the Spanish, Dutch, French, and English had many of their own. By the beginning of the 18th century, the supply of sugar could not keep up with the demand generated by the European consumption of jams, candies, **teas**, and **coffees**, and the price of sugar reached astronomical levels.

In 1747 a German chemist named Andreas Marggraf discovered that **beets** are a rich source of sugar. The sugar beet thrives in cooler climates, in northern and eastern Europe (as well as parts of northern Asia, northern Japan, and parts of North America), so the beet was quite common in Europe. A sugar beet processing factory was constructed in Prussia, and sugarcane's monopoly of the sugar industry was breached. To remove sugar from beets, the vegetables were washed, sliced, and pressed; the juice was filtered and concentrated by evaporation; sugar was extracted by crystallization. Small refinements to the process have been made since then. The sugar beet became even more important as a source of sugar during the Napoleonic wars, when the British blockade kept sugarcane sugar out of continental Europe. Sugar processed from sugarcane is indistinguishable from sugar processed from beets, and since the 19th century the beet sugar industry has grown to equal the cane sugar industry.

As a result of the growth of sugar beet processing in the 19th century, sugar started to become available to people of all economic classes. The invention of the Mason jar and the canning process in 1858 increased the demand for sugar—white sugar, that is, as neither brown sugar nor molasses is suitable for home canning. Since then, the availability and price of sugar has risen and fallen according to world economic conditions, sugar becoming scarce and expensive in wartime and common and less expensive at other times. Today, sugar is part of nearly every processed food, but the supply, about 134 million metric tons annually, manages to keep up with the demand. At present, sugarcane is cultivated primarily in Australia, Brazil, Cuba, and Thailand, and sugar beets primarily in northern Europe, Russia, the Ukraine, and the United States.

Sugar can be divided into the following categories:

- Raw sugars, yellow to brown in color, are made from clarified cane juice reduced to a crystalline solid; minimal chemical processing is involved.
- Mill white sugar (also known as plantation white sugar, crystal sugar, and superior sugar) is raw sugar that has been bleached white; the impurities have not been removed, and discoloration and clumping tend to occur.
- *Blanco directo* is made from cane juice that has had many impurities removed through chemical treatment.
- White refined sugar is made by purifying raw cane sugar, then decolorizing it by filtration methods. Beet sugar refineries usually produce white refined sugar directly. White refined sugar is commonly sold in granulated form, dried to prevent clumping, in different crystal sizes:
  - coarse-grained, for decorating desserts
  - normal-grained, for table use
  - finer grades, such as caster (used in baking) and superfine (used to sweeten drinks)
  - finest grades, such as powdered sugar, confectioners' sugar, and icing sugar, which are ground to a powdery consistency
  - sugar cubes, for standard convenience
- Brown sugar is made by removing the sugar before it has been bleached free of molasses or by introducing cane molasses syrup into white refined sugar.

Sugar is usually classified as a carbohydrate, and it generally contains no vitamins, minerals, or fiber but does contain loads of calories. In modern times, the overconsumption of sugar has been linked to increasing rates of diabetes and obesity. All sugars are used extensively in Middle Eastern cooking.

Sugar, Brown

Brown sugar is often used in baking. It results when **sugar** is removed from the refining process before all the color has been bleached out. It can also be made by coating the granules of white refined sugar with cane **molasses** syrup.

Sugar, Confectioners'

Confectioners' sugar is among the finest grades of white refined **sugar**. It is made when white refined sugar is ground to a powdery consistency. Confectioners' sugar is used in making candies, frosting, and other dessert items.

Vinegar

Quite simply, vinegar is **wine** that, left undisturbed, has gone sour. Vinegar was probably discovered by accident more than 10,000 years ago. Archaeologists believe that the ancient Babylonians used vinegar as a preservative (once they learned that it slows or stops the spoiling of food) and as a cleaning solution. In Greek mythology, Helen of Troy was said to have bathed in vinegar. The Greek physician Hippocrates prescribed vinegar for many ailments. Legend has it that Cleopatra, queen of Egypt, dissolved a string of pearls in vinegar, having wagered that she could consume a fortune in a single meal. According to stories, General Hannibal, when crossing the Alps to invade Rome, poured vinegar on heated boulders to crack them apart and remove them from the path of his elephants. Roman soldiers subsisted on cheap wine, which was probably vinegar in all but its name. The peoples of the Bible certainly relied upon vinegar; it is referred to as a drink (Numbers 6:3) and as a condiment (Ruth 2:14), though it is usually mentioned as a retribution or punishment for bad deeds (Psalm 69:21 and Proverbs 10:26), or as a way of mocking crucified prisoners (Matthew 27:34 and 48; Mark 15:36; Luke 23:36; John 19:29–30). The Talmud mentions vinegar as an ingredient for *haroset*.

During the 14th-century Black Death (Plague), desperate people tried to protect themselves by washing in vinegar. In the 17th century, vinegar served as a deodorant, scenting sponges that the aristocracy held to their noses to mask the odor of sewage in the streets. Naval crews used vinegar both as a preservative and as a cleaning agent for the decks of their ships. It is still a very effective and environmentally friendly household agent, used for cleaning windows, clearing drains (when mixed with **baking soda**), and softening fabrics during laundering, though today seldom used in this way. Doctors used vinegar to treat battlefield wounds during World War I, and white vinegar is still a good antiseptic treatment for rashes and insect bites. And vinegar will not go bad—it has an indefinite shelf-life and so is a ready topical medicine and a perfect preservative.

Usually 3–5 percent acetic acid by volume, vinegar can also contain tartaric acid, citric acid, and other acids. Vinegar is generally classified by its source:

- Malt vinegar is made by malting **barley**, turning the starch to **sugar**, brewing an ale from the sugar, then allowing the ale to turn into vinegar. Malt vinegar is the favorite condiment for fish and chips.
- Wine vinegar is made from allowing red or white wine to turn into vinegar. Special wine vinegars include those made from champagne and **sherry**.
- Apple vinegar (also called cider vinegar) is made from **cider** or **apple** must.
- White vinegar may be a simple solution of acetic acid in water, or it may be oxidized from distilled alcohol.
- **Balsamic vinegar** is a special, flavorful vinegar originally from Italy.
- Rice vinegar is made from **rice** wine. It may be red, black, or white, and is much used in Japan and China.
- Coconut vinegar comes from the sap of the **coconut** palm tree. It is popular in southeastern Asia and India.
- Cane vinegar is made from sugarcane juice, though it is not sweet at all.
- Raisin vinegar, made from **raisins**, is often called for in Middle Eastern recipes.
- Beer vinegar varies in flavor depending on the type of **beer** it is made from. It is popular in Germany, Austria, and the Netherlands.
- Honey vinegar, made from **honey**, is a rarity, produced mostly in Italy and France.
- Flavored vinegars are made by adding fruits, herbs, or spices to vinegar, usually white vinegar. Some common additives include **raspberries**, blueberries, strawberries, blackberries, **thyme, oregano, tarragon, rosemary, basil, shallots**, and **onions**.

In the kitchen, vinegar is an essential ingredient of vinaigrettes and most salad dressings. Pickling recipes, marinades, barbecue sauces, gelatin, and even meringue call upon vinegar. Condiments such as **ketchup, mayonnaise, mustard**, and salsa all contain vinegar.

Vinegar, Balsamic

Balsamic vinegar is a special dark-colored **vinegar** that was first produced in Modena, Italy, in the Middle Ages. Made from the concentrated juice (must) of white (often trebbiano) **grapes**, it has a complex flavor that is both rich and sweet, the result of years of aging in casks made from oak, **mulberry**, ash, chestnut, **cherry**, and **juniper**. Lower-quality Balsamic vinegar is aged for at least three years; the best-quality (*tradizionale*) may be aged for as long as twenty-five years and may sell for as much as $400 per bottle. There is also commercial-quality Balsamic vinegar, which has no legal aging requirements.

The best Balsamic vinegars are sometimes consumed alone or as a topping for strawberries and other fruits. The commercial-quality and lower-quality Balsamics are most often used in salad dressings, sauces, gravies, and marinades.

Worcestershire Sauce

Worcestershire sauce (also called Worcester sauce) is a fermented mixture of **vinegar, molasses, corn syrup, water, chili peppers, soy sauce, pepper**, tamarinds, anchovies, **onions, shallots, cloves**, and **garlic**. Created in the 19th century by the British during their rule of India, Worcestershire sauce became a commercial success when branded and marketed by Lea & Perrins in 1838.

Worcestershire sauce is used to flavor fish, **beef**, and pork, as a marinade or a cooking sauce; it is also an ingredient in the dressing for Caesar salad and in the **Bloody Mary** cocktail, as well as many Middle Eastern dishes.

Yam

The dozens of species of yams (*Dioscorea* genus) are believed to have originated in western Africa, where they still grow wild, and were probably first cultivated by 8000 B.C.E. The first written mention of yams occurs in a 3rd century B.C.E. Chinese poem. In between, the cultivation of yams spread eastward along the trade routes. Yams are now found around the world; because they can be stored for four to six months without refrigeration, they are still a food staple in large portions of Africa, Asia, and Oceania. Though yams are not mentioned in the Bible, they are very common in contemporary Middle Eastern cooking.

Yams usually have yellow or white flesh, though the outsides can be brown, white, yellow, or red. Generally, a yam will weigh between 2 and 8 pounds when harvested, though yam tubers of up to 150 pounds have been recorded.

Yams are high in vitamins A, B6, and C as well as calcium, potassium, and iron, and they are a good source of fiber. They can be baked and eaten plain or used in **breads** and other baked goods or in combination with **chicken** or other meat and vegetable dishes.

It is important to note that yams are not the same thing as sweet potatoes, which belong to the *Ipomoea* genus; that's why we put them at the end of the book—so you wouldn't get confused!

Yeast

Yeast is a general name for single-cell fungi that have the capability of multiplying extremely rapidly under certain conditions. Most yeasts are strains of *Saccharomyces cerevisiae*. It is important in the making of leavened (risen) **bread** and other baked goods. Yeast ferments the carbohydrates present in **wheat flour**, yielding alcohol and carbon dioxide. The gluten present in the flour traps the carbon dioxide in the dough, and the dough increases in volume. The alcohol evaporates during cooking. Yeast also makes the dough more elastic and sticky and creates unique flavors and aromas.

Though many Middle Eastern religious practices prescribe bread-making without yeast, it is a key ingredient of most Middle Eastern breads today.

Appendix A
Biblical Weights and Measures

Bible	American/British	Metric
Weight		
Talent	75 lb.	34 kg
Mina	1.25 lb.	0.6 kg
Shekel (2 bekahs)	0.4 oz.	11.5 g
Pim (⅔ shekel)	0.33 oz.	7.6 g
Bekah (10 gerahs)	0.2 oz.	5.5 g
Gerah	0.02 oz.	0.6 g
Dry Capacity		
Cor (Homer) (10 ephahs)	6 bushels	220 l
Lethek (5 ephahs)	3 bushels	110 l
Ephah (10 omers)	0.6 bushels	22 l
Seah (⅓ ephah)	7 qt.	7.3 l
Omer (1/10 ephah)	2 qt.	2 l
Cab (1/18 ephah)	1 qt.	1 l
Liquid Capacity		
Bath (1 ephah)	6 gal.	22 l
Hin (⅙ bath)	4 qt.	4 l
Log (1/72 bath)	0.33 qt.	0.3 l
Length		
Cubit	18 in.	0.5 m
Span	9 in.	23 cm
Handbreadth	3 in.	8 cm

Sources: *Bible Encyclopedia*, WebBible Encyclopedia, ChristianAnswers.net

❧ Appendix B ❧
Scripture Cake

Making a Scripture Cake is a fun way to become more acquainted with the scriptures and to learn more about what foods were important to the peoples of the Bible. There are many variations on this concept. Here are just two:

❧ Scripture Cake

1. 8 oz (225 g) Judges V:25, last clause (butter)
2. 8 oz (225 g) Jeremiah VI:20 (sugar)
3. 1 tablespoon (115 ml spoon) 1 Samuel XIV:25 (honey)
4. 3 Jeremiah XVII:11 (eggs)
5. 8 oz (225 g) 1 Samuel XXX:12, chopped (raisins)
6. 2 oz (50 g) Numbers XVII:8, blanched (almonds)
7. 8 oz (225 g) Nahum III:12 chopped (figs)
8. 1 lb (450 g) 1 Kings IV:22 (flour)
9. Season 2 Chronicles IX:9 (spices)
10. Pinch Leviticus II:13 (salt)
11. 1 teaspoon (15 ml spoon) Amos IV:5 (baking powder)
12. 3 tablespoons (45 ml) Judges IV:19 (milk)

Beat numbers 1, 2, 3 to a cream. Add 4, one at a time. Add 5, 6, 7 and beat well. Add 8, 9, 10, and 11, having mixed them together. Lastly add 12. Put in a lined tin and bake in a slow oven at 150°C, 300°F, for 1½ hours.

Source: Adapted from *The Scots Independent Newspaper Online—The Flag in the Wind*, www.scotsinde pendent.org. Friendship & Scripture Cake recipes reprinted by permission of Alastair McIntyre KTJ, FAS Scot. (www.scotsindependent.org)

❧ *Pennsylvania Dutch Scripture Cake*

½ cup Judges 5:25

2 cups 1 Kings 4:22

½ tsp. Leviticus 2:13

1 cup 1 Samuel 30:12 (first ingredient)

1½ cups Jeremiah 6:20

2 tsp. Luke 13:21

½ cup Genesis 24:11

1 cup 1 Samuel 30:12 (second ingredient)

3 Isaiah 10:14

1 Tbsp. Proverbs 24:13

½ cup Genesis 43:11

add spices (cinnamon) from 1 Kings 10:10

Preheat oven to 375°F. Blend butter, sugar, spices, and salt. Beat egg yolks and add to butter mixture. Sift in baking powder and flour; then add the water and honey. Put fruit and nuts through chopper and flour well. Follow Solomon's advice for making good boys. See first clause of Proverbs 23:14, then fold in stiffly beaten egg whites. Pour into greased and floured loaf pan. Bake for 1 hour.

Source: Pennsylvania Dutch Scripture Cake recipe reprinted by permission of Christian Crafters; obtained from www.christiancrafters.com , "Home of the Sunday School Teacher's Network."

Bibliography

About.com. Home Cooking. http://homecooking.about.com

Aish HaTorah. www.aish.com

All Recipes.com. http://bread.allrecipes.com/az/RmnvRssinBlckBrd.asp

Amplified Bible. The Lockman Foundation, 1987. www.Lockman.org

Beck, Barb. "Date-Manna Bread Recipe." FatFree.com: The Low Fat Vegetarian Recipe Archive. www.fatfree.com/recipes/breads-quick/date-manna-bread

Bible Gateway.com. www.biblegateway.com

Bodenheimer, F. S. "The Manna of Sinai." *The Biblical Archaeologist* 10 (1947).

Botanical.com. www.botanical.com

British Broadcasting Corporation. "Women's Lives." www.bbc.co.uk/religion/programmes/mary/evidence/8.shtml

Brown, Raymond E. *The Gospel According to John.* Vol. 29, The Anchor Bible Series. Garden City, N.Y.: Doubleday, 1978.

———. *An Introduction to the New Testament.* New York: Doubleday, 1996.

Carey, George. *Bible Study Notes: Life of Christ: John 2:1-11* www.geocities.com/npford/loc18.html?20052

Cayce, Edgar. *Edgar Cayce on Jesus and His Church.* New York: Warner Books, 1988.

Cheese Factory Restaurant. www.cookingvegetarian.com

Christian Answers.net. "Bible Encyclopedia." www.christiananswers.net/dictionary/weights.html

The Columbia Encyclopedia. 6th ed. New York: Columbia University Press, 2005.

Cox, Wade. "Wine in the Bible (No. 188)." Christian Churches of God. www.ccg.org/english/s/p188.html

Crawford, Patricia L. "Balm." In *Harper's Bible Dictionary.* Edited by Paul J. Achtemeier et al. San Francisco: Harper & Row, 1985.

Cutler, Daniel S. *The Bible Cookbook: Lore of Food in Biblical Times Plus Modern Adaptations of Ancient Recipes.* New York: William Morrow, 1985.

Daily Life through History. Westport, Conn.: Greenwood Press, 2005.

The Darby Translation of the Bible. www.biblegateway.com

Diamant, Anita, with Howard Cooper. *Living a Jewish Life: Jewish Traditions, Customs, and Values for Today's Families.* New York: HarperCollins, 1991.

"Did John the Baptist Eat Carob Tree Fruits or Bugs?" www.geocities.com/Athens/Parthenon/3664/locusts.html

Dodd, C. H. *The Interpretation of the Fourth Gospel.* Cambridge: Cambridge University Press, 1978.

Eager, George B. "Bread." In *The International Standard Bible Encyclopedia.* www.studylight.org/enc/isb

Farah, Madelain. *Lebanese Cuisine.* New York: Four Walls Eight Windows, 1985.

Fremlin, Maria. "Wings of Life Bread." http://maria.fremlin.de/recipes/wings.html

Garden Guides.com. www.gardenguides.com

Gernot Katzer's Spice Pages. http://webdb.uni-graz.at/~katzer/engl

Goodman, Naomi, Robert Marcus, and Susan Woolhandler. *The Good Book Cookbook.* Grand Rapids, Mich.: Fleming H. Revell, 1995.

Goodwin, Mimi, private correspondence. Recipe for *Mejeddarah.* Adapted.

Grieb, Ron. *Understanding God's Love: A Study of the Misunderstanding and Misrepresentation of God.* Casco, Mich.: Christian Traditions Publishing, 1999.

Grossinger, Jennie. *The Art of Jewish Cooking.* New York: Random House, 1958.

Grossman, Ruth, and Bob Grossman. *The Kosher-Cookbook Trilogy.* New York: Galahad Books, 1965.

Hauser, Benjamin Gayelord, and Ragnar Berg. *Dictionary of Foods.* New York: Benedict Lust Publications, 1970.

Heine, Peter. *Food Culture in the Near East, Middle East, and North Africa.* Westport, Conn.: Greenwood Press, 2004.

Herb Society of America. www.herbsociety.org

The Holy Bible: Douay-Rheims. London: Baronius Press, 2005.

The Holy Bible: King James Version.

The Holy Bible: New International Version (NIV). International Bible Society, 1984.

The Holy Bible: New International Version—United Kingdom (NIV—UK). International Bible Society, 1984.

Holy Land Olive Oil. www.holiveoil.com/services.html

Interactive European Network for Industrial Crops and Their Applications. www.ienica.net

Jamieson, Robert, A. R. Fausset, and David Brown. *A Commentary, Critical and Explanatory, on the Whole Bible.* New York: George H. Doran, 1921. www.ccel.org/ccel/jamieson/jfb.toc.html

The Jerusalem Bible.

Jewish Encyclopedia.com. www.jewishencyclopedia.com

Josephus, Flavius. *Antiquities of the Jews.* Trans. by William Whiston. www.ccel.org/j/josephus/JOSEPHUS.HTM

Judaism 101. www.jewfaq.org

Kalechofsky, Roberta, and Rosa Rasiel. *The Jewish Vegetarian Year Cookbook.* Marblehead, Mass.: Micah Publications, 1997.

Köhler-Rollefson, Ilse U. "Animals." In *Harper's Bible Dictionary.* Edited by Paul J. Achtemeier et al. San Francisco: Harper & Row, 1985.

Lehman-Wilzig, Tami. *Tasty Bible Stories: A Menu of Tales & Matching Recipes.* Minneapolis: Kar-Ben Publishing, 2003.

Margen, Sheldon. *The Wellness Encyclopedia of Food and Nutrition: How to Buy, Store, and Prepare Every Variety of Fresh Food.* New York: Rebus, 1992.

Marks, Gil. *Olive Trees and Honey: A Treasury of Vegetarian Recipes from Jewish Communities Around the World.* Hoboken, N.J.: Wiley, 2005.

McCormick.com. "The History of Spices." www.mccormick.com/content .cfm?ID=10109

McGee, Harold. *On Food and Cooking: The Science and Lore of the Kitchen.* New York: Charles Scribner's Sons, 1984.

McKibbin, Jean, and Frank McKibbin. *Cookbook of Foods from Bible Days.* Revised edition. Culver City, Calif.: Frank L. McKibbin, 1972.

Mitchell, Patricia. "Red Velvet Cake." www.texascooking.com/features/ may99redvelvet.htm

Morse, Kitty. *A Biblical Feast: Foods from the Holy Land.* Berkeley, Calif.: Ten Speed Press, 1998.

Musselman, Lytton John. "All the Plants of the Bible." http://web.odu/webroot/ instr/sci/plant.nsf/pages/allbibleplantslist

New Advent. www.newadvent.org

New Revised Standard Version of the Bible. Nashville: Catholic Bible Press, 1989.

Neyrey, Jerome. "Meals, Food and Table Fellowship." In *The Social Sciences and New Testament Interpretation.* Edited by R. L. Rohrbaugh. Peabody, Mass.: Hendrickson, 1996. www.nd.edu/~jneyrey1/meals.html

O'Brien, Marian Maeve. *The Bible Cookbook.* St. Louis: The Bethany Press, 1958.

Peake, Arthur S. *A Commentary on the Bible.* London: Thomas Nelson, 1960.

Peterson, Eugene H. *The Message: The Bible in Contemporary Language.* Colorado Springs: NavPress Publishing Group, 2002/2003.

Pett, Peter. "The Book of Genesis: A Commentary." http://www.geocities.com/ genesiscommentary

Quartz Hill School of Theology. www.theology.edu

Razzle Dazzle Recipes. www.razzledazzlerecipes.com

Reader's Digest Association. *Great People of the Bible and How They Lived.* Pleasantville, N.Y.: Reader's Digest, 1974.

RecipeGoldmine. www.recipegoldmine.com

Rinzler, Carol Ann. *The Complete Book of Food: A Nutritional, Medical, and Culinary Guide.* New York: World Almanac, 1987.

Roberts, Jonathan. *The Origins of Fruit and Vegetables.* New York: Universe, 2001.

Rodin, Cuia, and Tibor Rodin. *King Solomon's Feast: Culinary Delights from the Cuisine of Biblical Israel.* Self-published: 1994.

Rogov, Daniel. "Manna for Breakfast." www.stratsplace.com/rogov/israel/ manna_breakfast.html

Root, Waverley. *Food: An Authoritative, Visual History and Dictionary of the Foods of the World.* New York: Fireside, 1980.

Rylaarsdam, J. Coert, and J. Edgar Park. "The Book of Exodus." In *The Interpreter's Bible: A Commentary in Twelve Volumes.* Vol. I. New York: Abingdon-Cokesbury Press, 1952.

Schwabe, Calvin W. *Unmentionable Cuisine.* Charlottesville: University of Virginia Press, 1979.

Scots Independent. www.scotsindependent.org/features/food/german_cake.htm

"Shavouth: Holiday Laws and Customs." www.jewishholiday.com/shav65 laws.html

Shihab, Aziz. *A Taste of Palestine.* San Antonio, Tex.: Corona, 1993.

Small, Ernest, and Grace Deutsch. *Culinary Herbs for Short-Season Gardeners.* Missoula, Mont.: Mountain Press, 2001.

Smith, Jeff. *The Frugal Gourmet Celebrates Christmas.* New York: William Morrow, 1991.

———. *The Frugal Gourmet Keeps the Feast: Past, Present and Future.* New York: William Morrow, 1995.

Southern Illinois University–Carbondale. *Ethnobotanical Leaflets.* www.siu.edu/~ebl/leaflets/mustard.htm

Souvay, Charles L. "Plants in the Bible." In *The Catholic Encyclopedia.* Edited by Kevin Knight. 2003. www.newadvent.org From *The Catholic Encyclopedia,* vol. XXII. New York: Robert Appleton Company, 1911.

Stadd, Arlene. *Cooking with the Ancients: The Bible Food Book.* Aurora, Colo.: Glenbridge Publishing, 1997.

Swahn, J. O. *The Lore of Spices: Their History and Uses Around the World.* New York: Crescent Books, 1991.

Symington, J. Fife, III. "Governor's Cake." *The Arizona Republic* (September 4, 2004).

Tischler, Nancy M. *Men and Women of the Bible: A Reader's Guide.* Westport, Conn.: Greenwood, 2002.

Towner, W. Sibley. "Wedding." In *Harper's Bible Dictionary.* Edited by Paul J. Achtemeier et al. San Francisco: Harper & Row, 1985.

Truth in Heart.com. http://truthinheart.com/EarlyOberlinCD/CD/edersheim/IV.CHAPTERXIITH.htm

University of Pennsylvania Museum of Archaeology and Anthropology. "The Origins and Ancient History of Wine." www.museum.upenn.edu/new/exhibits/online_exhibits/wine/wineintro.html

von Rad, Gerhard. *Genesis: A Commentary.* Rev. ed. Philadelphia: Westminster Press, 1972.

Wells, Troth. *The New Internationalist Food Book.* Oxford: New Internationalist, 2000.

Wikipedia, the Free Encyclopedia. www.wikipedia.org

Williams, Michael E., ed. *The Storyteller's Companion to the Bible: Genesis.* Nashville: Abingdon, 1991.

World's Healthiest Foods. www.whfoods.com/index.html

Worldwide Gourmet. http://gourmet.sympatico.ca

Wycliffe New Testament. www.biblegateway.com

Zanger, Mark H. *The American History Cookbook.* Westport, Conn.: Greenwood Press, 2003.

Recipe Index

Recipes are listed under each category by order of appearance. Main entries in Recipe Index are set in **boldface** type.

Subject Index

Aaron, 49, 51, 52, 64, 152
Abigail, xvi, xix, 83–84, 85, 86–88, 92, 95, 96
Abimelech, King, 14
Abraham, xvi, xix, 3–6, 14–15, 25, 26, 36, 50, 64, 76, 96, 188, 213, 232, 297; as Abram, 3–6; as father of the Arab peoples, 5, 14; as father of the Jewish peoples, 5
Absalom, 96, 279
Agag, 84
Age of Exploration, 225
Ahab, King, 118
Akhenaten, 50
Alexander the Great, xix, 142, 175–76, 254, 315, 362
Alexandra, Queen (Hasmonean), 150
Amalekites, 84
Amenhotep IV, 50
Ammon, 75
Ammonites, 84
Andrew (disciple of Jesus), 198
Antiochus IV Epiphanes, King, 176
Antipater, King, 150
Apicius, 247
Apocrypha (Pseudepigrapha), 166
Aramaic, 165
Aristotle, 333

Ark, of the Covenant, 64, 72, 96; disappearance of, 126
Artaxerxes I, King, 125, 126, 141
Artaxerxes II, King, 141
Artemis, 220
Asenath, 37
Asher, 36
Ashkenazi Jews, 88
Assyria, empire of, 126, 302
Astor, John Jacob, 341
Aten (Aton), 50–51
Aztecs, 209, 221, 281, 300, 315, 352, 353, 356

Babylon. See Babylonia
Babylonia, xix, 3–4, 126, 140, 227, 231, 235, 249, 277, 291, 301, 302, 303, 313, 327, 365
Bathsheba, 96, 108
Beersheba, 28
Benjamin, 36, 37, 38, 40; tribe of, 84
Beth-el (Bethel), 36, 37, 118, 119
Bethlehem, 75, 76, 279
Bilhah, 36
Birthright, 13, 15–16, 25; as indicated by passing of coat, 37, 118, 168
Bitter herbs, 223, 232, 233, 234, 235, 243, 309, 314. See also Passover

Black Death, 264, 365
Blessing: of children, 24, 25, 27–28; of food, xiii, xv; of individuals, 36; of nations, 25, 108
Boaz, 75–76, 77–78, 82 n.2, 84
Boston Tea Party, 340
Brahma, 237
Bread: importance of, xv, 26, 28, 33 n.2, 179; as term of sustenance, 77
British East India Company, 328, 340, 341; beginning as John Company, 340, 341
Brooklyn Papyrus, 65
Buddha, 237, 261, 339

Caesar, Julius, xx
Cambyses II, 141
Canaan, 4, 37, 64, 65, 96, 188, 343
Canaanites, 14
Carmel, Mount, 118, 267
Carver, George Washington, 348
Cato, 224, 228, 234
Celebrations: Dedication of the Firstborn, 52; Feast of the Unleavened Bread, 52
Chanukah. See Hanukkah
Charlemagne, 286, 313
Charles II, king of England, 340
Chaucer, Geoffrey, 233
Chevreul, Michel, 346

About the Authors

ANTHONY F. CHIFFOLO, Editorial Director of Praeger Publishers, has a master's degree in the classics of Western Civilization from St. John's College in Annapolis, Maryland. He is the author of *100 Names of Mary: Stories and Prayers, Advent and Christmas Wisdom with Padre Pio, Advent and Christmas with the Saints, Be Mindful of Us: Prayers to the Saints* and the compiler/editor of *Padre Pio: In My Own Words, Pope John Paul II: In My Own Words, Pope John XXIII: In My Own Words,* and *At Prayer with the Saints.* He is the co-author, with Rayner W. Hesse, Jr., of *We Thank You, God, for These: Blessings and Prayers for Family Pets.*

RAYNER W. HESSE, Jr. (The Rev. Dr.), is the author, with Anthony F. Chiffolo, of *We Thank You, God, For These: Blessings and Prayers for Family Pets.* A graduate of both Union Theological Seminary and The General Theological Seminary in New York, he most recently completed his doctoral work (D.Min.) in liturgy and philosophy of religion at New York Theological Seminary. An accomplished chef and biblical scholar, Fr. Hesse is an ordained Episcopal priest serving a parish in New Rochelle, New York, where he is currently at work on a third book to be published in 2007.